Russia, the European Union and the CIS

Russia, the European Union and the CIS

Eric Engle (Ed.)

eleven international publishing

Published, sold and distributed by Eleven International Publishing
P.O. Box 85576
2508 CG The Hague
The Netherlands
Tel.: +31 70 33 070 33
Fax: +31 70 33 070 30
e-mail: sales@budh.nl
www.elevenpub.com

Sold and distributed in USA and Canada
International Specialized Book Services
920 NE 58th Avenue, Suite 300
Portland, OR 97213-3786, USA
Tel.: 1-800-944-6190 (toll-free)
Fax: +1 503 280-8832
orders@isbs.com
www.isbs.com

Eleven International Publishing is an imprint of Boom uitgevers Den Haag.

ISBN: 978-94-90947-52-1

Printed in The Netherlands

Preface

This work presents a collection of essays about Russian Law and Economics with respect to the Russian federation's relations to the European Union and the Commonwealth of Independent States (CIS). The work confronts the challenges facing a transition economy in its struggle for economic development through market forces and its efforts to impose the rule of law, not men, on a former dictatorship. The topics addressed range from Russia's relationship to the EU and other CIS states to a variety of commercial law topics: key contemporary issues in Russian intellectual property, tax, and M&A law are addressed by Russian jurists writing in English. The problems of corruption or bureaucracy are addressed directly and openly in the hope that increased EU and US cooperation with the Russian Federation will lead to better international relations.

The author undertook this work while teaching law at Pericles LL.M. Institute in Moscow: the edited works are by Pericles' alumni. The author wishes to thank Pericles Dean Marian Dent for her kind understanding. I hope my editing these works as to grammar and scientific method makes the material more accessible to non-Russian speakers. The authors' insights are their own, and any remaining errors in grammar are really my fault. I hope the materials will interest jurists intrigued by the problems and possibilities facing and presented by the Russian federation for global governance.

Finally, please note, in keeping with the times and the fact that this work is international, many of the citations are to sources on the internet. In the event such links go "stale" the reader is kindly referred to the "wayback machine" an internet archive at <http://waybackmachine.org> or <http://archive.org>. Likewise "stale" links may also be searched for on google using the cache: operator. With such resources one may generally find any URL from at least the year 2000. I ask the reader's comprehension of the fact that Western citation formats are not generally known to Russian jurists but in all cases the referenced works can be found. Thank you for reading, which we hope you will enjoy.

For my friend, Natalia Kravtsova.

Dr.Jur. Eric Engle, LL.M.
Berlin, 2012

Table of Contents

Part I
The EU and Russia

1 The EU, Russia, and the Commonwealth of Independent States (CIS)

Eric Engle

1 Introduction

The European Union builds peace through interdependence and prosperity by transferring elements of state sovereignty to intergovernmental and supranational bodies. The EU is the world's most advanced and successful example of transnational governance: it is a key vector of globalization. An unparalleled success, the EU presents a model for transnational governance. Its rules and institutions can be emulated in other regions of the world[1] such as Eastern Europe.

This chapter compares the institutions and objectives of the USSR, the EU, and the CIS to understand the differing origins and competing tendencies of these alternative models of transnational governance. Understanding the systemic differences and commonalities of those models enables contextualizing past history and thus improves our understanding of current relationships of the former Soviet Republics to the EU. Hopefully, understanding the historical sources and development of transnational relations in Eastern Europe will in turn enable better international relations between the EU, the Russian Federation, and other former Soviet Republics and the United States.

2 Comparing Teleologies of Transnational Governance: Goals and Structures

Understanding the past helps us to appreciate the present and then to form the future. First, we compare the goals and structures of the USSR, the EU, and the CIS. By disaggregating the differing origins and competing tendencies of these distinct models of transnational governance we can see their commonalities and the historical breakdowns in order to attain improved relations by understanding shared goals and methods to those goals.

---

1 See Eric Engle, *Europe Deciphered: Ideas, Institutions and Laws,* Fletcher Forum of World Affairs, Vol. 33, pp. 63-84, (2009). Available at <http://papers.ssrn.com/sol3/papers.cfm?abstract_id=1336490>.

2.1 *The Structure and Teleology of the USSR*

The USSR was a one-party system. A workers' and peasants' dictatorship in name,[2] directed and led by the Communist Party of the Soviet Union (CPSU). The CPSU regarded itself as a vanguard party, the most advanced elements (intelligentsia) of the most advanced class (the proletariat), subject to democratic centralism and exercising a dictatorship on behalf of the proletariat (workers and peasants). In western terms, the CPSU was a centralized, hierarchical party of elites directing a centrally planned economy via dictatorship. The party elite of the CPSU (the "nomenklatura") claimed to govern on behalf of and for the benefit of the workers and peasants, *i.e.* the peoples of the Soviet Union. The dictatorship of the party on behalf of the workers and peasants was justified as necessary to work revolutionary changes on their behalf. And indeed, the initial performance of the USSR was breathtaking. The USSR eradicated illiteracy and literally doubled average life expectancy[3] and also ended the chronic famines endemic to Tsarist Russia. Leninism also instituted sex equality.[4] In real human terms such as average life expectancy and literacy rates Leninism was unquestionably progress as compared to Tsarism.

Figure 1.1 Dynamics of Literacy

Dyanamics of Literacy 1897-1979: Population Aged 9-49, in Percentages

Population		1879	1920	1926	1939	1959	1970	1979
Rural	*M*	35.5	52.4	67.3	91.6	99.1	99.6	99.6
	F	12.5	25.2	35.4	76.8	97.5	99.4	99.5
	All	23.8	37.8	50.6	84.0	98.5	99.5	99.6
Urban	*M*	66.1	80.7	88.0	97.1	99.5	99.9	99.9
	F	45.7	66.7	73.9	90.7	98.1	99.8	99.9
	All	57.0	73.7	80.9	93.8	98.7	99.8	99.9
Total	*M*	40.3	57.6	71.5	93.5	99.3	99.8	99.8
	F	16.6	32.3	42.7	81.6	97.8	99.7	99.8
	All	28.4	44.1	56.6	87.4	98.5	99.7	99.8

Source: Narodnoe obrazovanie, nauka i kul'tura v SSSR: Statisticheskii shornik (Moscow. 1977, 9; SSSR: zarubezbnye strany, 1987: Statisticheskii sbornik (Moscow, 1988), 83.

2 Art. 1 of the 1936 Constitution of the USSR, stated "The Union of Soviet Socialist Republics is a socialist state of workers and peasants." <www.departments.bucknell.edu/russian/const/36cons01.html> (last visited 16 January 2011).

3 Stephen White, Russia Goes Dry: Alcohol, State and Society, p. 43, (1996).

4 See, *e.g.*, Gail Warshofsky Lapidus, Women in Soviet society: Equality, Development, and Social Change, p. 136 (1978).

The CPSU justified its dictatorship as the best way to obtain the well-being of the workers and peasants[5] and also as necessary to prevent and win any future world war. Over time however, the Soviet system degenerated and increasingly worked to the benefit of the party establishment (the "nomenklatura")[6] at the expense of the broad masses of workers and peasants. Meanwhile, the threat of invasion diminished. From this perspective, which I call dual delegitimation, we can better understand the sudden, unexpected, and relatively bloodless restoration of capitalism[7] in Russia. The system, *in its own terms*, lost legitimacy as being no longer necessary (defence against a war which never came) or effective (consumer well being was simply higher in the west, and the nightmare of Tsarist famine illiteracy and inequality was long past). These systemic facts help explain the near bloodless dissolution of the Soviet system.

Soviet foreign policy was less aggressive than perceived by the US foreign policy elites, particularly the military, at the time. Rather than relentlessly seeking to inflame global revolution at every turn in a zero-sum struggle with the West, the USSR first sought to build socialism in one country,[8] and then in its own sphere of influence: to construct a stable autarchic system. The Soviets sought autarchy as the means to self defense.

Geopolitically, the Soviet system can be described as a series of concentric rings. At the centre was the USSR; then Eastern Europe;[9] then Third World Marxist states, and finally Third World non-Marxist allies. The closer a country was geographically to the Soviet centre, the greater the level of integration into the autarchic economy. Western efforts to

5 "Article 1. The Union of Soviet Socialist Republics is a socialist state of the whole people, expressing the will and interests of the workers, peasants, and intelligentsia, the working people of all the nations and nationalities of the country." 1977 Constitution of the USSR, Part I. Available at: <www.departments.bucknell.edu/russian/const/77cons01.html#chap01> (last visited 17 January 2011).

6 See generally, Michael Voslensky, Nomenklatura: The Soviet Ruling Class (1st ed.), Doubleday (1984).

7 Capitalism is a system of economic production predicated on the private ownership of capital. It is distinct from state capitalism wherein capital is held by the state or through public-private partnerships. Capitalism is also defined as an industrial rather than a feudal mode of production. The Tsarist economy was semi-feudal and industrializing. Further, many of its economic projects involved heavy state participation (state capitalism). However, the ownership of capital in the hands of a financial elite distinguishes Tsarist semi-feudal (state) capitalism from the Soviet planned economy. Of course, strong state participation in the economy, directly and indirectly, remains a mark of the Russian economy. However, private ownership of capital and the role of the Orthodox Church as spiritual guide of the nation were definitively restored in the post Soviet era. Thus I refer to this process as "capitalist restoration" rather than "capitalist instauration". See, *e.g.*, Steven Rosefielde, Comparative Economic Systems: Culture, Wealth, and Power in the 21st Century, p. 183 (2002).

8 Josef Stalin, *The October Revolution and the Tactics of the Russian Communists* in Problems of Leninism, by J.V. Stalin, Foreign Languages Press, Peking, 1976, p. 117. (1924). Available at <www.marxists.org/reference/archive/stalin/works/1924/12.htm> (last visited 16 Januray 2011).

9 Joseph G. Whelan, Michael J. Dixon, The Soviet Union in the Third World: Threat to World Peace?, p. 8 (1986).

"roll back" Marxism were generally unsuccessful,[10] perhaps because the Soviet system *was* autarchic. The failure of "roll back" ultimately led to the "Brezhnev doctrine", wherein the USSR declared the attainment of "socialism" in any country as irreversible.[11]

To attain autarchic economic development the USSR implemented an import substitution industrialization (ISI) model for economic development. ISI had already been used in the West for the industrialization of the US and Japan.[12] However, the USSR justified its version of ISI by rationales of substantive equality and solidarity, and contrasted those with the formal freedoms conditioned by economic inequality which justified western (at times social) democracies.[13] Russia's approach to ISI was, within its own terms, rational. The Soviet leadership considered obtaining and maintaining the autarchy of the USSR a necessary, legitimate and attainable goal.[14] Given the historical fact that Russia has suffered invasion after invasion, the Soviet goal of economic autarchy as a means to national security, though definitively economically suboptimal to trade, was politically justifiable, albeit increasingly economically inapt.

Pursuant to the ISI strategy, a ruble currency economic zone was created and the ruble was inconvertible. Capital restrictions were the norm. So were border controls such as customs duties and passport checks. A policy of autarchy complemented military security by enabling independent political choices. Military security was seen by the Soviet leadership as a precondition to economic security and well being. To circumvent the problem of a lack of foreign currency and the inability to use the ruble for currency exchanges overseas, and related problems arising from the nature of a closed economic system, barter in and for real goods (counter-trade) was taken up by and between the COMECON countries. For example, the USSR would barter with Cuba, trading sugar for finished Soviet goods.[15] Barter also occurred at the micro-economic level, though not as a legitimate de jure instrument of state policy, but as a de facto necessity of everyday life, albeit of questionable legality.[16] "Gifts" however could be justified as a "social" and "fraternal" act under the

10 Peter Grose, Operation Rollback: America's Secret War Behind the Iron Curtain, p. 210 (2001).

11 This policy was known as "The Brezhnev Doctrine". See, *e.g.*, Matthew J. Ouimet, The Rise and Fall of the Brezhnev Doctrine in Soviet Foreign Policy (2003).

12 For an exposition of the import substitution industrialization model of development see generally, David M. Trubek, Alvaro Santos, The New Law and Economic Development: A Critical Appraisal (2006).

13 Eric Engle, Marxism, Liberalism, And Feminism (Leftist Legal Thought), p. 33-35 (2010).

14 David Childs, Thomas A. Baylis, East Germany in Comparative Perspective, p. 190 (1989).

15 José F. Alonso and Ralph J. Galliano, *Russian Oil-For-Sugar Barter Deals 1989-1999* in Cuba in Transition: Volume 9, Papers and Proceedings of the Ninth Annual Meeting of the Association for the Study of the Cuban Economy (ASCE) (1999). Available at <http://lanic.utexas.edu/la/cb/cuba/asce/cuba9/alonso.pdf>.

16 See, *e.g.*, Jim Leitzel, Russian Economic Reform, p. 128 (1995). Also see, Byung-Yeon Kim, *Informal Economy Activities of Soviet Households: Size and Dynamics*, Journal of Comparative Economics, Volume 31, Issue 3, September 2003, pp. 532-551.

Marxist logic of transforming monetary economic compulsion into cooperative voluntary social acts. However, with capitalist restoration the primitive version of a "gift economy" became warped into generalized bribery, undermining the rule of law in the post-Soviet era.

Preferential tariff treatment for the COMECON and Soviet client states was a key feature of the international trade policy of the Socialist bloc.[17] High tariff barriers were created to protect the autarchic COMECON home market.[18] These tariff barriers would also encourage infant industries. Non-tariff technical barriers such as restrictions on imports for health and safety reasons also served the ISI logic. Meanwhile, intellectual property would be either unprotected or weakly protected in order to use Western innovation to support the USSR.[19] For example, software piracy of Western computer technology software and microchip technology was the norm during the Soviet era[20] and intellectual property law enforcement in Russia remains a sore spot in US-Russian relations to this day. Most importantly, the taxing and subsidization system of the centrally-planned economy aimed to accumulate the surplus capital needed for economic development through the creation of infrastructure (*e.g.*, housing, roads, airports) via forced saving[21] but also, more ominously, for military production.

The political and legal institutions in the USSR and its satellites paralleled those of the West. Legal and institutional parallels included: the Warsaw Treaty Organization (the Warsaw Pact), which paralleled the North Atlantic Treaty Organization (NATO); the Council for Mutual Economic Assistance (COMECON, also known as CMEA), for its part, paralleled the European Economic Community (EEC). Other parallels could be found

17 See, *e.g.*, Adam Zwass, The Council for Mutual Economic Assistance: The Thorny Path from Political to Economic Integration, M.E. Sharpe, Armonk, NY (1989); Marie Lavigne, International Political Economy and Socialism, Cambridge Univ. Press, (1985), p. 175.

18 COMECON (also known as the CMEA) was the USSR's effort to form a common market within the Soviet bloc. See, *e.g.*, J. J. Brine, COMECON: The Rise and Fall of an International Socialist Organization (1992).

19 Intellectual property remains but weakly protected in the Russian federation and the their successor states to the USSR. "[C]ounterfeiting and piracy activity in Russia remains on a high level. The lack of effective enforcement affect Russian markets on a large scale. To be fully integrated in the world trading system, to continue to attract foreign investment and to prevent major losses for right-holders, Russia has to implement all its international obligations, in particular the ones related to Intellectual Property Rights and their Enforcement." European Commission, *Trade: Dialogues (Intellectual property)*, at <http://ec.europa.eu/trade/creating-opportunities/trade-topics/intellectual-property/dialogues/#_russia> (last visited 7 February 2011).

20 See, *e.g.*, Shane Hart, *Computing in the Former Soviet Union and Eastern Europe*, Crossroads, Volume 5 Issue 3, March 1999.

21 For a detailed explanation of the ISI model in the context of Soviet development theory see, Eric Engle, *A Social-Market Economy for Rapid Sustainable Development*, Gujarat National Law University, Journal of Law, Development and Politics, Vol.2, pp. 42-62, (2009). Available at <http://papers.ssrn.com/sol3/papers.cfm?abstract_id=1424695>.

fairly readily, and in my opinion Soviet socialist legalism should be seen as a variant of civilianist law.

Legal and political parallels arose because each system sought the same goals (economic development, technical progress, national security) albeit by somewhat different methods and justified by differing rationales; the Soviet system was an authoritarian egalitarian variant of late modernity that sought to attain economic development using the Western import substitution industrialization (ISI) model. The Soviet systemic rationales were substantive equality and social solidarity; the West's were freedom, property and individual rights. These rationales were also principles for organizing production and social life generally.

The Soviets, like the West, sought the same goals: to obtain a better life for workers (the people) and physical (military) security (*i.e.*, *defense*). However, the means to those ends differed. The USSR sought to obtain prosperity not through the capitalist anarchy of production but through centralized economic planning. Similarly, the USSR sought to attain security through autarchy (isolation and independence) rather than through economic interdependence; economic interdependence was the path to peace taken by the west, as exemplified by the EU and WTO.

Legal and institutional parallels between the Soviets and the West included: the Warsaw Treaty Organization (the Warsaw Pact), which paralleled the North Atlantic Treaty Organization (NATO); the Council for Mutual Economic Assistance (COMECON, also known as CMEA), for its part, paralleled the European Economic Community (EEC). Other parallels could be found fairly readily, and in my opinion Soviet socialist legalism should be seen as a variant of civilianist law.

The key problem of the soviet economy was the fact that it was defined around building up a military-industrial complex to fight and win a World War III if ever attacked again: autarchy as a means to security. Tragically,[22] in pursuit of its military defense, the USSR and its Warsaw Pact allies wasted almost all their surplus production on unproductive military spending.[23] Ultimately, the US response to the failure of rollback and the Brezhnev

22 Recall that tragedy, strictly speaking, means the *inevitable* downfall of a *hero* (or anti-hero) due to his *excess* of virtue. In the Soviet Union "defense of the motherland" taken to its excess became paranoia, crippling production and dooming the system to (inevitable) collapse. However, the West did not win the cold war: rather, the Soviets lost it.

23 "By the mid-1980s, the Soviet Union devoted between 15 and 17 percent of its annual gross national product to military spending, ... Until the early 1980s, Soviet defense expenditures rose between 4 and 7 percent per year." Global Security Org, Russian Military Spending, at <www.globalsecurity.org/military/world/russia/mo-

doctrine was to compete in fields where the USSR could not compete due to technological inferiority or the structure of a closed dictatorship. The US' own arms buildup aimed to bankrupt the USSR by forcing it into an unsustainable arms race, a policy that worked.[24] The resulting economic strains led to constant shortages that seriously undercut the USSR's claim to be creating a workers' paradise with the highest standard of living for ordinary people on earth.[25] The USSR was undermined by economic dislocations, the inability of the planned economy to deliver high quality goods on time where most needed, and the increasing strain of militarism. "The party of Lenin", despite such stunning initial success, was ultimately unable to match capitalism in the quality and abundance of consumer goods.[26] This, coupled with the increasing tendency of the nomenklatura to serve its own goals rather than to seek the well being of all the Soviet peoples, and the fact that the US, unlike Nazi Germany was not in fact threatening to invade the USSR to seize resources led to a crisis of purpose, a crisis of legitimacy, and capitalist restoration.

2.2 The Objectives of the EU

The EU aims to form a single, integrated European market in order to: (1) break the link between territory and trade which drove Europe into at least two global wars; and (2) generate the prosperity through trade that results from specialization in production, economies of scale, and reduced transaction costs.[27] At one extreme, Euro-Federalists have cautiously and tentatively argued for the formation of a "United States of Europe".[28] The Euro-Federalists' ultimate goal is both unrealistic and undesirable: recreating mercantilist nation states as mercantilist continental empires would only lead to more global conflict.[29]

---

budget.htm> (last visited 16 January 2011); also see: Anders Åslund, Building Capitalism: the Transformation of the Former Soviet Bloc, Cambridge University Press, (2001), p. 131.

24 Ruud van Dijk (Ed.), Encyclopedia of the Cold War, Volume 1, *Strategic Defense Initiative*, Routledge (2008) p. 862-863.

25 *E.g.*, "Communism is Soviet power plus the electrification of the whole country." -Vladimir Ilyich Lenin. That is, the Soviet system justified itself as the fastest route to development, which it was for at least one generation. However, ultimately, the system lost legitimacy as it became clear and clearer that the west produced better quality consumer goods and in greater numbers.

26 See especially, Alex F. Dowlah, John E. Elliott, The Life and Times of Soviet Socialism, p. 182 (1997).

27 For a deeper synopsis of this author's views on the ideas, institutions, and laws behind the EU see Eric Engle, *Europe Deciphered: Ideas, Institutions and Laws,* Fletcher Forum of World Affairs, Vol. 33, pp. 63-84, (2009). Available at <http://papers.ssrn.com/sol3/papers.cfm?abstract_id=1336490>.

28 See, *e.g.*, Alberta M. Sbragia, Euro-Politics: Institutions and Policymaking in the New European Community p. 260 (1992).

29 Eric Engle, *The EU Means Business: A Survey of Legal Challenges and Opportunities in the New Europe*, 4 DePaul Bus. & Com. L.J. 351, 352-353 (2006). Available at: <http://papers.ssrn.com/sol3/papers.cfm?abstract_id=1020467>.

However, there were good practical reasons for the EU's creation. The EU's objectives, also (and more importantly) included preventing another European war and improving the well-being of all workers.[30] Those objectives were attained through the functionalist method of forming specialized institutions defined around particular goals to take advantage of unbiased expert judgment. This expert judgment in specific sectors in turn enabled the EU to attain socially desirable goals in the common interest of all Europeans in an incremental step-by-step fashion. The functionalist method first pooled together the military industries: coal, steel, and atomic power via the European Coal and Steel Community (ECSCE)[31] and the European Atomic Energy Community (EURATOM).[32] European states also formed a customs union, the European Economic Community (EEC) to disaggregate national cartels, which were seen as a cause of wars for market share because trade and territory of these war industries had been linked.[33] The customs union aimed to attain a single integrated market via the free movement of goods, workers, capital, and enterprises (the four freedoms). Ultimately, the EU evolved into a supranational body with a common currency (the Euro), common citizenship and passports, common borders (the Schengen Area), and to some extent a common foreign and security policy.[34] As a confederation,[35] the EU began to share many elements of classical Westphalian nation-states.[36]

30 Treaty of Rome, Preamble, 25/III/1957. Available at <http://ec.europa.eu/economy_finance/emu_history/documents/treaties/rometreaty2.pdf>. The Rome Treaty was succeeded by the Treaty of Amsterdam (Maastricht) and then the Treaty of Lisbon which reiterated those goals: "The Union's aim is to promote peace, its values and the well-being of its peoples." Article 2 (1), Treaty of Lisbon, (2007/C 306/01). Available at <http://europa.eu/lisbon_treaty/index_en.htm>.

31 The ECSCE merged into the EU.

32 The EURATOM's Atomic Energy Commission (AEC) maintains a separate legal existence as an international organization. See generally, European commission, "The European Atomic Energy Community (EURATOM)". Available at <http://ec.europa.eu/energy/nuclear/euratom/euratom_en.htm> (last visited 24 January 2011).

33 Namely, the unity of trade and territory under the Westphalian state system led to war because any state which wished to expand its economy also had to expand its territory. See, *e.g.*, Eric Engle, *Europe Deciphered,* 33 Fletcher Forum of World Affairs 63 (Fall 2009).

34 Thereto, see generally, Eric Engle, *I Am My Own Worst Enemy: Problems and Possibilities of European Foreign Policy Vis-a-Vis the United States,* St. Thomas Law Review, Vol. 18, p. 737, (Spring 2006). Available at <http://papers.ssrn.com/sol3/papers.cfm?abstract_id=1020482>.

35 See, *e.g.*, Eric Engle, *Theseus's Ship of State: Confederated Europa between the Scylla of Mere Alliance and the Charybdis of Unitary Federalism.* 8 Florida Coastal Law Review, 27 (2006). Available at <http://ssrn.com/abstract=1020468>.

36 See, generally, Eric Engle, *The Transformation of the International Legal System: The Post-Westphalian Legal Order,* 23 QLR 23 (2004). Available at <http://papers.ssrn.com/sol3/papers.cfm?abstract_id=1020475>.

2.3 The Objectives of the CIS

The CIS arose in the chaotic aftermath of the collapse of the USSR.[37] In contrast to the USSR or the EU, the CIS never had well-articulated goals. While one faction of the former Russian nomenklatura may well have seen the CIS as the Soviet Union by other means, another faction of Russians (the former economic criminals) may well have seen the CIS as merely a vast economic opportunity. Even if we presuppose the unity of Russian nationalist leaders, the fact that such unity centered on "great Russian nationalism" rather than "proletarian internationalism" indicates that the centralizing tendencies of the CIS were disunited and unattractive to the newly independent national states. I simply do not see a unity of factions nor of objectives on the part of the CIS leaders. Nevertheless, even if there were a unity, if only of great Russian factions and objectives, that unitary vision was not able to attract adhesion or persuade the newly independent national republics in, *e.g.* former Soviet Central Asia, to submit to some variant of confederation featuring a customs union and/or common currency and/or common defensive alliance.[38]

This lack of a compellingly attractive central vision, of shared goals and objectives for the CIS, crippled it as an institution for transnational governance. Lacking a common teleology or goal, the CIS degenerated into the political overseer of the peaceful dissolution of the USSR[39] and, to a certain extent, the introduction of market mechanisms to replace the

---

37 "Shortly after the collapse of the Soviet Union most of its successor states, with the exception of the Baltic States, joined the Commonwealth of Independent States (CIS). At the same time many CIS countries opened up their trade regimes by dismantling various trade restrictions, state trading monopolies, multiple exchange rate regimes as well as formal tariff barriers. However, in the course of the 1990s pressure for the protection of domestic industries has increased. Import tariffs on "sensitive imports", such as refined sugar, have started to pop up. By far the most serious barriers to trade and the ones most frequently used are non-tariff barriers. The ever more complex and constantly changing trade regimes of many CIS countries have also opened the door for corruption and smuggling." Michael Roberts and Peter Wehrheim, *Regional Trade Agreements and WTO Accession of CIS Countries*, SpringerLink – Intereconomics, Volume 36, Number 6, p. 315 (2001). Available at <www.springerlink.com/content/41642065037ll583/> (last visited 6 December 2010).

38 Stephen K. Batalden, Sandra L. Batalden, The Newly Independent States of Eurasia: Handbook of Former Soviet Republics, p. 19. (1997). (Factional conflict within the RSFSR at formation of CIS); Vladimir Shlapentokh, Christopher K. Vanderpool, Boris Zusmanovich Doktorov (eds.), The New Elite in Post-Communist Eastern Europe, p. 57 (1999) (Lack of vision); Scott L. Greer, Questioning Geopolitics: Political Projects in a Changing World-System (2000). (factionalism within the nomenklatura).

39 "Ten years after the break up of the USSR, CIS countries are still struggling to find the appropriate format to govern their mutual trade relations. At present a patchwork of half-implemented bilateral agreements and a series of paper framework agreements govern intra-CIS trade relations. Most of the RTAs among CIS Member States remain de jure agreements. If one were to characterise this institutional framework, one might term it 'managed disintegration'". Michael Roberts and Peter Wehrheim, *Regional Trade Agreements and WTO Accession of CIS Countries*, SpringerLink – Intereconomics, Volume 36, Number 6, p. 323 (2001). Available at <www.springerlink.com/content/41642065037ll583/> (last visited 6 December 2010).

planned economic system. Consequently, in Western literature the CIS is typically described as "moribund"[40] and can accurately be compared to the present day British Commonwealth.

2.3.1 The Breakdown of the CIS

The CIS failed to evolve into a viable transnational governing institution due to a lack of a common vision[41] and inexperience in transnational institutionalism,[42] particularly with regards to market liberalization.[43] The CIS was confronted with the simultaneous tasks of privatization, political and economic liberalization, and the implementation of the rule of law. At the same time, the CIS lacked experience and experts in transnational governance beyond the context of a strong vertical hierarchy of a one-party dictatorship. Consequently, liberal western transnational governance models such as those of the European Communities could not inform the CIS's already overwhelmed managerial class. Moreover, some of the new managerial class were Soviet era "economic criminals",[44] while others were former nomenklatura. Consequently, factionalism soon ensued both between and within these two historically conflicting groups. The CIS's failure is unsurprising, and was perhaps even inevitable, given those conditions.[45]

Lacking a common vision, the CIS defaulted into the role of the clearinghouse for the USSR's remarkably peaceful dissolution via two distinct factors: (i) privatization; and (ii) the devolution of former federal powers to individual Republics.[46]

---

40 See, *e.g.*, Global Security, *Commonwealth of Independent States (CIS)*, at <www.globalsecurity.org/military/world/int/cis.htm> (last visited 7 December 2010).

41 "The CIS was burdened with ambivalent goals. On the one hand, it aimed to assist the newly independent countries to gain economic independence, while on the other hand it was the intended institution to bring the newly independent states together in an economic union. The ambivalent character of the CIS, and the increasing self-consciousness, both politically and economically, of the newly independent states, resulted in numerous bilateral and multilateral agreements at the same time." Joop de Kort and Rilka Dragneva, *Russia's Role in Fostering the CIS Trade Regime*, Department of Economics Research Memorandum 2006.03, p. 9. Available at: <http://
ssrn.com/abstract=1440809>.

42 See, *e.g.* Margot Light, *International Relations of Russia and the Commonwealth of Independent States* in Eastern Europe and the Commonwealth of Independent States (Europa Publications, 1999) p. 21.

43 Philip Hanson, *The Economics of the Former USSR: An Overview* in Eastern Europe and the Commonwealth of Independent States (Europa Publications, 1999), p. 79.

44 See, *e.g.*, Olimpiad Solomonovich Ioffe, Mark W. Janis, Soviet Law and Economy, Dordrecht [Holland]; Boston: M. Nijhoff, (1987). p. 177; Charles A. Schwartz, *Economic Crime in the USSR: A Comparison of the Khrushchev and Brezhnev Eras*, 30 ICLQ, 281-296 (April 1981).

45 Nonetheless, its failure was remarkable in that it contributed to the peaceful transition from one-party dictatorships to independent republics with varying degrees of democratic participatory government.

46 Stephen Kux, *From the USSR to the Commonwealth of Independent States: Confederation or Civilized Divorce?* in Joachim Jens Hesse,Vincent Wright (eds.) Federalizing Europe? (Oxford: 1996) p. 325, 346-347. Also see Stephan Kux, *Confederalism and Stability in the Commonwealth of Independent States*, 1 New Eur. L. Rev. 387 (1992-1993).

The institutional problems mentioned contributed to the breakdown of CIS. For example, the CIS's transnational trade policy was characterized by incoherence. Numerous overlapping multilateral and bilateral treaties covered similar issues,[47] leading to economic disputes due to the contradictory obligations imposed by the various treaties. However, these overlapping multilateral and bilateral treaties also left many issues unaddressed.[48] For example, the CIS' agreements were not sophisticated enough to take into account non-tariff trade barriers such as health, safety, and technical restrictions to trade.[49] Ultimately, conflicting rules, gaps in rules coverage, and non-enforcement[50] gutted the CIS treaties of efficacy, created legal uncertainty, and increased transaction costs.[51] The CIS' institutions and rules were simply ineffective.[52] The CIS states were unable to effectively transpose EU-style transnational trade governance to help it develop coherent trade relationships due to incoherent rules and absent institutionalism. Lacking effective rules and institutions, a political approach predominated, which only further impeded any effort by the CIS partners to maintain productive synergies such as a customs union, a common currency,

---

47 "What can be observed in the CIS is that economic cooperation takes the form of overlapping bilateral and multilateral agreements of very distinct legal quality. From an economic point of view it does not make sense that countries that have concluded a multilateral free trade agreement, as the CIS countries did in 1994, an agreement that they amended in 1999, subsequently conclude bilateral free trade agreements with their partners as well. It creates overlap, increases transaction costs, and obfuscates the status of multilateral and bilateral agreements." See Joop de Kort and Rilka Dragneva, *Russia's Role in Fostering the CIS Trade Regime*, Department of Economics Research Memorandum 2006.03, p. 1. Available at: <http://ssrn.com/abstract=1440809>.

48 "The agreements that are concluded often are partial and selective, while their ratification and implementation also is a mixed affair". Joop de Kort and Rilka Dragneva, *Russia's Role in Fostering the CIS Trade Regime*, Department of Economics Research Memorandum 2006, 03, p. 1. Available at: <http://ssrn.com/abstract=1440809>.

49 "The CIS trade regime can be described as a symbiosis between bilateral and multilateral regimes, both of which can be described as weak regimes. Bilateral agreements cover some key free trade rules, such as tariffs, but remain minimal and quite basic. Non-tariff barriers, for instance, are generally left out, as are liberalisation of services or intellectual property to name a few issues that have become important in international trade agreements. Disputes are generally resolved through consultations." Joop de Kort and Rilka Dragneva, *Russia's Role in Fostering the CIS Trade Regime*, Department of Economics Research Memorandum 2006.03, p. 3. Available at: <http://ssrn.com/abstract=1440809>.

50 "Though most CIS countries have FTAs with each other on a bilateral basis, not all of them are practically implemented or enforced." Michael Roberts and Peter Wehrheim, *Regional Trade Agreements and WTO Accession of CIS Countries*, SpringerLink – Intereconomics, Volume 36, Number 6, p. 319 (2001). Available at <www.springerlink.com/content/41642065037ll583/> (last visited 6 December 2010).

51 "[F]ragmentation poses a danger of rule clashes, patchy implementation, and a non-transparent and complex administration of the regime." Joop de Kort and Rilka Dragneva, *Russia's Role in Fostering the CIS Trade Regime*, Department of Economics Research Memorandum 2006.03, p. 2. Available at: <http://ssrn.com/abstract=1440809>.

52 "90 per cent of all multilateral documents that create the legal base of the CIS, and there are more than 1,000 of them, are ineffective. According to many observers, the CIS seems to have failed in becoming an effective framework of economic cooperation and (re)integration." Joop de Kort and Rilka Dragneva, *Russia's Role in Fostering the CIS Trade Regime*, Department of Economics Research Memorandum 2006.03, p. 1. Available at: <http://ssrn.com/abstract=1440809>.

and common health and safety standards. Moreover, the frequent use of reservations by CIS Member States not only rendered agreements all but pointless, but also impeded any serious form of legal stability from taking root into CIS institutions.[53] In sum: CIS institutions and rules were simply ineffective.

Any effort to bring the USSR's customs and monetary union into the CIS era was thus doomed for several interlocking reasons. There was an absence of useful legal concepts such as "basic economic rights" (the four freedoms)[54] as a necessary means to the desirable end of economic integration to obtain peace and prosperity. Absent legal concepts in the CIS treaties such as subsidiarity, proportionality, and acquired community positions (*acquis communautaire*[55]) further crippled the CIS because those are methods of coordinating supranational and intergovernmental tendencies in order to attain by accretion the objectives of economic integration. Finally, CIS institutions such as the Economic Court of the CIS were weak or entirely absent[56] because of an absent common will, an absent common goal, and absent common concepts.

Nevertheless, although the CIS lacked the institutional expertise and juridical structure to transform the USSR into something like the EEC, this does not mean that it is currently impossible or undesirable. Accordingly, this chapter considers the Eurasian Economic

---

53 "The CIS applies the 'interested party' principle, which implies that a state could choose not to participate in a certain agreement or decision without afflicting its validity." Joop de Kort and Rilka Dragneva, *Russia's Role in Fostering the CIS Trade Regime*, Department of Economics Research Memorandum 2006.03, p. 1. Available at: <http://ssrn.com/abstract=1440809>.

54 The central concept to the foundation of the European Union as an economic area are the four freedoms (basic rights): the free movement of goods, workers, capital and of enterprises among the Member States. See generally, *e.g.*, Eric Engle, Europe Deciphered: Ideas, Institutions and Laws, 33 Fletcher Forum of World Affairs, 63 (2009). Available at SSRN: <http://ssrn.com/abstract=1336490>.

55 Jorgensen, Knud Erik, *The Social Construction of the Acquis Communautaire: A Cornerstone of the European Edifice*, European Integration online Papers (EIoP), p. 11. Volume 3 Issue 4 (1999) available at: <http://eiop.or.at/eiop/texte/1999-005a.htm> (Nietzsche-Foucauldian genealogical method); BBC, "Acquis Communautaire" (30 April, 2001), *available at*:< http://news.bbc.co.uk/1/hi/in_depth/europe/euro-glossary/1216329.stm>.

56 "[T]he CIS presents a mix of, often overlapping, bilateral and multilateral agreements. The picture gets even more complicated as bilateral and multilateral agreements often differ in the strength of commitment they require from the signatories. Bilateral agreements rarely envision a mechanism for resolving disputes between its parties, relying on negotiations to do so. Multilateral agreements on the other hand often do attempt to strengthen the bindingness of the commitments undertaken. In 1993, the Treaty of the Economic Union even went as far as to strengthen the role of the Economic Court, by requiring that 'if the Economic Court recognises that [...] a Member State has not fulfilled its obligation ensuing from the Treaty, this state is obliged to take measures connected with the implementation of the decision of the Economic Court'.3 A year later, in 1994, a Free Trade Agreement (FTA) was concluded which 'undermines' the position of the Economic Court" Joop de Kort and Rilka Dragneva, *Russia's Role in Fostering the CIS Trade Regime*, Department of Economics Research Memorandum 2006.03, p. 2. Available at: <http://ssrn.com/abstract=1440809>.

Community (EurAsEC) to see whether and how the CIS can take up EU principles and implement them.

2.3.2 The Eurasian Economic Community (EurAsEC)[57]

Following the instauration of market mechanisms to replace the planned economic system, and because of the continual success of the EU as an institution of transnational governance, the Russian Federation, Belarus and Kazakhstan together instituted a customs union known as the "Eurasian Economic Community."[58] The EurAsEC could, and should, look directly to the EU's growth and evolution as a source of inspiration and also for basic legal concepts such as:

- Direct effect of treaty provisions (that private persons have directly enforceable rights and duties under the EurAsEC treaty).
- The four freedoms (free movement of goods, labor capital, workers and enterprises).
- Acquis communautaire (the idea that each step toward a single integrated market is irreversible, and that new adherents to the EurAsEC must agree to abide by the existing acquis.
- "General principles of international law" as a source of EurAsEC law.
- The principle of legality (that EurAsEC institutions should be legal, not political).
- Functionalism (that the EurAsEC institutions should be built out incrementally to progressively attain a single integrated market).

Economic development occurs more quickly through open borders. Thus, though one can critique the rule of law and democracy in the former Soviet republics, the way ahead is through free trade. Economic development is the most practical and effective way to build stronger and more democratic institutions in the former Soviet republics because wealth creates the conditions that enable genuine protection of human rights.[59] The authoritarian

57 "[A] customs union within the EurAsEC framework, with the Republic of Belarus, the Republic of Kazakhstan and the Russian Federation as initial members. Other EurAsEC Member States will join the customs union when their economies are ready to take this step." ЕврАзЭС, <www.evrazes.com/en/about/> (last visited 6 December 2010).

58 "Russia and two other CIS countries – Kazakhstan and Belarus – established a customs union (CU) in 1995. The Kyrgyz Republic joined in March 1996 and Tajikistan joined in 1999. The CU's text provided for discontinuation of all trade tariffs between member countries, tariffs for trade with other countries were adjusted to one level, [*i.e.*, harmonized into a common external tariff] and the system of privileges was unified. In addition, certain measures were taken to unify tax policy (tax rates and application of indirect taxes). The agreements on the customs union called for coordination of customs, excise, and value-added dues" Michael Roberts and Peter Wehrheim, *Regional Trade Agreements and WTO Accession of CIS Countries*, SpringerLink – Intereconomics, Volume 36, Number 6, p. 321 (2001). Available at <www.springerlink.com/content/41642065037ll583/> (last visited 6 December. 2010).

59 "Living in the post-Cold War era has lent some air of stability--a peace dividend--to life in Russia. This may have a positive effect on the development of the economy and democratic institutions." NIC Conference

democracies in the former Soviet Republics are not *systematic* violators of *the most basic* human rights.[60]

Functionalist incrementalism would be more effective at securing human rights protection than extreme methods.[61] Economic integration (through freer trade) and improved economic performance are positively correlated.[62] Improved economic performance and improved protection of human rights are also positively correlated.[63] Consequently, a policy of constructive engagement[64] through aid and trade can help to improve economic well being and will lead to the improved protection of human rights and the institution of the rule of law in the former Soviet republics.

Supranational and intergovernmental governance worked well in the EU to leverage its Member States and their immediate neighbors out of war.[65] Those same methods – economic integration to increase prosperity to foster peace and the progressive realization of human rights[66] – can and should be used in the former Soviet republics into the rule of

---

Report – Russia in the International System. Available at: <www.dni.gov/nic/confreports_russiainter.html> (last visited 17 January 2011).

60 "[T]he election of President Medvedev in 2008 has led to gradual changes in the previously more hard-line policy regarding human rights in EU-Russia relations. The new foreign policy doctrine appears to emphasise less confrontational and more pragmatic relations with partners such as the EU with the aim of promoting Russia's modernisation." Eleanor Bindman, Russia's response to the EU's human rights policy", openDemocracy, 1 October 2010. Available at <www.opendemocracy.net/od-russia/eleanor-bindman/russia%E2%80%99s-response-to-eu%E2%80%99s-human-rights-policy> (last visited 9 February 2011).
"In 2010 Russia demonstrated increased openness to international cooperation on human rights …
In January 2010 – after years of delay – Russia ratified Protocol 14 to the European Convention for Human Rights, becoming the last Council of Europe (CoE) Member State to do so. Protocol 14 streamlines the case review process at the ECtHR and strengthens the enforcement mechanisms of the CoE's Committee of Ministers. …
In 2010 Russia showed some improved cooperation on human rights, but Russia's international partners did not do enough to encourage human rights reform." Human Rights Watch, *World Report 2011: Russia* (2011). Available at: <www.hrw.org/en/world-report-2011/world-report-2011-russia> (last visited 9 February 2011).

61 Elena Klitsounova, *Promoting human rights in Russia by supporting NGOs: how to improve EU Strategies*, CEPS Working Document 287 (2008).

62 See, *e.g.*, United Nations, Assessment of Trade Policy Trends and Implications for the Economic Performance of the ESCWA Region, E/ESCWA/EDGD/2009/1, p. 3 (14 April 2009).

63 Clemens L. J. Siermann, Politics, Institutions, and the Economic Performance of Nations, p. 131 (1998).

64 Sanford J. Ungar and Peter Vale, South Africa: *Why Constructive Engagement Failed*, Foreign Affairs, Winter 1985/86. Available at <www.foreignaffairs.com/articles/40525/sanford-j-ungar-and-peter-vale/south-africa-why-constructive-engagement-failed> (last visited 16 Januray 2011).

65 See, *e.g.*, Paul P. Craig, Gráinne De Búrca, EU Law: Text, Cases, and Materials, p. 3-6. (2008).

66 Štefan Füle, EU Commissioner for Enlargement and Neighbourhood Policy, "The EU: a Force for Peace, Stability and Prosperity in Wider Europe", EU@UN, 30 November 2010 at Columbia University, New York. At: <www.europa-eu-un.org/articles/fr/article_10447_fr.htm> (last visited 6 February 2011).

law and protection of human rights.[67] Free trade generates economic prosperity, and economic prosperity in turn generates improved protection of human rights. Thus, free trade improves protection of human rights.

2.3.3 Comparing CIS and EU Institutions

Institutionally, the USSR was, at least nominally, a workers' and peasants' dictatorship. Its stated purpose[68] was to prevent the wars for market share that capitalism unleashed in economic crises at the trough of business cycles.[69] Both the EU and the USSR sought to prevent war and attain well being for ordinary workers. However, the similar teleology was to be attained by a different means. In the USSR an advanced vanguard party would exercise a dictatorship on behalf of the proletariat.[70] While we can criticize the idea of a vanguard party exercising a dictatorship on behalf of workers and peasants, we should also understand that the USSR's proletarian dictatorship shared the same stated objectives as the EU. Marx predicted that business cycle causes war for market share, to burn off surplus production, and to employ the unemployed.[71] The USSR, like the EU,[72] sought to prevent wars for market share to advance the well-being of all citizens. While the USSR, following Marx's prescription to transform the state into civil society,[73] sought to end market relations entirely[74] to attain the goal of peace and prosperity, the EU sought to use

67 "Following the collapse of the Soviet Union and the ascendancy of Boris Yeltsin, US policy could be defined in brief as one of constructive engagement, in which the United States aggressively and assiduously worked to secure Russian integration with the world economy, Russian political, economic and legal reform, and democratization." John Pearce Hardt, (ed.) Russia's uncertain economic future, Joint Economic Committee, Congress of the United States, p. 121 (2003); "both Russia and China may be susceptible to a strategy aimed at their inclusion in cooperative international structures. To that end, two Eurasian power triangles must be steadily managed and, over time, more directly connected: one involving the United States, the European Union and Russia; and the other involving the United States, Japan and China. For that linkage to be effective, the constructive engagement of Russia is essential." Zbigniew Brzezinski, *Living With Russia*, The National Interest, #61, (Fall 2000); Jackie Gower, Graham Timmins, Russia and Europe in the Twenty-First Century: An Uneasy Partnership, pp. 169-170 (2009).

68 See generally, Vladimir Ilyich Lenin, Imperialism, the Highest Stage of Capitalism (1916). Available at: <www.marxists.
org/archive/lenin/works/1916/imp-hsc/ch09.htm> (last visited 17 January 2011).

69 See, *e.g.*, Karl Marx, Friedrich Engels, The Communist Manifesto, Chapter 2 (1848). Available at: <www.marxists.org/archive/marx/works/1848/communist-manifesto/ch02.htm> (last visited 16 January 2011), Karl Marx, Capital. See also Vladimir Lenin, What Is To Be Done; Vladimir Lenin, State and Revolution; Vladimir Lenin, Imperialism: Highest Stage of Capitalsm.

70 See, *e.g.*, Peter. Burger, Theory of the Avant-Garde, University of Minnesota Press, 1 February 1984.

71 Karl Marx, Friedrich Engels, The Communist Manifesto, p. 11 (Echo, 2009).

72 See, *e.g.*, Damian Chalmers, Gareth Davies, Giorgio Monti, European Union Law: Text and Materials, p. 7 (2010).

73 Friedrich Engels, Karl Marx, Socialism: Utopian and Scientific, p. 68 (Mondial 2006).

74 See, *e.g.*, Soviet Constitution of 1936, Art. 4 ("The socialist system of economy and the socialist ownership of the means and instruments of production firmly established as a result of the abolition of the capitalist system of economy, the abrogation of private ownership of the means and instruments of production and

market forces to attain those same goals.[75] Paradoxally, the EU and USSR both sought to transform the state (coercion) into society (voluntarism) – but through the exactly opposite means.

Like the EU, the USSR was multinational, multilingual, and had attained a monetary union with the free movement of goods, labor, and capital. But the USSR did not in fact attain the best standard of living for workers: life expectancy was only a few years lower than in the West, and double that of Tsarist Russia.[76] Leisure was assured, but consumer goods were always in short supply.[77] Quality of goods suffered from production deadlines at the end of the five year planning cycles when production goals had to be met but improved over time.[78] In sum, the quality of Soviet life did not match Western European standards. This was mostly because so much of the government's resources were wasted on building a military-industrial complex that did not advance the well-being of Soviet citizens.

Moreover, the planned economy faced an increasingly complex task: the centralized coordination of production and distribution of a growing variety of goods. Central planning of a primitive industrializing economy with only a few basic inputs is considerably easier than for a diversified industrial economy with scores then hundreds of consumer goods. The Soviet planned economy succeeded at shifting the USSR from a semi-feudal economy producing but a score of basic goods into an industrial economy. However, the newly created industrial economy produced a myriad of different goods.[79] This production diversity doomed the centrally planned economy. Namely, an ever greater variety of products made central planning increasingly complex and thus less efficient at coordinating production and consumption. Soviet production was not entirely inefficient: Soviet weaponry was cheap, durable, easily maintained and reliable. The USSR was the first country to put a satellite into space, and later a man into orbit. However, the USSR's centrally planned economic production system was more appropriate for a semi-feudal

the abolition of the explotation of man by man, constitute' the economic foundation of the U.S. S.R. 1936"). Available at <www.departments.bucknell.edu/russian/const/36cons01.html> (last visited 11 February 2011).

75 See, *e.g.*, Treaty of Rome, Preamble, 23 March 1957. Available at <http://ec.europa.eu/economy_finance/emu_history/documents/treaties/rometreaty2.pdf>.

76 Stephen White, Russia Goes Dry: Alcohol, State and Society, p. 43, (1996).

77 Robert Whitesell, *Why Does The Soviet Economy Appear To Be Allocatively Efficient?* Soviet Studies, 42 #2, April 1990 (259-268). Available at: <http://ideas.repec.org/p/wil/wilcde/113.html>.

78 Donald D. Barry (ed.), Soviet Law after Stalin: Social Engineering Through Law, Part 2, p. 202 (1978). (Rising quality of Soviet goods between 1960s and 1970s).

79 Eric Engle, *A Social-Market Economy for Rapid Sustainable Development*, Gujarat National Law University, Journal of Law, Development and Politics, Vol.2, pp. 42-62, (2009). Available at: <http://papers.ssrn.com/sol3/papers.cfm?abstract_id=1424695>.

industrializing society with few goods than for a highly developed industrial economy producing a myriad of goods.[80]

The institutions of a single party dictatorship and the teleology of the USSR were not apt to liberalism.[81] Thus, the customs and monetary union of the CIS quickly degenerated into national economies with separate currencies and tariff barriers still trying to implement the ISI development model – a model that neoliberalism had long surpassed.[82] The establishment of inter CIS customs and tariff barriers raised transaction costs and reduced economies of scale. Restructuring a centrally planned dictatorial economy centered on autarchy and war into a consumer oriented networked globalizing economy exacerbated those problems. The result was suboptimal economic performance.[83] At times the newly independent Republics were trying to implement outdated and inefficient liberal or Soviet models of economic development; at other times, they became disposable experiments in neoliberalism. All too often the results were chaos, corruption, asset stripping, and economic failure,[84] which contributed to *declining* average life expectancy in the post-Soviet years.[85] These results explain why multiparty liberal democracy did not take root in some of the former Soviet republics. The return of one-party rule in some former Soviet republics after the collapse of the USSR resulted from the chaos of the failed Soviet planning model, the failed ISI model and mixed bag results from neoliberal experimentation. The CIS's lack of institutional experience and personnel expertise in the principles and practices of liberal markets and transnational governance in any context other than that of a single party dictatorship in turn explains the failure of the CIS Member States to have adopted EU governance models in the late 1990s.

---

80 See generally, Ludwig von Mises, Economic Calculation in the Socialist Commonwealth (1920). Available at: <http://mises.org/econcalc.asp> (last visited 9 February 2011).

81 I mean liberalism in the sense intended by Aristotle and Locke; an open democratic form of governance in which people are free to enter into economic transactions as they themselves choose. See, John Locke Second Treatise of Civil Government (1690). Available at <www.constitution.org/jl/2ndtreat.htm>.

82 See, *e.g.* Friedman, Milton. Capitalism and Freedom (University of Chicago Press, 1962). While I critique certain points of Friedman (See Eric Engle Lex Naturalis, Ius Naturalis (2010) p. 220 *et seq.*), Friedman's views on monetary policy seem entirely correct to me and replaced the failed theory of John Maynard Keynes's General Theory of Employment, Interest and Money (1936).

83 See, *e.g.*, World Bank, Belarus: Prices, Markets, and Enterprise Reform (1997) p. 1.

84 "By the beginning of 1997 the Russian economy had perhaps reached its lowest point. GNP fell by 6% in 1996, compounding a decline of more than 50% since 1991 (although the shadow economy has expanded). Many enterprises are on the brink of collapse; the proportion of loss-making enterprises in the main economic sectors is approximately 43%." International Labor Organization, *Privatization: Lessons from Russia and China-Employment Sector*. Available at: <www.ilo.org/public/english/employment/ent/papers/emd24.htm> (last visited 24 January 2011).

85 See, *e.g.*, D A Barr and M G Field, *The Current State of Health Care in the Former Soviet Union: Implications for Health Care Policy and Reform*. American Journal of Public Health, Vol. 86, Issue 3 307-312, 1996. p. 308.

3 Concepts in Transnational Governance

This section sets out the relationships between the rule of law, the economy, the protection of human rights, and democracy. It outlines ideas about political legitimation and presents practical methods to advance transnational relations to better understand how international relations between the US, the EU and the former Soviet Republics can be improved.

3.1 *Historical Materialism Revisited*

A key question for transnational governance is: how to untangle the relationships among the rule of law, democracy, the economic system, and human rights? The rule of law, democracy, free trade, and protection of human rights are all positively associated: improving the protection of one tends to improve protection of the others.[86] Is there any hierarchy ordering their relations? I hypothesize that the rule of law is needed for an effective economy, and that a productive economy and the rule of law in turn leads to the protection of human rights.

I argue that democratic institutions are less important to the protection of human rights or the attainment of the rule of law than is usually thought to be the case.[87] In practice, democratic institutions are generally used to reinforce and legitimize policies formed by elites rather than to form public policies.[88] Most legislative bills are introduced not by democratic referenda but by elected republican representatives. Policies are typically proposed by elites[89] and are then taken up or rejected by masses through the democratic process.[90] The West tends to equate democracy with the rule of law,[91] and wrongly presumes that the democratic process is necessary to the rule of law and protection of human rights.

86 See, *e.g.*, Eugene Cotran, Adel Omar Sherif, Democracy, the Rule of Law and Islam – pp. 202-204 (1999); Amazu A. Asouzu, International Commercial Arbitration and African States: Practice, Participation and Institutional Development, p. 42 (2001). Jeremy Waldron, *The Concept and the Rule of Law*, 43 Ga. L. Rev. 1 (Fall, 2008).

87 See, *e.g.*, Thomas Carothers, *The Rule of Law Revival*, 77 For. Aff. 95 96-97 (1998).

88 Joseph A. Schumpeter, Capitalism, Socialism, and Democracy p. 269-283 (1942). Eva Etzioni-Halevy, Fragile Democracy: The Use and Abuse of Power in Western Societies p. 16 (1989); David Held, Models of Democracy p. 164 (2006). In the context of Russia see Richard Ahl, Harry Eckstein, Philip G. Roeder, Can Democracy Take Root in Post-Soviet Russia?: Explorations in State Society Relations, p. 134 (1998).

89 See generally, Charles Wright Mills, Alan Wolfe, The Power Elite (2000).

90 Anne Peters argues, as does this chapter, for "legitimation ex post" *i.e.* legitimation by success. See: Anne Peters: Elemente einer Theorie der Verfassung Europas, 517, 580 (2001). Thereto also see: Michel Rosenfeld, Constitutionalism, Identity, Difference, and Legitimacy: Theoretical Perspectives, p. 186 (1994); Alan Keenan, Democracy In Question: Democratic Openness in a Time of Political Closure p. 28 (2003).

91 See, *e.g.*, Richard Bellamy and Dario Castiglione, *Constitutionalism and Democracy – Political Theory and the American Constitution*, 27 Brit. J. Pol. Sci. 595 (Oct., 1997).

I maintain that the rule of law leads to a productive economy.[92] The rule of law and a productive economy together in turn foster democratic processes and the real protection in practice of substantive human rights. These ideas can be summed up as "key points":

- the rule of law is necessary for a productive open market;[93]
- a market economy with social protections favors prosperity;
- economic prosperity favors protection the protection of human rights; and
- democratic deficit can be ex post facto legitimized by the success of public policies that were politically unpopular at the time of their enactment.

Rather than seeing democratic processes as the source of human rights protection or a necessary precondition to the rule of law, I argue that the rule of law and economic development positively correlate[94] and are preconditions to the effective and meaningful defense of human rights. I also argue that democratic legitimation can be an outcome of economic and legal development.[95]

The aforementioned sequence reiterates the historical materialist argument that economic processes ultimately drive legal and ideological rationalizations and justifications of any given political system.[96] The dialectical materialist refinement of that argument is to note

---

92 "For more than half a century, a prevailing view motivating Western foreign aid approaches was that rule of law correlated in some positive and significant way with economic development and an attractive business climate for foreign investment ... More recent literature in this field, however, has led to growing skepticism about the validity and general application of the assumptions that served as the touchstones for Western development initiatives. Debate continues, for example, over whether a causal relationship between rule of law and a successful market economy exists and, if so, in which direction that causation runs, whether these variables may be mutually reinforcing, what key elements characterize a rule- of-law system, and how does one explain away the many anomalies."
David Silverstein, Daniel C. Hohler, *A Rule-Of-Law Metric for Quantifying and Assessing the Changing Legal Environment of Business*, 47 Am. Bus. L.J. 795, 818-819 (Winter 2010).

93 See, *e.g.*, Edgardo Buscaglia, *Judicial Corruption in Developing Countries: Its Causes and Economic Consequences*, UN CICP-14 (2001) p. 6-7. Available at <www.unodc.org/pdf/crime/gpacpublications/cicp14.pdf>.

94 Frank Richardson, *Pro Bono Work Has Burgeoned Over the Past Few Years Both Geographically and in Its Legal Range*, 64 No. 4 Int'l B. News 26 (August, 2010). (Positive correlation between rule of law and economic performance; negative correlation between corruption and economic performance).

95 There is a plethora of literature, much of it contradictory, on the relationships among the rule of law, prosperity, democracy, and human rights. Examples include: Stephan Haggard *et al.*, *The Rule of Law and Economic Development*, 11 Ann. Rev. Pol. Sci. 205 (2008); Susan D. Franck. *Judicial Independence and Legal Infrastructure: Essential Partners for Economic Development: Foreign Investment, Investment Treaty Arbitration, and Rule of Law*, 19 Pac. McGeorge Globai Bus. & Div. L.J. 337, 342-343 (2007); James R. Jones, *Open Markets, Competitive Democracy, and Transparent and Reliable Legal Systems: The Three Legs of Development*, 83 Chi.-Kent L. Rev. 25 (2008); Randall Peerenboom. *Social Networks, Rule of Law and Economic Growth in China: The Elusive Pursuit of the Right Combination of Private and Public Ordering*, 31(2) Global Econ. Rev. 3 (2002); John Hewko. *Foreign Direct Investment: Does the Rule of Law Matter?* (Carnegie Endowment for Int'l Peace, Democracy and Rule of Law Project. Carnegie Papers No. 26. 2002).

96 G. A. Cohen, *Base and Superstructure: A Reply to Hugh Collins*, Oxford J Legal Studies (1989) 9(1): 95-100. Available at <http://ojls.oxfordjournals.org/content/9/1/95.full.pdf>.

that the economic base (the forces of production) generally determine the legal forms of the superstructure, but that exceptionally, at particular times and under certain conditions, the superstructure (ideology) can determine the base:[97] that the material forces of production *generally* constitute and constrain the ideological superstructure which rationalizes them. *Exceptionally,* at certain times and places in history, the ideological superstructure can, to some extent, influence and compel the structure of the material forces of production. Marxism aimed to act as a catalyst for the natural and inevitable movement of history by intervening at these exceptional points in social life "at the margins".[98] Perhaps the vanguard party's altruism outran the basic needs for consumption of the productive base it was leading. Perhaps the vanguard party became corrupted. Perhaps both explanations apply. Nevertheless, I conclude that vanguard parties exercising a dictatorship on behalf of the proletariat are very effective at ending illiteracy and starvation and at introducing gender equality, but are not terribly effective at coordinating production and consumption in a complex consumer economy.[99]

The rule of law, economic development via free trade and open markets, human rights protection, and democracy all correlate positively and are mutually reinforcing.[100] However, I postulate their priority as follows: without basic laws, economic development is impossible due to physical insecurity and legal uncertainty. Without economic development, human rights protection is impossible or at least meaningless. Meanwhile, democratic processes require a basic legal system and at least minimal economic well-being. Human rights protections without economic development are sub-optimal. For example, the protection of the freedom of religion in the face of starvation is merely the right to last rites so to speak. While dying with dignity is not utterly meaningless, would it not be better to choose life, somehow? By placing survival rights, such as the right to food,[101] ahead of psychological rights, or even political rights, we would be likely better able to protect people in real terms.

---

97 The dialectical relationship between the material forces of production (base) and the ideological relations of productions (superstructure) is a basic tenet of Marxism. See, Karl Marx, A Contribution to the Critique of Political Economy, preface (1859). Available at <www.marxists.org/archive/marx/works/1859/critique-pol-economy/preface.htm> (last visited 9 February 2011).

98 See generally, Karl Marx, Capital, Chapter 24 Section 1. Available at: <www.marxists.org/archive/marx/works/1867-c1/ch24.htm> and *Id.* Afterword to the Second German Edition (1873). Available at: <www.marxists.org/archive/marx/works/1867-c1/p3.htm>. Also see Friedrich Engels, Dialectics of Nature (1883) available at: <www.marxists.org/archive/marx/works/1883/don/index.htm>.

99 See generally, Eric Allen Engle Marxism, Liberalism, Feminism: Leftist Legal Thought (2010).

100 *E.g.*, NAFTA, see, Pamela K. Star, *The Two "Politics of NAFTA" in Mexico*, 16-FALL L. & Bus. Rev. Am. 839, 841 (Fall 2010). (Trade liberalization, economic performance, democratization correlated positively).

101 See, *e.g.*, UN EcoSoc, Report by the Special Rapporteur on the right to food, Mr. Jean Ziegler (2001)E/CN.4/2001/53 7 February 2001. Available at <http://graduateinstitute.ch/faculty/clapham/hrdoc/docs/foodrep2001.pdf>. Clearly a well functioning economy facilitates the furtherance of the right to eat.

This hierarchy of concepts is interrelated. Democracy, productive open markets, protection of human rights, and the rule of law are all positively correlated, and mutually reinforcing. As Russia increasingly implements the rule of law, transaction costs in Russia will be reduced which will strengthen the Russian economy. This in turn creates an environment where it is possible to envision better human rights protections and increases the needed material resources for the real protection and enjoyment of human rights.

3.2 *Functionalism*[102]

Functionalism argues that institutions should be understood and formed in terms of the functions that they aim to fulfil.[103] Functionalist approaches to transnational governance seek to safeguard peace by drawing nations together[104] rather than splitting them apart.[105] Functionalism forms specialized institutions incrementally[106] to attain specific practical purposes.[107] Functionalism linked to market liberalism seeks to obtain peace by generating prosperity and economic interdependence to obviate war by delinking trade and territory.[108] One tenet of functionalism is that economic and political integration is best achieved not

102 As a theory of sociology, functionalism analogizes society to an organism, with each member having particular functions, like organs of a body. See, *e.g.*, Kent McClelland, *Functionalism*, (2000), at: <http://web.grinnell.edu/courses/soc/s00/soc111-01/IntroTheories/Functionalism.html>.

103 "The core idea of functionalism is that international governance should be organized according to 'tasks' and 'functional lines.'" José E. Alvarez, Steve Charnovitz, *Triangulating The World Trade Organization*, 96 Am. J. Int'l L. 28, 48 (2002).

104 "Functionalism is a theory of international organization which holds that a world community can best be achieved not by attempts at the immediate political union of states, but by the creation of non-political international agencies dealing with specific economic, social, technical, or humanitarian functions. Functionalists assume that economic, social and technical problems can be separated from political problems and insulated from political pressures." Bartram S. Brown, *The United States and the Politicization of the World Bank* 14-15 (1992).

105 "The logic behind the approach is to prevent war not negatively – by keeping states apart – but positively by engaging them in cooperative ventures … to establish functionally specific agencies, initially in what were then seen as non contentious areas like welfare. These were to transcend national boundaries and be managed by rational technocrats (not swung by the vagaries of political ideology and power hungry political parties) owing their allegiance to a functionally specific organization not to a given nation state. … Their tasks will cover those areas of the economy essential to running military machines. Governments, deprived of control over those areas, will be unable to pursue war and will eventually be left to manage residual areas not covered by functional bodies …" J. Lodge, The European Community and the Challenge of the Future (Pinter, 1993) p. xix.

106 "[F]unctionalism … has enabled the incremental, progressive development of the European Union." Sabino Cassese, *European Administrative Proceedings*, 68-WTR Law & Contemp. Probs. 21, 23 (2004).

107 "Functionalism starts from the premise that by promoting functional cooperation among states it may be possible to deter them from settling disputes over competition for scarce resources aggressively" J Lodge, The European Community and the Challenge of the Future (Pinter, 1993) p. xix.

108 There is a vast literature on functionalism. For an early example see, *e.g.*, Ernst B. Haas, The Uniting of Europe; Political, Social, and Economic Forces, 1950-1957. (Stanford: Stanford University Press 1958).

at one fell swoop with grandiose and impossible ideas,[109] but rather through incremental efforts in diverse fields.[110] Functionalism is realistic and pragmatic: it seeks to attain the possible, here and now, rather than utopian dreams that do not materialize. Its methods obtain political legitimacy after the fact because of the success of the institution at achieving practical goals.[111] Ultimately, functionalists aim to prevent war not by keeping states apart, but by drawing them together by establishing transparent, responsible, and effective transnational governance structures in specific sectors. Neo-functionalism takes functionalism one step forward, involving political decision-making and seeking political integration.[112]

Just as functionalist methods were successfully applied to create the EEC and grow them into the EU, so can they be used to build stable prosperous transnational governance among the former Soviet Republics to foster the rule of law and protection of human rights by increasing economic prosperity. Specifically, the functionalist method would focus on developing in Eastern Europe the idea of the rule of law. First, the idea of an impartial independent judiciary seeking to implement the national will as expressed in legislation. Second, the idea of law as more than mere positive command – law as persuasive attractive moral appeal. Third, the idea of legal certainty. This requires further construction of a but partially existent legal culture. In Estonia, for example, Soviet era judges were effectively shunted aside to secondary tasks, retrained, and entered retirement or academia. New judges were selected from shockingly young candidates. To a much lesser extent that is also happening in Russia. However, the lack of institutional retraining initiatives extended from the US or EU can be partly to blame. Educating and reforming an entire legal culture is necessary, but initiatives to do so are starkly lacking. With the formation of a neutral independent unbiased judiciary it would then be possible to form transparent responsible

109 Hans J. Morgenthau, *Positivism, Functionalism, and International Law*, 34 AJIL 260, 283 (1940). ("Grandiose legalistic schemes purporting to solve the ills of the world have replaced the less spectacular, painstaking search for the actual laws and the facts underlying them.").

110 There is a vast literature on functionalism which this essay merely sketches. For an early example see:

111 "The neo-functionalist theory that has driven much of European integration, for example, posits that supranational institutions formed for fairly narrow purposes will attract political support over time and will thereby be able to expand their functions." Ernest A. Young, *The Trouble With Global Constitutionalism*, 38 Tex. Int'l L.J. 527, 540 (2003).

112 "Neofunctionalists have a common starting point with functionalists in their attachment to learning processes, allegedly apolitical, technocratic socio-economic welfare functions, consensus-building and functional specificity, neofunctionalists adopt a pluralist perspective. They argue that competitive economic and political elites mediate in the process and not only become involved in it but become key players. ... Neo-functional integration sees integration as a process based on spillover from one initially non-controversial, technical sector to other sectors of possibly greater political salience, involving a gradual reduction in the power of national government and a commensurate increase in the ability of the centre to deal with sensitive, politically charged issues." J. Lodge, The European Community and the Challenge of the Future (Pinter, 1993) p. xix.

and effective institutions. A functionalist approach would then seek to protect human rights sequentially, focusing first on survival rights, then on the economic rights, progressively attaining an ever greater protection of human rights: the hierarchy of norms[113] to attain the hierarchy of needs.[114] I have argued elsewhere for hierarchizing some of the basic human rights as follows: the right to one's own life, then the right to food,[115] then the right to shelter, then political rights and cultural rights.[116] In other words, one's basic needs in the hierarchy must be met before the more advanced and complex needs can be satisfied.[117] All these rights are vital to a good life, but some are naturally prior to others as a matter of fact. From the Russian perspective, establishing a judiciary or administrative institution is easy: The President and Prime Minister issue an order. But how to form an *independent* and *unbiased* judiciary? From the EU perspective, forming judicial expertise is nothing difficult, merely a matter of training in western legal methods. Joint EU-Russian judicial and administrative bodies might allow the positive implementation of such neutral unbiased adjudication. Then the EU judges would be able to compare experiences methods and ideas with their Russian counterparts. The EU and US do what they can to train and retrain Russian jurists. All this is meant to merely to *suggest* possible ways forward and also to indicate the extent of the problem.

3.3 *Ex Post Legitimacy and Democratic Deficit in the EU*

Democratic deficit in the EU was no obstacle to economic and political integration because of legitimation after the fact. As long as processes are transparent (*i.e.* open, governed by the rule of law) and not tainted with secrecy and deception (*i.e.* political), policies can attain legitimacy after their implementation by virtue of their efficacy.

113 For a history of the hierarchical evolution of human rights see; Eric Allen Engle, *Universal Human Rights: A Generational History*. 12 Ann. Surv. Int'l & Comp. L. 219, (2006). Available at <http://ssrn.com/abstract=1020464>. For a discussion on the logical hierarchization of human rights see Eric Engle Lex Naturalis, Ius Naturalis, Chapters 12 and 13, p. 363 *et seq.* (2010).

114 See, *e.g.* Jim Ife, Human Rights and Social Work: Towards Rights-Based Practice (2001). p. 83.

115 "Everyone has the right to a standard of living adequate for the health and well-being of himself and of his family, including food, clothing, housing and medical care and necessary social services, and the right to security in the event of unemployment, sickness, disability, widowhood, old age or other lack of livelihood in circumstances beyond his control." U.N., The Universal Declaration of Human Rights Article 25.(1). Available at: <www.un.org/en/documents/udhr/index.shtml> (last visited 7 February 2011).

116 Amitava Mukherjee, Hunger: Theory, Perspectives and Reality, p. 83-84 (2002).

117 S. N. Chaudhary (ed.) Human Rights and Poverty in India: Theoretical Issues and Empirical Evidences, p. 24 (2005).

The EU was a long term project driven by elites with minimal mass support.[118] It was built gradually and sequentially using the functionalist method that focused first on aggregating the war industries, and then on dissolving national cartels by building a single integrated market for goods, labor, capital, and services. The war industries were made subject to common control not to prepare for a war against the Soviet bloc, but to prevent yet another Western European War. While NATO greatly facilitated the development of the EU by providing a defensive umbrella under the premise of collective security, two World Wars had already shown that collective security alone was not sufficient to prevent war. Something beyond nation-state alliances was necessary to achieve lasting peace.

The EU was built without mass public support often thought needed for political legitimization. Despite this democratic deficit, the EU emerged to become one of the world's most competent and effective transnational organizations. One of the lessons of the EU for the former Soviet Republics is that, the problem of democratic governance in the former Soviet republics is surmountable. We can and should draw all the lessons from the experiences of the EU. Democratic institutions in Eastern Europe can be built gradually over time using functionalist methods. Transnational governance via functionalism will generate the economic well-being necessary to create a foundation for eventual respect of human rights

We now turn our attention to the relationship between the EU and Eastern Europe in order to understand exactly how Eastern Europe can take up EU models of governance to build effective transparent participatory state systems governed by the rule of law in order thereby to enjoy economic prosperity and improved human rights protections.

4 The EU and Russia

> *"We propose the creation of a harmonious economic community stretching from Lisbon to Vladivostok"* – Vladimir Putin[119]

The success of the EU as an example of transnational governance and the growing number of Eastern European legal scholars familiar with the basics of EU law explain the growing acceptance of the EU in the former Soviet republics. The Russian Federation's ultimate

118 Whole forests have been felled to rehash the famous issue of "democratic deficit". See, *e.g.*, Paul C. Adams, Atlantic Reverberations: French Representations of an American Presidential Election, p. 50 (2007). Jeffrey J. Anderson, Regional Integration and Democracy: Expanding on the European Experience, p. 1 (1999).

119 Der Spiegel, *'From Lisbon to Vladivostok': Putin Envisions a Russia-EU Free Trade Zone*, 11/25/2010. Available at <www.spiegel.de/international/europe/0,1518,731109,00.html> (last visited 6 December 2010).

long-term goal with the EU is to form an economic union to achieve trading synergies and encourage technological innovation[120] in order to generate economic development. As Schumpeter rightly noted, wealth is generated by innovation.[121] EurAsEc and the EU complement each other[122] because each aims at the same goals: to attain economic development via free trade and economic integration in order to create the economic base needed for the protection of human rights, to guarantee of the rule of law and obviate the risk of war. EurAsEc could develop independently of the EU. However, the logic of economic synergy resulting from specialization and economies of scale enjoyed as a result of free trade explains why both transnational organizations are more effective cooperating rather than competing with each other. These economic benefits are further augmented by the fact that good foreign relations means fewer resources wasted on weapons.

France's Nicholas Sarkozy supports Russia's desire for economic integration with Europe, as does Italy's Silvio Berlusconi.[123] As earlier noted, the desire for increased economic integration is partly driven by the fact of growing trade between Russia and Europe. This growing trade reflects the comparative advantage of Russia in hydrocarbons[124] and, to a lesser extent, atomic energy, and the asymmetric European comparative advantage in certain industrial goods. Though Western Europe is even more dependent on imported petroleum than the US, there are alternatives to Russian natural gas. Solar energy has become much more efficient in the past decades.[125] Wind turbines too are increasingly competitive. Though Germany currently essentially rejects atomic energy[126] for environ-

120 Valentina Pop, *Putin proposes Russia-EU union* 26.11.2010 @ 09:29 CET EUobserver available at <http://euobserver.com/19/31361> (last visited 6 December 2010).

121 Joseph Schumpeter, The Theory of Economic Development. (1934).

122 European Parliament resolution of 17 June 2010 on the conclusions of the EU/Russia summit (31 May-1 June 2010) (P7_TA-PROV(2010)0234 para. G. Available at: <www.europarl.europa.eu/document/activities/cont/201006/20100624ATT76660/20100624ATT76660EN.pdf>.

123 See, *e.g.*, RIA Novosti, "Berlusconi wants EU-Russia visa regime to be scrapped" 18/04/2008 at <http://en.rian.ru/world/20080418/105424007.html> (last visited 24 January 2011).

124 "The European Union's relationship with Russia is one of its most important and most complicated. Strong trade and energy ties bind both although many in the EU are concerned about Moscow's human rights record." European Parliament, *Balance human rights & energy with Russia says Knut Fleckenstein MEP*, at <www.europarl.europa.eu/sides/getDoc.do?language=EN&type=IM-PRESS&reference=20100618STO76329> (last visited 26 January 2011).

125 "The expansion of renewable energy sources in Germany has been an exemplary success. Since 2000, renewable energies' contribution to final energy supply has increased 2.5-fold to a level of 10.3 %. In the electricity sector, the German Government had originally aimed to achieve a 12.5 % renewables' share of gross electricity demand by 2010. This target was already surpassed, considerably, by 2007. In 2009, a share of over 16% had been reached." German Federal Ministry for the Environment Nature Conservation, and Nuclear Safety, Renewable Energy Sources in Figures p. 8 (2010). Available at: <www.erneuerbare-energien.de/files/english/pdf/application/pdf/broschuere_ee_zahlen_en_bf.pdf.>

126 "Every [sic] since Chernobyl puffed its radioactive plume over Europe in 1986, Germany has been deeply suspicious of nuclear power. Opposition to Atomkraft is at the center of the country's green movement, and almost a decade ago the country decided to phase out its nuclear plants by 2021. Eben Harrell, *Germany*

mental reasons, France uses it extensively.[127] It is even possible, albeit expensive, to liquefy coal into petroleum products.[128] Likewise, ethanol has been used successfully in Brazil as an alternative automotive fuel.[129] Thus, energy dependence of countries such as the United States or Germany on petroleum imports is only relative. Russian energy exports are driven not by geopolitical ambitions, but by the practical fact of who will pay the most.[130] Recall that, during the Cold War, the USSR did not participate in the Arab oil embargos and continued to sell petroleum to the US.[131] This experience shows that energy issues are not determinative of foreign relations between the Russian Federation and other states but merely constrain outcomes because of the fact that energy dependence is *relative* not absolute. While the importance of those economic relationships is obvious, they are not the EU's primary legal concern. Nor are these economic relationships the driving force of efforts toward *de jure* economic integration of Russia into the EU or the WTO. Meanwhile, *de facto* economic integration is, and will be, pushed forward regardless of political issues.

Mutual economic interests between the EU and Russia are leading to *de facto* economic integration. Europe is dependent on Russian primary resources and exchanges them for investments in Russia's secondary and tertiary markets.[132] This creates conditions under which the rule of law is likely to be increasingly respected because 1) increasing wealth makes respect for the rule of law greater; 2) foreign investors do not wish to see their economic interests nationalized; and 3) International commerce requires legal stability so that contracts clear quickly and efficiently. All this wealth creation in turn indirectly makes the real protection of human rights much likelier in practice. I argue here that *de jure* economic integration will accelerate the inevitable process of *de facto* economic integration *and* help contribute to the formation of the rule of law in the former Soviet republics at least in an exemplary fashion, though hopefully also through formation of institutions and comparison of expertise.

Decides to Extend Nuclear Power – Ecocentric – TIME.com, (6 September 2010). <http://ecocentric.blogs.time.com/2010/09/06/germany-decides-to-extend-nuclear-power/> (last visited 7 February 2011).

127 "France derives over 75% of its electricity from nuclear energy. This is due to a long-standing policy based on energy security." World Nuclear Association, *Nuclear Power in France*, (Updated 21 January 2011). At <www.world-nuclear.org/info/inf40.html> (last visited 7 February 2011).

128 SouthAfrica.info, *Sasol's Synthetic Fuels Go Global*, 16 March 2007. At <www.southafrica.info/business/success/sasol-130307.htm> (last visited 7 February 2011).

129 Larry Rohter, *With Big Boost from Sugar Cane, Brazil Is Satisfying its Fuel Needs*, New York Times, <www.nytimes.com/2006/04/10/world/americas/10brazil.html?_r=1&pagewanted=1&sq=Bush%20Brazil%20ethanol&st=nyt&scp=5> (10 Apr 2006).

130 Marshall Goldman, Petrostate pp. 136-170 (2010)

131 Yaacov Ro'i, The Limits to Power: Soviet Policy in the Middle East, pp. 96-98 (1979).

132 See, *e.g.*, Interview of Finnish Prime Minister Matti Vanhanen, *Europe and Russia's Resources "We Are Mutually Dependent on Each Other"* Spiegel, 14 July 2006, <www.spiegel.de/international/spiegel/0,1518,426555,00.html> (last visited 11 February 2011).

What about human rights? Often people think "either economics or human rights". That is a false dichotomy. In fact, trade leads to prosperity resulting in better protection of human rights.[133] Trade also leads to interdependence making war unprofitable. Accordingly, the EU seeks to create an open integrated market with the Russian Federation. Both partners desire increased integration because the EU is Russia's main trading partner,[134] and because the level of trade between the EU and Russia continues to grow very rapidly.[135]

Key institutions created to channel EU-Russia relations include the EU-Russia Partnership and Cooperation Agreement (PCA), the four "common spaces" pursuant to the PCA, and the Northern Dimension. Finally, to understand how the EU relates to other former Soviet Republics that are not EU Member States, we must also understand the EU's Eastern Partnership program.

4.1 *The EU's Concerns with Respect to the Russian Federation*

In order to understand the relations between the EU and the Russian Federation, we must understand the perceptions of the EU towards the Russian Federation. The issues that cause concern among the EU's leadership or its citizens with respect to the Russian Federation are political, economic and legal in nature. This section briefly summarizes the EU's position on all three issues to show how the three issues, albeit discrete, interact to a significant degree. Ultimately, this section illustrates how the EU and Russia are moving closer to each other on a variety of fronts in the post-Soviet era.

---

133 See, *e.g.*, Isfahan Merali, Valerie Oosterveld, *Giving Meaning to Economic,Ssocial, and Cultural Rights*, p. 74 (2001); Adam Gearey, *Globalization and Law: Trade,Rights, War*, p. 133 (2005); Fabrice Lehmann, Jean-Pierre Lehmann, Peace and Prosperity Through World Trade, p. 279 (2010).

134 "The EU is by far Russia's main trading partner, accounting for 52.3% of its overall trade turnover in 2008. It is also by far the most important investor in Russia." European Commission, *Trade : Russia (Bilateral relations)*, available at <http://ec.europa.eu/trade/creating-opportunities/bilateral-relations/countries/russia/index_en.htm> (last visited 6 December 2010).

135 "Trade and investment between the EU and Russia are substantial and growing, and it is in our mutual interest that this trend should continue. Russia is our third most important trading partner and we see growth rates of up to 20% every year. Energy is a major factor, but impressive growth figures have also been seen in services. With its sustained high growth rates and emerging middle class, Russia is an important emerging market on our doorstep that offers opportunities to EU enterprises. The EU is the major investor in Russia, accounting for 80% of cumulative foreign investment" Europa, Press Releases, *Review of Russia-EU Relations*, <http://europa.eu/rapid/pressReleasesAction.do?reference=MEMO/08/678&format=> (last visited 6 December 2010).

4.1.1 Political Concerns

Politically, the EU's concerns with respect to the Russian Federation go to questions of the rule of law, democracy,[136] and the protection of human rights.[137]

As to the rule of law, a Russian procedural rule of law state enables construction of durable and predictable *legal* institutions, rather than uncertain *political* ones, with the aim of transforming zero-sum political interactions into positive-sum economic interactions. Corruption in the domestic governance of the Russian Federation is a real problem for EU's relationship with the Russian Federation because corruption threatens the security of economic relations.[138]

Democracy, in turn, is not merely an issue of the legitimacy of state power. The existence of democratic institutions is also taken – to some extent erroneously – as evidence or guarantor of the rule of law.[139] The EU's concern with democracy in the Russian Federa-

136 "The EU has supported the development of democracy, the protection of human rights and the development of a healthy civil society in Russia notably through the European Initiative for Democracy and Human Rights (EIDHR)." European Union – EEAS (European External Action Service) | *Freedom, Security and Justice*, <www.eeas.europa.eu/russia/common_spaces/fsj_en.htm> (last visited 6 December 2010).

137 With democracy, respect for human rights, fundamental freedoms and the rule of law an essential element of EU-Russia relations, it is only natural that these issues are regularly discussed at all levels. In 2005 regular, six-monthly EU-Russia human rights consultations were established. They have provided for a substantial dialogue on human rights issues in Russia and the EU and on EU-Russian cooperation on human rights issues in international fora. The EU also maintains a regular dialogue with both Russian and international NGOs on human rights issues. Issues that the EU raises with Russia in the human rights consultations include: the human rights situation in Chechnya and the rest of the North Caucasus, including torture and ill-treatment; freedom of expression and assembly, including freedom of the media; the situation of civil society in Russia, notably in light of the laws on NGOs and extremist activities; the functioning of the judiciary, including independence issues; the observation of human rights standards by law enforcement officials; racism and xenophobia; legislation relating to elections. For its part the Russian side raises matters of concern to it in developments inside the EU. The EU has supported the development of democracy" European Union – EEAS (European External Action Service), *Freedom, Security and Justice*, <www.eeas.europa.eu/russia/common_spaces/fsj_en.htm> (last visited 6 December 2010).

138 Council of the European Union, *European Union Action Plan on Common Action for the Russian Federation on Combating Organized Crime* (2000/C 106/02) Available at: <http://eur-lex.europa.eu/LexUriServ/LexUriServ.do?uri=OJ:C:2000:106:0005:0012:EN:PDF>.

139 European Parliament resolution of 17 June 2010 on the conclusions of the EU/Russia summit (31 May-1 June 2010) (P7_TA-PROV(2010)0234 Conclusions of the EU/Russia Summit) ("1. Reaffirms its belief that Russia remains one of the EU's most important partners in building long-term cooperation and a commitment to working together to address common challenges by means of a balanced, results-oriented approach based on democracy and the rule of law"). Available at: <www.europarl.europa.eu/document/activities/cont/201006/20100624ATT76660/20100624ATT76660EN.pdf>.

tion[140] can be seen as a proxy for concerns about the rule of law.[141] However, *equating* democracy and the rule of law – and they do *correlate* – means that failure to attain the former is seen, wrongly, as *necessarily*, *i.e.inevitably*, impinging on attainment of the latter. That can prevent progress. The rule of law is a precondition to stable business relations, which in turn generates prosperity[142] leading in turn to effective human rights protection.[143] Democratic legitimation can thus be after the fact and is not a *necessary* precondition indispensable to improving human well being in real terms.

As to human rights, not only are open governance institutions and processes needed for the economy,[144] but the rule of law is also crucial for human protection.[145] Poverty resulting

140 See, *e.g.*, Maria Elena Efthymiou, *Fact Sheets on the European Union: Russian Federation*, 07/2009. ("The fundamental values and principles of democracy, human rights, the rule of law and the market economy underpin the EU-Russia bilateral relationship and its legal basis, the Partnership and Cooperation Agreement (PCA). Russia and the EU are committed to work together to combat new threats to international security, such as terrorism, organised crime, illegal migration and trafficking in people as well as drugs." <www.europarl.europa.eu/parliament/expert/displayFtu.do?language=en&id=73&ftuId=FTU_6.4.2.html> (last visited 25 January 2011).

141 See, *e.g.*, European Parliament resolution of 17 June 2010 on the conclusions of the EU/Russia summit (31 May-1 June 2010) (P7_TA-PROV(2010)0234 Conclusions of the EU/Russia Summit) ("F. whereas, as a member of the Council of Europe and of the Organisation for Security and Cooperation in Europe (OSCE), Russia has committed itself to protect and promote human rights, fundamental freedoms and the rule of law, and to respect the sovereignty of its European neighbours; whereas EU-Russia relations have faced a number of serious challenges over the last few years, notably as regards concerns about democracy and human rights in Russia"). Available at: <www.europarl.europa.eu/document/activities/cont/201006/20100624 ATT76660/20100624ATT76660EN.pdf>.

142 "Property rights are not guaranteed and can easily be violated via the corrupt police, courts and other government agencies. As a result, free markets cannot function and the best competitor is not the most efficient but the one with the best connections." Oleg Kozlovsky, *Kozlovsky on Russia's Failed Democracy*, <http://boycottsochi.eu/breaking-human-rights/401-kozlovsky-on-russias-failed-democracy> (last visited 26 January 2011). While I respectfully think Mr. Kozlovsky overstates the case, his identification of the rule of law as a needed precondition to the most productive open market economy is accurate. However, I argue that even a corrupt yet productive economy will generate improved human rights protection and the rule of law indirectly over time, but not as rapidly as a "clean" economy would. Corruption is a significant transaction cost and a source of inefficiency.

143 "The EU places emphasis on the promotion of democracy, the rule of law and good governance in general, as well as respect for human rights and fundamental freedoms." EU, Country Strategy Paper 2007-2013: Russian Federation, p. 3. (2007). At <http://ec.europa.eu/external_relations/russia/docs/2007-2013_en.pdf>.

144 "Growth requires specific economic institutions: the protection of ownership rights and of competition, the fulfillment of contracts (*i.e.* an independent and effective court system)." Sergei Guriev, *Tackling corruption in the Russian economy* openDemocracy, 12 November 2009. At <www.opendemocracy.net/od-russia/sergei-guriev/tackling-corruption-in-russian-economy> (last visited 26 January 2011).

145 "Democracy and human rights are considered to be fundamental prerequisites for a sustainable development and long-term peace." Murad Tangiev, *Political Leadership and Transitional Democracy in the Russian Federation: Challenges and Prospects* Journal of Peace Conflict & Development Issue 11, November 2007, p. 3. Available at <www.peacestudiesjournal.org.uk/dl/PCD%20ISSUE%2011%20ARTICLE_Political%20Leadership%20and%20Transitional%20Democracy%20in%20Russia_Murad%20Tangiev.pdf>.

from legal uncertainty and corruption reduces the real level of protection of human rights and the legitimacy of Russian democracy.[146]

The relationships between the rule of law, a productive economy (which results from an open market, free trade, and the rule of law), democracy, and the attainment of human rights are mutually reinforcing but intertwined in complex ways which are difficult to definitively untangle, prioritize, and hierarchize. However, the rule of law, a productive economy, democracy, and the attainment of human rights are all positively associated: improvement in one tends to encourage improvement in the others.

4.1.2 Economic Concerns

As earlier mentioned, the economic context of Russian-EU trade can be summed up as "raw materials for finished goods": a normal pattern of trade between developed and developing countries.[147] In other words, the EU and the Russian Federation have an economic relationship based on interdependence. Nevertheless, Russian-EU trade has not, to present, coalesced into a binding legal document or relationship[148] beyond the existing partnership and cooperation agreement.

One key to a post war 21st century is economic interdependence rather than isolation. Trading states have a strong incentive to renounce war against each other.[149] For example, the US, unlike the EU does not trade heavily with the Russian Federation.[150] Perhaps as a

146 *E.g.*, "declining state capacity, fiscal austerity, and growing social inequality, characteristic features of many of the new democracies, translate into gross violations of the rights of socially vulnerable groups." Jonathan Weiler, *Human rights in post-Soviet Russia*, Demokratizatsiya, available at: <http://findarticles.com/p/articles/mi_qa3996/is_200204/ai_n9062371/> (last visited 26 January 2011).

147 "The Russian Federation is the 3rd biggest world trade partner of the EU. Energy represents 65% of total EU imports from Russia. Russia is the biggest oil, gas, uranium and coal exporter to the EU. In 2007, 44.5% of total EU's gas imports (150bcm), 33.05% of total EU's crude oil imports, and 26% of total EU coal imports came from Russia. In total, around 24% of total EU gas sources are originating from Russia. In general, energy dependency varies significantly between different Member States / regions in the EU.
The EU is by far the largest trade partner of the Russian Federation: 45% of Russia imports originate from the EU, and 55% of its exports go to the EU, including 88% of Russia's total oil exports, 70% of its gas exports and 50% of its coal exports. The export of raw materials to the EU represents around 40% of the Russian budget, and the EU represents 80% of cumulative foreign investments in Russia." European commission, *Energy: EU-Russia Energy Relations* at <http://ec.europa.eu/energy/international/russia/russia_en.htm> (last visited 7 February 2011).

148 "[F]ollowing the gas crisis from 2009, it is essential to reinforce mutual confidence and to establish a strong and stable legal framework for EU-Russia energy relations." European Commission, *Energy: EU-Russia Energy Relations* at <http://ec.europa.eu/energy/international/russia/russia_en.htm> (last visited 7 February 2011).

149 Paul D'Anieri, International Politics: Power and Purpose in Global Affairs, p. 188 (2009); Brink Lindsey, Against the Dead Hand: The Uncertain Struggle for Global Capitalism, p. 71 (2002).

150 For example, in 2010 the US exported but 5.3861 billion dollars of goods to Russia and improted only 23.7004 billion dollars of goods from Russia. US Census Bureau FTD – Statistics – Country Data – US Trade Balance

consequence, US analysts seem to overemphasize security aspects of the West's relationships to Russia.[151]

4.1.3 Legal Concerns

The EU's legal concerns with Russia touch a myriad of issues. This section addresses only some of the most salient ones. One concern is criminality,[152] which includes arms and drug trafficking.[153] Human migration is also a concern, with fears that Russian workers might flood European labor markets.[154] However, these fears are not in fact particularly realistic.

---

with Russia (2011). At <www.census.gov/foreign-trade/balance/c4621.html#2010> (last visited 9 February 2011); "Russia is currently our 23rd largest goods trading partner with $36.1 billion in total (two way) goods trade during 2008. Goods exports totaled $9.3 billion; Goods imports totaled $26.8 billion. The US goods trade deficit with Russia was $17.4 billion in 2008.

Russia was the United States' 28th largest goods export market in 2008.=

US goods exports to Russia in 2008 were $9.3 billion, up 26.8% ($2.0 billion) from 2007, and up 262% from 1994 (the year prior to Uruguay Round). ...

Russia was the United States' 17th largest supplier of goods imports in 2008."

Office of the United States Trade Representative, Russia. At <www.ustr.gov/countries-regions/europe-middle-east/russia-and-eurasia/russia> (last visited 9 February 2011).

151 Errors in US analysts of Russian capabilities and intentions are a fairly consistent historical fact. See, *e.g.*, Athan G. Theoharis, Richard H. Immerman, Loch Johnson, Kathryn Olmsted, John Prados (eds.) The Central Intelligence Agency: Security Under Scrutiny p. 143 (2006); Norman A. Graebner, Richard Dean Burns, Joseph M. Siracusa, Reagan, Bush, Gorbachev: Revisiting the End of the Cold War (Praeger Security International) 2, 47 (2008). That resulted from 1) individualist method which does not consider historical tendencies of groups 2) presuming the opponent has the same experiences and objectives (failure in opponent modeling) 3) presuming the opponent is an (implacable) adversary and cannot be a partner. These sorts of errors are the result of applying the outmoded realist state centric view of the world to international relations. Thereto, see generally, Eric Engle, *Beyond Sovereignty? The State After the Failure of Sovereignty,* (2008). 15 ILSA J. Int'l & Comp. L. 1 (Fall 2008). Available at SSRN: <http://ssrn.com/abstract=1269445>; Eric Engle, The Transformation of the International Legal System: The Post-Westphalian Legal Order. 23 Quinnipiac L. Rev. 23, 2004. Available at http://ssrn.com/abstract=1020475 ; Eric Engle, Europe Deciphered: Ideas, Institutions and Laws, 33 Fletcher Forum of World Affairs, 63 (2009). Available at SSRN: <http://ssrn.com/abstract=1336490>; Eric Engle, Contemporary Legal Thought in International Law: A Synopsis, Harvard European Law Association WPS, (2010).

152 "POLAND is pushing for citizens of the Russian enclave of Kaliningrad to have visa-free travel, despite fears this could increase smuggling and illegal migration into the European Union." *EU immigration fears over Polish visa deal with Russik,* The Independent.ie, <www.independent.ie/world-news/europe/eu-immigration-fears-over-polish-visa-deal-with-russia-2475682.html> (last visited 25 January 2011).

153 "Our cooperation contributes to the objective of building a new Europe without dividing lines and facilitating travel between all Europeans while creating conditions for effectively fighting illegal migration. Moreover, the EU has a considerable interest in strengthening cooperation with Russia by jointly addressing common challenges such as organised crime, terrorism and other illegal activities of cross-border nature." European Union – EEAS (European External Action Service), *Freedom, Security and Justice,* available at <www.eeas.europa.eu/russia/common_spaces/fsj_en.htm> (last visited 6 December 2010).

154 "The visa barrier between the EU and its eastern neighbors has been growing stronger since the 1990s as a result of Europe's fear of a wave of poor immigrants from the East. As it turns out, this fear was unjustified. Even after Poland joined the EU and all restrictions on Polish immigration were lifted, Poles continued to immigrate to other European countries legally for jobs they had already secured and with enough travel money in their pockets.

Most people are not criminals, and most criminals are eventually caught. The EU's eastward expansion did not lead to the flooding of Western European labor markets with cheap Eastern labor. Western European fears of a flood of Eastern European workers have shown themselves to be unrealistic and overstated. Like most modern industrialized countries, the Russian Federation faces net labor inflows rather than outflows.[155] In fact, about ten million illegal workers from China and Northern Korea work in the Russian Federation. Russian-EU economic integration will not lead to a flood of Russian labor into the EU.

The aforementioned political, economic and legal concerns return us to the question of the relationships between the rule of law, democracy, the economic system, and human rights questions to which we now focus our attention.

4.2 The EU-Russia Partnership and Cooperation Agreement (PCA)

The EU and the Russian Federation aim to create an open integrated market. Just as the EU created a single integrated market in order to generate prosperity and interdependence to obviate and avert war, so too do the EU and Russian Federation seek to create an integrated market.[156] This open and integrated market is to be attained via the Partnership and Cooperation Agreement, which is the principal legal instrument governing EU-Russia relations.[157] The EU also uses PCAs to relate to several other former Soviet republics.[158] The PCAs seek, via functionalist incrementalism, to create over time the same base as found in the EU: a customs union featuring the free movement of goods and capital, the

---

There was no wave of immigrants from Belarus, Ukraine or Russia, even though Ukrainians, for example, can get a Schengen visa from Poland free of charge." *Russia-EU summit: Is Russia part of Europe?* RIA Novosti, <http://en.rian.ru/analysis/20100602/159271249.html> (last visited 25 January 2011).

155 "The chairman of the Federal Migration Service said that there were up to 15 million illegal workers living in present-day Russia. About 80 percent of them come from the countries of the former USSR." Russian Translation Service, *Russian Cultural Updates*, available at <www.english-to-russian-translation.com/russian-translation-news-091105.html> (last visited 24 January 2011).

156 "The overall objective of the Common Economic Space is the creation of an open and integrated market between the EU and Russia." European Commission, *EU-Russia Common Spaces Progress Report2009*, p. 5. (March 2010). Available at <www.st-gaterus.eu/_media/commonspaces_prog_report_2009_en.pdf.>.

157 Agreement on partnership and cooperation establishing a partnership between the European Communities and their Member States, of one part, and the Russian Federation, of the other part EUR-Lex – 21997A1128(01) – EN, <http://eur-lex.europa.eu/LexUriServ/LexUriServ.do?uri=CELEX:21997A1128 (01):EN:NOT> (last visited 6 December 2010).

158 The EU has signed PCAs with almost all of the former Soviet Republics. For the listing and the contents of the various PCAs see *E.U., Partnership and Cooperation Agreements (PCAs): Russia, Eastern Europe, the Southern Caucuses and Central Asia*, at: <http://europa.eu/legislation_summaries/external_relations/relations_with_third_countries/eastern_europe_and_central_asia/r17002_en.htm> (last visited 17 January 2011).

right to establish enterprises, and eventually to include the exchange of professional services and workers.

The EU-Russia PCA forms the basis of the four "common spaces" between the EU and the Russian Federation[159] resulting in an effective institutional framework functioning through the Permanent Partnership Council.[160] At the 2003 Petersburg Summit, the EU and Russia agreed to strengthen cooperation by creating four "common spaces" in the framework of the Partnership and Cooperation Agreement.[161] These are:

1. The Common Economic Space, covering economic issues and the environment;
2. The Common Space of Freedom, Security and Justice;
3. The Common Space of External Security, including crisis management and non-proliferation; and
4. The Common Space of Research and Education, including cultural aspects.

This approach can be seen to parallel the "pillar" structure that was one aspect of the EU prior to the entry into force of the Lisbon Treaty. The Russian Federation wants to be treated as an equal partner to the EU. Thus, a pillar approach, rather than the European Neighborhood Policy (ENP), was set out. However, the pillar approach in fact parallels the ENP approach:[162]

159 "The Partnership and Co-operation Agreement (PCA) which entered into force in 1997 has been the framework of the EU-Russia relationship for a decade. The agreement regulates the political, economic and cultural relations between the EU and Russia and is the legal basis for the EU's bilateral trade with Russia. In 2003 the EU and Russia agreed to create four EU-Russia "common spaces", within the framework of the existing Partnership and Co-operation Agreement (PCA). The Common Economic Space (CES) aims at increasing economic cooperation with creating grounds for establishing a more open and integrated market between the EU and Russia." Joseph Francois, Miriam Manchin, *Economic Impact Of A Potential FTA Between The EU and CIS*, CASE Network Reports No. 84 p. 102 (2009). Available at <www.case-research.eu/upload/publikacja_plik/23704363_CNR_84_final.pdf>.

160 "EU-Russia relations are based on the Partnership and Cooperation Agreement (PCA) in force since 1997, which was further complemented by the Four Common Spaces in 2005. This results in an institutional framework which in many respects works well, particularly at political level through the Cooperation Council (now Permanent Partnership Council in Foreign Ministers' format)." Europa, Press Releases, *Review of EU-Russia Relations*, <http://europa.eu/rapid/pressReleasesAction.do?reference=MEMO/08/678&format=> (last visited 6 December 2010).

161 European Union – EEAS (European External Action Service),*EU-Russia Common Spaces*, available at <www.eeas.europa.eu/russia/common_spaces/index_en.htm> (last visited 6 December 2010).

162 "Russia is not part of the European Neighbourhood Policy. Its relationship with the EU is defined as a Strategic Partnership, consistent with the ENP but evolving along different lines." ENPI, *Commission Report Reviews Progress Under EU-Russia Common Spaces*, <www.enpi-info.eu/maineast.php?id=21349&id_type=1> (last visited 6 December 2010).

4.2.1 Common Economic Space

The essence of the European Union is a "single integrated market". The EU-Russian common economic spaces seeks to attain "an open integrated market". Formation of the common economic space requires the "gradual approximation of legislation".[163] Legal harmonization is one means to the end of improving the rule of law in Russia. Legal harmonization increases legal certainty and reduce transaction costs as does the suppression of tariff barriers, quantitative restrictions, and legal provisions with similar effect.

4.2.2 Common Space on Freedom, Security and Justice

This common space essentially governs police cooperation.[164] It is here where the EU addresses its concerns earlier mentioned of criminality.[165] The essence of this common space is cooperative – it is largely a political arrangement rather than a legal one. As to *freedom* that goes to the issue of visas: travel to and from Russia is still generally subject to visas. Secondarily is the ongoing concern of unauthorized migration. As to security, the problem of counterterrorism is central, but also anti-crime efforts. As to justice, the primary human rights issues involve press freedoms and overreactions against terrorism by organs of the Russian state, secondarily the concern with ultra-nationalist violence appears thereunder.[166]

4.2.3 Common Space on External Security

This common space parallels the former common foreign and security policy (CFSP) pillar of the EU.[167] The goals here are non-proliferation of weapons of mass destruction (especially nuclear weapons), anti-terrorism collaboration, and EU-Russia security cooperation.

---

163 European Union – EEAS (European External Action Service), *Common Economic Space*, available at: <www.eeas.europa.eu/russia/common_spaces/economic_en.htm> (last visited 6 December 2010).

164 "The EU and Russia agreed at the St. Petersburg Summit of May 2003 to create in the long-term a 'Common Space on Freedom, Security and Justice'. A road map agreed in 2005 sets out the objectives and areas for cooperation in the short and medium term. Its gradual development takes place in the framework of the Partnership and Cooperation Agreement." European Union – EEAS (European External Action Service), *Freedom, Security and Justice*, available at <www.eeas.europa.eu/russia/common_spaces/fsj_en.htm (last visited 6 December 2010).

165 "Our cooperation contributes to the objective of building a new Europe without dividing lines and facilitating travel between all Europeans while creating conditions for effectively fighting illegal migration. Moreover, the EU has a considerable interest in strengthening cooperation with Russia by jointly addressing common challenges such as organised crime, terrorism and other illegal activities of cross-border nature." European Union – EEAS (European External Action Service) | Freedom, security and justice, <http://eeas.europa.eu/russia/common_spaces/fsj_en.htm> (last visited 26 January 2011).

166 See generally, European Commission, Eu-Russia Common Spaces Progress Report 2009 p. 41-43 (March 2010). Available at: <http://eeas.europa.eu/russia/docs/commonspaces_prog_report_2009_en.pdf>.

167 "The EU and Russia have agreed to reinforce their cooperation in the area of external security" European Union – EEAS (European External Action Service), *External Security*, available at: <www.eeas.europa.eu/russia/common_spaces/external_security_en.htm> (last visited 6 December 2010).

Today, the EU and the Russian Federation cooperate militarily in certain peacekeeping missions in Africa pursuant to the common space of external security.

4.2.4 Common Space of Research and Education, Including Cultural Aspects

This common space seeks to foster intellectual exchanges and encourage scientific and technical innovation as a key contributor to economic growth.[168] From the Russian perspective, it involves developing the Skolkovo research and industrial park, which is considered the Russian Silicon Valley.[169]

4.3 The Northern Dimension

The Northern Dimension is a regional political framework established to govern the Baltic and Arctic regions,[170] most notably to focus on environmental pollution and cleanup issues that particularly concern radioactive waste[171] resulting from the decommissioning of Soviet-era nuclear vessels, and related issues such as health and maritime transit.[172] The Northern Dimension's objective is to promote environmentally sustainable development throughout the region.[173]

168 "In the area of research and development the objective is to enhance EU-Russia cooperation in mutually agreed priority fields"European Union – EEAS (European External Action Service), *Research and Development, Education, Culture*, available at: <www.eeas.europa.eu/russia/common_spaces/research_en.htm> (last visited 6 December 2010).

169 *Russia to spend $132 million on Skolkovo research hub in 2010,* RIA Novosti, at <http://en.rian.ru/business/20100729/159987299.html> (last visited 7 December 2010).

170 "The Northern Dimension Policy of the European Union answers to the EU's intensive cross-border relations with Russia in the Baltic Sea and Arctic Sea regions." E.U., *Northern Dimension*, available at: <http://ec.europa.eu/delegations/russia/eu_russia/fields_cooperation/regional_issues/northern_dimension/index_en.htm> (last visited 6 December 2010).

171 "Nuclear Safety projects" E.U., *NDEP: Northern Dimension Environmental Partnership*, <www.ndep.org/projectsnuclear.asp?type=nh&cont=prjh&pageid=21> (last visited 6 December 2010).

172 "To facilitate project implementation within the framework of the ND policy, partnerships on the following issues were created: the environment (NDEP), public health and social wellbeing (NDPHS), culture (NDPC) and transport and logistics (NDPTL)." European Union – EEAS (European External Action Service), *Northern Dimension*, <http://eeas.europa.eu/north_dim/> (last visited 6 December 2010).

173 "The mission of the NDPHS is to promote the sustainable development of the Northern Dimension area by improving peoples' health and social well-being." Northern Dimension Partnership in Public Health and Social Well-being, *NDPHS – ABOUT NDPHS – Background, Mission, Priorities, Strategy, Actors and Activities*, <www.ndphs.org/?about_ndphs> (last visited 6 December 2010).

4.4 The Eastern Partnership

The EU frames its relations with the Ukraine, Moldova, and the Caucasian republics within the its Eastern Partnership framework.[174] The *Joint Declaration of the Prague Eastern Partnership Summit* stated that "The main goal of the Eastern Partnership is to create the necessary conditions to accelerate political association and further economic integration between the European Union and interested partner countries."[175] To attain this goal of open borders and economic integration to foster economic development and ultimately political stability, the respect of human rights and the rule of law, "[t]he European Commission proposed a 'differentiated, progressive, and benchmarked approach' to the new neighbors which was specified in the European Neighborhood Policy (ENP) Strategy."[176] To promote this strategy, the EU has jointly mobilized aid and trade as rewards for the attainment of the rule of law and human rights protections to EU standards.[177]

The Eastern Partnership has sometimes been perceived as a point of contention between the EU and the Russian Federation by both Russia and the EU. Each side inaccurately perceived the other as trying to carve out "spheres of influence" to "freeze out" the other.[178] However, the obstacles that had been hindering improved economic integration will be increasingly surmounted by visionary leadership at the EU and in Russia and the other former Soviet Republics. This is because of increased transnational institutional awareness

174 The European Commission put forward concrete ideas for enhancing our relationship with: Armenia, Azerbaijan, Belarus, Georgia, Moldova and Ukraine. This would imply new association agreements including deep and comprehensive free trade agreements with those countries willing and able to enter into a deeper engagement and gradual integration in the EU economy. European Union – EEAS (European External Action Service), *Eastern Partnership*, available at <http://eeas.europa.eu/eastern/index_en.htm> (last visited 6 December 2010).

175 Europa, *Joint Declaration of the Prague Eastern Partnership Summit*, Europa, Press Releases, Prague, 7 May 2009, <http://europa.eu/rapid/pressReleasesAction.do?reference=PRES/09/78&format=HTML&aged=0&language=EN&guiLanguage=en> (last visited 6 December 2010).

176 Joseph Francois, Miriam Manchin, *Economic Impact of a Potential FTA Between The EU And CIS*, CASE Network Reports No. 84 p. 9 (2009). Available at: <www.case-research.eu/upload/publikacja_plik/23704363_CNR_84_final.pd>.

177 See, *e.g.*, EU, *European Neighbourhood and Partnership Instrument: Georgia National Indicative Programme 2007-2010*, p. 4. Available at: <http:/ec.europa.eu/world/enp/pdf/country/enpi_csp_nip_georgia_en.pdf>.

178 See, *e.g.*, Valentina Pop, *EU expanding its 'sphere of influence,' Russia says*, E.U. Observer 21 March 2009. At: <http://euobserver.com/9/27827>(last visited Jan. 17, 2011); EU, *Motion for a resolution on the EU-Russia Summit* – B7-0297/2010, available at <www.europarl.europa.eu/sides/getDoc.do?type=MOTION&reference=B7-2010-0297&language=EN> (last visited 17 January 2011) ("whereas there is a latent dispute between the EU and Russia on creating spheres of influence in the common neighbourhood; whereas this competition prevents the solution of frozen conflicts and risks to create new one's; whereas the European Union and the Russian Federation could and should play together an active role in promoting peace and stability in the common neighbourhood,"); Directorate General, External Policies of the Union, EU Policy Department, External Policies, The Future of EU-Russia Relations (2009) p. 15-16. Available at: <www.europarl.europa.eu/meetdocs/2004_2009/documents/dv/pe407011en_wilsonpopes/pe407011en_wilsonpopescu.pdf>.

and improved mutual understanding. Most importantly, it is also because of the mutual recognition that EU cooperation with the formation of EU-modeled transnational governance in the Russian Federation and former Soviet Republics are complementary and not conflicting.

4.5 WTO Accession

The EU sees Russian accession to the WTO as a means to the end of increased prosperity through freer trade and the construction of legal institutions for the formation of a Russian rule of law state.[179] So does the United States.[180] For its part, the Russian Federation wished to join the WTO[181] and coordinated its accession with EurAsEC[182] and the EU[183] toward

179 European Parliament resolution of 17 June 2010 on the conclusions of the EU/Russia summit (31 May-1 June 2010) (P7_TA-PROV(2010)0234 Conclusions of the EU/Russia Summit) ("G. whereas Russia's accession to the World Trade Organisation (WTO) would make a substantial contribution to further improving economic relations between the EU and Russia, subject to a binding commitment on Russia's part to full compliance with and implementation of WTO undertakings and obligations, and would pave the way for a far reaching, comprehensive economic integration agreement between the two partners on the basis of genuine reciprocity, and whereas Russia established a customs union with Kazakhstan and Belarus on 1 January 2010"). Available at <www.europarl.europa.eu/document/activities/cont/201006/20100624ATT76660/20100624ATT76660EN.pdf>.

180 "We note the importance of our relationship with Russia. A stable, prosperous and democratic Russia remains in our common interest. We seek in our relations with Russia to promote common values such as political pluralism, the rule of law, and human rights, including freedom of media, expression and assembly, and note our concerns in these areas. We will continue to work with Russia in areas of mutual interest, including non-proliferation, counterterrorism, energy security and regional issues, such as the resolution of frozen conflicts. We will also continue to work with Russia towards its accession to the World Trade Organization." EU, *2007 EU- U.S. Summit Promoting Peace, Human Rights and Democracy Worldwide*, p. 2. (2007) Available at: <www.eeas.europa.eu/us/sum04_07/statement_political_security_issues.pdf>.

181 Deputy Prime Minister Alexander Zhukov stated clearly: "Russia's WTO accession is our foreign economic policy priority". Official Website of the Government of the Russian Federation, <http://government.ru/eng/docs/13142/> (last visited 7 February 2011).

182 "We believe that we have come close to meeting every requirement for this. Moreover, I can tell you that, as our negotiators report, in practical terms we have agreed, at least with the European Union (EU), on every major issue. I hope that we will document this in the near future. And, finally I'd like to comment on an issue that is worrying many people. I'm referring to our Customs Union, which is to be followed by the Common Economic Space (CES), and that will mean further integration with Belarus and Kazakhstan. I see here a lot of my acquaintances and even friends. And this is what I want to tell you: I think you should be grateful to us for our enormous and complicated work on coordinating the positions of our partners from Belarus and Kazakhstan. ... the process of coordinating those positions, which are almost identical to WTO rules, was indeed complicated and exhausting. This means that our partners in Europe ... will be able to work, in the near future, both in Belarus and in Kazakhstan by nearly common rules, rules that are very close to WTO requirements. If you study in detail what we are negotiating, you will see that there are practically no deviations from WTO rules." Vladimir Putin, *Prime Minister Vladimir Putin meets with representatives of the German business community*, 26 november, 2010. At <http://premier.gov.ru/eng/events/news/13120/> (last visited 7 February 2011).

183 EUROPA, *Joint Statement of the Delegations of the Russian Federation and of European Union on the occasion of the conclusion of the bilateral talks on the key issues in the accession of the Russian Federation to the WTO,*

that goal. This chapter argues that free trade leads to specialization and economies of scale, and that the rule of law increases legal certainty and reduces transaction costs. This in turn leads to increased prosperity and reduced likelihood of war. The EU and EurAsEc seek the same goals of greater prosperity and political security through free trade. Thus, the EU and EurAsEc are complimentary to each other and are not in conflict with each other.[184] The WTO extends this logic of free trade as the path to peace and prosperity to the global level.[185] The Russian Federation's accession to the WTO reflects and leads to increased acceptance by the West of the Russian Federation's economic growth and future potential.

Following derailment of Russia's WTO accession process because of its 2008 war with Georgia, the Russian Federation has finally concluded its accession to the WTO Treaty.[186] The EU and Russia worked out their differences[187] and the Russian Federation finally joined the WTO.[188] Both the EU and the Russian Federation considered Russian adhesion to the WTO as desirable since it creates new economic opportunities on both sides of the

IP/10/1599 Date: 24/11/2010 ("Both sides are confident that this agreement will greatly facilitate the overall process of accession of Russia to the WTO"). At <http://europa.eu/rapid/pressReleasesAction.do?reference=IP/10/1599&format=HTML&aged=0&language=EN&guiLanguage=en> (last visited 7 February 2011).

184 European Parliament resolution of 17 June 2010 on the conclusions of the EU/Russia summit (31 May-1 June 2010) (P7_TA-PROV(2010)0234 para. G. Available at: <www.europarl.europa.eu/document/activities/cont/201006/20100624ATT76660/20100624ATT76660EN.pdf>.

185 WTO, *10 benefits – 1. Peace*, at: <www.wto.org/english/thewto_e/whatis_e/10ben_e/10b01_e.htm> (last visited 6 February 2011). Also see: Adam Smith, An Inquiry into the Nature and Causes of the Wealth of Nations Ch. 1, para. 3 (University of Chicago Press 1976) (1776) (noting an example of increased production in a pin factory due to specialization); David Ricardo, On the Principles of Political Economy and Taxation 7.13-7.16 (John Murray 1817), available at: <www.econlib.org/library/Ricardo/ricP2a.html#Ch.7,%20On%20Foreign%20Trade> (last visited 30 March 2006); WTO, *Comparative Advantage*, at: <www.wto.org/english/res_e/reser_e/cadv_e.htm> (last visited 6 February 2011).

186 "Both sides are confident that this agreement will greatly facilitate the overall process of accession of Russia to the WTO, and they re-affirm their shared commitment to continue working in a constructive and co-operative spirit on the remaining questions in this multilateral process to achieve this goal as soon as possible." E.U., *Creating Opportunities – Bilateral Relations- Countries-Russia*, available at: <http://trade.ec.europa.eu/doclib/press/index.cfm?id=660&serie=385&langId=en> (last visited 6 December 2010).

187 Lyudmila Alexandrova, *No key differences left at Russia's talks on WTO membership* 27.11.2010, Itar-Tass World Service, <www.itar-tass.com/eng/level2.html?NewsID=15722387> (last visited 6 December 2010).

188 RIA Novosti, *Russia, Economy, Europe, WTO – Russia to Sign WTO Accession Document with EU Next Week – EU Official :: JRL 11/29/10*, <www.cdi.org/russia/johnson/russia-wto-europe-nov-366.cfm> (last visited 6 December 2010).

ledger.[189] Russian adhesion to the WTO was not impeded by Russia's existing free trade areas such as EurAsEC,[190] because each follows the same logic.

5 CONCLUSIONS

This chapter argued that EU governance models can be applied by the Russian Federation and other former Soviet Republics in their relations to each other and the EU. To make that case, it compared the objectives and institutional structure of the USSR, the EU, and the CIS. The USSR and EU alike tried to react to the problem of war and to obtain the best standard of living possible for their people. Nevertheless, they pursued these objectives in radically different ways. Recognizing that both the USSR and EU shared common goals helps us to contextualize the USSR's collapse and the CIS' failure. It also enables us to propose workable governance models based on the extensive historical experiences of the EU in transnational governance. Such institutions and rules can serve as a basis for the formation of the rule of law in Eastern Europe which in turn will generate economic prosperity, especially through trade liberalization, which in turn will improve the real protection of basic human rights there and also make conflict less likely due to interdependence. Understanding the mutually reinforcing character of a market economy, the rule of law, and human rights protection enables all actors to seek out the best rules and processes to obtain optimal outcomes for all people and peoples. Common teleologies,

---

189 "Both sides stressed their strong expectation that the rapid accession of Russia to the WTO will greatly contribute to the opening of new opportunities to do business with and in Russia and strengthen the international competitiveness of the Russian economy by harmonising its economic regime with global trading rules." *Joint Statement of the Delegations of the Russian Federation and of EU on the Occasion of the Conclusion of the Bilateral Talks on the Key Issues in the Accession of the Russian Federation to the WTO*, 24/11/2010. Available at: <http://trade.ec.europa.eu/doclib/docs/2010/november/tradoc_147047.pdf>.

190 "Normally, setting up a customs union or free trade area would violate the WTO's 'most-favoured-nation' principle which assures equal treatment for all trading partners. However, three WTO articles provide derogations from this principle. Article XXIV of the GATT (complemented by an 'Ad Art XXIV', and updated by the 1994 Understanding) allows regional trading arrangements to be set up under certain conditions. Article XXIV contains the primary provisions covering customs unions (CUs), free trade areas (FTAs) and interim trade agreements (necessary for the formation of CUs and FTAs). It is based on four main criteria: Duties and other restrictive regulations of commerce must be eliminated (XXIV:8) on 'substantially all trade' between constituent territories of a customs union or free trade area. Interim arrangements leading to the formation of a free trade area or customs union should exceed ten years only in exceptional circumstances. Furthermore, Article V of the General Agreement on Trade in Services allows WTO members to sign regional agreements on services provided that such agreements have substantial sectoral coverage, eliminate existing discriminatory measures and/or prohibit new or more discriminatory measures. Finally, the 'Enabling Clause' allows derogations from the most-favoured nation treatment principle in favour of developing countries and permits preferential arrangements among developing countries in goods trade." Michael Roberts and Peter Wehrheim, *Regional Trade Agreements and WTO Accession of CIS Countries*, SpringerLink – Intereconomics, Volume 36, Number 6, p. 316 (2001). Available at: <www.springerlink.com/content/41642065037ll583/> (last visited 6 December 2010).

coupled with conflicting methods of competing governance models contextualize historical experiences: understanding these broad tendencies enables mutual understanding which enables us to build bridges instead of walls.

2 A Comparison of the European Union and Eurasian Economic Community

Prospects of Cooperation

Pavel Kislovsky

1 Introduction

1.1 History of Formation and Development

1.1.1 The European Union

The European Union (EU) was founded on 5 May 1950 when French Foreign Minister Robert Schuman proposed integrating the coal and steel industries of Western Europe. This lead to the Paris Treaty, creating the European Coal and Steel Community (ECSC), in 1951, with six members: Belgium, France, Italy, Luxembourg, the Netherlands and West Germany.[1]

The next important step in the formation of what is now the European Union was the signature on 25 March 1957 of the treaty of Rome (Rome treaty) which established the European Economic Community (EEC), the European Atomic Energy Community (Euratom) among the members. This started the removal of trade barriers between the Member States and the creation of a 'common market'. In this year the statute of European Court of Justice was also approved.[2] In December 1991, the project of the treaty on European Union was adopted and signed in 1992 with entry into force on 1 November 1993. The EU leaders agreed to create an Economic and Monetary Union, with a single currency managed by a European Central Bank.

1 S.D. Primbetov, Европейский Союз и Евразийское Экономическое Сообщество -использование опыта и перспективы сотрудничества *(European Union and Eurasian Economic Commonwealth – usage of the experience and perspective of cooperation)*, <www.kisi.kz/img/docs/906.pdf> (27 May 2003).

2 *The history of European Union*, <http://europa.eu/abc/history/1945-1959/1957/index_en.htm> (last accessed 11 January 2011).

1.1.2 The Eurasian Economic Community

While the international processes were deepening and expanding in Europe, in the USSR there was a growing political and economic crisis. As a result, the deeply integrated Soviet system dissolved. The USSR broke into separate countries.

On 8 December 1991 in Belarus, near Belovegskay, the heads of three republics – Belarus, Ukraine and Russian – signed an epochal agreement. This document stated the termination of the USSR and declared the formation of the Commonwealth of Independent Countries (CIS).[3] Later, on 21 December 1991 in Alma-Ata the heads of 11 countries adopted the Almatinskaya declaration that upheld the decision on formation of the superior body of the Commonwealth that was called the Council of the heads of the countries. Later Georgia joined these accords.[4]

Thus, the CIS was organized as the regional international organization with the purpose of creation auspicious conditions for establishing new independent countries, the legal formation of their state system, their international identification, and making treaties between these newly independent countries. Thereby, the CIS finalized the process of political and economical separation of the ex-union republics in a peaceful, civilized form.[5]

By the end of 1993, the new independent countries strengthened their political sovereignty, established state institutions, including national finance-economic systems, and became part of the international community. For all these and other reasons the CIS countries increasingly diverged, especially economically, with regard to cooperation. The CIS lacked any economic, or political mechanism with which to ensure the development of the cooperation between the members.

Because of the low effectiveness of the CIS, in January 1995 Russia and Belarus signed the Treaty on Custom Union.[6] One year later Russia, Belarus, Kazakhstan and Kyrgyzstan signed the Treaty on deepening of integration in economic and humanitarian spheres.[7]

---

3 Ровно 15 лет назад распался СССР *(Fifteen years ago the USSR broke up)*, <www.tass-ural.ru/details/49540.html> (posted 8 December 2006).

4 On 18 August 2009 Georgia terminated participation in the Commonwealth after the conflict in South Ossetia. See, *e.g.* <http://cis.minsk.by/main.aspx?uid=8926>.

5 S.D. Primbetov, *supra* n 1.

6 СОГЛАШЕНИЕ о Таможенном союзеот 20 января 1995 года (*The Treaty on Custom Union)* (20 January 1995), RG, 28 January 1995 (Russia), available at: <www.tsouz.ru/Docs/IntAgrmnts/Pages/Dogovor_2001 1995.aspx>.

7 Договор – от 29 марта 1996 г. Договор об углублении интеграции в экономической и гуманитарной областях *(The Treaty between Russian Federation, Belarus Republic, Kazakhstan Republic and Kirgizstan Republic on deepening of economic and humanitarian integration)*, (29 March 1996), Diplomaticheski vestnik (Diplomatic bulletin), No 4, (Russia) available at: <http://spravka-jurist.com/base/part-rq/tx_xswffu.htm>.

On 26 February 1999 the above mentioned states plus the Republic of Tajikistan signed the Treaty on Custom Union and Common Free Market Zone.[8] In October 2000 the heads of the Member States of the Custom Union, on the basis of the decision of the Custom Union formation, decided to establish an international economic organization and thus signed the Treaty on establishing the Eurasian economical community (EurAsEC).[9]

Within 2007-2009 the legal basis for the building of the union custom zone between Russia, Belarus and Kazakhstan was formed. Since the June 1, 2010 the customs union territory has started its activity.[10]

2 Comparison of Oganizational Mechanisms of the EU and the EurAsEC

2.1 *Parliament of the EU and the Inter-Parliamentary Assembly of the EurAsEC*

The Parliament of the EU and the Inter-Parliamentary Assembly of the EurAsEC do not fully reproduce national parliaments. They both have limited authority in comparison with parliaments of states. They both have restricted legislative power, they do not have executive organs, and they do not have the parliamentary powers which are typical for a state parliament.

Despite the limitations on the EU Parliament there is one feature that makes this organ absolutely unique. The EU Parliament is elected by the citizens of the Union through direct universal suffege. Thus, the EU Parliament is the independent supranational organs of the community; this is a unique case in the history of the Member States.

8 ДОГОВОР о Таможенном союзеи Едином экономическом пространствеот 26 февраля 1999 года *(The Treaty on Custom Union and Free Market Zone)* (26 February 1999), SZ RF, No. 43, item 3983 (1999) (Russia), available at: <www.tsouz.ru/Docs/IntAgrmnts/Pages/Dogovor_26021999.aspx>.

9 ДОГОВОР об учреждении Евразийского экономического сообщества (с изменениями и дополнениями от 25 января 2006 годаи от 6 октября 2007 года) *(the Treaty on establishment of the EurAsEC)* (October 10, 2000), SZ RF, No. 7, Item 632 (Russia), available at: <www.tsouz.ru/Docs/IntAgrmnts/Pages/Dogovor_EvrAzES.aspx> {hereinafter the Treaty on establishment of the EurAsEC}.

10 N.J. Kaveshnikov, Институциональная структура Евразийского экономического сообщества *(Institutional structure of the Eurasian economic commonwealth)*, <www.perspektivy.info/rus/ekob/institucionalnaja_struktura_jevrazijskogo_ekonomicheskogo_soobshhestva_2010-06-30.htm> (posted 6 June 2010).

The number of members of the Europarliament is limited to 732 representatives with a definite number from each state. The parliamentarians are elected for a term of five years.[11]

The EU Parliament acts as an independent institution formed on the basis of will of the people of the Union. In contrast, the Inter-Parliamentary Assembly of the EurAsEC is the organ that is formed by the parliaments of the members of the community from the parliamentarians of such states. The members of the Inter-Parliamentary Assembly do not meet on a daily basis: it holds its session annually.[12]

The Inter-Parliamentary Assembly of the EurAsEC is the organ of cooperation between the legislative authorities of the Member States of the EurAsEC; its main tasks are coordination of the legislative activity of the national parliaments of the Member States; adoption of model laws and codes; assistance in building organizational and legal conditions to conform the Member States' law according to the treaties.[13]

Functionally, the main difference between the EU Parliament and the Inter-Parliamentary Assembly of the EurAsEC is that the EurAsEC parliament does not act as an independent supranational organ. It is an organ of intergovernmental cooperation among the parliaments of the EurAsEC Member States. Projects of law and codes drafted and approved by the Inter-Parliamentary Assemble have a voluntary character and do not have binding legal effect within the territory of the community until the national parliaments adopt them through the procedure of national legislation.

In contrast to the EurAsEC, the EU legislation can have direct effect within the territory of the EU. The EU parliament has the authority to consider and approve EU legislation (Regulations) which has direct legal effect within the territory of the EU.

The EU Parliament at the beginning of its development had primarily advisory functions; later and at the present time the EU Parliament increasingly actively takes other socially important prerogatives.

---

11 *The Treaty establishing the European Community* art. 189-190 (25 March 1957), Official Journal of the European Union C 321, available at <http://eur-lex.europa.eu/LexUriServ/site/en/oj/2006/ce321/ce32120061229en00010331.pdf> {hereinafter the Treaty establishing the European Community}.

12 *The Treaty on establishment of the EurAsEC, supra* n. 9, at Art. 6; *Reshenie Mezgossoveta EurAsEC No 52 o Mezgparlamentskoy asamblee Evraziiskogo ekonomicheskogo prostranstva (Decision of the Intergovernmental Council of the EurAsEC No 52 regarding the Inter-Parliamentary Assemble of the EurAsEC)* (13 May 2002), Informatcionniy bulletin EurAsEC (Informational bulletin of the EurAsEC), 2003, No 3 (Russia), (available at Research legal system ConsultansPlus) {hereinafter Decision of the Intergovernmental Council No 52}.

13 *Decision of the Intergovernmental Council of the EurAsEC No 52, supra* n. 12, at Chapter II Art. 1.

As a result of its evolution, the EU Parliament not only has advisory functions but also has certain (in concert with the EU Council and the Commission) legislative, control, and budgetary authority; the Europarliament also has authority in foreign-policy communication of the EU and relations with the other institutions of the Community and public officers.[14]

The Inter-Parliamentary Assemble of the EurAsEC resembles the EU Parliament before 1979. At that time, the members of the EU Parliament were drawn from the membership of the national legislatures. The EurAsEC Inter-Parliamentary Assembly is at the beginning of its formation as an independent supranational organ. Its development will mostly depend on the legislative development of the EurAsEC Community and especially on the formation of directly effective legislation for the territory of the Community.

The other problem that EurAsEC may face in the formation of the independent parliament is that on the territory of the Member States there is weak political activity. Many specialists note that one of the main problems of the credibility of the EU Parliament as an independent organ is that the electorate does not take an interest in this organ as the political institution during elections.[15] Because we see such allegations about "democratic deficit" in politically active Europe we can rightly wonder how much stronger they would apply to the politically less experienced EurAsEC. New fragile democracies thus have a greater risk of accusations of "democratic deficit" in their intergovernmental and supernational associations such as EurAsEC. The Member States of the EurAsEC are characterized as states without political competition and with a unidirectional political system: a top-down hierarchical system which tends to favor the incumbent party; that exacerbates the problem of "democratic deficit". Effective outcomes may legitimate the results but the policy formation may suffer from inflexibility or limited inputs as a result.

The weakness of the EuraAsEC Inter-Parliamentary Assembly is also conditioned by the limited competence of this organ. The Inter-Parliamentary Assembly is not involved in creation of the Intergovernmental Council decisions and treaties between the countries. At the present moment the function of the Inter-Parliamentary Assembly is limited to drafting model codes and legislation[16] for uptake and emulation by the Member States.

14 M.N. Marchenko, E.M. Deriabina, *Pravo Evropeiskogo Soyuza. Voprosi istorii i teorii (The law of the European Union – the questions of the history and theory)*, Prospekt. 283 (2010) (citing R. Folsom, *European Union Law in a Nutshell*, pp. 40-47 St. Paul 1995).

15 *Id.* at p. 274.

16 N.J. Kaveshnikov *supra* n. 10.

2.2 The Council of the EU and the Intergovernmental Council of the EurAsEC

According to Articles 3 and 5 of the Treaty on establishment of the Eurasian economic community, the Intergovernmental Council of the EurAsEC is the highest organ of the EurAsEC. It composed from the heads of the Member States and the heads of the executive of these states.[17]

The Intergovernmental Council is responsible for consideration of the principle questions regarding the Community. It determines the strategy, direction and perspective of integration development; it makes decisions concerning the mutual trade, realization of the goals and objectives of the EurAsEC, regulation of the custom policy regarding non-Member States etc.[18]

The Constituent Agreement makes certain connections between the highest organ of the EurAsEC and the other organs. The Intergovernmental Council forms the Integration Committee commission, applies to Inter-Parliamentary Assembly and the Court of the Community with inquiries. The Integration Committee is accountable to the Intergovernmental Council. The Intergovernmental Council presents candidates for judges to the Inter-Parliamentary Assembly.

In fact the Intergovernmental Council is the only organ that has the power to make decisions obligatory to the Community. All decisions of the Intergovernmental Council are made through consensus.

The EU Council, unlike the Intergovernmental Council, is formed on the level of ministers of the Member States. The work of the Council is organized by its President who holds this post on the basis of rotation within the period of six months.[19] At least twice a year the EU Council meets under the chairmanship of the head of state or Government of the Member State which holds the Presidency of the Council.[20]

The main functions of the EU Council according to the Treaty are the promotion of the integration process, the development of the EU Community and definition of the general

17 *The Treaty on establishment of the EurAsEC, supra* n. 9, at Arts. 3, 5.

18 *Id.*

19 *The Treaty establishing the European Community, supra* n. 11, at Art. 203.

20 *The Treaty on European Union* Art. 4 (7 February 7 1992), Official Journal of the European Union C 321, available at: <http://eur-lex.europa.eu/LexUriServ/site/en/oj/2006/ce321/ce32120061229en00010331.pdf>) {hereinafter the Treaty on European Union}.

political guidance of the EU Community.[21] For the achievement of these aims the Council has the power to coordinate the general economic policies of the Member States and to make decisions. The Council may impose certain requirements in respect of the exercise of these powers. The Council may also reserve the right, in specific cases, to exercise directly implementing powers itself.[22]

Combining legislative and executive-administrative control functions, the Council of the EurAsEC and the EU Council generally resemble each other, with this exception: decisions of the EU Council de jure do not have obligatory character. Acts made by the EU Council must be approved by the procedure of the Parliament.

2.3 The EU Commission and the Integration Committee of the EurAsEC

The Integration Committee of the EurAsEC is the standing organ of the EurAsEC. It is composed from the deputies of the executive branches of the Member States. The Integration Committee is accountable before the Intergovernmental Council. Among the main tasks of this organ are assuring cooperation of the EurAsEC organs, drafting decisions and documents for the Intergovernmental Council, and ensuring realization of the decisions.[23]

The Integration Committee may decide to establish auxiliary organs in the form of the commissions that are formed on the basis of the sectoral principle. At the present moment there are seventeen councils on the level of ministers of heads of the state organs and five commissions on different aspects of trade policy.[24]

The secretariat of Integration Committee was established to ensure the activity of the Integration Committee. The Secretariat organizes work as projects, consultations and negotiations, prepares analytic overviews, organizes legal and economic expertise etc. The staff of the Integration Committee is formed on a national quota based on the population of the Member States. The officers of the Secretariat are approved by the decision of the Integration Committee at the presentation of the Member State organs.[25]

---

21 *Id.*

22 *The Treaty establishing the European Community, supra* n. 11, at Art. 202.

23 *The Treaty on establishment of the EurAsEC, supra* n. 9, at Art. 6

24 N.J. Kaveshnikov *supra* n. 10.

25 *Pologenie ob Integratsionnom Komitete Evraziiskogo ekonomicheskogo prostranstva (utv. Resheniem Mezgossoveta EurAsEC No 6) (Regulation of Integration Committee of the EurAsEC (approved by Decision of the Intergovernmental Council of the EurAsEC No 6)),* Chapter V (31 May 2001), Informatcionniy bulletin EurAsEC (Informational bulletin of the EurAsEC), 2001, No 1 (Russia), (available at Research legal system ConsultansPlus) {hereinafter Decision of the Intergovernmental Council No 6}.

In contrast to the Integration Committee, the EU Commission is an independent organ which has its own power of the decision. It participates in the shaping of measures taken by the Council and by the European Parliament. It is forbidden for the members of the Commission in the performance of these duties to seek or take instructions from any government or from any other body. The Council and the Commission consult each other and settle by common accord their methods of cooperation.[26]

There must be at least one citizen from each Member State. Heads of State or Government nominate the person it intends to appoint as President of the Commission, who must in turn be approved by the European Parliament. Then, each Member State propose members of the Commission from its state and the Council together with the nominee for President adopt the list of the other persons whom it intends to appoint as Members of the Commission. The nominated President and other Members of the Commission are subject of approval by the European Parliament.[27]

The Integration Committee is more similar to the Council of Ministers of the EU regarding general questions. But there is an essential difference: the Integration Committee considers questions, reconciles drafts of the decision, prepares proposals, and informs the Council but it does not make decisions. All decisions in the EurAsEC are made on the level of the Intergovernmental Council. Decisions made by auxiliary organs of the Committee are realized not by these organs but by its members on the level of the heads of the organs of Member States. Thus, implementation of the law of the EurAsEC into the national law is made on the national level without the strict control from the independent authority.[28]

2.4 *The European Court of Justice and the EurAsEC Court*

The EU court system consists of the two instances. These are the Court of Justice and the Courts of First instance which was established at the insistence of the Court of Justice and is considered as an extension of the ECJ.[29]

The Court of Justice has broad jurisdiction. It considers and decides the questions concerning the failure to comply with the EU Treaty and fulfillment of obligations under this Treaty; it reviews the legality of acts adopted by the EU organs and hears actions against the European Parliament, the Council or the Commission concerning the infringement

---

26 *The Treaty establishing the European Community, supra* n. 11, at Arts. 211, 213, 218.

27 *Id.*, at Art. 214.

28 S.D. Primbetov *supra* n. 1.

29 S.J. Kashkin *et al., Pravo Evropeiskogo Souza (Law of the European Union),* 77 (3d ed., Prospekt, 2011).

of the Treaty. The ECJ also gives preliminary rulings concerning the interpretation of this Treaty, the validity and interpretation of acts of the institutions of the Community and of the European Central Bank, the interpretation of the statutes of bodies established by an act of the Council and decides the disputes relating to compensation for damage caused by intuitions of the EU Community or its servants and *et al.*[30]

The Court of the First Instance has jurisdiction on most questions subject to the jurisdiction of the Court of Justice with the exception of questions concerning: interpretation of the establishing treaties, acts adopted by the institutions of the Community and the European Central Bank, statutes of bodies established by an act of the Council, and questions concerning disputes between the Member Stated which relate to the subject matter of this Treaty. Decisions made by the Court of First Instance may be appealed to the Court of Justice.[31]

The EurAsEC Court ensures the uniform application of the Treaty on the EurAsEC, the other treaties in the framework of the EurAsEC, and decisions made by organs of the EurAsEC. It also considers economic questions between Member States concerning realization of the legal basis of the EurAsEC and gives interpretation and opinions.[32] The decisions made by the EurAsEC court are final and subject of execution in accordance with the national law of Member States within three months from the moment when the decision was made.[33]

Compared with the Court of Justice, the EurAsEC court has rather limited competence. The EurAsEC does not have jurisdiction on disputes between private persons, unlike the European Court of Justice. The Court of the EurAsEC may have the right to consider other disputes arising out from the treaties executed within the framework of the EurAsEC, but only if it is stipulated in such treaties. At present there are 93 effective treaties within the framework of the EurAsEC as well as the treaty establishing the EurAsEC itself: however, only five of those treaties provide for adjudication by the EurAsEC court. In over ten years the Court has decided only two cases.[34] The statistic is telling regarding the lack of effectiveness of the EurAsEC court system.

---

30 *The Treaty establishing the European Community*, *supra* n. 11, at Arts. 230, 232, 234-235.

31 *Id.*, at Art. 225.

32 *The Treaty on establishment of the EurAsEC*, *supra* n. 9, at Art. 8.

33 *Statut Suda Evraziiskogo Ekonomicheskogo prostranstva (priniat Resheniem Megossudarstvennogo Soveta EurAsES No 502) (Statute of the EurAsec court (adopted by the Decision of the Intergovernmental Council of the EurAsEC No 502 on the new redaction of the Statute of the EurAsEC court))*, Art. 22 (5 July 2010), (was not published, available at Research legal system ConsultansPlus) {hereinafter Decision of the Intergovernmental Council No 502}.

34 N.J. Kaveshnikov *supra* n. 10.

Moreover, the legal consequences of the decisions made by the Court of the EurAsEC are unclear. The Statute of the Court says that the decision made by the Court is final – but not binding – but that each Member State *shall* execute the decisions of the Court. At the same time, according to the Statute of the Court, the EurAsEC Court shall provide a recommendation concerning the measures for execution of its judgment. Such a conception differs from the legal power of the decisions made by the European Court of Justice. The European Court of Justice has definite sanctions for failure to execute its decisions such as penalties; the decisions made by the Court of Justice concerning the legality of national law in light of the EU law have direct effect and are not required to be confirmed by national institutions.

3 Prospects of Cooperation

At present it is hard to talk about large-scale cooperation between the EurAsEC and the EU for several reasons. First, the EurAsEC was registered by the UN as an international organization only in May 2003. The EurAsEC is in the process of formation and has not entered into cooperation with non-member countries or international organizations. Secondly, the EurAsEC and the EU have different organizing principles. The EurAsEC and its organs, unlike the EU, cannot be called a supranational organization. Finally, the EurAsEC does not have separate finance resources. The only resources it has are the contributions of EurAsEC Member States.

Unlike the EurAsEC, international cooperation by the EU is central to the organization and covers both economic and political spheres. The main form of cooperation is participation in multilateral negotiations and conclusion of treaties. The making of such treaties shows that the EU is a subject of international law.[35]

So far there is still only limited cooperation between the EU and the EurAsEC. However, the cooperation between the Member States of the EurAsEC and the EU is very progressive especially with Russia.

> Russia is one of the EU's key trading partners and trade between the two economies has showed steep growth rates until mid 2008… The EU is by far Russia's main trading partner, accounting for 52.3% of its overall trade turnover in 2008. It is also by far the most important investor in Russia. It is estimated that up to 75% of foreign direct investments stocks in Russia come from the

35 S.D. Primbetov *supra* n. 1.

> EU Member States… The Partnership and Co-operation Agreement has been the framework of the EU-Russia relationship for more than a decade. It was signed in 1994 and entered into force on 1 December 1997.[36]
>
> The agreement foresees the possible establishment of a free trade area between the parties…
>
> At the St. Petersburg Summit in May 2003 the EU and Russia agreed to reinforce co-operation with a view to creating four EU/Russia common spaces, within the framework of the existing Partnership and Co-operation Agreement. The Common Economic Space aims at increasing opportunities for economic operators, a further step towards establishing a more open and integrated market between the EU and Russia. The overall objective of the Common Economic Space is to put in place the conditions for increased and diversified trade and creating new investment opportunities by pursuing economic integration, elimination of trade barriers, regulatory convergence, market opening, trade facilitation and infrastructure development by closer co-operation, exchange of information and sharing of best practices.[37]

At the EU-Russia Summit in Moscow on 10 May 2005 the Roadmap on the Common Economic Space was adopted.[38] "The document sets out a number of principles and priority activities. It also sets up dialogues on the following trade related issues: Investment dialogue, IPR dialogue, Public Procurement Dialogue, Regulatory Dialogue on Industrial Products and Industrial and Enterprise Policy Dialogue, Energy Dialogue, Competition Dialogue, Macroeconomic and Financial Services Dialogue, Trade Facilitation and Customs."[39]

4 Conclusion

The institutional structure of EurAsEC has been formed on the basis of the EU experience. Commentators on the EurAsEC repeatedly say this.[40] For example, the chairperson of the Committee on CIS of the Federation Council Mr. Gustov V.A. argues that the legal basis

36 *The European Union and the Russian Federation*, <http://ec.europa.eu/trade/creating-opportunities/bilateral-relations/countries/russia/> (last accessed 11 January 2011).

37 *Id.*

38 See *The Joined Statement The Roadmap on the Common Economic Space*, (last accessed 23 May 2003) <http://eeas.europa.eu/russia/docs/roadmap_economic_en.pdf>.

39 *Russia*,<http://ec.europa.eu/trade/creating-opportunities/bilateral-relations/countries/russia/index_en.htm> (last accessed 11 January 2011).

40 Konstantin Gaaze, Воссоздание СССР по образу и подобию Евросоюза *(Reconstruction of the USSR in the image and likeness of the EU)*, <http://slon.ru/articles/329088/>, (posted 19 March 2010).

of regional integration that has been actively developed for the last years in the world is generally a reflection of the EU practice on formation and development of the EU Community.[41] However, in this case, some variants to the EU structure are made.

The main difference is that in the present form the EurAsEC does not stipulate the creation of the supranational organs. The experience of the EU shows that the delegation of some national functions to the EurAsEC is necessary. It is a very delicate question that will take some period with several interim stages.

Another major difference of the institutional structures of the two communities is that the EurAsEC does not have an organ which would ensure the interests of the Community. In the EU the EU Parliament and the European Commission are the organs that defend the interests of the whole Community. Basically, the EU is a balance of institutions that represent general interests of the Community and the interests of the Member States. In the EurAsEC, neither the Inter-Parliamentary assemble nor the Integration Committee can currently be called organs that express the general interest of the EurAsEC.

It is clear that for further realization of the principles of free market zone of the Eurasian Economic Community the Member State of the EurAsEC will have to change their approach to the formation of the institutions and vest some national authority in the organs of EurAsEC. The experience of the EU shows that creation of effective independent Community organs with real powers is the key factor in building a truly integrated economic community.

41 V.A. Gustov, *Na puti k sozdaniu tamozennogo souza Evraziiskogo ekonomicheskogo soobschestva (On the way of formation of the custom union of the EurAEC)*, 19 (Evraziiskaya integratsia: ekonomika, provo, politika No3, 2008).

3 The EU-Russia Relationship

Svetlana Voronova-Yaremenko

1 Introduction

In this chapter we look at the EU-Russia relationship from the Russian perspective, to understand why the EU and Russia have failed to achieve their major goals so far. This chapter summarizes reasons for failures and recommendations on how to avoid future frustration.

The main idea of this chapter is that Russia is a unique country in many ways including its history, market development, the people's mentality, and elites' attitudes towards the world and its role and place in it. Attempts to apply Western patterns and standards to Russia have always failed, both when undertaken by Russia itself or imposed from without. That is why the EU and Russia did not achieve many of their goals with respect to each other, so far, resulting in frustration, particularly from the EU's side. Russia does not and most probably will never fit EU standards, notwithstanding their high quality and Russia's good will efforts to comply with these standards. But that does not decrease mutual interdependence and does not abolish the necessity to develop EU-Russia relations on the basis of mutual respect of each others' particularities.

2 Background of the Present EU-Russia Relationship

This section presents the basics of the EU-Russia relationship and is based on "the key idea that EU-Russia interdependence cannot be avoided and will only get stronger in the future."[1] Relations with Russia are of crucial importance for the EU.[2] First of all, because Russia is the EU's biggest neighbour, secondly because Russia is the third largest trading partner of the EU, the fourth largest trading partner of the Eurozone and an essential energy supplier to the EU. The Economic and Social Committee pointed out that relations with Russia are among the EU's priorities, and over the last few years have become even

1 Thomas Gomart, *EU-Russia Relations Toward a Way Out of Depression*, (2008), <www.ifri.org/files/Russie/Gomart_EU_Russia.pdf>.

2 Recommendation to the Council on the new EU-Russia agreement – European Parliament recommendation to the Council of 2 April 2009 on the new EU-Russia agreement (2008/2104(INI)) OJ 2010 C137E/29.

more important.[3] The Committee added some more reasons for this. Historical links are the first one: "[f]or hundreds of years, relations between Russia and other countries have had a decisive influence on the development of the whole of Europe."[4] The second reason is that Russia was the main component of the former Soviet Union and the third one is that Russia is a nuclear power.

From the Russian side, the EU is very important trade and investment partner. The EU is the major investor in Russia, accounting for 80% of cumulative foreign investment. The EU's investments are very important for the development of the Russian's economy, its diversification and modernization.[5] The EU is also a source of technology and know-how for Russia.[6]

Finally, Russia is a member of various European organizations, for examples the Council of Europe and the Organization for Security and Cooperation in Europe (OSCE).

2.1 *The EU-Russia Partnership and Cooperation Agreement*

The legal basis for EU-Russia relations is The EU/Russia Partnership and Cooperation Agreement (PCA)[7] which was negotiated in 1992-1994 and entered into force on 1 December 1997. According to Article 106, the PCA is concluded for an initial period of ten years and is "automatically renewed year by year provided that neither Party gives the other Party notice of denunciation of the Agreement at least six months before it expires". At the Sochi Summit in May 2006, the EU and Russia agreed that the PCA would remain valid until a New Agreement enters into force.[8]

The PCA provides a political, economic and cultural framework for EU-Russian relations. It sets up trade, investment and harmonious economic relations. Among the main values provided in the PCA are: respect for democratic principles and human rights, the commit-

3 OJ 1998 C138/166, Resolution on the Commission communication 'The future of relations between the European Union and Russia and the action plan 'The European Union and Russia : the future relationship' (COM(95)0223 C4-0217/95 6440/96 – C4-0415/96).
4 OJ 1998 C138/166, Resolution on the Commission communication 'The future of relations between the European Union and Russia and the action plan 'The European Union and Russia : the future relationship' (COM(95)0223 C4-0217/95 6440/96 – C4-0415/96).
5 Communication from the Commission to the Council – Review of EU-Russia relations {SEC(2008) 2786}
6 Rolf Schuette, *E.U. -Russia relations Interests and Values—A European Perspective,* Carnegie Papers (2004).
7 OJ 1997 L327/1, Agreement on partnership and cooperation establishing a partnership between the European Communities and their Member States, of one part, and the Russian Federation.
8 Commission staff working document accompanying the communication from the Commission to the Council – Review of EU-Russia relations pursuant to conclusions of the Extraordinary European Council of 1 September 2008 {COM(2008) 740 final}.

ment to promote international peace and security, and the principles of market economy and sustainable development. The PCA sets out in detail economic provisions including trade in goods, business, establishment, trade, and services and provides in less detail for cooperation on prevention of illegal activities, as well as general provisions on cultural cooperation and financial cooperation.[9] The PCA's declared objectives are to strengthen political and economic freedoms and to support Russia's efforts to consolidate its democracy, to develop its economy, and to complete its transition into a market economy.[10]

The PCA also provides for institutional framework for EU-Russia relations: the Cooperation Council (now Permanent Partnership Council in Foreign Ministers' format),[11] the Cooperation Committee and the Parliamentary Cooperation Committee.

The PCA forms the legal basis necessary for the development of cooperation between the EU and Russia.[12]

The legal framework of relations between EU and Russia established in the PCA was complemented by the Four Common Spaces in 2005.

2.2 The Four Common Spaces[13]

At the St. Petersburg Summit in May 2003, the EU and Russia agreed to set up long term cooperation in four common spaces in the framework of PCA: a common economic space; a common space of freedom, security and justice; a space of co-operation in the field of external security; and a space of research, education, and cultural exchange.

At the Moscow Summit in May 2005 the parties adopted a single package of Road Maps for the creation of the four common spaces. The Road Maps set out further specific objectives, and determine the actions necessary to make the common spaces a reality. They

9 Commission staff working document accompanying the communication from the Commission to the Council – Review of EU-Russia relations pursuant to conclusions of the Extraordinary European Council of September 1, 2008 {COM(2008) 740 final}.

10 Rolf Schuette, *E.U. -Russia relations Interests and Values—A European Perspective,* Carnegie Papers, 14 (2004).

11 Communication from the Commission to the Council – Review of EU-Russia relations {SEC(2008) 2786}.

12 OJ 1998 C138/166, Resolution on the Commission communication 'The future of relations between the European Union and Russia and the action plan 'The European Union and Russia : the future relationship' (COM(95)0223 C4-0217/95 6440/96 – C4-0415/96).

13 European Union Preparatory Acts, Communication from the Commission to the Council and to the European Parliament on relations with Russia, EU: COM(2004) 106, Celex No. 504DC0106, p. 1

thereby determine the agenda for co-operation between the EU and Russia for the medium-term.[14]

The main goal of the four common spaces was establishing better relations between EU and Russia. According to some authors it was the first attempt to identify a rational, long-term strategy for EU-Russian cooperation.[15]

2.2.1 Common Economic Space

The common economic space is based on well developed trade and investment relations between the EU and Russia. The EU and Russia rightly regard each other as important trade partners and are becoming important investment partners as well. Russia is the EU's third largest trade partner after the USA and China. Total trade among EU and Russia amounted to 232 billion euros in 2007 (compared with 130 billion in 2004).[16]

The EU has always declared that its main goal is to eliminate all obstacles for bilateral trade and investment, to create an open and integrated market, and to assist the development of a Russian market economy.[17] This objective is the key idea of the common economic space between EU and Russia. "The common economic space aims to remove barriers to trade and investment and promote reforms and competitiveness, based on the principles of non-discrimination, transparency, and good governance"[18] which are the main ideas of free movement of goods among EU Member States.

Russia is a huge market for EU companies. The range of goods exported by the EU to Russia is diverse. It includes machinery and transport equipment (39%), chemicals (13%), manufactured goods (11%), and food and live animals (6%). Russia exports mainly energy/mineral fuels (65.7%) to the EU.[19] So, notwithstanding the mutual importance of common economic space for both parties, I believe the EU benefits even more from this alliance than Russia.

---

14 Russia-European Union relations, Wikipedia, <http://en.wikipedia.org/wiki/Russia_%E2%80%93_European_Union_relations>.

15 Rolf Schuette, *E.U.-Russia relations Interests and Values—A European Perspective,* CARNEGIE PAPERS, 2004, (p. 2).

16 Commission staff working document accompanying the communication from the Commission to the Council – Review of EU-Russia relations pursuant to conclusions of the Extraordinary European Council of 1 September 2008 {COM(2008) 740 final}.

17 Rolf Schuette, *E.U. -Russia relations Interests and Values—A European Perspective,* Carnegie Papers (2004).

18 Russia-European Union relations, Wikipedia, <http://en.wikipedia.org/wiki/Russia_%E2%80%93_European_Union_relations>.

19 Commission staff working document accompanying the communication from the Commission to the Council – Review of EU-Russia relations pursuant to conclusions of the Extraordinary European Council of 1 September 2008 {COM(2008) 740 final}.

The common economic space sets forth a wide range of targets: regulatory policy, investment issues, competition, financial services, telecommunications, transport, energy, outer space activities, etc. Great significance in the common economic space is attached to environmental problems including nuclear safety. EU-Russia mutual interests under the common economic space also include new investment opportunities, common transport, telecommunications, and energy networks.

In my view, though the common economic space is much more in the EU's interest so far, there is also a big potential for developing the Russian economy and integrating it into the world's business community not only as a raw material supplier but as a producer of high technology products, aero-space technology, and food and consumer goods.

2.2.2 Common Space of Justice, Freedom and Security

The issues of the common space of Justice, Freedom and Security belong to cooperation in Justice and Home Affairs.[20] The basis for this common space is respect for human rights, democracy and the rule of law. The Common space of Justice and Home Affairs includes interests of Russia and the EU which coincide: visa matters, fighting international organized crime and terrorism, preventing illegal migration and immigration, judicial training of Russian legal experts in the EU, transit of persons and goods to and from Kaliningrad and similar issues.

As contacts between the EU and Russian citizenry are increasing due to trade, tourism and education an important priority in the EU-Russian relationship is to ease people-to-people contacts. This issue is implemented in the EU-Russia Agreements on Visa Facilitation and Readmission, which entered into force on 1 June 2007.

These agreements are the first step undertaken by the EU and Russia towards visa liberalization. Russia's objective is to obtain a visa free regime for Russian citizens in the EU.

The EU's interests, in contrast, are contradictory. On the one hand the EU wants facilitated travel of EU citizens to Russia and to eliminate the complicated registration procedures in Russia. On the other hand, there is a fear on the EU's side that visa liberalization can create a flood of low qualified workers and criminals to the EU. Therefore the EU wants to enable Member States to return undesired aliens back to Russia. One more problem in

20 Rolf Schuette, *E.U. -Russia relations Interests and Values—A European Perspective,* Carnegie Papers (2004).

this area is that the EU rules of work admission for foreign workers are not fully harmonised yet.[21]

Drug-fighting is another common field of interest of both sides. A Memorandum of Understanding between the European Monitoring Centre on Drugs and Drugs Addiction and the Russian Federal Drugs Control Service was signed in 2007. The MoU facilitates exchanges of information between the two agencies in order to prevent drug traffic.[22]

Preventing international crime is one more crucial area of cooperation between the EU and Russia. This problem includes terrorism, illegal immigration and trafficking in human beings, money laundering, counterfeiting currencies and documents. The existing strategic cooperation agreement covers such fields. EU-Russian cooperation in the fight against terrorism is based on the 2002 Joint Statement on Counter-terrorism and the relevant provisions of the road maps for the Common Spaces of Freedom, Security and Justice and of External Security.[23]

The field of Justice and Home Affairs also includes border issues. The EU seeks to ensure the legal security of its external borders. This question thus implicates relations between Russia and the Baltic States (Estonia, Latvia and Lithuania). The border demarcation agreement between Russia and Estonia has been signed, but Russia's ratification is pending. The border agreement between Russia and Latvia was ratified in 2007. Russia's border agreement with Lithuania has been ratified, but the border is not yet properly demarcated. Clarifying the border issue and Russian ratification is in the EU's interests. These agreements address the exact position of the borders between the Baltic states and Russia.

Though big steps were made in developing of Common space of Justice, Freedom and Security, there are nevertheless still some undecided problems. For example, access to asylum procedures and documentation of refugees and asylum seekers is still incompletely regulated. Many asylum seekers in the EU originate from Russia. For the years 2005, 2006 and 2007 Russia ranked second among countries of origin of asylum seekers in the EU.[24]

In order to implement the road map and address problems in the area of Justice and Home Affairs, EU and Russian representatives met on 13 October 2005. They agreed to organize

---

21 Commission staff working document accompanying the communication from the Commission to the Council – Review of EU-Russia relations pursuant to conclusions of the Extraordinary European Council of 1 September 2008 {COM(2008) 740 final}.

22 *Id.*

23 *Id.*

24 *Id.*

regular bi-annual meetings to bring together experts in counter-terrorism, cyber-crime, document security and judicial cooperation.[25]

2.2.3 Common Space of External Security

The Common Space of External Security roadmap points out the shared responsibility of the and Russia in the international order. This road map is covered by the EU's second pillar, the Common Foreign and Security Policy. For the EU, peace and security in its neighbourhood is one of the most important areas of concern. Though the EU and Russia disagree on some international issues – historically, *e.g.*, the Federal Republic of Yugoslavia; currently, the situation in Abkhazia[26] and South Ossetia – the EU admits that "Russia is a key geopolitical actor, whose constructive involvement in international affairs is a necessary precondition for an effective international community."[27]

The PCA set forth the relevant goal of cooperation between the EU and Russia to "bring about an increasing convergence of positions on international issues of mutual concern, thus increasing security and stability." The Common Space of External Security's issues are often discussed by the parties at multiple levels: twice-yearly Summits; regular meetings of Foreign Ministers; monthly PSC Troika meetings with Russia, Political Directors meetings, twice-yearly human rights consultations, as well as working level contacts. These contacts help to develop mutual understanding between the parties on the different international issues.

From the EU's perspective, the Common Space of External Security includes two areas: "international issues, including regional conflicts; and the domestic situation in Russia itself, that is, on questions of the 'common European values,' such as democracy, human rights, and the rule of law, and how they have been implemented or not in Russia."[28]

The focus of the Common Space of External Security is on international issues. The EU is an active international actor on the political level. "The EU engages with Russia on Iran, the Middle East, Afghanistan, the Balkans (…) in the Middle East Peace Process and on non-proliferation in Iran."[29] Moreover, the parties have to meet "new global challenges and threats (for example, the fight against international terrorism, and disarmament and the non-proliferation of weapons of mass destruction)".[30] As to domestic issues, Russia

25 Russia – European Union relations, Wikipedia, <http://en.wikipedia.org/wiki/Russia_%E2%80%93_European_Union_relations>.

26 Communication from the Commission to the Council – Review of EU-Russia relations {SEC(2008) 2786}.

27 *Id.*

28 Rolf Schuette, *E.U. -Russia relations Interests and Values—A European Perspective,* Carnegie Papers (2004).

29 Communication from the Commission to the Council – Review of EU-Russia relations {SEC(2008) 2786}.

30 Rolf Schuette, *E.U.-Russia relations Interests and Values—A European Perspective,* Carnegie Papers (2004).

often feels subjected to severe criticism from the EU. Examples include the conflict in Chechnya and similar issues of domestic security. On the other hand, the EU itself does not always abide by its stated "common values". For example, the abuse of the human rights of Russian minorities in the Baltic States. In Estonia for example those Russian nationals who do not speak Estonian do not have the right to Estonian passports – and thus are denied EU Citizenship. Such discrepancies lead to disagreements between the EU and Russia.

But, notwithstanding such sad misunderstandings in international and domestic affairs, the EU and Russia cannot do without each other. Cooperation requires continuing political dialogue between the parties at many levels and respect of each others position. "[B]oth sides should have an interest and feel a responsibility to create stability and build security in their immediate neighborhood (…) both sides would benefit from such cooperation".[31]

In short, cooperation in international affairs is in the mutual interest of the EU and Russia. Even if the parties cannot always come to the agreement in these area, Russia's cooperation is necessary for the EU to attain Peace, safety and stability in the region. Therefore, the EU cannot avoid cooperation which Russia in this field.

2.2.4 Common Space of Research and Education, Culture

Cooperation in the field of research, education and culture is another strong mutual interest of Russia and the EU. This field is addressed by the common space of research, education and culture. Both Russia and the EU wish to deepen and broaden their existing cooperation in research, science, and technology.

The framework of research cooperation is the EC-Russia Science and Technology Cooperation agreement, which is in force since 2004. On the institutional level there are regular meetings of the Joint EC-Russia Steering Committee; meetings of FP7 National Contact Points; participation of Russian Federation entities in FP7; setting-up and organisation of meetings of joint EC-Russia thematic research working groups. Cooperation in research area includes not limiting aeronautics research (the EC & Euratom FP7 Work Programmes; Partnership between the European Space Agency and Rosaviakosmos); nuclear safety (the Agreement for cooperation between the European Atomic Energy Community (Euratom) and the Russian Federation in the field of nuclear safety) etc.

In the field of science, Russia is a party to the International Science and Technology Centre (ISTC). The ISTC "is an intergovernmental organization established in 1992 through an

31 *Id.*

agreement signed by the European Community and the European Atomic Energy Community (acting as one party), the USA, Canada, Japan, and the Russian Federation."[32] The ISTC carried on more than 2600 projects during the past fourteen years involving weapons scientists.

In the education area, Russia participates in various EU-funded programmes, notably Tempus and Erasmus Mundus. Moreover, contacts between the EU and Russian students and teachers and student mobility have increased over past few years. "In 2008, Russia's allocation translated into at least 570 scholarships and three new partnerships of EU-Russia universities."[33]

The EU and Russia also carry on some joint education projects. For example, the European Studies Institute (ESI) in Moscow. ESI provides a one-year postgraduate Master's programme in EU studies, the Institute's main goals are: (1) developing a cadre of officials who are familiar with EU issues; (2) to increase various debates on EU-Russia relations.

Cultural co-operation has started with the Kajaani process in 2006.[34] The cultural issues are covered by EU-Russia joint working group on culture established in 2007. The main aim of the group is to promote artistic and cultural projects, cooperation between cultural institutions and at UNESCO etc by means of drawing up relevant Action Plan.[35]

The creation of the common space of research, education and culture was in the mutual interests of the EU and Russia. The EU sees cooperation in this area as a way to promote a common European identity and to strengthen Russian civil society, "common European values," and the freedom of expression and free media.[36] For Russia, it is new opportunity in sharing experience with the well developed EU society.

3 Mutual Interests

There are strong mutual interests in EU-Russia relations. The first area is growing economic interdependence due to increased trade and investment flows. The EU's goal of eliminating

32 Commission staff working document accompanying the communication from the Commission to the Council – Review of EU-Russia relations pursuant to conclusions of the Extraordinary European Council of 1 September 2008 {COM(2008) 740 final}.

33 *Id.*

34 Communication from the Commission to the Council – Review of EU-Russia relations {SEC(2008) 2786}

35 Commission staff working document accompanying the communication from the Commission to the Council – Review of EU-Russia relations pursuant to conclusions of the Extraordinary European Council of 1 September 2008 {COM(2008) 740 final}.

36 Rolf Schuette, *E.U. -Russia relations Interests and Values—A European Perspective,* Carnegie Papers (2004).

all obstacles for bilateral trade and investment and to assist the development of a Russian market economy is in Russia's interests as well. The second common area of concern is security and prosperity on the European continent. Common transport, telecommunications, and energy networks are some more common areas of the EU-Russia interest. Fighting against international terrorism and organized crime also requires joint EU-Russian efforts.

Therefore, the EU and Russia have many common interests. Coordinating and improving attainment of common goals however is hindered if Russia and the EU pursue opposing objectives or try to carve out spheres of influence in the former Soviet republics.[37] Cooperation and common interests are the keys to conflict resolution. However, while there are many common interests between the two partners, some are more important for one party than the other. This asymmetric reality explains why despite common interest conflict subsists.

3.1 Russian Interests

One of Russia's greatest long-term objectives is to integrate its economy into the world economy. It is in Russia's interest to modernize its economy and integrate it into the global economy with the help of the EU which is economically and technologically advanced and is the biggest Russian trade partner. In March 2008, Dmitry Medvedev in his speech outlined that "after almost a century of isolation and self-isolation" Russia is returning "to global Politics and [the] global economy." It is necessary to remember that the Russian economy has never been as integrated into the world economy as it is today.[38] Medvedev stated that Russia sought to build up an equal cooperation with the EU including in the energy sector.[39]

Russia needs to integrate into the global economy in order to get market access for its products, including exports of its raw materials. The EU is a big market for Russian primary exports, especially energy. Russia also wishes to improve the conditions for trade in nuclear materials.[40] Russia has a strong interest in increasing its nuclear generating capacities and enlarging its fuel supply market.[41]

37 The EU and Russia: our joint political challenge Speech by Peter Mandelson Bologna, 20 April 2007, <http://trade.ec.europa.eu/doclib/docs/2007/april/tradoc_134524.pdf>.

38 Thomas Gomart, *EU-Russia Relations Toward a Way Out of Depression,* (2008), at p. 3, <www.ifri.org/files/Russie/Gomart_EU_Russia.pdf>.

39 *Id.*

40 Communication from the Commission to the Council – Review of EU-Russia relations {SEC(2008) 2786}.

41 Commission staff working document accompanying the communication from the Commission to the Council – Review of EU-Russia relations pursuant to conclusions of the Extraordinary European Council of 1 September 2008 {COM(2008) 740 final}.

Among Russian's short-term objectives is visa abolition with the EU: the visa regime generates a perception that the EU regards Russia as "second rate" and "not really European".[42] Aside from real inconvenience, the visa regime wounds national pride. Some steps were undertaken at improvements here. The EU and Russia entered into the Visa Facilitation Agreement (VFA). The goal of the VFA is to make life easier for travellers, including those from the EU itself. At the same time, the EU prevented illegal migration in the Readmission Agreement with Russia.

Russia attaches great importance to its relations with the EU. In its 1999 "Medium-Term Strategy" (MTS), Russia stated it aims at the "development and strengthening of a strategic partnership" with the EU. According to the MTS, EU-Russian's relations should be based on trade, investment, finances, infrastructure projects, science and technology, property rights, transboundary contacts, and law enforcement.

But Russia also states in the MTS that it wants to build its relations with the EU "without an officially stated objective of Russia's accession to or association with the E.U." This may be both to avoid (or because) of (further!) wounds to national pride, and also because Russia perceives itself as "a world power situated on two continents". Russia wishes to retain its freedom to implement its domestic and foreign policies without deep interference from Brussels. Further, Russia perceives itself as a Eurasian state, the largest country of the CIS, and thus seeks to retain a certain independence with respect to international organizations.[43] While the EU is very important to Russia, Russia wants to remain independent and seeks for mutually advantageous cooperation in the fields of common interests.

3.2 EU Interests

The EU is still trying to understand where the EU's own interests in relations with Russia now lie.[44] At the same time, the EU admits that "good-neighbourly relations between the EU and Russia are of particular importance to the stability, security and prosperity of Europe."[45] In its relations with third states, the EU is always trying to pursue common values, such as "democracy, respect for human rights and the rule of law".[46] The EU wants

42 Thomas Gomart, *EU-Russia Relations Toward a Way Out of Depression,* (2008), at p. 16, <www.ifri.org/files/Russie/Gomart_EU_Russia.pdf>.

43 Rolf Schuette, *E.U. -Russia relations Interests and Values—A European Perspective,* Carnegie Papers (2004).

44 Communication from the Commission to the Council – Review of EU-Russia relations {SEC(2008) 2786}.

45 EU-Russia Summit 26-27 June 2008 – European Parliament resolution of 19 June 2008 on the EU-Russia Summit of 26-27 June 2008 in Khanty-Mansiysk, OJ 2009 C286E/35.

46 Recommendation to the Council on the new EU-Russia agreement – European Parliament recommendation to the Council of 2 April 2009 on the new EU-Russia agreement (2008/2104(INI)) OJ 2010 C137E/29

to apply the same standards to its relations with Russia. The EU also wishes to see Russia develop "into a state, economy, and society on the European or western model".[47]

All major EU documents on Russia contain an extensive catalogue of objectives.[48] They can be understood as seeking the goal of "a stable, democratic and prosperous Russia, firmly anchored in a united Europe free of new dividing lines, is essential to lasting peace on the continent."[49] Pragmatically speaking, Russia is the EU's single largest energy supplier[50] and this compels the EU to partner with Russia.[51] As to the environment, EU concerns with respect to Russia include reducing pollution,[52] including nuclear waste and nuclear safety, climate change is also a concern.[53] Another point of common interest is the treatment of the Kaliningrad exclave.[54]

As can be seen, Russia and the EU have mutual yet asymmetric interests. Understanding the commonality and asymmetry is key to managing their mutual interactions.

4 CONCLUSION

In conclusion, the EU wishes to transform into a state like an EU member or candidate. For its part however, Russia however does not seek EU membership and sees itself as an independent world power.[55] Yet, because of their common interests in trade, and because Russia needs the EU for continued economic development,[56] both Russia and the EU seek to form a "strategic partnership" however ambiguously defined. Despite any wish to autarchy, Russia is compelled by demographic and economic factors into strategic partnerships.[57]

---

47 Rolf Schuette, *E.U. -Russia relations Interests and Values—A European Perspective,* Carnegie Papers No. 54 (2004), p. 13.

48 See, *e.g.*, Communication from the Commission to the Council – Review of EU-Russia relations {SEC(2008) 2786}; Commission staff working document accompanying the communication from the Commission to the Council – Review of EU-Russia relations pursuant to conclusions of the Extraordinary European Council of September 1, 2008 {COM(2008) 740 final}; EU-Russia Summit 26-27 June 2008 – European Parliament resolution of 19 June 2008 on the EU-Russia Summit of 26-27 June 2008 in Khanty-Mansiysk, OJ 2009 C286E/35.

49 Schuette, p. 16.

50 Schuette, p. 28.

51 Schuette, p. 22.

52 EU-Russia Summit on 18 November 2009 in Stockholm – European Parliament resolution of 12 November 2009 on the preparations for the EU-Russia Summit in Stockholm on 18 November 2009, OJ 2010 C271E/2.

53 See generally, Rolf Schuette.

54 Commission staff working document accompanying the communication from the Commission to the Council – Review of EU-Russia relations pursuant to conclusions of the Extraordinary European Council of 1 September 2008 {COM(2008) 740 final}.

55 Schuette, p. 18.

56 Schuette, p. 28.

57 Thomas Gomart, *EU-Russia Relations Toward a Way Out of Depression,* (2008), at p. 8, <www.ifri.org/files/Russie/Gomart_EU_Russia.pdf>.

Russia is a unique country in many ways. Its history development, people's mentality, attitude towards the world and its role and place in it are often different to that of western Europe. In many cases, Russia does not benefit from its unique characteristics. Attempts to apply Western patterns and standards to Russia have always failed, whether undertaken by Russia itself or imposed from without. This is probably because of the unique geographic and demographic characteristics alluded to above. The EU and Russia have not achieved their goals so far because trying to apply a (developed) Western European model to a (developing) Eurasian country leads to frustration on the side of the EU Russia does not and most probably will never meet EU norms exactly as desired by the EU, notwithstanding good faith and reasonability. However, economic and historic asymmetry causing incongruent expectations does not change the fact of mutual dependence: Russia and Europe need each other. Thus, they will be forced to somehow get along.

I agree with Peter Mandelson's view that "the EU needs a strong partnership with a confident and stable Russia."[58] The EU seeks security and prosperity in its neighbourhood and is trying to strengthen and even deepen its relations with Russia – its biggest neighbour and key partner. As a Russian citizen and patriot I appreciate these efforts very much. However, looking to the problem from Russia, I can see that not all of the EU's expectations can be met. Russia values its autarchy more highly than rules of law or EU values. Notwithstanding that fact, Russia and the EU *must* cooperate in pursuing their common interest, somehow. That can best be achieved by mutual respect and understanding, especially of differences.

58 The EU and Russia: our joint political challenge, Speech by Peter Mandelson Bologna, 20 April 2007, at 4. <http://trade.ec.europa.eu/doclib/docs/2007/april/tradoc_134524.pdf>.

4 Renegotiation of the EU-Russia Partnership and Cooperation Agreement

Andrey Remnev

1 Introduction

Currently there is a big debate on what the future of EU-Russia relationship should be. There are different points of view on this issue. Each of them has the right to be considered carefully and can bring a lot of benefits to both parties. However there are also many discrepancies in political, social, economic and spiritual spheres which do not give us the possibility to use the full potential of our relationships. In this chapter we shall take a glance at the hardships and achievements which both parties have come to so far in their cooperation, and on the basis of such knowledge try to sketch the future way of bringing mutual relationships to a new level.

2 The EU-Russia Partnership and Cooperation Agreement: Principles and Goals

The Partnership and Cooperation Agreement (hereinafter PCA) between Russia and the EU was concluded in 1997 for a ten-year-period with possible annual renewal until 2008. The EU has concluded eight other PCAs with some of the former Republics of the Soviet Union.

The aims of these partnerships in general were "to provide a suitable framework for political dialogue, to support the efforts made by the countries to strengthen their democracies and develop their economies, to accompany their transition to a market economy, to encourage trade and investment, to provide a basis for cooperation in the legislative, economic, social, financial, scientific, civil, technological and cultural fields."[1] However, the PCA with Russia also aimed at establishing a free trade area.[2] The general

1 Partnership and Cooperation Agreements. Summary. available at: <http://europa.eu/legislation_summaries/external_relations/relations_with_third_countries/eastern_europe_and_central_asia/r17002_en.htm>.
2 *Id.*

principles of all PCAs were respect of democracy, principles of international law and human rights.[3]

The parties in 2007 decided to prolong the agreement for one more year, but during that period they failed to come to any new version of partnership and cooperation agreement. That happened due to the fact that the results of first Partnership and Cooperation Agreement cannot be estimated as entirely successful. Some goals were successfully attained, others were not.

Russia has received a lot of investments from the European Union which helped her to start re-building its economy. Many Europeans were coming to Moscow and Saint-Petersburg and other cities of Russia as tourists or workers, and many Russians have visited the EU. The European Union and Russia became more open to each other. Nevertheless, still many problems could be seen. Russia did not agree with the European Union on many political issues such as policy in relation to the European Energy Charter, Kosovo, the Baltic States and many other issues. The European Union, in its turn, had lots of claims to Russian policy towards Iran, Serbia, human rights issues in the country and so on. All these discrepancies in both parties' views and opinions became big obstacles in their relationships. Therefore, it is hard for Russia and European Union to come to a new agreement on partnership and cooperation which could help to reduce tensions between the parties.

3 Four Common Spaces: Goals and Results

Efforts were made to establish closer relationships. The authorities of Russia and European Union considered that the PCA had great potential of developing the relationships, but had not been actually fully working in practice. So, they decided to make the relationship between the parties more specific and therefore more integrated. In 2003 at the Saint Petersburg Summit (May, 2003) Russia and European Union agreed to create four "common spaces" in the framework of existing Partnership and Cooperation Agreement:[4]

1. The Common Space of Freedom, Security and Justice.
2. The Common Space of External Security.
3. The Common Economic Space
4. The Common Space of Research, Education Including Cultural Aspects.

3 *Id.*

4 European Union – EEAS (European External Action Service), EU-Russia Common Spaces, available at: <www.eeas.europa.eu/russia/common_spaces/index_en.htm> (last visited 18 December 2010).

The Common Space of Freedom, Security and Justice

The Common Space of Freedom, Security and Justice defines key areas for cooperation between Russia and the EU such as freed movement of persons, the fight against terrorism and organized crime, including combatting drug trafficking and money laundering, corruption, and trafficking in human beings as well as providing for judicial cooperation.[5] Oversight on their implementation is exercised by the Russia-EU Permanent Partnership Council on Freedom, Security and Justice.

3.1 *The Common Space of External Security*

The main objectives of the Common Space of External Security are to ensure active cooperation in order to strengthen the central role of the United Nations and to enhance the effectiveness of international and regional organizations, in particular the OSCE and the Council of Europe, as well as regimes and treaties, which make an important contribution to the establishment of a more just and secure world; to strengthen bilateral interaction and dialogue on security and crisis management; to promote the processes of regional cooperation in a mutually beneficial manner and to prevent the spread of practices that fuel racism, racial discrimination, xenophobia and related intolerance.[6]

3.2 *The Common Economic Space*

The objective of the Common Economic Space is the creation of an open and integrated market between Russia and the EU based on the principles of non-discrimination, transparency and good governance. The Common Economic Space is aimed at increasing opportunities for economic operators, promoting trade, facilitating the establishment of companies, and strengthening cooperation in various sectors, from agriculture to information technologies and space. Ultimately, the Common Economic Space is called to strengthen the competitiveness of mutually complementary economies of Russia and the EU, currently it focuses on problems of modernization and transition to the "economy of knowledge".[7]

5 Road Map on the Common Space of Freedom, Security and Justice, available at: <http://russianmission.eu/en/common-space-freedom-security-and-justice> (last visited 18 December 2010).

6 Road Map on the Common Space of External Security, available at: <http://russianmission.eu/en/common-space-external-security >(last visited 18 December 2010).

7 Road Map for the Common Economic Space – Building Blocks for Sustained Economic Growth, available at <http://russianmission.eu/en/common-economic-space> (last visited 18 December 2010).

3.3 *The Common Space of Research and Education, Including Cultural Aspects*

Ultimately, the Common Space of Research and Education, including Cultural Aspects, aims at promoting economic growth, strengthening competitiveness, optimizing links between research and introduction of innovations, and to stimulate close cooperation in the field of education, including continuous integration for higher education and free academic mobility between Russia and the EU countries.[8]

In summary, all the common spaces show that although there were no major breakthroughs, day to day business was conducted efficiently under all the common spaces. Progress continues to be made, but much remains to be done and some important points agreed in principle are yet to be implemented in practice. The Common Spaces became the framework for establishing better relationships between European Union and Russia. However, they are not legally binding and represent only the list of objectives which the Parties agreed upon. In 2005 the road maps were signed in order to promote the common objectives in practice. The PCAwas prolonged in 2007 for one year and has expired in 2008, but the objectives which were settled in the common spaces are still pursued by both parties.

4 Perspectives on the New Russia and European Union Agreement

Since 2008 the EU and Russia are working together in order to find the appropriate form of mutual cooperation and partnership. They are trying to find the solution which would satisfy both parties and intensify our relationships. There are different formats being proposed in which the relationships between Russia and the European Union should be continued.

Among them are:
- Partnership and Cooperation Agreement similar to the previous one;
- Strategic Partnership and Cooperation Agreement;
- Free Trade Area Agreement and others.

Any of these versions can be realized at some point. However, there are several important principles which should be taken into account while negotiating the future agreement.

8 Road Map on the Common Space of Research and Education, Including Cultural Aspects, available at <http://russianmission.eu/en/common-space-research-and-education-including-cultural-aspects> (last visited 18 December 2010).

One of the principles is the *acquis communautaire*[9] – the principle of acquired community positions. This principle is used usually during negotiations with candidate to Member States, however, from our point of view it would be very useful to use it during negotiations on Russia-EU agreement. Why shouldthe EU and Russia in the contex of the PCA not use the concept of the *acquis*?

The essence of this principle means that as soon as parties have mutually agreed on some issues, they stay on them in the further process of negotiations in order to move forward in their relationships.

Such a principle should help both Russia and EU to overcome deadlock which sometimes happens during negotiations. It can help to outline the issues which shall serve as starting points for further developing of the relationships and therefore they should be considered closely.

The other principle which is also very important is the principle of mutual interest. This principle serves the important function of using a fair approach to mutual positions in negotiations on the agreement – the duty of good faith and fair dealing. The Parties, in order to sign the final draft of the agreement, should be convinced that the agreement serves their mutual interests and does not diminish them somehow. This principle also helps the negotiating parties to find a compromise in complex issues.

One more important principle is the principle of functionalism. It is the principle the core idea of which is that international governance should be organized according to "tasks" and along "functional lines".[10] Functionalists assume that economic, social and technical problems can be separated from political problems and insulated from political pressures[11] to generate unbiased neutral expertise in particular sectors – and to generate mutual trust and interdependence thereby. The European Union and Russia should create such institutions which would separate economic, social and technical issues from politics and would anchor and deepen the mutual cooperation of the parties.

Aside from principles there are some issues which should be taken into account while developing the new Russia-European Union Agreement:

---

9 European Union Internet Dictionary, available at <http://en.euabc.com/word/12> (last visited 18 December 2010).

10 Jose E. Alvarez, Steve Carnovitz, *Triangulating The World Trade Organization*, 96 Am. J. Int'l L. 28, 48 (2002).

11 Bartram S. Brown, *The United States and the Politicization of the World Bank* 14-15 (1992).

1. First of all, is the human rights aspect. The respect for human rights should not only be declared as a goal, the agreement should also include an enforcement mechanism which can be used if the rights are being violated.[12]
2. Secondly, is the rule of law and legislation harmonization aspect. The parties should clearly understand that the agreement will be workable only in case of support by local legislation and uniform standards which should be harmonized in both parties in order to be effective and fair.[13]
3. Thirdly, visa free travel for Europeans and Russians. It is fully understandable that visa free travel is not realistic, but the parties can make essential contributions to opening borders. Visa facilitation for students, researches and businessmen should be a priority in order to promote contacts among people.[14]
4. Finally, the EU-Russia relationship should be based on the principles of common integrated and open markets and reciprocity of investment rights between the partners and therefore both partners should guarantee the property rights of foreign investors.[15]

There are, of course, many more issues which are important in order to make the relationships sustainable, but the above mentioned ones should become the main objectives of the new agreement.

5 DREAM OF A COMMON ECONOMIC COMMUNITY

Currently there are proposals from the Russian authorities to create "a harmonious economic community stretching from Lisbon to Vladivostok".[16] This can be considered as an ultimate goal to which the parties are to strive to and which recharge the new wave of industrialization.

Mr. Putin wrote: "A 'harmonious economic community stretching from Lisbon to Vladivostok' would imply strategic alliances in key industries, such as shipbuilding, car manufacturing, space exploration and the pharmaceutical industry. In my view, we need to address the question as to how we can trigger a new wave of industrialization across the European continent".[17]

12 Recommendation to the Council on the new EU-Russia Agreement, OJ C 137 E, 27May 2010, p. 34.

13 *Ibid*, p. 35.

14 *Ibid*, p. 36.

15 *Ibid*, p. 37.

16 Der Spiegel, *"From Lisbon to Vladivostok": Putin Envisions a Russia-EU Free Trade Zone*, 25 November 2010, available at <www.spiegeel.de/international/europe/0,1518,731109,00.html>.

17 Valentina Pop, Putin proposes Russia – EU union 26 November 2010 @ 09:29 CET EUobserver available at <http://euobserver.com/9/31361> (last visited 18 December 2010).

This is an ambitious goal but is attainable, particularly since Russia is finally gaining admission to the World Trade Organization. Accession to WTO will help form common standards with other members of WTO and by virtue of that reduce most of the barriers which prevents creating an Economic Community with the European Union.

The other issue is that Russia is trying to create a customs union with Belarus and Kazakhstan (EurAsEC). This could create major obstacles in developing Russia-EU relationships. The countries of the union would have to establish common standards which will be new for the EU and the negotiation process could tighten up further.

In this respect there are two possible ways for Russia and European Union to develop their relationship: either in a "union-country" form or "union-union" form. Bearing in mind the close ties of Russia with the countries of Commonwealth of Independent states the second variant seems to be more realistic.

6 Conclusion

Russia and the European Union do not have a long history of cooperation with each other. They are moving forward in that respect developing their relationships and they need time for that.

The first PCA was a kind of pilot project through which the parties tried to understand each other and to find the solution for peaceful and prosperous co-existence. In the end, Russia and the European Union came to the conclusion that cooperation is advantageous to the both sides. Therefore, they should strive to work out the most acceptable variant. At the same time, the European Union should take into account that Russia wants to establish a Customs Union with Belarus and Kazakhstan which may make conclusion of PCA not possible in the nearest future. The question of the coordination of the EU and the EurAsEC is a key issue in contemporary international relations. These international organizations can be complementary, not conflicting, and can also be brought in line not only with each other but also within the greater context, de jure or de facto, of the WTO. That is the question for diplomacy.

5 Kaliningrad: The Hostage of Europe or a Chance for Partnership?

Anna Grishchenkov

1 Introduction

In 2001 the EU Commission, in Communication to the Council, first discussed in full the ideas of future cooperation between the EU and Kaliningrad Oblast with regard to the pending enlargement of the EU: Poland and Lithuania joined EU in 2004 and Kaliningrad Oblast in turn was surrounded by the EU and separated from the other parts of Russia. However, to present, the way of cooperation between EU and Kaliningrad Oblast has not yet been found. I argue that the main reason of that is that the EU and Russia have different approaches to this cooperation and different fears: asymmetry as to goals and methods. These different approaches and fears together prevent the EU and Russia from a successful partnership. In this chapter I compare the EU and Russian viewpoints on the EU-Kaliningrad relationship. I argue that to find the solution which will be fruitful for both the EU and Russia it is necessary to understand that the EU and Russia are not enemies but equal partners. Kaliningrad Oblast should become a model for the possible partnership of the EU and Russia and the first step to be done is to end the "isolation" of the Kaliningrad.

2 Brief Analysis of Kaliningrad Oblast' Geographical and Historical Specifics: A Knot of Different Interests (Russia, EU, Germany and Lithuania)

Kaliningrad is a seaport and the administrative center of Kaliningrad Oblast, the Russian Exclave between Poland and Lithuania on the Baltic Sea. The original name of the town is Königsberg. The town was founded in 1255 and was part of Prussia and then Germany until 1945, but was largely destroyed during the World War II. It became the part of the Soviet Union in 1945 in accordance with decisions of the Potsdam Conference.

Due to the collapse of the Soviet Union in 1991, the Kaliningrad Oblast became an exclave, geographically separated from the rest of Russia.[1] The Kaliningrad region of the Russian

1 See at <http://en.wikipedia.org/wiki/Kaliningrad>.

Federation became futher isolated from Russia as a consequence of the EU enlargement in 2004 when Poland and Lithuania joined EU in 2004.[2]

As enlargement drew nearer, increasing attention of the EU was being focused on the region.[3] In 2001 the EU Commission, in Communication to the Council, first discussed in full the ideas of future cooperation between the EU and Kaliningrad Oblast with regard to the pending enlargement.

However, not only EU attention is focused on Kaliningrad. Kaliningrad was originally the German town, so it is a sphere of interest of Germany. According to some Russian authors, in November, 2004 the opposition fraction of *Christlich Demokratische Union Deutschlands (CDU)* attempted to put into the question the practicability of maintaining Kaliningrad as a part of the Russian Federation. In the statement made to the federal chancellor Gerhard Shroder members of the Bundestag named Kaliningrad as a Königsberg Oblast and asked to think about the transformation of the Oblast into the eurozone "Prussia" (Borussia).[4]

Kaliningrad is also an area of interest of Lithuania, who considers this region to be closely related to Lithuania culturally, because before becoming German, this region was originally inhabited by the Prussians as well as by Lithuanians. In Lithuanian literature this region sometimes is called "Lithuania Minor" and considered to have been the birthplace of the nation's literature, literary language and national press.[5]

Such political, cultural and geographical specifics make the Kaliningrad status even more complicated.

3 Brief Analysis of the EU-Russia Relationship

The European Union and the Russian Federation have a strong trade relationship. Russia is one of the EU's key trading partners. The EU is by far Russia's main trading partner, accounting for 52.3% of its overall trade turnover in 2008. It is also by far the most important investor in Russia. It is estimated that up to 75% of FDI stocks in Russia come from the EU Member States.[6]

2 See at <www.eeas.europa.eu/russia/kaliningrad_en.htm>.

3 Communication from the commission to the Council: The EU and Kaliningrad (2001).

4 See, *e.g.*, Sergey Kortunov, *Kaliningrad as a gate to Big Europe*. Available at <www.globalaffairs.ru/number/n_4210>.

5 See, *e.g.*, Darius Furmonavicius, *Konigsberg /Karaliaucius/ Kaliningrad region: settlement of sovereignty will end Second World War*. Available at <http://aei.pitt.edu/6491/>.

6 See, *e.g.*, <http://ec.europa.eu/trade/creating-opportunities/bilateral-relations/countries/russia/index_en.htm>.

The cooperation between EU and Russia is based on a Partnership and Co-operation Agreement concluded in 1994 (PCA). The PCA came into force on 1 December 1997 for an initial duration of ten years, with the option to be extended. The provisions of the PCA cover a wide range of policy areas to be included in a political dialogue: trade in goods and services; business and investment; financial and legislative cooperation; science and technology; education and training; energy, nuclear and space cooperation; environment, transport; culture; and cooperation on the prevention of illegal activities.[7]

At the St. Petersburg Summit in May 2003, the EU and Russia agreed to reinforce their co-operation by creating in the long term four 'common spaces ' in the framework of the Partnership and Cooperation Agreement: *The Common Economic Space, The Common Space of Freedom, Security and Justice, The Common Space of External Security, The Common Space on Research, Education, Culture.* The London Summit in October 2005 focused on the practical implementation of Road Maps for the four Common Spaces.[8]

Negotiations on a New EU-Russia Agreement were launched at the Khanty-Mansyisk Summit in June 2008. The New Agreement should update and replace the existing Partnership and Cooperation Agreement. It should provide a comprehensive framework for EU-Russia relations, and include substantive, legally binding commitments in all areas of the partnership, including political dialogue, JLS issues, economic cooperation, research, education and culture, as well as solid provisions on trade, investment and energy.[9]

Premier-minister of the Russian Federation Vladimir Putin in November, 2010 proposed to create a harmonious economic community stretching from Lisbon to Vladivostok.[10] However, nothing significant has been done until the present moment and there are still a lot of questions which need to be resolved before this economic community can come into being, specifically:

- energy issues between Russia and EU;
- visafree travel between Russia and EU;
- entry of the Russia into WTO, which *appears* resolved at the time of this writing.

---

7 See *The European Union and Russia – Statistical Comparison*, available at <http://epp.eurostat.ec.europa.eu/cache/ITY_OFFPUB/KS-77-07-231/EN/KS-77-07-231-EN.PDF>.

8 *Ibid.*

9 See, *e.g.*, <http://eeas.europa.eu/russia/index_en.htm>.

10 See, *e.g.*, Eric Engle, *To Russia With Love: The EU, Russia, and Special Relationships.* Available at <http://papers.ssrn.com/sol3/papers.cfm?abstract_id=1721485>.

Kaliningrad can become a model of the future partnership, however, to find a solution first of all it is necessary to understand the interests and fears of the both sides (the EU and Russia, accordingly).

4 Kaliningrad Oblast Seen from the EU

In 2001 the EU Commission, in Communication to the Council, first discussed in full the ideas of future cooperation between the EU and Kaliningrad Oblast with regard to the pending enlargement of the EU.[11] The Communication outlined ideas and options for discussion between the parties and discussed the following issues.

4.1 *Difficulties to Give Any Special Status to Kaliningrad*

The Commission mentioned that from time to time, proposals had been made for a special trade regime for Kaliningrad. Since Kaliningrad was an integral part of Russia, it would be difficult to grant any special status, such as free trade or a customs union. This would raise a number of political and legal issues apart from the fact that Russia was unlikely to grant the necessary degree of autonomy to Kaliningrad because of the Russian orientation toward greater centralization; Russia is a relatively centralized federation.

4.2 *Main Problems of the Region*

The EU Commission mentioned that unemployment and poverty have increased dramatically in Kaliningrad since 1991 and the main welfare indicators suggested that the standard of living is below the Russian average. Responsibility for the economic development of Kaliningrad lies with the central authorities in Moscow and the local authorities in the region. Kaliningrad was dependent on budgetary allocations from Moscow and on its trade and economic links with the rest of the country. As yet, Russian regional policy was less developed than that of the EU, in terms of financial transfers and investment incentives and current Russian policy is oriented towards greater centralization. Nonetheless, there is much that the central and local authorities can do to stimulate economic development. As elsewhere in Russia there is a need for a stable and secure legal and institutional environment. Good corporate governance, fair and efficient enforcement of legislation (*e.g.* to guarantee the protection of shareholder and investor rights, bankruptcy, auditing and accounting), enterprise restructuring and the further development of SMEs. Market institutions should be strengthened, *e.g.* in the financial sector and the tax system.

11 Communication from the commission to the Council: The EU and Kaliningrad (2001).

As elsewhere in Russia there is a need for action to combat illegal activities, which were likely to affect neighbouring EU Member States. Strong action is needed by the federal authorities, for example to enact and enforce legislation and international conventions. The Task Force on Organised Crime in the Baltic Sea Region could make a valuable contribution to tackling these problems. On the local level co-operation should be developed to deal with problems such as car crime and then be extended to other areas.

The EU Commission made *the following suggestions for future cooperation with regard to enlargement.*

Kaliningrad's own development and its involvement in the wider region depends on the strengthening of the rule of law, and the broad implementation of good governance principles, particularly through promoting institution building and civil society development. The EU could contribute to this process by encouraging Kaliningrad's participation in EU projects for public administration and judicial reform, and participation of local civil servants in training programmes. Regional and local budget management and management of municipal services could be supported.

Through the Tacis Local Support Office, established in Kaliningrad in December 2000, the participation of local actors in partnership programmes with EU organizations and people-to-people activities will be promoted, including training institutions, NGOs, trade unions, media, professional organisations, enterprises, municipalities and courts.

Ten years after the Communication to the Council have passed, but the relationship between the EU and Russia (and Kaliningrad Oblast accordingly) is one of the biggest and most complicated challenges in European politics and foreign policy. It affects every significant European and Russian interest – energy, climate change, trade, security, crime, migration, even the Middle East, Iran, and the Balkans.[12]

Politically, the concerns of the EU with respect to the Russian Federation go to the question of the rule of law, democracy and the protection of human rights.[13]

Among other fears of EU there is a fear of potential danger for security of EU, a fear of illegal activities (arms trafficking, drug dealers, prostitution), which can affect neighbouring

12 Russia and the EU: building trust on a shared continent, speech by Peter Mandelson, available at <http://trade.ec.europa.eu/doclib/docs/2008/june/tradoc_139377.pdf>.

13 See, *e.g.*, Eric Engle, *To Russia With Love: The EU, Russia, and Special Relationships.* Available at <http://papers.ssrn.com/sol3/papers.cfm?abstract_id=1721485>.

EU Member States.[14] Thereto, one also notes concern over the idea that Eastern Europe workers might flood Western European labor markets.[15]

The absence of unanimity among the EU Member States as to ways of cooperation with Russia (specifically, intra-EU discord between Western and Eastern Europe members) complicates the EU-Russia relationship. For example, there are ongoing popular demands in Lithuania to formally condemn as crime acts committed by the Soviet regime such as the occupation and annexation of the country to the Soviet Union.[16]

As EU Trade Commissioner Peter Mandelson stated in his speech, "managing challenges as complex as the regional questions in the South Caucasus, Iran or Kosovo is much more difficult in the absence of enduring trust in the relationship. The same can be said in the economic sphere, whether we look at the EU's increasing dependence on imports of energy, or Russia's wish to re-structure and modernize its industrial base, services sector and infrastructure. Some in Europe think Russia seems to be more interested in investing in future leverage than in future energy production. That Gazprom's strategic spending spree abroad contrasts with the lack of investment at home. And in Russia, there is resentment that the openness of Europe's market is constrained, that regulatory changes are being adopted to prevent foreign companies expanding in the single market, and that we are after Russia's resources without any concern for her well-being. Let's be honest: each suspects the other of employing double standards, of using the energy weapon as an instrument of politics."[17]

So, Russia has its own concerns with regard to Kaliningrad and the EU.

5 Kaliningrad Oblast Seen from Russia

During 2001-2010. Russia concerns were (and are) the following:

14 Communication from the commission to the Council: The EU and Kaliningrad (2001).

15 See, *e.g.*, Eric Engle, *To Russia With Love: The EU, Russia, and Special Relationships*. Available at <http://papers.ssrn.com/sol3/papers.cfm?abstract_id=1721485>.

16 See, *e.g*, <www.google.ru/#sclient=psy&hl=ru&newwindow=1&q=russia+and+lithuania&aq=0&aqi=g1g-o1&aql=&oq=Russia++and+Lithuani&pbx=1&fp=4ca3834baa662a8>.

17 Russia and the EU: building trust on a shared continent, speech by Peter Mandelson, available at <http://trade.ec.europa.eu/doclib/docs/2008/june/tradoc_139377.pdf>.

5.1 *Possibility of the Separation of Kaliningrad Oblast from Russia*

As far as Kaliningrad has been a Russian city for a very short period of time (from 1945), there are always some concerns about possibility of the separation of Kaliningrad Oblast from Russia. Views of some Lithuanian authors, proposing to consider a sovereignty of Kaliningrad Oblast,[18] can be treated as proof that fears of Russia are not baseless.

Thus, Russia fears a potential threat of the formation of the so-called "Baltic/Black sea belt" of Russia's isolation. Some authors think that this was the major reason for the Russian Federation to conclude the "Treaty on formation of the Russian Federation – Belarus union" in 1999, which can be viewed as a "Russian response" to geopolitical changes around Kaliningrad and an attempt of Russia to strengthen its position in the region. In particular, the Treaty suggests, "pulling the Kaliningrad special defense region out of military and strategic isolation".[19]

Another Russia policy that influences the relationship with the EU is *a necessity of strong stand by Russia in foreign policy because of the fear of being taken advantage of*. Such is the legacy of neoliberal asset-stripping.

From the military point of view, Kaliningrad is not only an anachronistic military base, but also the headquarters of the Russian Baltic fleet. In such a situation, Kaliningrad's isolation from the other parts of Russia is constructed by Russia as the biggest danger, which is seen as threatening Russia's territorial integrity, sovereignty, and national security.[20]

Another Russian concern is a *fear of loss of cultural and spiritual connections between Kaliningrad and other parts of Russia.*

For example, in 2002 the Kaliningrad bureaucracy proposed to the federal government to start an educational program for Kaliningrad youth to familiarize them with Russia (!).[21]

---

18 See, *e.g.*, Darius Furmonavicius, *Konigsberg /Karaliaucius/ Kaliningrad region: settlement of sovereignty will end Second World War.* Available at <http://aei.pitt.edu/6491/>.

19 See, *e.g.*, Viktoriya Topalova, *The Kaliningrad Question: Discourses of Insecurity in the Context of European Integration.* Available at <http://aei.pitt.edu/2963/>.

20 See, *e.g.*, Viktoriya Topalova, *The Kaliningrad Question: Discourses of Insecurity in the Context of European Integration.* Available at <http://aei.pitt.edu/2963/>.

21 See, *e.g.*, Sergey Kortunov, *Kaliningrad as a gate to Big Europe.* Available at <www.globalaffairs.ru/number/n_4210>.

5.2 *Barriers for Free Movement of Goods and People Between Kaliningrad and Other Parts of Russia*[22]

Kaliningrad Oblast's geographical situation leads to barriers for free movement of goods and people between Kaliningrad and other parts of Russia.

Russian politicians stressed more than once that it is an insult for Russian people to obtain EU visa to get home from the other parts of Russia.[23]

Until now Kaliningrad residents have not received any favorable visa regime.

They not only lost their right to obtain free Polish and Lithuanian visas, they also have to explain the reasons for their trip and to pay the consulate fee to transit the EU. Moreover, to visit Ukraine or Belarus they have to pay to obtain a Polish or Lithuanian transit visa.

In 2010 Kaliningrad residents even appealed to the EU and asked for a visa-free regime for them. Kaliningrad residents wrote the following: "European institutions should pay special attention to our region. European authorities should recognize a special position and status of the Kaliningrad region, specific local problems faced by residents and authorities. The European Union should be interested in that the visa regime for Kaliningraders become liberal, ideally – visa-free. Human communication between citizens of the EU and Kaliningraders should become the main foundation for the stability of bilateral relations. Statements by European diplomats and politicians, heard in recent years, demonstrate, that the European Union understood and largely shared that view. However, progress in this matter does not exist, despite all the smiles and the minister's statements. After all, even if it is impossible to solve the problem at once in full, quite realizable numerous intermediate variants which are really facilitating Kaliningraders the entrance to EU and are not creating any threats and damage to EU safety exist. We are ordinary citizens, not the official persons or representatives of big business, so the EU might take the responsibility for braking vicious circle of «symmetry» decisions with the Russian government. It will be a farsighted step".[24]

The practical questions of border control and free movements of persons and goods are the major concerns for the Russian officials.

---

22 See, e.g., Yury Borko, Russia and the EU: the Kaliningrad Dilemma. Available at <http://aei.pitt.edu/1993/>.

23 See, *e.g.*, Viktoriya Topalova, *The Kaliningrad Question: Discourses of Insecurity in the Context of European Integration*. Available at <http://aei.pitt.edu/2963/>.

24 See, *e.g.*, Kaliningrad, the prisoner of Europe. Kaliningraders appealing to EU: Tear down this "Iron Curtain". Available at <www.dvornik.ru/issue/740/27301/>.

2001-2010. Russian visions of EU-Russian relationship with regard to Kaliningrad Oblast:

With regard to the mentioned above fears and concerns there are three possible ways ahead for the EU-Russian relationship. These are:[25]

- Cold peace;
- Stagnation;
- Partnership.

5.3 *Cold Peace*

This is the worst scenario possible as a result of unfavourable globalization. As a response to global challenges (terrorism, immigration and worsening ecology) the main global players will come to a policy of isolation, animosity and suspiciousness. In such a case, alienation between the EU and Russia will increase and will be expressed in diametrically opposite policies with regard to Moldova, Ukraine, Belarus and Caucasian republics. Visa, custom and trade barriers will be created and near-bordered territories will suffer. Trade disputes between EU and Russia on different matters (from the steel to energy tariffs) will prevent Russia's entry into WTO.

5.4 *Stagnation*

This scenario is a continuation of the current relationship between EU and Russia and an increasing stagnation. The weakness of cooperation institutes, fruitless meetings among leaders, and a bureaucratic war of words lead to deteriorating the dialog between EU and Russia. EU policy with regard to Russia becomes inconsistent and will vary from the traditional and too personal approach of France, Germany and Italy to the historical distrust to Russia from the new members of EU (Eastern European countries).

As a result, out of the four "common spaces" a small partnership only with regard to two 'common spaces' (economy and humanitarian issues) will continue. The spaces of the internal and external security will turn into an arena of disputes and such issues like visa and immigration and competition among EU and Russia for influence on members of CIS will come into the first place.

25 Full description of these ways see in Kaliningrad Partnership in EU – Russian Relationship: Road Map Into the Future (2005). Available at <www.recep.ru/files/publ/kaliningrad_ru.pdf>.

5.5 *Partnership*

This scenario is a strategic project and is also the most desirable strategic decision. Under this scenario the dialog between the EU and Russia develops goes beyond the scope of the current partnership and good neighbourhood. In such a case, the deepened dialog would lead to the creation of a free trade zone and at the end of the day to the single integrated market. For Russia it will be connected with significant institutional changes and step-by-step adoption of part of the *acquis communautaire* and with partial coordination with the EU legal norms in aid of creation of the minimal legal base for free-trade zone. The principle of the four "common spaces" would be used fully. As for economy, EU will be able to participate in modernization of Russia – not only through direct investments, but through creation of favourable institutional conditions for modernization, through opening EU markets for Russia and through assisting in increasing rates of growth of the Russian economy. As for external policy, the model of security based on the cooperation will be created. In the area of internal policy, the issue of the visa-free trips will change from discussions into the practical realization which will increase the development of the fourth space (the humanitarian exchanges).

The project "Kaliningrad partnership" can be done only within "partnership" scenario but can become a model for the whole partnership idea.

6 CONCLUSION

Both the EU and Russia have some fears with regard to each other. They each have different approaches to the Kaliningrad problem. Russia believes that the EU should solve this issue, because the issue was created by the EU enlargement. The EU supposes that Kaliningrad is mostly a Russian problem which the EU can help to solve but is not obliged to.[26] I think that it is necessary to share responsibility with regard to Kaliningrad Oblast between the EU and Russia. Three groups of interests must be harmonized: federal (Moscow), regional (Kaliningrad) and European.[27] It is necessary for both sides (EU and Russia) to understand that Russia and EU are not source of danger for each other but present potential opportunities and can be partners.

Isolated, Kaliningrad is impoverished. An "island" of poverty surrounded by prosperity is a risk to the EU because of criminality. The solution is to end Kaliningrad's isolation.

26 See, *e.g.*, Sergey Kortunov, *Kaliningrad as a gate to Big Europe*. Available at <www.globalaffairs.ru/number/n_4210>.

27 Sergey Kortunov, *Kaliningrad as a gate to Big Europe*. Available at <www.globalaffairs.ru/number/n_4210>.

The possible approaches can be a creation by EU and Russia of a special Kaliningrad Oblast passport giving a right to visa-free travel for limited durations or including Kaliningrad Oblast into the visa-free zone. In any case, practical measures can and must be undertaken to generate greater trust and easier travel.

6 Separation of Vertically Integrated Undertakings and Rights of Foreign Investors in the Context of the Third Energy Package

Larisa Logvinova

The Third Energy Package was one of the most monumental events of the previous year in EU energy politics. The Third Energy Package includes the following documents:

- Directive 2009/73/EC of the European Parliament and of the Council of 13 July 2009 concerning common rules for the international market in natural gas and repealing Directive 2003/55/EC (hereinafter – "Gas Directive of the EU");
- Directive 2009/72/EC of the European Parliament and of the Council of 13 July 2009 concerning common rules for internal market in electricity and repealing Directive 2003/54/EC (hereinafter – "Energy-Electricity Directive of the EU");
- Regulation No. 715/2009 of the European Parliament and of the Council of 13 July 2009 on conditions of access to the natural gas transmission networks and repealing Regulation (EC) No. 1775/2005;
- Regulation No. 714/2009 of the European Parliament and of the Council of 13 July 2009 on conditions of access to the networks for cross-border exchanges in electricity and repealing Regulation (EC) No. 1228/2003;
- Regulation No. 713/2009 of the European Parliament and of the Council of 13 July 2009 establishing an Agency for the Cooperation of Energy Regulators.

The Third Energy Package entered into force in 3 September 2009, however it will apply from the 3 March 2011 (after the term of implementation of Gas and Energy-Electricity has expired).

Here we will focus on two issues:

1. The issue concerning the new aspect – the 'effective unbundling' concept and 'third countries clause', as it is one of the most speculative now.
2. The analysis of the legitimacy of those two aspects in the context of European and international law.

I. The Third Energy Package provides the complex of measures to reform so-called 'vertically integrated undertakings'. Under the 'vertically integrated undertakings' the Gas Directive means "a natural gas undertaking or a group of natural gas undertakings where the same person or the same persons are entitled, directly or indirectly, to exercise control, and where the undertaking or group of undertakings perform at least one the functions of transmission, distribution, LNG or storage, and at leas one of the functions of production or supply of natural gas".[1]

This complex of measures provides the separation of two types of activity: natural monopoly (transportation) and competitive ones (production and supply). The Member States have an option to choose different models of separation:

- 'ownership unbundling' model;
- two alternative models: 'independent system operator', and 'independent transmission operator'.

The first model is applied to all new transmission systems after 3 September 2009. The other models are applied to vertically integrated undertakings, which on 3 September 2009 own transmission systems.

(1) The model of 'ownership unbundling' prohibits the same persons to own voting shares in undertakings performing the functions of production and supply, on the one hand, and undertakings on energy transmission, on the other part.[2]

The implementation of this model will bring to the full disintegration of the vertical integrated undertakings. Undertaking should either transfer the transmission system to an independent person or separate into several companies held by different owners performing transmission and production (supply) of energy.

The Third Energy Package however is silent on the issue with respect to the rights of the production-supply undertakings relating to the system operator. On the one hand, from Article 9 (1) (b) and (2)[3] it follows that such undertakings have no rights with respect to the system operator, including voting rights. On the other hand, from the preamble of the Gas Directive (point 8) it is clear that it is possible to hold a non-controlling interest in the operator undertaking.

---

1 Gas Directive of the EU, cl. 2 (20).
2 Gas Directive of the EU, cl. 9 (1) (b).
3 Gas Directive of the EU, cl. 9 (2).

The geographical sphere of the effect of 'ownership unbundling' is also not very clear. When the Gas Directive says production-supply undertaking are prohibited to have rights in transmission operators (and vice-versa), it is not clear whether the case is about the undertaking and the operator that are located in one Member State or in different ones. This conflict *might* be resolved by reference to the goals of the Union to create a single integrated European market.

(2) The alternative models of 'independent system operator' and 'independent transmission operator' permit combining within one group of persons the ownership of production-supply and transmission business, provided that the control of the owner of the energy transmission system is terminated completely ('independent system operator' model) or is substantially limited ('independent transmission operator' model).

(a) In the model of 'independent system operator', the transmission system nominally remains in the ownership of the vertically integrated undertaking. However, practically all rights of holding and using of the transmission system are transferred to a legal entity not connected with the vertically integrated undertaking – to the independent system operator.

Such independent system operator is appointed by the Member State with the proposal of a vertically integrated undertaking and shall be approved by the Commission. Independent system operators perform all complex management of the system: they provide third parties with the access to the network, perform the operator functions, and realize the investment planning. The vertically integrated system shall give assistance to independent system operator as well as finance the investment projects initiated by them.

The basic difference of the 'independent system operator' from the 'ownership unbundling' model is that the transmission system remains in the hands of the vertically integrated undertaking and vertical integration is removed because the owner may not further control the transmission system.

This model of 'independent system operator' is based on the experience of Scotland, where the company "National Grid" manages the networks of the vertically integrated companies "Scottish Power" and "Scottish & Southern Energy", companies which are not connected with it.

(b) In the "independent transmission operator" model, the transmission system is transferred to the ownership and management of a legal entity that is part of the vertically integrated undertaking – the independent transmission operator.

The main issue here is that independent transmission operator and vertically integrated undertaking are affiliated with each other. Such a connection could potentially lead to discrimination against third parties. In order to avoid such a situation, the Gas Directive provides a range of measures, ensuring the autonomy of the operator in the following:

- The independent transmission operator is apportioned with own technical, personnel and financial resources that are necessary for performing transmission activity.
- The independent transmission operator is maximally isolated from the vertically integrated undertaking (separate corporate identity, office).
- Management and personnel are maximally independent of each other (appointed by the regulator, etc.)

In order to control the fulfilment of these measures the Compliance program is implemented. The Compliance program determines measures in order to avoid discrimination. This Compliance program is approved by the regulator, special Compliance officer controls the fulfilment of the program.

Independent transmission operators perform their current business independently. Key personnel issues are resolved with the participation of the regulator. The vertically integrated undertaking has no possibility to influence informally the management of the independent transmission operator.

This model is the most popular in Europe and was proposed by France and Germany as the model alternative to ownership unbundling. However, this model has been transformed into a complex model that will be difficult to implement. In this regard, the vertically integrated undertaking would better abandon the transmission system rather than implement the model of 'independent transmission operator'.

There are several exemptions from the separation requirements related to the new transmission systems and isolated or emergent markets:

(a) Pursuant to Article 36 of the Gas Directive of the EU major new gas infrastructure such as interconnectors, LNG and storage facilities may upon request be exempted for a defined period of time from the provisions of separation.[4] This measure is necessary to incite the investment activity of the vertical integrated companies.

The Gas Directive allows for exemptions from those rules for major new gas infrastructure. Member States or the national regulators can grant those exemptions, if specific criteria

4 Gas Directive of the EU, Art. 36.

are fulfilled. The Commission has to be notified of an exemption and, within two months, can request that the decision be amended or withdrawn.

The Commission shall approve the issue of providing the exemption and the Commission has a right to provide or not to provide such exemption considering several criteria:
- the investment must enhance competition in gas supply and enhance security of supply;
- the level of risk attached to the investment is such that the investment would not take place unless an exemption was granted;
- the infrastructure must be owned by a natural or legal person which is separate at least in terms of its legal form from the system operators in whose systems that infrastructure will be built;
- charges are levied on users of that infrastructure;
- the exemption is not detrimental to competition or the effective functioning of the internal gas market, or the efficient functioning of the regulated system to which the infrastructure is connected.[5]

However there is great discretion for the Commission to decide whether to approve the exemption or not. For example the Commission first approved the exemption for the Bulgarian project Nabucco, but then amended its decision because of the following reason:

> "The Commission thus notes that several of the markets which will be provided with gas from the Nabucco pipeline are today dominated by a single market player being the vertically integrated OMV including its subsidiary Econgas and that the dominant upstream supplier for gas imported into Austria is Gazprom. There is thus a risk that additional gas from the Nabucco pipeline may strengthen one or more dominant positions."[6]

This means that any project that is on the post-investment stage (after the investment decision has been approved) cannot qualify for the exemption. At the same time there are no intermediate clauses that would automatically exempt from the separation requirement the projects which were initiated within the previous legal regime.

It is interesting that the list of objects for potentially exemptions is closed. This list does not include transmission systems connecting Member States with third countries. Theo-

5 <http://ec.europa.eu/energy/infrastructure/infrastructure/gas/gas_exemptions_en.htm>.

6 Paragraph 33 of the decision of the Commission,available at <http://ec.europa.eu/energy/infrastructure/infrastructure/gas/gas_exemptions_en.htm>.

retically it could lead to an imbalance of the law regime of cross-border projects, which would connect Member States between each other and with third countries.

There are several important open questions concerning the exemptions:
- It is not clear, whether the exempted undertaking is not covered with the norms related to the alternative models (independent system operator and independent transmission operator) or the alternative models are applied to it.
- If not, it is not clear, whether such norms will apply to the exempted undertaking after the expiration of the term of exemption.

If the alternative models are not applied to the project, then after the exemption period has expired the vertically integrated undertaking will have to abandon the rights to the transmission system. Such perspective could negatively effect the commercial incentives for the realization of the project.

(b) Article 29 of Gas Directive of the EU provides the right to postpone the application of the separation rule to Member States whose markets are isolated or emergent. This exemption will remain until the markets reserve such characteristics.

The market is isolated when it is not connected with the interconnected system of the EU and has one major external gas supplier (with the participation interest more that 75%). The market is emergent when first supply was less than 10 years before.[7]

Isolated markets are Finland, Estonia, Lithuania and Cyprus.

II Third Countries Clause

For the first time the Third Energy Package introduced on the EU level restrictions of the rights of foreign investors; the so-called third countries clause. The term of the implementation of this clause is until 3 March 2013.

Such provisions have the purpose to prevent control of transmission systems or their owners by companies from non-EU countries until they fulfill certain conditions, *i.e.* a national regulator will have the right to refuse certification of a transmission system operator controlled by "a person or persons from a third country", if:

7 Gas Directive of the EU, Art. 49.

- this company does not comply with the unbundling requirements, and
- its market entry would jeopardise the Member State's or the EU's security of supply.[8]

The merit of the clause is the following: transmission system operators controlled by the foreign investors may be certified by the Commission only in case they show that their certification will not affect the security of energy supply. However, there is no determination of the term 'security of energy supply' and it is not determined how the operators could demonstrate the lack of such risk.[9]

This requirement is not applied to the operators controlled by the investors of the EU, *i.e.* the clause infringes the national treatment regime, because constitutes the exemption of restrictive nature. This clause is applied not only to the new operators but also to existing operators. This could destabilize the current relationships in the market.

The regulator of the Member State, when the operator is located, takes the decision of the certification, but before this it shall ask the opinion of the Commission. The consequences of the rejection are not provided in the Gas Directive of the EU and shall be determined on the national level. Probably the operator that has no certification will not have the right to engage in transmission activity.

III Analysis of the Legitimacy of Separation Rules and Third Parties Clause in the Contest of European and International Law

The question of the legality of the separation rules and third parties clause is the subject of serious discussions. There are critical opinions of these concepts of the Third Energy Package from the part of the Brussels lawyers, which address the infringement of European and international law.[10]

In the context of the European law, the critics say that there is no legal basis for the approval of the Third Energy Package and that the approval of the Third Energy Package breaches basic EU principles of law: proportionality, and free establishment of companies, free movement of capital, legal transparency.

---

8 Datamonitor Position paper. End Game: What Now for Europe's Energy Markets? O4/2009. BFEN0457. Uploded from <www.europeanenergyreview.eu/data/docs/Viewpoints/datamonitor_en090430.pdf>.

9 Gas Directive of the EU, Art. 11.

10 Willems A.R., Sul J., Benizri Y. Unbundling As a Defence Mechanism Against Russia: Is the EU Missing the Point? *Oil, Gas & Energy Law Intelligence*. May, 2009. Vol. 7, Issue 2.

The general rule is that only Member States have the right to challenge the rules of secondary EU law at the ECJ and only within two months of the date of their publication.[11] The potential claimants have not used their right yet – because the Third Energy Package is a political compromise between the Member States and the EU institutions during long and difficult negotiations.

At the stage of the implementation of the Third Energy Package rules private persons whose interests are affected will have the right to challenge the respective norms in national courts. In this case, national courts would appeal to the EU Court in order to obtain prejudicial decisions on issues of construction and validity of the EU law rules.[12]

The answer to the question whether the Third Energy Package is coherent with international rules depends on the investment treaties of the EU and its Member States. Power undertakings of the EU with foreign investments exist within a special regime, provided by those international treaties and are secured by international arbitration. This special regime makes their position more favourable than the position without such foreign investment.

In the case that separation of undertakings will cause the substantial forfeiture of control or investment value, such can be qualified as a measure having expropriation effect. The legitimacy of the expropriation depends on the fulfilment of the conditions including non-discriminatory nature, due process, and just compensation. In this regard property is protected against expropriation by the duty to pay full, prompt and effective compensation (Energy Charter Treaty Article 13). Such duty also extends to 'regulatory takings', *i.e.* government regulatory action that is in its impact equivalent to expropriation. This obligation does not mean expropriation is prohibited, but that full compensation has to be paid. This is probably the current standard of customary international law (based on the so-called 'Hull formula').[13]

The application of separation rules to the vertically integrated undertaking with foreign investments can destabilize current ownership relations and breach the indicated international rules.

Implementation of the third countries clause will cause breach of national treatment with respect to the transmission system operators with foreign investments. National treatment is provided by ECT (clause (10) (7)), many bilateral investment treaties, and the Partnership

11 Treaty on the Functioning of the European Union, Art. 263.
12 Treaty on the Functioning of the European Union, Art. 263.
13 Konoplyanik, Andrei; Wälde, Thomas (2006). "Energy Charter Treaty and its Role in International Energy". *Journal of Energy & Natural Resources Law* (International Bar Association) 24 (4): 523-558.

and cooperation agreement between Russia, EU and Member States 1994 (clause 28 (2)). Foreign investors whose investments are covered by national treatment have the right to non-application of the third countries clause.

Conclusion

The discussion about the relation between the Third Energy Package rules and international obligations of the EU and its Member States have been transferred into a political area.

From the Tenth Progress Report of the EU-Russia Energy Dialogue we can see two opposing viewpoints. The EU believes that with the adoption of the Third Energy Package the EU is consolidating its efforts towards achieving a fully effective market-opening and a single European electricity and gas market. However, according to the assessment of Russia, the current situation is characterized by an unfavourable investment climate for developments in the energy sector of the EU Member States. In particular, the adoption of the third Energy Package by the EU significantly limits the activities of Russian fuel and energy companies in the EU market, directly affecting their interests. The EU side does not share such an assessment. It rather considers the Third Package, which is fully in compliance with the Community's bilateral and international legal commitments, to provide an attractive and stable regulatory framework also for Russian investments into the EU electricity and gas sector.[14] Because of the political nature of this conflict, this chapter offers little prognostication and instead limited analysis to outlining the conflict and the competing positions. Hopefully at least that level of analysis is useful to analysts and practitioners.

14 EU-Russia Energy Dialogue. Tenth Progress Report. November 2009. Available at <http://ec.europa.eu/energy/international/bilateral_cooperation/russia/doc/reports/progress10_en.pdf>.

7 Conflict of Jurisdiction in the EU: A Trend Towards Extraterritoriality

Yuri Klyuchnikov

1 Extraterritoriality

Extraterritorial application of law is a well known feature of contemporary international law. This phenomenon has public law and private law features.

The private law aspect of extraterritoriality is easily understandable: all of private international law is about it. Rules of private law are applicable outside the borders of the state that originated these rules – the particular cases of such application are determined by conflict of laws norms.

On the other hand, extraterritorial application of public law norms is a sphere of acute legal and political conflicts. The recent example is the extradition of Russian citizen Victor Bout from Thailand to the USA. The USA asserted extraterritorial application of US criminal laws in situation where the allegedly criminal acts were committed outside of the USA by a foreign citizen.

The rules dealing with jurisdiction of national courts over commercial and other civil matters are on the borderline of private and public law extraterritoriality. The possibility to exercise jurisdiction to adjudicate is itself a public law matter, though the issues over which jurisdiction may prescribe substantive rules are related only to private law. Thus, jurisdiction to adjudicate (*i.e.* over private matters) is a fertile field for scientific research of extraterritoriality trends. Its analysis is more integral than the analysis of separate jurisdictional issues (prescriptive jurisdiction, jurisdiction to enforce, etc.).

Extraterritoriality, explained in practical terms, means that a state deals with some matter closely connected with another state as though such matter has a close territorial connection to the first state. This happens because sovereign interests in the modern world tend to expand, which, in its turn, is a consequence of economic integration-globalization.

2 Regulation of Jurisdiction over Civil and Commercial Claims in the EU

Implications for Extraterritoriality

European integration leads to an expansion of Member States' sovereign interests beyond their national borders. Therefore, the development of the European Union inevitably leads to an increase of extraterritorial application of national laws of Member States. This chapter proves the trend towards extraterritoriality in EU through analysis of jurisdiction in civil and commercial matters, which, as explained above, is at the border of public law and private law and thus of universal research interest.

In the early years of EU history, civil and commercial jurisdiction was regulated by the Brussels Convention on jurisdiction and the enforcement of judgments in civil and commercial matters, signed on 27 September 1968[1] (hereinafter, the Brussels Convention). Through numerous developments (which are not analyzed in this chapter) the Brussels Convention evolved into the Lugano Convention on jurisdiction and the recognition and enforcement of judgments in civil and commercial matters, signed on 30 October 2007[2] (hereinafter, Lugano Convention). These Conventions formed the so called "Brussels Regime" along with Regulation (EC) No 44/2001 on jurisdiction and the recognition and enforcement of judgments in civil and commercial matters(22 December 2000)[3] (hereinafter the Brussels I Regulation).

The evolution of jurisdictional rules in Europe can be briefly described as follows: The Brussels Convention established jurisdictional principles for the six original Member States of European Community and was later replaced by Brussels I Regulation; the Lugano Convention, then extended the application of the Brussels I Regulation to the relations between Member States of the EC and Denmark, Norway, (now, Member States) Iceland and Switzerland (non Member States). The Lugano Convention, substantially reproduces the Brussels I Regulation's provisions.[4]

The territorial spheres of application of Brussels and Lugano Conventions do not coincide. However, I think that it is methodologically correct to compare the provisions of Brussels and Lugano Conventions, because the Lugano Convention absorbed the current EU

1 OJ L 299, 31 December1972, pp. 32-42.
2 OJ L 339, 21 December 2007, pp. 3-41.
3 OJ L 12, 16 January 2001.
4 See Explanatory Report by Professor Fausto Pocar, Official Journal of the European Union, 23 December 2009, C 319/1, C 319/4.

jurisdictional approach and the structure of the two treaties is quite similar. Moreover, a considerable but not excessive period of time passed between signing of the two Conventions making it possible to conclude a certain trend in the extraterritoriality approach.

This chapter demonstrates the extraterritoriality trend in the EU by a comparative analysis of the Brussels and Lugano conventions. This thesis is further is supported by opinions of other scholars.

3 The Scope of the Conventions: Territorial and Personal

The first and perhaps most important difference between the Brussels and Lugano Conventions concerns the definition of territories which are affected by the treaties. The Brussels Convention from this point of view is a standard international treaty. It uses the term "Contracting State" and, accordingly, deals with issues of jurisdiction over persons domiciled in a Contracting State. The Lugano Convention, on the other hand, uses another term – "State bound by this Convention." At first glance, there is little or no difference between two terms. But the Lugano Convention, unlike Brussels Convention, provides a definition of the relevant term. Under Article 1 (3) of Lugano Convention "… the term 'State bound by this Convention' shall mean any State that is a Contracting Party to this Convention or a Member State of the European Community. *It may also mean the European Community*" (emphasis added).

In other provisions, the Lugano Convention uses terms such as "persons domiciled in a State bound by this Convention," "place in a State bound by this Convention," linking the place of, *e.g.*, delivery or other performance with judicial jurisdiction. The fact that the term "State bound by this Convention" may have the meaning (at the time of signing of the Lugano Convention) of the European Community, gives, to my mind, a rather strong argument for the fact of extraterritorial application of jurisdiction of the Member States *via* the EEC (now EU). Speaking with a good bit of simplification, if the place of performance is somewhere in EU, the Member State's court essentially becomes part of EU law enforcement. Thus, the Member State may assert its jurisdiction according to its sovereign interests. For me, this is a proof of extraterritorial possibilities conferred to European states, though the doctrinal basis for application of this approach has yet to be formed. In the present moment, the official construction of the provision on parties bound by the Convention is that "certain of the Convention's obligations may apply directly to the Community itself, or may concern the recognition and enforcement of judgments delivered by the Court of Justice or by other Community courts".[5] Regarding the application of Brussels and Lugano Conventions to specific persons, the concept of domicile of legal persons evolved. Thus, under Article 53 of Brussels Convention, "the seat of a company or other legal person or association of natural or legal persons shall be treated as its domicile." Article 60 of Lugano Convention broadens[6] the notion of domicile, including in it not only the place of its statutory seat, but also the place of its central administration or principal place of business. The notions of "seat" and "statutory seat" are not equal, and thus the difference between the two domicile definitions may be not so striking. However, it is hard to challenge the fact that Lugano Convention gives additional possibilities to qualify legal entities as domiciled in a particular contracting state, thereby extending the reach of national rules of law extraterritorially, using the "nationality" principle of jurisdiction.

There are also provisions in the Conventions concerning court jurisdiction in special cases.

4 Jurisdiction over Torts: Enhancement of Effects Doctrine

One of such special cases is jurisdiction over torts. Article 5 (3) of Brussels Convention provides that a person domiciled in one contracting state may be sued in another "in matters relating to tort, delict or quasi-delict, in the courts for the place where the harmful event occurred." "This place may either be the place of the event giving rise to the damage or the place where that damage *actually* occurred"[7] (emphasis added). Article 5 (3) of Lugano Convention repeats the wording of the Brussels Convention, but with one meaningful addition – "in the courts for the place where the harmful effect occurred *or may occur*" (emphasis added).

This modification is an evidence of proliferation of the so called "effects analysis " in European law. Among several jurisdictional bases (*e.g.*, jurisdiction over the state's own-territory and over its own-nationals is well-rooted and indisputable) jurisdiction based on the effects of the transaction, sometimes called "effects jurisdiction" or "effects doctrine",

5 *Ibid*, C 319/5.

6 The analysis of jurisdiction broadening is given in: Explanatory Report by Professor Fausto Pocar, Official Journal of the European Union, 23 December 2009, C 319/8.

7 Alexander Klauser, Bernhard Girsch, Monika Gudenus, Peter Polak, referring to Judgment of ECJ of 30 November 1976, Case 21/76, *Mines de Potasse d'Alsace,* (1976) ECR 1735, Overview of Austrian Agency Regulation/ International Agency and Distribution Law [2008] Vol. I, P. I/130, available at <www.books.google.com>.

has been the most disputable basis of jurisdiction. Currently, it is recognized that, though the "effects analysis " remains controversial, almost all jurisdictions apply it in some form.[8]

Under the traditional "effects analysis" a state may assert jurisdiction over some action when the consequences of that action are suffered in the territory of that state or by its nationals. An extreme – and controversial – form of "effects" based jurisdiction provides that jurisdiction may be exercised when there may be even *potential* effect for the territory or the nationals of the state. The Lugano Convention adopted this extreme approach. This shows the extraterritoriality trend in the EU.[9]

However, the application of the "effects" approach to tort jurisdiction is not unlimited. Speaking of the construction of the wording "the place where the harmful effect ... may occur", Professor Pocar points out that "in line with the approach taken by the Court of Justice ... it must be the place where there is a danger of immediate damage, and not a place where there may be indirect financial damage."[10]

5 Immovable Property: *Lex Situs* Is Still Important, but No Longer Absolute

Another special case where extraterritorial law may be found is in Article 6 (4) of Lugano Convention which addresses the commonly accepted basis of jurisdiction is jurisdiction over disputes concerning immovable property. The general approach is that the courts of a state where immovable property is located have exclusive jurisdiction in suits involving such property. The Lugano Convention goes further however, and establishes an alternative basis for jurisdiction, linking claims over real estate to other possibly related claims. Under Article 6 (4) "[a] person domiciled in a State bound by this Convention may also be sued ... in matters relating to a contract, if the action may be combined with an action against the same defendant in matters relating to rights in rem in immovable property, in the court of the State bound by this Convention in which the property is situated." Practically, this means that a state where mortgaged property is located may extend its jurisdiction extraterritorially, adjudicating claims concerning, *e.g.*, loan agreements secured by mortgage.

8 Report of the Task Force on Extraterritorial Jurisdiction, available at <www.ibanet.org>, p. 13 (no data on authors or publication details).

9 It must be said, however, that even in the pre-Lugano 2007 period ECJ interpreted Article 5 (3) of Brussels Convention as not presupposing the existence of damage. See *Verein fur Konsumenteninformation v. Henkel*, ECJ Case C-167/00, [2002] ECR I-8111, available at <www.eur-lex.europa.eu>.

10 Explanatory Report by Professor Fausto Pocar, Official Journal of the European Union, 23 December 2009, C 319/16.

However, application of *lex situs* to disputes concerning immovable property is no longer absolute. As was mentioned above, jurisdiction over immovable property is customarily and historically exclusive. The Brussels and Lugano Conventions in Articles 16 (1) and 22 (1) respectively contain almost identical provisions which provide, that in proceedings which have as their object rights in rem in immovable property or tenancies of immovable property, the courts of the state bound by the convention in which the property is situated shall have exclusive jurisdiction, regardless of domicile of the parties.

The Lugano Convention, however, in the same article provides for a very characteristic exception to this general rule. Under the exception:

> "in proceedings which have as their object tenancies of immovable property concluded for temporary private use for a maximum period of six consecutive months, the courts of the State bound by this Convention in which defendant is domiciled shall also have jurisdiction, provided that the tenant is a natural person and that the landlord and the tenant are domiciled in the same State bound by this Convention."

Analysis of this rule demonstrates that jurisdiction is tied to the state of defendant's domicile, while in other places the Convention speaks of landlord and tenant. The term "defendant" may not coincide with "landlord" or "tenant." For example, "proceedings which have as their object tenancies of immovable property" may relate to rights of third parties in respect of real estate. Consequently, we observe here a tendency towards dissociation of court jurisdiction from the place where the immovable property is located. Thus, extraterritoriality of jurisdiction is at least implicit here.

6 Other Special Cases of Jurisdiction

Both the Brussels and Lugano Conventions contain rules establishing jurisdiction over certain special matters.

However, the Lugano Convention contains an entirely new section concerning jurisdiction over individual contracts of employment. The general approach of the Lugano Convention is quite common for employment disputes: the employer generally may be sued in courts of the state where he is domiciled (or where employer's branch, agency or other establishment is located). The Lugano Convention, however, introduces a special rule reflecting modern employment trends. In accordance with Article 19 (2) of Lugano Convention, an employer may be sued in the state bound by the convention, other than the state of domicile,

> "(a) in the courts for the place where the employee habitually carries out his work or in the courts for the last place where he did so; or (b) if the employee does not or did not habitually carry out his work in any one country, in the courts for the place where the business which engaged the employee is or was situated."

This provision, to my mind, serves to the current tendency on the job market, where an employee may not be tightly linked to one particular place of employment (tele/commuting, interims, part timers, etc.). Consequently, there is the additional possibility for essentially extraterritorial jurisdiction of courts (*i.e.* over non-nationals and in respect of issues not directly related to the state of the court). This, nonetheless, does not affect jurisdiction over employees: according to Article 20 (1) of Lugano Convention "[a]n employer may bring proceedings only in the courts of the State bound by this Convention in which the employee is domiciled." Thus, in cases of suits against employees there are no extraterritoriality options.

Recognition and enforcement of foreign judgments is also a sphere where issues of extraterritoriality may be raised. Judgments held in one contracting state are given extraterritorial effect in other contracting states. Though the relevant Conventions regulate jurisdiction over commercial and other civil matters, such judgments may relate to private as well as public law issues. For example, breach of administrative procedure may impact the resolution of commercial disputes. Therefore, public law sometimes gains extraterritorial effect through recognition and enforcement of private law decisions.

International treaties, such as the Brussels and Lugano Conventions, provide for mutual recognition and enforcement of judgments, as a general rule. The evolution of the approach may be found only in exceptions to that general rule – cases where a judgment shall not be recognized. Here, the Lugano Convention as compared to Brussels Convention provides that the judgment shall not be recognized if such recognition is not only contrary, but *manifestly* contrary to public policy in the state in which recognition is sought (Article 34 (1)). This modification is considered by scholars as stressing "the exceptional nature of recourse to this ground for refusal."[11] Moreover, failure to duly serve process is a basis for

11 Fausto Pocar, *The new Lugano Convention on Jurisdiction and the Recognition and Enforcement of Judgments in Civil and Commercial Matters,* 10 Yearbook of Private Int'l. L., 13 (2008). Available at <www.books.google.com>.

non-recognition not in any case, but only where "the defendant failed to commence proceedings to challenge the judgment when it was possible for him to do so." By establishing exceptions to the special cases of non-recognition of foreign judgments, the Lugano Convention extends possibilities for extraterritorial application of national laws within the EU.

7 CONCLUSION

From this study of the evolution of jurisdictional rules in EU, I conclude that there is a clear trend towards extraterritorial application of EU substantive law (in Germanic terms *Materielles Recht*). This tendency attracts its share of attention in European doctrine and US doctrine as well.

As Laura Tomasi (representative of European doctrine) points out, "it can be submitted that extension of EC instruments on conflicts of jurisdiction to non purely intra-Community cases ... is somewhat in line with a generalized tendency to widen EC law['s] spatial scope vis-à-vis situations connected (also) with third states. The core idea underlying such expansion of EC law scope is to grant and offer 'EC law protection' to natural and legal persons having certain degree of *proximité* with the Community territory."[12]

John Fitzpatrick (University of Connecticut School of law) in 2007 – that is, even prior to Lugano, analyzing jurisdictional tendencies in Europe, stressed that the relevant norms of jurisdictional conventions "specifically [prohibit] exorbitant bases of jurisdiction existing in national legal systems. However, this prohibition only applies to defendants domiciled in one of the signatory countries. Therefore, the internal law of the forum state, including its exorbitant bases of jurisdiction are explicitly approved when applied to parties domiciled in non-EC states. [...] A general comparison of US law to the [EU law] indicates that Europe and America are moving in opposite directions concerning exorbitant assertion of jurisdiction over foreign defendants. The United States Supreme Court in recent years has constantly struck down excessive assertions of jurisdiction over foreigners by state courts. The basis for this denial is the due process clause .... In contrast, the EC ... [has] expanded the reach of excessive assertions of jurisdiction ...."[13]

---

12 Laura Tomasi, *The Application Of Ec Law To Non Purely Intra-Community Situations,* (2008), p. 94. Available at <www.books.google.com>.

13 John Fitzpatrick, *The Lugano Convention and Western European Integration: A Comparative Analysis of Jurisdiction and Judgments in Europe and the United States.* 8 Conn. J. Int'l L. 695, 703, 726. In that article at footnote 34 Fitzpatrick also explains the notion of "exorbitant jurisdiction", that "can be defined as those assertions of jurisdiction that are not generally recognized by accepted principles of international law."

The analysis of the modern jurisdictional regulation under Lugano Convention as compared to pre-existing regulation gives strong arguments to assert *a firm tendency toward extraterritorial application of legal norms in the EU*. Despite the importance of the issue, this trend has not yet received due attention in legal scholarship. However, this is well understandable, as the Lugano Convention only entered into force on 1 January 2010. This chapter looks at the extraterritoriality trend through the evolution of European jurisdictional rules. Further doctrinal research of this trend is to be expected as ever greater trade and communication create more and more cross-jurisdictional transactions.

Part II
Russia and the European Court of Human Rights

8 Russia and the European Court of Human Rights

Ilya Korotkikh

1 Introduction

"We propose the creation of a harmonious economic community stretching from Lisbon to Vladivostok," Putin writes. "In the future, we could even consider a free trade zone or even more advanced forms of economic integration. The result would be a unified continental market with a capacity worth trillions of euros."[1] These current ideas of the Russian Prime Minister are consequences of convergence process between Russia and the EU.

Since the early 1990s Russia is rushing to become a part of European family. Some steps highlighted the process of convergence of Russia and EU. The first step was the conclusion in 1994 of the Partnership and Co-operation Agreement between Russia and the EU,[2] which established a base for relationships. The second one was the ratification in 1998 by Russia of Convention for the Protection of Human Rights and Fundamental Freedoms[3] (the Convention) that opened to Russia a window to European rule of law through European Court of Human Rights (ECHR).

"Prior to ratification, the period of 1992-1996 was characterized by a huge volume of legislative activity and search of ways by legal system democratization. The cooperation of Russia and Europe was highlighted by changing of view about human rights in Russian legal ideology and legal system. Russian legislation and legal science began using the well-known term 'human rights'."[4]

But what was changed in the Russian legal system after joining to the Convention? And how does Russia meets to the ECHR's requirements? This chapter answers the questions

1 *'From Lisbon to Vladivostok' Putin Envisions a Russia-EU Free Trade Zone*, <www.spiegel.de/international/europe/0,1518,731109,00.html> (accessed 18 December 2010).
2 *The Partnership and Co-operation Agreement between Russia and EU*, (24 June 1994).
3 *Convention for the Protection of Human Rights and Fundamental Freedoms*, (4 November 1950).
4 O. Doronina & V. Kalinin, *Vlijanie evpopeyskih standartov v Oblasti prav cheloveka na Rossiyskoe zakonodatelstvo I pravoprimenitelnuyu praktiku [Impact of European standards in the area of human rights on the Russian legislation and case law]*, 1 Advokatskaya praktika, (January 25, 2008) (available at Consultant plus, legal database).

and observes Russian problems in the ECHR and the requirements to Russian complaints tried before the ECtHR.

2 The Russian Legal System After Joining to the Convention

2.1 The ECHR's Jurisdiction over Russia

"Upon the Convention ratification, Russia declared that acknowledges 'ipso facto' and without any special approval the jurisdiction of ECHR by all issues of construing and applying the Convention by cases of violations by Russia of the Convention provisions."[5]

Under Article 1 of the Convention,[6] the High Contracting Parties shall secure to everyone within their jurisdiction the rights and freedoms defined in Section I of this Convention. The High Contracting Parties undertake to abide by the final judgment of the Court in any case to which they are parties.[7]

It means that the Convention provisions that Russia is obligated to fulfil are to conform with judgements of ECHR. Under Article 15 of the Russian Constitution,[8] the provisions of the Convention are part of the legal system of Russia, therefore, the ECHR's judgments are binding for the legal system and Russian courts.

So, the first impact on the Russian justice system is that Russian judges have to follow the ECHR's practice when they try a case. The ECHR practice is laid down on the basis of a judgment regardless of the legislator's opinion. That is a new source of law, which develops the court system in new ways without the interference of other government branches. In addition, the ECHR's practice imparts the court system with independence when national law contravenes the Convention and the ECHR's decisions, or where there are gaps in the law.

The second impact of the ECHR on Russian justice is the implementation by the Russian courts of standards required by the Convention and expressed in the ECHR's practice.

5 *Federal Law on the Ratification of European Convention of Human Rights*, N 54-FZ, SZ RF. N 14, Art. 1 (20 February 1998) (Russia).
6 *Convention for the Protection of Human Rights and Fundamental Freedoms*, Art. 1.
7 *Id.*, Art. 46.
8 *Constitution of RF*, Art.15 (12 December 1993) (Russia).

Standards include the right to a fair trial, an independent and impartial judge;[9] a public hearing[10] and reasonable time of trial.[11]

2.2 *Russian Problems in ECHR*

About 25% of the cases heard before the ECHR are from Russia.[12] Analysis of judgments against Russia revealed tendencies which the ECHR highlights regarding the protection of human rights in Russia.

The first problem is a violation of the principle of legal certainty.

The principle presumes predictability of judgements' results. In the case *Ryabykh v. Russia*[13] the ECHR held there was a violation by Russia of that principle.

The facts of the case follow: the judge of the local court decided to compensate Ms. Ryabykh for the bank deposit that she lost by fault of the State bank. Despite numerous reversals of the decision, the judge again and again stood by its decision. Finaly, in six years after the first decision the Supreme court of the region closed the case when Ms. Ryabykh and the Government of Belgorod region signed an amicable settlement agreement.

The ECHR held:

> One of the fundamental aspects of the rule of law is the principle of legal certainty, which requires, among other things, that where the courts have finally determined an issue, their ruling should not be called into question .... Legal certainty presupposes respect of the principle of res judicata, that is the principle of finality of judgments. This principle insists that no party is entitled to seek a review of a final and binding judgment merely for the purpose of a rehearing and a fresh decision of the case. Higher courts' power of review should be exercised for correction of judicial mistakes, miscarriages of justice, and not to substitute a review. The review cannot be treated as an appeal in disguise, and the mere possibility of two views on the subject is not a ground for re-

9 *Sutyazhnik v. Russia,* 8269/02, ECHR, 2009.
10 *Zagorodnikov v. Russia*, 66941/01, ECHR, 2007.
11 *Kormacheva v. Russia*, 53084/99, ECHR, 2004.
12 O. Snezhko, *Defekti Rossiyskogo pravosudiya v resheniyah evropeyskogo suda po pravam cheloveka [Defects of the Russian justice under judgments of ECHR]*, 19 Konstitucionnoe I municipalnoe pravo, (15 October 2007) (available at Consultant plus, legal database).
13 *Ryabykh v. Russia*, 52854/99, ECHR, 2004.

> examination. Departures from that principle are justified only when made necessary by circumstances of a substantial and compelling character.[14]

The second problem is repetitive accusations.

A vivid example of the problem is the case of twins Irina and Elena Smirnova.[15] Over nine years of police investigation, the sisters were arrested four times and Elena was imprisoned for four years. In its decision, the ECHR held Russia liable for the violation of the rights to freedom, to safety, to respect of private life and to a fair trial within a reasonable time.

The issue of whether a period of detention is reasonable cannot be assessed in abstract. Whether it is reasonable for an accused to remain in detention must be assessed in each case according to its special features. Continued detention can be justified in a given case only if there are specific indications of a genuine requirement of public interest which, notwithstanding the presumption of innocence, outweighs the rule of respect for individual liberty.[16]

The third problem is slowness and inefficiency of the justice.

Partly, the reason for that problem is that the Russian courts are overloaded. But the ECHR does not excuse that. For example, Russia paid € 2400 to Alexandr Plaksin[17] because he litigated for five years, with no final decision. The ECHR considered that the case about property damage is not so difficult to go on for five years. Therefore, the right of Plaksin to a reasonable time of proceedings was violated.

The fourth problem and the most outrageous is non-execution of judgements.

2.2.1 The Pilot-Judgment Against Russia (the Problem of Non-Execution of Judgments in Russia)

The famous case *Burdov v. Russia* (No. 2)[18] laid down the dispute between Russia and the ECHR. The facts of the case follow. Beginning from 1997, the applicant brought numerous lawsuits against the State authorities about recovering the social benefits to which he is entitled as a participant of works in the Chernobyl nuclear plant disaster. The courts granted his suits, but many judgements were not executed during a long period. In 2000,

14 *Id*, cl.51.
15 *Smirnova v. Russia*, 46133/99 & 48183/99, 2003.
16 *Id*, cl.61.
17 *Plaksin v. Russia*, 14949/02, ECHR, 2004.
18 *Burdov v. Russia (N 2)*, 33509/04, ECHR, 2009.

he brought the first complaint to the ECHR on the ground of non-execution of a judgement. The ECHR "[h]eld that there had been violations of Article 6 of the Convention and of Article 1 of Protocol No. 1 on account of the authorities' failure for years to take the necessary measures to comply with these decisions."[19] The Government paid the applicant the sum of satisfaction provided for in the ECHR's judgment and in domestic decisions. From 2003 to 2006, the applicant repeatedly had to litigate (five times) their claim against the Government for social benefits. The courts granted audience to his suits, but all judgements were not executed.

In 2008, Burdov submitted the complaint to ECHR:

> [T]hat the authorities' prolonged failure to comply with the binding and enforceable judgments in his favour violated his right to a court under Article 6 of the Convention and his right to the peaceful enjoyment of his possessions under Article 1 of Protocol No. 1, which in so far as relevant read as follows:
>
> Article 6 § 1 "In the determination of his civil rights and obligations ..., everyone is entitled to a fair and public hearing within a reasonable time by {a]... tribunal ..."
>
> Article 1 of Protocol No. 1 "Every natural or legal person is entitled to the peaceful enjoyment of his possessions. No one shall be deprived of his possessions except in the public interest and subject to the conditions provided for by law and by the general principles of international law".[20]

The ECHR granted the complaint of the applicant, having stated:

> 65. The right to a court protected by Article 6 would be illusory if a Contracting State's domestic legal system allowed a final, binding judicial decision to remain inoperative to the detriment of one party. Execution of a judgment given by any court must therefore be regarded as an integral part of the "trial" for the purposes of Article 6 (see Hornsby v. Greece, 19 March 1997, § 40, Reports of Judgments and Decisions 1997-II).
>
> 66. An unreasonably long delay in enforcement of a binding judgment may therefore breach the Convention (see Burdov v. Russia, No. 59498/00, ECHR

19 *Id*, cl.9.
20 *Id*, cl.46.

> 2002-III). The reasonableness of such delay is to be determined having regard in particular to the complexity of the enforcement proceedings, the applicant's own behaviour and that of the competent authorities, and the amount and nature of the court award (see Raylyan v. Russia, No. 22000/03, § 31, 15 February 2007).
>
> 86. In view of the foregoing, the Court concludes that by delaying the execution of the ... judgments ... the authorities failed to respect the applicant's right to a court. There is accordingly a violation of Article 6 of the Convention.
>
> 87. Given that the binding and enforceable judgments created an established right to payment in the applicant's favour, which should be considered as a "possession" within the meaning of Article 1 of Protocol No. 1 (see Vasilopoulou v. Greece, No. 47541/99, § 22, 21 March 2002), the authorities' prolonged failure to comply with these judgments also violated the applicant's right to peaceful enjoyment of his possessions (see Burdov, cited above, § 41). There is accordingly also a violation of Article 1 of Protocol No. 1.[21]

But after rendering the decision by the complaint of the applicant, the ECtHR rendered a "pilot-judgment" about the obligation of Russia within six months to adopt and implement "[a] remedy which secures genuinely effective redress for the violations of the Convention on account of the State authorities' prolonged failure to comply with judicial decisions delivered against the State or its entities."[22] In addition, the ECtHR suspended trying the cases against Russia where the grounds were the same as in *Burdov*.

The ECtHR in its decision explained a "pilot-judgment" as follows:

> 126. In order to facilitate effective implementation of its judgments along these lines, the Court may adopt a pilot-judgment procedure allowing it to clearly identify in a judgment the existence of structural problems underlying the violations and to indicate specific measures or actions to be taken by the respondent state to remedy them .... [A]nother important aim of the pilot-judgment procedure is to induce the respondent State to resolve large numbers of individual cases arising from the same structural problem at the domestic level, thus implementing the principle of subsidiarity which underpins the Convention system .... The object of the pilot-judgment procedure is to facilitate

21 *Id*, cl.65, 66, 86, 87.

22 *Id*, cl.141.

> the speediest and most effective resolution of a dysfunction affecting the protection of the Convention rights in question in the national legal order (see Wolkenberg and Others v. Poland (dec.), No. 50003/99, § 34, ECHR 2007-... (extracts)). While the respondent State's action should primarily aim at the resolution of such a dysfunction and at the introduction, where appropriate, of effective domestic remedies in respect of the violations in question, it may also include ad hoc solutions such as friendly settlements with the applicants or unilateral remedial offers in line with the Convention requirements. The Court may decide to adjourn examination of all similar cases, thus giving the respondent State an opportunity to settle them in such various ways (see, mutatis mutandis, Broniowski, cited above, § 198, and Xenides-Arestis v. Turkey, No. 46347/99, § 50, 22 December 2005).
>
> 128. If, however, the respondent State fails to adopt such measures following a pilot judgment and continues to violate the Convention, the Court will have no choice but to resume examination of all similar applications pending before it and to take them to judgment so as to ensure effective observance of Convention ....[23]

In pursuit of the case *Burdov v. Russia* (No. 2) on 30 April 2010, Russia adopted the on Compensation for Violation of Right to Justice on Reasonable Time and Right to Execution of Judgment on Reasonable Time.[24] Under the law, a court awards compensation for failure to enforce judgment within a reasonable time. Also, changes in the Codes about trial and arbitration procedures were adopted which established the reasonable time of trial and arbitration.

After adoption of the law and the changes, domestic political disputes about the jurisdiction of the ECtHR over Russia erupted.

On meeting with judges of Constitutional Court of Russia (the highest court in Russia) President Medvedev said:

"I think that in our contacts with foreign partners and European institutes we primarily have to act in compliance with the powers that we [Russia] transferred to ECHR. As I think

23 *Id*, cl.126-128.

24 *Federal Law on Compensation for Violation of Right to Justice on Reasonable Time and Right to Execution of Judgment on Reasonable Time*, N 68-FZ, (30 April 2010) (Russia).

we never transferred a power and part of our sovereignty that allow to a international court [ECHR]or foreign country to render decisions that change our national law.

By the way, some European countries that more integrated in European institutions uphold this position.

This issue requires additional analysis and discussion with European partners. Sometimes it has significant importance for our country. We will not close eyes to this kind of things. I want that the judges of Constitutional court who present here, the chiefs of the Supreme and High *Arbitrazh* courts do understand my position, because I am a guarantor of the Constitution. We will react on this kind of things."[25]

The words show that Russian politicians (perhaps also the people) are angry about the pilot-judgment and probably Russia in the future will use the right not to fulfill pilot-decisions. However, the fact undoubtedly will undermine the credibility of Russia before the European countries.

3 Access of Russian Complaints to ECHR

Under Article 34 of the Convention,[26] the Court may receive applications from any person, non-governmental organization, or group of individuals claiming to be the victim of a violation by one of the High Contracting Parties of the rights set forth in the Convention or the Protocols thereto. Under Article 34, the ECtHR tries those cases where the Government of a country, participating in the Convention, violated the rights of an applicant protected by the Convention. An applicant can be a commercial company.

Under Article 35 (1) of the Convention,[27] the Court may only deal with the matter after all domestic remedies have been exhausted, according to the generally recognised rules of international law, and within a period of six months from the date on which the final decision was taken.

The most important condition of the article is that all domestic remedies should be exhausted. Under the ECHR's practice, in Russia the court of last resort is a regional court in cases of common jurisdiction and an appeals court in *arbitrazh*. After trying the cases

25 *Meeting with the judges of the Constitutional Court*, <http://президент.рф/новости/9792> (accessed 18 December 2010).
26 *Convention for the Protection of Human Rights and Fundamental Freedoms*, Art.34.
27 *Convention for the Protection of Human Rights and Fundamental Freedoms*, Art.35 (1).

in the courts judgments become binding. The main criteria to determine whether all domestic remedies have been exhausted is a final legal judgment.

In addition, the ECtHR is very skeptical about the Russian courts supervisory review and does not treat those courts as courts of final resort.[28]

4 Conclusion

This chapter has explored the impact of the ECHR on Russia. Through the ECtHR's judgments, problems of the Russian justice system were revealed: lack of legal certainty, preponderance of accusation, non-execution of judgments, slowness and inefficiency. Judgments of the ECtHR are an effective way for establishment of and control over the European principles of justice. The pilot-judgment by the case *Burdov v. Russia (No. 2)* forced Russia to adopt and change laws about reasonable time and proper execution of national judgments. At the same time, there are threats from Russian politicians to step aside from execution of the future ECHR's pilot-judgments. That would seriously undermine the credibility of Russia with respect to other European countries.

28 See, *e.g.*, *Ryabykh v. Russia*, 52854/99, ECHR, 2004.

9 ECtHR Judgments and Russian Legislation

Aijamal Umarova

1 Introduction

The Convention for the Protection of Human Rights and Fundamental Freedoms[1] ("the European Convention") is a basic European treaty.[2] Judgments of the European Court of Human Rights and Fundamental Freedoms ("the ECHR") are important and influential. ECHR judgments are final.[3] Thus, the implementation of the ECtHR's judgments in the Russian Federation[4] is vital to the rule of law.

The implementation of the ECHR's judgments is one of the problems widely discussed today by Russian lawyers due to the fact that there are many lacunae and even defects in Russian legislation. As a result, there is no unified procedure to enforce ECtHR judgments in Russia at this moment.[5] The implementation of the ECtHR's judgments in the Russian legal order needs improvement. However, there are some steps forward in developing the current situation. *E.g.*, Abdumajitova stated "it would be interesting to see the progress that has been achieved by the Russian Federation in its compliance with the judgments of the Court"[6]. This chapter presents a brief summary of recent changes in Russian legislation which concerned the rehearing (reopening) procedure as one of individual measures.

---

1 Council of Europe, *European Convention for the Protection of Human Rights and Fundamental Freedoms*, 4 November 1950, ETS 5, available at: <http://conventions.coe.int/treaty/Commun/QueVoulezVous.asp?NT=005&CL=ENG>.

2 Variychuk, E., The Implementation of the Judgments of the European Court of Human Rights in Russia, IPRA Research Paper (undated) (available at: <http://soc.kuleuven.be/iieb/ipra2008/papers/index.php?action=paperauthor>>. [hereinafter Variychuk].

3 Abdumajitova, N., 2007. Compliance with judgments of the European Court of Human Rights in the Russian Federation, p. 1 (available at: <www.duo.uio.no/sok/work.html?WORKID=65930&lang=en>). ("The judgments of the European Court of Human Rights are final if the cases are not appealed and referred to the Grand Chamber within three months") [hereinafter Abdumajitova].

4 Probably, all these refer to Russian federation history of the acceptance to the Council of Europe. See Abdumajitova, *supra* note 3 at 1 ("The Russian Federation was accepted to the Council of Europe despite the fact that its legislation, except its Constitution and its law enforcement practice, did not comply with the Council of Europe's standards on human rights ").

5 See Variychuk, *supra* note 2 at p. 2.

6 See Abdumajitova, *supra* note 3 at p. 1.

2 Overview of the Legal Framework

2.1 *The European Convention*

The European Convention[7] was adopted on 4 November 1950 by the Council of Europe and came into force on 3 September 1953. Article 46 of the Convention sets forth an obligation to comply with the ECHR' judgment in any case to which the Contracting State is a party. The obligation stemming from the judgment of the Court falls into three categories: just satisfaction, individual measures, or general measures.[8] Implementation of these measures in the national legal order is necessary to fulfil the primary task of the Contracting Parties to the European Convention, which is to secure the rights and freedoms of everyone within their jurisdiction.[9]

2.2 *Russia's Ratification*

The Russian Federation ratified the European Convention on 5 May 1998. Thus, Russia declared that it recognizes ipso facto and without special agreement the jurisdiction of the ECtHR with regard to the interpretation and implementation of the European Convention and its Protocols in the cases of alleged breaches of the European Convention by Russia.[10]

2.3 *Legal Grounds for Implementation of the ECHR's Judgments in the National Legal System of the Russian Federation*

Since Russia is a party to the European Convention, the European Convention's norms are binding on Russia. This conclusion is based upon the rule of Article 15(4)[11] of the Constitution[12] of the Russian Federation, according to which generally recognized principles

7 See *supra* note 1.

8 See Abdumajitova, *supra* note 3 at p. 1.

9 See Abdumajitova,*supra* note 3 at p. 1.

10 See Variychuk, supra note 2 at 1.

11 RF Const., Art. 15(4) ("Generally recognized principles and norms of the international law and international agreements of the Russian Federation are constituent part of its legal system. If an international agreement of the Russian Federation establishes other rules differing from those provided by the law, the rules of the international agreement are to be applied").

12 The Constitution of the Russian Federation was adopted by national voting on 12 December 1993. See RF Const. (available at <www.constitution.ru/en/10003000-01.htm>).

and norms of international law and international treaties of the Russian Federation shall be deemed an integral part of its legal system.[13]

Moreover, Article 46(3) of the Constitution contains a relevant provision concerning individual complaints to international bodies, which states: "Everyone shall have the right to appeal, according to international treaties of the Russian Federation, to international bodies for the protection of human rights and freedoms, if all the existing internal state means of legal protection have been exhausted."

Therefore, this article indirectly requires that international human rights principles be respected at the national level in the first instance.[14]

3 Rehearing (Reopening) Procedure as One of the Individual Measures

As mentioned above, there are three categories (just satisfaction, individual measures and general measures) of the obligation stemming from the ECHR's judgment. It is a common view among Russian lawyers that the Russian federation generally has no problems with *just satisfaction* and *general measures.*[15]

The problem with *individual measures* is more complicated.[16] However, from the juridical point of view one of the most interesting individual measures taken during the enforcement of the ECHR's judgments is rehearing of the case by a domestic court.[17] The execution of the individual measure is necessary in some cases to address national mechanisms for

13 Musin, V.A., 2007. Recent Case Law of the European Court of Human Rights: an Overview. International Journal of Legal Information, Vol. 35: Iss. 2, Article 11, p. 262 (Available at: <http://scholarship.law.cornell.edu/ijli/vol35/iss2/11>). [hereinafter Musin].

14 Burkov, A., 2010. "Impact of the Convention for the Protection of Human Rights and Fundamental Freedoms on the Russian Legal System", *The EU-Russia centre review*, May 2010, Iss. 14 p. 31 (available at: <www.eu-russiacentre.org/reviews>).

15 See Variychuk, *supra* note 2 at 2 ("Considering the problem of the enforcement of the Court's judgments it is essential to remember that the European Court of Human Rights in its judgments awards not only pecuniary damages to the victim but also prescribes the necessity of individual and general measures to be taken within a country to put an end to the violations of the rights found by the European Court and to prevent similar violations. There is no doubt that what one notices first of all is that the European Court of Human Rights awards to the applicant a "just satisfaction", *i.e.* a fixed sum of money as physical and moral damages suffered through the violation of the Convention and legal costs incurred with regard to this violation. And in Russia there is usually no problem with enforcing this part of the European Court's judgment. Russian authorities pay such sums of money in time. There are actually no complaints about non-payments or delay of the damages").

16 See Musin, *supra* note 13 at p. 273.

17 See Variychuk, *supra* note 2 at p. 3.

restoration of an individual's rights and freedoms which have been violated.[18] As noted by Abdumajitova,"the reopening of the domestic procedure is a form of individual measure which the State frequently takes".

In order to review a Russian Court's judgment on the basis that it is inconsistent with the European Court judgment against Russia, a relevant norm of Russian procedural law is needed, issued upon a complaint of the applicant who lost their case in Russian Court.[19] There are three procedural codes in Russia: the Code of Civil Procedure (GPK RF), the Code of Arbitral Procedure (APK RF) and the Code of Criminal Procedure (UPK RF). In Russian law the issue of rehearing of the case is decided in different ways. The present legislation of the Russian Federation allows for the reopening of a final judicial decision in the national legal system through the Code of Criminal Procedure and the Code of Arbitration Procedure. Both laws foresee the reopening of the procedure on the basis of new circumstances which include a finding of the Court's judgment a violation of the Convention.[20]

3.1 RF Criminal Procedure Code (UPK RF)

Article 413 of the UPK, RF states: "one of the grounds for rehearing the case on new circumstances is a breach of the Convention set by the European Court of Human Rights. The reopening of crimina procedure in favour of a convicted person is not time barred. The day a criminal case is reopened will be the day when a judgment of the European Court becomes final."[21] Under the Russian legal system, the right to initiate the reopening of criminal proceedings belongs to the Prosecutor.[22] In situations when the reopening of criminal procedure follows the judgment of the European Court, the review of the criminal case is carried out by the Presidium of the Supreme Court of the Russian Federation. After examination of the case, under Article 415(5) the Presidium of the Supreme Court, as a result, annuls or alters the judgment concerned.

3.2 RF Arbitration Procedure Code (APK RF)

This Code deals with resolution of cases related to business activities. A similar provision can be found in Article 311 of the APK RF: if the European Court finds that there was a

18 See Abdumajitova, *supra* note 3 at p. 29.
19 See Musin, *supra* note 13 at p. 273.
20 See Abdumajitova, *supra* note 3 at p.29.
21 UPK RF, Art. 414(1).
22 See Abdumajitova, *supra* note 3 at p. 29.

breach of the Convention during the national arbitration and the plaintiff appealed to the European Court of Human Rights this case has to be reheard on newly-discovered circumstances.[23]

According to this Code, an application for the reopening of a judicial decision has to be lodged by the parties to the dispute within three months from the day that new circumstances have become known.[24] The Court that altered or passed the previous decision reviews the application for the reopening of the judicial decision.[25] If the court annuls the previous judicial decision, the court has a right to reconsider the case in the same proceeding, unless there are protests of parties to do so.[26]

3.3 *RF Civil Procedure Code (GPK RF)*

However, there is no such provision in the present UPK RF: Article 392 does not contain a clear provision which allows the reopening of domestic procedure on the basis of the ECHR judgment. There is no similar norm in the Code. However, from Musin's point of view, the Code provides for an analogy of lex (positive law) and jus (justice).[27] Therefore, it is possible at his point to apply in such cases the above mentioned norm of the APK by analogy of lex.[28] It will be a review of the Russian Court judgment upon newly-discovered circumstances that may only be initiated by a litigant's motion to be filed with the Court which issued the judgment.[29]

It should be noted that for a long time among scientists there was no agreement on the legal consequences of the European Court of Human Rights in Civil Procedure.[30] Some believed that the finding of a violation of this court is the basis for the correction of judicial error in the procedure of supervisory review (nadzor),[31] whereas others believed such

23 See Variychuk, *supra* note 2 at p. 3.
24 APK RF, Art. 312(1).
25 See Abdumajitova, *supra* note 3 at p. 29.
26 APK RF, Art. 317.
27 GPR RF, Art. 1(4).
28 See Musin, *supra* note 13 at p. 274.
29 GPR RF, Art. 394.
30 Sultanov, A.R., 2010. A new milestone in the execution of judgments of the European Court of Human Rights: importance and legal implications of the Constitutional Court of the Russian Federation dated February 26, 2010 No. 4-P. *Journal of Comparative Constitutional Review*, 4, pp.142-154.
31 Blazheev, V.V. 2008. Revision of judicial decisions on newly discovered evidence in the mechanism of judicial protection of rights and lawful interests of citizens and organizations. *Laws of Russia: experience, analysis, and practice*, 11. See also Ershov, V.V. 2007. The legal position of the European Court of Human Rights. *Russian justice*, 1, p. 31. See also Aliev, T.T., 2007. *Production of newly discovered evidence*. Moscow, pp. 98-99. See also Terekhova, L.A., 2007. *The system of review of judicial decisions in the mechanism of judicial protection*. Moscow, p. 82.

violation would entail instead the review procedures for Newly Discovered-circumstances;[32] meanwhile, others suggested the creation of a special procedure for the revision of the judgment's entered into force[33]. But even before the ruling by the Strasbourg court, some researchers tended to see the possibility of using the procedures for review of newly discovered-circumstances.[34] It is regarded as a deficiency of law which has to be eliminated because such a differentiated approach of the Russian legislator seems strange, as all these codes are procedural.[35]

With respect to the mentioned point, Mrs. Lyudmila Zharkova, Judge of the Constitutional Court of Russia, was interviewed and publicly asked why "attempts to complement article 392 GPK RF with relevant amendments had been made, but the results were not succeed",[36] and could Mrs. Zharkova "explain this reluctance to adopt such amendments". Judge Zharkova answered:

> Reasons for exclusion from the legislative draft submitted by the Supreme Court's to federal legislator, (amendments to Art. 392(2) GPR RF, similar to that contained in Art. 311(7) APK RF) the Constitutional Court failed to set it during the proceedings.
>
> Perhaps, in contrast with the criminal procedure regulations (according to which determining by ECHR the violation of the Convention provisions while

---

32 Lesnitskaya, L.F., 2008. *Some problems in the revision of judgments in the court of general jurisdiction.* Moscow, pp.368-369. See also Osokina, G.L., 2007. *Civil Procedure.* Moscow, p.737. Commentary to the Civil Procedural Code of the Russian Federation. Editon by V.M. Zhuykova, M.K. Treushnikova. M., 2007, p. 823; see also Yurova, N.M., 2008. *International civil procedural law: theoretical foundations of implementation of the norms in the legal system of the Russian Federation.* Moscow:Wolters Kluwer. p. 228. See also Vorontsova, I.V., Solov'eva T.V., 2009. *Regulation of the European Court of Human Rights in Civil Procedure of the Russian Federation.* Moscow, pp. 12-15. See also Degtyarev, S.L., 2007. *Implementation of the judiciary in civil matters: theoretical and applied problems.* Moscow, p. 353. See also Sultanov, A.R., 2009. On the revision of judicial decisions of courts of general jurisdiction, as the adoption of individual measures necessary for the fulfillment of Russia the European Court of Human Rights. *Arbitration and Litigation,* 6-7, pp. 24-27.

33 See the draft "*On Making Amendments to the Criminal Procedural Code of the Russian Federation Arbitration Procedure Code and Civil Procedural Code of the Russian Federation.*" This project is dedicated to the review procedure of judicial decisions in relation to the European Court of Human Rights was drafted chair of European Law, Russian Academy of Justice, Mr P. Laptev. Special issue of the journal "Russian Justice" pp.73-76. See also: the draft "*On amendments and additions to the Civil Procedure Code*", 2009 *Russian justice,* 2, p.93.

34 Blazheev, V.V., 2010. Mechanism for the enforcement of judgments of the European Court of Human Rights, adopted in civil cases against the Russian Federation. *Law and the State: Theory and Practice,* 2, p. 38. See also Aliev, T.T., 2010. The problem of classification revision on the grounds of newly discovered circumstances with court orders, entered into force in civil court proceedings. *Arbitrationand civil procedure,* 2, p. 26.

35 See Variychuk, *supra* note 2 at p. 4.

36 Interview by Bodrjagina O. with Zarkova L.M., Pres. Of Rus. (May, 2010) (available at: <www.gazeta-yurist.ru/article.php?i=1184>).

considering the Court's criminal case shall be treated as new-discovered circumstance (Art. 413(4) of the UPK RF)), there was disagreement on the legality of classifying the ECHR's decision to the grounds for rehearing of decisions on new-discovered circumstances. There were fears that appropriate amending Art. 392 GPK RF would follow reviewing all cases, including decisions on family and labor disputes, and that 'undermine the national system of justice.'

In December 2008, the State Duma of the Russian Federation [Russian Parliament] informed the Constitutional Court that there are no barriers for amending Art. 392 GPK RF, however the legislator hasn't turned to this issue.

4 The Constitutional Court of the Russian Federation Issued a Judgment No.4-P

On 26 February 2010 the RF Constitutional Court (the "Constitutional Court") delivered its judgment No.4-P "On the matter relating to checking of constitutionality of Article 392(2) of the GPR RF in connection with the complaints of A.A. Doroshka, A.E. Kot and E.Yu. Fedotova".[37] By this judgment, Article 392(2) of the GPR RF has been held to be consistent with the Constitution of the Russian Federation. However, the Constitutional Court has pointed out that, in order to secure proper legal regulation, "the parliament has the obligation to introduce 'a mechanism of execution of final judgments of the European Court of Human Rights which would allow adequate redress for violations of rights determined by the European Court of Human rights'."[38]

The Constitutional Court noted the ECHR decision and that the ECHR is an integral part of the Russian legal system and should be taken into account by the legislative and other governments.[39] The Constitutional Court has held that the non-inclusion of the said reason in Article 392(2) of the GPK RF may not be regarded as permission for a common court to deny re-trial, in connection with newly discovered facts, of a matter in which ECHR has found a violation of the Convention. The Constitutional Court referred to a pilot judgment, Burdov against Russia[40] (No. 2), indicating that the commitment of the Russian

37 The detailed Constitutional Court press release available at <www.londonmet.ac.uk/fms/MRSite/Research/HRSJ/EHRAC/Advocacy/Constitutional%20Court%20press%20release%20(civil%20cases)%2026_2_10.doc>. (unofficial translation)

38 See *supra* note 14 at p. 33.

39 Timofeev M., 2010. Russian Constitutional Court: The European Court judgments are considered as "newly discovered circumstances" in civil cases. *Journal of the European Human Rights Advocacy Centre (EHRAC)*. (available at <www.kavkaz-uzel.ru/articles/172493/#5>).

40 *Burdov v. Russia* (No. 2) 2) (No. 33509/04, 15 January 09).

authorities to comply with a final ruling of the ECHR includes not only monetary compensation, but also individual and general measures.[41] The ECHR merely states the fact of a violation of the Convention. The respondent Government is obligated in such event to take measures ensuring the restoration of a citizen's infringed rights, in particular, by establishing of adequate opportunities for re-trial of matters within the legal system, including re-opening of proceedings in the judicial instances where the violation took place. Thus, the Constitutional Court has pointed out that a person, upon whose application the ECHR resolution was issued, should be afforded an opportunity to apply to a competent court with a request for review of court rulings issued in his matter and be sure that his request will be considered. Otherwise, everyone's right to protection by court would be diminished and limited.[42] The Constitutional Court said that the discrepancy between what the ECHR decision falls under the category of "new circumstances" under the APK, but not on the GPK, which in fact establishes a different level of protections for human rights in civil proceedings that cannot be justified by the specific cases that are considered in courts of general jurisdiction.[43]

The Constitutional Court has resolved that the constitutional meaning of Article 392(2) of the GPR RF as revealed by the Resolution, is obligatory for all and precludes any other interpretation thereof in law enforcement practice.[44]

In connection with the above the Judge of the European Court of Human Rights on the behalf of Russia, Mr. Kovler A.I., on the Constitutional Court Judgment No. 4-P said:

> "*As for the 'absolute guarantee' that the national court to reconsider the case after the decision of the ECHR, had to disappoint you: the ECHR is not a 'fourth instance' in relation to national courts and can not give them instructions to reconsider the particular case. ECHR was conceived as a subsidiariy remedy and remains so to this day*. [emphasis added].
>
> Another thing is that the Court may note that the national law there is a means of correcting violations, including a retrial. We do that in criminal and arbitration cases, referring respectively to the art. 413 Criminal Procedure Code and art. 311 Arbitration Procedure Code. Already there are examples of review of judicial decisions in criminal cases. If a corresponding entry will be included

41 See *supra* note 39.
42 Law firm Andrey Gorodissky & Partners, Newsletter review, 2010, item 2 (available at <www.agp.ru/eng/infoletters.aspx?ob_no=461&page=1&d_no=728&print=1>). Начало формы
43 See *supra* note 39.
44 See *supra* note 41.

in Art. 392 Civil Procedure Code, we also point to this possibility in their decisions. But first I must wait until such a rule."[45]

I think is also important that ECHR has already influenced Constitutional Court Judgments: the ECHR in Section 207 of the Regulation on the case *Jehovah's Witnesses of Moscow v. Russia*[46] dated 10 June 2010 recommended a possible way for the execution of its decisions[47] in accordance with Article 46 of the Convention for the revision of the newly discovered evidence of a prior judicial acts on the basis of interpretation of Article 392 of GPK RF. This was given by the Constitutional Court of the Russian Federation in its decision No.4-P:

> It should be noted that, in accordance with the Constitutional Court Decision No. 4-P on February 26, 2010, the European Court are binding for the Russian Federation, and the establishment of the European Court of violations of the European Convention and its Protocols constitute grounds for reconsideration of Civil Affairs in accordance with Article 392 GPK RF and review of decisions of national courts in light of the Convention's principles established by the European Court. The Court finds that such revision would be an ideal means for correcting violations identified by the European Court in this Ordinance. However, the respondent State reserves the right, under the supervision of the Committee of Ministers, to elect any additional means to perform its obligation under Article 46 of the European Convention, provided that such methods do not contradict the conclusions set out in the Decision of the Court (see paragraph 249 Decision of the Grand Chamber of the European Court in Skotstsari and Dzhyunta against Italy (Scozzari and Giunta v. Italy [GC]) Complaints No. 39221/98 and 41963/98).

Another step developing these changes in the current situation is the fact that the Plenum of the Supreme Court's on 15 July 2010 submitted to the Russian Parliament a draft version of the amendments to the GPK RF, changing the procedure for the review of civil cases.[48] According to the Russian Parliament website this legislative draft has been registered under number 407795-5 and sent to the Chairman of the Parliament on 16 July 2010.[49]

45 Interview by Bodrjagina O. with Kovler A.I., Pres.Of Rus. (January, 2010) (available at <www.gazeta-yurist.ru/article.php?i=955>.

46 *Jehovah's Witnesses of Moscow v. Russia* (application no. 302/02) (available at <http://cmiskp.echr.coe.int/tkp197/view.asp?action=html&documentId=869689&portal=hbkm&source=externalbydocnumber&table=F69A27FD8FB86142BF01C1166DEA398649>).

47 See *supra* note 30 at p. 17.

48 Available at <www.gazeta-yurist.ru/new.php?i=11453>.

49 Available at <http://asozd2.duma.gov.ru/main.nsf>.

5 CONCLUSION

The legislator should determine the effect of procedural rulings by the ECHR, based on the competence of the court, so that national courts are bound to the decisions at Strasbourg and do not try to insist on its erroneous interpretation of the obligations arising from participation of Russia in the Convention. More efforts and willingness of the Russian authorities on compliance with the judgments of the European Court are required in order to ensure the protection of rights and freedoms of each human being under the jurisdiction of the Russian Federation.

We can see that during this year Russian legislation made a huge step in forward with respect to European treaties. However, progress should not be limited to changes to the Code of Civil Procedure of the Russian Federation. A special federal law dedicated to the problems of the enforcement of the European Court's judgments in Russia is needed. Currently no such law exists. Hopefully, reform minded Russian lawyers will draft model laws for the Duma to consider.

10 Expropriation of Agricultural Land and the ECHR

Ekaterina Lapidus

1 Introduction

Currently Russian draft law proposes that the agricultural land which has not been used by its owner for agricultural purposes during five year term shall be expropriated ("Russian draft law"). Unfortunately, there is no official text of the draft available. Hence, a significant number of news articles about the draft propose that two routes of the expropriation mechanism are possible: (1) expropriation without the compensation; and (2) expropriation with compensation.

The European Convention on Human Rights (Art. 1 to Protocol No 1 to the Convention) ("ECHR" and "Art. 1 to Prot. No 1" respectively) and the majority of the case law provide that no expropriation can be carried out without compensation to the owner of the expropriated property. However, the recent case law changed the above mentioned approach and found that in case there are "exceptional circumstances" the expropriation can be carried out without compensation to the owner of the expropriated property.

The Russian Federation is a party to the ECHR and, therefore, shall observe its provisions. Hence, Russian domestic courts are, in theory, bound by the European Court on Human Rights decisions.

2 Two Possible Variants of the Expropriation Mechanism Provision

The Russian draft law provides that the agricultural land which has not been used by its owner for agricultural purposes during five year term shall be expropriated. Unfortunately, there is no official text of the draft available. Hence, a significant number of news articles about the draft assume that the two routes of the expropriation mechanism are proposed by the legislators: (1) expropriation without compensation; and (2) expropriation with compensation.

2.1 *Expropriation Without Compensation*

There are a number of articles which proposes that the above mentioned expropriation would be carried out without the compensation.

In particular, certain articles state that "the draft law on the expropriation of the agricultural land provides for the confiscation mechanism."[1]

The confiscation of the property is regulated by Article 243 of the RF Civil Code. This article provides that:

> "In the instances provided for by a law property may be withdrawn without compensation from the owner by decision of a court in the form of a sanction for the commission of a crime or other violation of law (confiscation).
>
> In the instances provided for by a law, confiscation may be made in an administrative procedure. The decision concerning confiscation adopted in an administrative procedure may be contested in a court."

So: does it mean that the failure to observe the use of the land requirement shall be qualified as a "crime or other violation of the law?"

2.2 *Expropriation for Fair Compensation*

A number of news articles states that the draft law provides for a fair compensation mechanism for expropriation.

In particular, one of the articles states that "The draft law provides that the agricultural land may be expropriated from individuals and legal entities only by means of court procedure, and from state and municipal organizations by means of administrative procedure. The expropriated land plot has to be sold by means of public auction and the ex-owner is entitled to the amount received from the auction save for the expenses for the organization of the auction and the required for this cadastral works."[2]

---

1 See *The Deputies defined the expropriation mechanism (Author unknown).* Available at: <www.bfm.ru/news/2010/11/26/deputaty-opredelili-mehanizm-izjatija-zemel.html> (last visited 14 December 2010).

2 See Dmitriy Kazmion, Elena Vinogradova, Anton Filatov, *Plough the land or you may lose it*, Vedomosti, No. 224 (2742) dated 26 November 2010. Available at: <http://old.vedomosti.ru/newspaper/article.shtml?2010/11/26/250555> (last visited 14 December 2010).

It should be noted that if the legislator follows the above mentioned route (*i.e.* the expropriation of the land with compensation), such procedure probably would be regulated by new provisions[3] to the RF Civil Code which are part of the Russian draft law on the expropriation of the agricultural land.

3 The ECHR's Requirements

3.1 Legislation – Article 1 of Prot. No 1 to ECHR

The right to quiet enjoyment of property is regulated by Article 1 to Prot. No 1 to ECHR. This chapter also proposes and assumes that no property owned by an individual or legal entity can be expropriated without compensation.

Note, generally, that the "…rights contained in the Convention and its protocols can be grouped according to their status. There are those provisions containing absolute rights, such as Article 3, whilst there are others, like Article 1, which operate with limitations. The form in which the limitations are set out in the provisions of the Convention and its protocols is inconsistent. The limitations in Article 1 have always made it difficult to argue successfully that the provision has been violated."[4]

Article 1 of Protocol 1 to the ECHR states:

> "Every natural or legal person is entitled to the peaceful enjoyment of his possessions. No one shall be deprived of his possessions except in the public interest and subject to the conditions provided for by law and by the general principles of international law."

Article 5 of Protocol 1 to the ECHR provides that the provisions of Articles 1 of this Protocol shall be regarded as additional article to the ECHR and all the provisions of ECHR shall apply accordingly, although "[T]he preceding provisions [see Art. 1 of Prot. No 1] shall not, however, in any way impair the right of a state to enforce such laws as it deems necessary to control the use of property in accordance with the general interest or to secure the payment of taxes or other contributions or penalties."[5]

---

3 Currently the official text of such provisions is not available.

4 See E.H.R.L.R. 2002, pp. 67-79, available at WESTLAW.

5 See Ulrike Deutsch, *Expropriation without compensation – the European Court of Human Rights sanctions German legislation expropriating the heirs of "New Famers.* Available at:<www.germanlawjournal.com/article.php?id=639> (last visited 14 December 010).

3.2 *Case Law – Application of Article 1 of Prot. No 1 by the old European Commission of Human Rights and the European Court of Human Rights*

Regarding the approach used by the old European Commission of Human Rights and the European Court of Human Rights to complaints made under Article 1 of Prot. No 1:

3.2.1 General Approach

> "The old European Commission of Human Rights and the European Court of Human Rights have had many years to develop a systematic approach to Art.1 of Prot. No 1".

3.2.2 Complex Formula for Assessing Any Complaint under Aricle1 to Prot. No 1

There is "...a complex formula for assessing any complaint under Article 1. It is only by satisfying all the criteria that make up this formula that an applicant can hope to sustain this or her claim."[6]

3.2.3 First Criterion

"The first criterion to satisfy is that the dispute involves 'possessions'"[7] *i.e.* property.

3.2.4 Second Criterion

"The Court next moves on to consider the respective elements of Article 1. It is settled law that these compromise three distinct rules. They can be described as the 'Sporrong' rules, since they are set out in the leading judgment of that name.[8] The Court said: 'The first rule, which is of a general nature, enounces the principle of peaceful enjoyment of possessions; it is set out in the first sentence of the first paragraph. The second rule covers deprivation of possessions and subject it to certain conditions; it appears in the second sentence of the same paragraph. The third rule recognizes that the States are entitled, amongst other things, to control the use of property in accordance with the general interest, by enforcing such laws as they deem necessary for the purpose; it is contained in the second paragraph.'"[9] [internal citations omitted]

6 See E.H.R.L.R. 2002, pp. 67-79, available at WESTLAW.
7 See *id.*
8 *Sporrong and Lonnroth v. Sweden* (1983) 5 E.H.R.R. 35
9 See E.H.R.L.R. 2002, 67-79, available at WESTLAW.

Regarding the three rules "the European Court of Human Rights[10] reiterates its case law that Art. 1 of Prot. No 1 comprises three distinct rules: first the principle of peaceful enjoyment of property (para. 1, first sentence), second the subjection of the deprivation of property under certain conditions (para. 1, second sentence) and third the right of Contracting States to control the use of property in accordance with the general interest (para. 2)."[11]

"[N]umerous cases have concerned a control of use under the third rule. Control measures within the meaning of Article 1 are those measures that substantially interference with a person's peaceful enjoyment of his possessions but which fall short of deprivation. Control measures can be positive requirements or negative restrictions."[12] "In *Air Canada*, it was the scheme of the domestic legislation making the release of the aircraft subject to a payment of a sum of money that amounted to a control of use of property[13]. In *Mellacher v. Austria* the control of use was the reduction in rent that was imposed on landlords by the coming into force of the 1981 Rent Act".[14] [internal citation retained as footnote].

3.2.5 Third Criterion

> "Having established that one of the rules applies to the case before it, the Court then moves on the remaining criteria. These are, first, the assessment of whether the interference is in accordance with the law, and, second, whether it is in the public or general interest. Finally, everything leads, as the road do to Rome, to whether or not the interference complained of strikes a fair balance '"between the demands of the general interest of the community and the requirements of the protection of the individual's fundamental rights.'"[15] In other words, is there a reasonable relationship of proportionality between the means employed and the aim pursued? This is known as the '"fair balance"' test, and there will have been a violation if it has not been met."[16] Note that the above described remaining criteria also can be summarized as follows: "According to the case

10 See Eur. Court H.R., *Jahn and other v. Germany* (note 2), para. 78.

11 *Id.*

12 See E.H.R.L.R. 2002, 67-79, available at WESTLAW. Also see: *Air Canada v. United Kingdom* (1995) 20 E.H.R.R. 150.

13 *Air Canada v. United Kingdom* (1995) 20 E.H.R.R. 150.

14 12 E.H.R.R. 391, para. 44 (1990).

15 *Sporrong and Lonnroth v. Sweden* (1983) 5 E.H.R.R. 35.

16 See E.H.R.L.R. 2002, 67-79, available at WESTLAW.

> law of the European Court of Human Rights, an interference with the right to property must be lawful, pursue a legitimate aim and be proportionate."[17]

This is of course the internationally well known general principle of proportionality of law.

3.2.6 Lawful

> "The first requirement of Art.1 of Prot. No 1 is that any deprivation of property must be based on law."[18]

3.2.7 Legitimate Aim

> "The Court must examine whether the aim of the provisions was in the public interest."[19]

3.2.8 Proportionality

The principle of proportionality means the proportional means to the ends, where the means should be rational and necessary, and the ends – legitimate, permissible and (strictu sensu) least invasive.

> "...[t]here must be a reasonable relationship of proportionality between the aim of a measure depriving a person of his possession and the means employed to achieve this aim. Article 1 of Prot. No 1 does not establish the payment of compensation compulsory."[20]

That is, we are examining the issue whether the expropriation meets the test of proportionality, *i.e.* has been carried out with appropriate (market value) compensation.

Thus, in order to establish that the Russian draft law corresponds to the ECHR's provisions (Art. 1 to Prot. No 1), we shall first examine whether there is a dispute which involves "possessions", secondly, to determine if and how one of the "Sporrong rules" applies to

17 See Ulrike Deutsch, *Expropriation without compensation – the European Court of Human Rights sanctions German legislation expropriating the heirs of "New Famers"*. Available at: <www.germanlawjournal.com/article.php?id=639> (last visited 14 December 2010).

18 See *id.*

19 See *id.*

20 See Ulrike Deutsch, *Expropriation without compensation – the European Court of Human Rights sanctions German legislation expropriating the heirs of "New Famers"*. Available at: <www.germanlawjournal.com/article.php?id=639> (last visited 14 December 2010).

the case, and, finally, whether the interference with the right to property was lawful, pursued a legitimate aim and was proportionatal – or not.

3.3 *Application of Article 1 of Prot. No 1 by the Domestic Courts*

"The domestic courts are not, of course, [strictly] bound by the Strasbourg jurisprudence; they are only obliged to take it into account.[21] [That is,]It has been suggested at the highest levels that the domestic courts might use the powers afforded to them under the 1998 Act to "provide *greater* protection for human rights ...than is strictly required by case law emanating from Strasburg".[22] After all, the Convention only "provides a floor and not a ceiling for rights."[23] (emphasis added).

Following Wilson and Wallbank, we are now begging to have an idea of the approach of the domestic courts in deciding cases based on Article 1. "It is obvious that the Strasbourg approach is not being strictly applied. This may even be justifiable. Nevertheless, the problem for advisers if this pattern continues is that, invoking Sir Nicholas Bratza's metaphor, they will have little idea how the house has been designed let alone where the ceiling is to be found."[24]

4 APPLICATION OF ECHR PROVISIONS TO THE TWO POSSIBLE SCENARIOUS OF THE RUSSIAN DRAFT LAW

Whether the future law on the expropriation of the agricultural land will satisfy the requirements of the European Convention on Human Rights provided that that such expropriation is to be carried out for [fair] compensation?

4.1 *The Principle of Expropriation for Compensation*

In this chapter, we assume that (1) the future dispute under Russian draft law involves "possessions" (*i.e.* first criteria of the complex formula for assessing any complaint under Art. 1 of Prot. No 1, see section 3 above); (2) the respective element of Article 1 of Prot. No 1 is present ("Sporrong rules") (*i.e.* second criteria of the complex formula for assessing

21 25701/94, November 23, 2000 [GC]. Human Rights Act 1998, s. 2(1).
22 For a useful list of "possessions" under this head, see *Compensation for Interference with Property,* loc.cit., at p. 546. Sir N. Bratza, *The Implications of the Human Rights Act of 1998 for Commercial Practice* [2000] 1 E.H.R.L.R. 1 at 4.
23 *Sporrong and Lonnroth v. Sweden* (1983) 5 E.H.R.R. 35.
24 See E.H.R.L.R. 2002, 67-79, available at WESTLAW.

any complaint under Art. 1 of Prot. No 1, see Section III above); (3) the interference in question is lawful and pursues a legitimate aim (*i.e.* third criteria of the complex formula for assessing any complaint under Art. 1 of Prot. No 1, see section 3 above).

Thus, we are not going to consider the above mentioned issues. However, we will concentrate on the last test within the third criteria – proportionality.

The "proportionality test" examines whether the expropriation was carried out with or without reasonable compensation. "[O]ne clear rule which has emerged is that, where an applicant has been deprived of his property, a violation will be found unless compensation is paid."[25]

The European Commission of Human Rights defined that "[T]here is inherent in Art. 1 of Prot. No 1 a right to compensation for the taking of property of anyone within the jurisdiction of a Contracting State where and insofar as the payment of compensation is *necessary* to preserve the appropriate relationship of *proportionality* between the interference with *individual's right* and the *public interest*."[26] (emphasis added).

4.2 *Fair compensation*

4.2.1 What is "Fair" and What Should Be Criteria for the Qualification the Land as "Fair"?

Compensation methods with regards to the arable land during the process of the expropriation of such land may include (1) Income Capitalization Method; and (2) Market Comparative Method.[27]

> "A fair, just or adequate compensation should seek to meet one primary policy objective: it should reflect a careful *balancing of the interests of the parties*. The minimum condition for the flow and security of international direct capital is that its benefits be equitably distributed between the host country and the investor and his home country, so that all parties would have an interest in maintaining this economic relationship. Equitable distribution of benefits

25 See *Holy Monasteries v. Greece* (1995) 20 E.H.R.R. 1.

26 See (1985) 7 E.H.R.R. 56.

27 See Xue Minchuan, *Compensation method and rational standard of arable land expropriation*. Available at: <http://ideas.repec.org/a/ags/asagre/53519.html> (last visited 14 December 2010)

would eliminate the economic incentive for expropriation and reduce the usual controversy over compensation."[28]

4.2.2 What About the Bargaining Power of the Government Versus the Owner?

"When the Dutch government wants to initiate a new public project, it often has to buy land from the citizens. In cases like this, the citizen in question and the government face a situation of bilateral monopoly and the price the government has to pay in exchange for the ownership of the land depends on the bargaining power of the two agents."[29]

There are "two interesting phenomena about the bargaining process between the government and farmers in The Netherlands. First, almost all cases are solved via a settlement by agreement between the parties, *i.e.* the mere threat of a decision by court is enough to come to an agreement. Second, in some cases all farmers accept the first offer by the government; in other cases the government has to make several offers before all farmers accept."[30]

Therefore, the Russian draft law on expropriation of agricultural land will satisfy the requirements of ECHR provided that the fair compensation mechanism for the expropriation of property is included.

4.3 Whether the Future Law on the Expropriation of the Agricultural Land Will Satisfy the Requirements of the European Convention on Human Rights Provided that such Expropriation Is to Be Carried Out Without Compensation?

As we concluded in Section III above, in order to establish that the draft law corresponds to ECHR's provisions (Art. 1 to Prot. No 1), we shall first examine whether there is a dispute which involves "possessions", secondly, to establish that one of the "Sporrong rules" applies to the case, and, finally, an interference with the right to property must be lawful, pursue a legitimate aim and be proportionate.

For the purposes of the current article, we assume that (1) the future dispute under the Russian draft law involves "possessions" (*i.e.* first criteria of the complex formula for

---

28 Onyeonoro S. Kamasu, Compensation for expropriation in the third world, Rutgers University (Newark). Available at <www.springerlink.com/content/vr700q3040767852/>, last visited on 14 December 2010).

29 See Marten C.W. Janssen, Christian Gerth, Lonneke Jansen, Marinka Niehoff, *The price of land and the process of expropriation*, Economist 144, No 1, 1996. Available at <www.springerlink.com/content/n67747q06t875435/> (last visited on 14 December 2010).

30 See *id.*, p. 10.

assessing any complaint under Article 1 of Prot. No 1, see Section III above); (2) the respective element of Article 1 of Prot. No 1 is present ("Sporrong rules") (*i.e.* second criteria of the complex formula for assessing any complaint under Article 1 of Prot. No 1, see Section III above); (3) the interference in question is lawful and pursues a legitimate aim (the third criteria of the complex formula for assessing any complaint under Article 1 of Prot. No 1, See Section III above).

Thus, we are not going to consider the above mentioned issues. Rather, we will concentrate on the last test within the third criteria – proportionality.

According to the general rule developed the European Court of Human Rights "[t]he expropriation of property by the state has been held to be justified by the Court where there is payment of compensation, thus preventing a violation of Art.1 of Prot. No1. In the Grand Chamber decision of *Jahn v. Germany* (46720/99) (2006) 42 E.H.R.R. 49 (ECHR (Grand Chamber)), the Court for the first time found that exceptional circumstances existed which justified expropriation without any balancing payment."[31]

"[O]ne clear rule which has emerged is that, where an applicant has been deprived of his property, a violation will be found unless compensation is paid."[32]; "This principle has been applied consistently, including in the few cases which have emerged from the circumstances originally envisaged by the Convention founders... A recent decision seems to suggest that the approach of the Court is changing, however. In *Jahn v. Germany*, the Grand Chamber considered an expropriation of property by an unelected government."[33]

In *Jahn v. Germany*, the applicants "contended that they had been deprived of their property in violation of their rights under Art.1 of Protocol No 1, and looked to the European Court of Human Rights for redress. After the Court applied the 'Sporrong rules', it then turned to the next three elements test. 'Where a deprivation has taken place, ... the Court must consider first whether the deprivation is lawful, secondly whether it is in the public interest, and finally whether it strikes a fair balance between the needs of the State and the rights of the individual; ...The basic rule informing the fair balance test for Art.1 of Protocol No1 is that where deprivation has taken place, compensation must be paid. The taking property without payment of an amount reasonable related to its value will normally constitutes a disproportionate interference, and a total lack of compensation can be considered justifiable under the Convention only in exceptional circumstances.[34] No compen-

31 See E.H.R.L.R. 2007, 3, 295 -303.
32 See *Holy Monasteries v. Greece* (1995) 20 E.H.R.R. 1.
33 See E.H.R.L.R. 2007, 3, 295 -303.
34 *Holy Monasteries v. Greece* (1995) 20 E.H.R.R.1.

sation had been made available to the applicants. The question was therefore: did circumstances exceptional enough to justify this lack of compensation exist?"[35] [internal citation retained].

The three principal factors which the court considered amounted to exceptional circumstances in *Jahn* (see above) were "[f]irst, the Modrow Law was passed by an unelected legislature during a period of major political and constitutional unpheaval. The applicants accordingly could not, according to the Grand Chamber, have had any certainty in its continued application. Secondly, the period of time between the Modrow Law coming into force and the 1992 Act taking effect was very short. Thirdly, the 1992 Act was motivated by reasons of social justice. The applicants had benefited from a 'windfall' at the time of the Modrow Law and some of the reassigned land would be redistributed amongst farmers (as opposed to remaining in the ownership of the State)."[36] On that basis, the Grand Chamber concluded that the lack of compensation in such circumstances can be qualified as a fair balance.

Note that *Jahn* is not the first case on which the Court has been faced with an application arising from such a major change of regime (See *Former King of Greece v. Greece* (2003) 36 E.H.R.R.CD 43 and *Broniowski v. Poland* (2005) 40 E.H.R.R.21). However, in the two mentioned cases with the similar circumstances the decision was opposite (the fair balance assumed the compensation) to the decision in *Jahn*.

"Jahn is the first decision in which the Court has justified a deprivation of property without compensation on the basis of the exceptional circumstances in which state action took place. The question must inevitably be asked: in what other situations might such exceptional circumstances be deemed to exist? It is a question which cannot be answered with any certainty."[37]

Therefore, in case a Russian draft law will be passed with the provision that no compensation shall be paid for the expropriation, the question may remain the same as in *Jahn*, *i.e.* did circumstances exceptional enough to justify this luck of compensation exist, and if the answer to the question is positive (such exceptional circumstances are present), then the draft law will most likely be satisfying the requirements of ECHR (although no compensation is paid to the owners of the expropriated agricultural land).

---

35 See E.H.R.L.R. 2007, 3, 295 -303.

36 See E.H.R.L.R. 2007, 3, 295-303.

37 See *id.*

5 Conclusion

Given the above analysis, we conclude that the answer to the question whether the future law on the expropriation of the agricultural land will satisfy the requirements of the European Convention on Human Rights depends on inclusion of the compensation mechanism for the expropriation of the property provided that there are no "exceptional circumstances" according to which such expropriation can be carried out without compensation.

Part III
Intellectual Property

11 Russian Intellectual Property Law: Parallel Imports and Regional Trade

Valeriya Irugova

1 Theoretical Background of IP Law Protection in Russia

In 24 November 2006 the State Duma adopted the Fourth part of the Civil Code of the Russian Federation, which provides: "Rights on the results of intellectual activity and on means of individualization". In particular, this document defined such terms as *copyright* (intellectual property right on a work of science, literature and art),[1] *patent* (intellectual property rights on an invention, useful model, industrial design),[2] *right on means of individualization*, in particular, *trademark* (a trademark, namely an indication which serves as a mean of individualization of goods of legal entities and individual entrepreneurs).[3]

The owner of a trademark has the right to use it, namely to place it on goods, labels and packing which are produced and/or offered for sale, and/or sold, and/or demonstrated on exhibitions and fairs or are otherwise introduced into commerce.[4]

Consequently, a person who infringes the intellectual property rights on a trademark by using it in one of the aforementioned ways without the owner's consent is liable to reimburse the owner either by monetary compensation or restitution.[5]

However, theoretical declarations are not always easily implemented in practice.

2 Practical Problems of Implementation

It is no secret that Moscow is flooded with counterfeit goods. The internet is a crazy-quilt with offers to purchase goods of well-known brands at the lowest prices. Watches, bags,

1 Clause 1, Art. 1255, Chapter 70.
2 Clause 1, Art. 1345, Chapter 72.
3 Clause 1, Art. 1477, Chapter 76.
4 Clause 2, Art. 1484, Chapter 76.
5 Art. 1515, Chapter 76.

clothes, footwear, accessories, etc. of high-class brands are waiting for customers in the narrow metro passages and in the huge trade centres.

On the one hand, customers themselves provoke this counterfeit flood. If demand decreases and the buying audience chooses goods of the same quality and price, but unmarked with fashionable labels, instead of their imitations, the offer of counterfeit goods will probably decrease as well.

On the other hand, the authorities whose function is to restrain the illegal turnover of counterfeit goods, to exempt them and initiate lawsuits, turn a blind eye on the infringers in exchange for a bribe.

The other reason for such an unfriendly attitude to the protection of IP rights in Russia is recent initiatives of legislator.

Since 2008 the customs authorities initiated a mass attack on parallel imports. They confiscated not only counterfeit goods; they also confiscated original goods which were imported to the territory of Russian Federation – without the consent of the owners of those trademarks which were placed on the goods to such importation. The Highest *Arbitrazh* Court and the Highest Court of Russian Federation prepared a draft decree which clarified the implementation of the Fourth part of the Civil Code, mentioned above. Clause 63 of this decree stated that the import of original goods without the owner's consent is an infringement, even if it was bought directly from the owner abroad. However, the representatives of the Federal Antitrust Service and the State Duma opposed this initiative.[6]

After that, court practice started to develop in favour of parallel importers. The famous case about the counterfeit Porsche Cayenne auto parts gave birth to the decision of the Presidium of the highest *Arbitrazh* Court of Russian Federation, A40-928/08-145-128 from 3 February 2009. In accordance with this decision, administrative liability accrues only if the counterfeit goods (goods which bear a trademark on them) were illegally imported. Original (non counterfeit) goods, purchased abroad, cannot be confiscated.[7]

As a result of this decision, court practice became uniform and the Russian courts refused administrative lawsuits in parallel import cases brought by the customs authorities. However, administrative compensatory remedies, such as fine and confiscation, are still enforceable if the goods in question are counterfeit. In other cases of IP rights infringement

6 <www.tks.ru/news/nearby/2010/04/14/0006>.
7 *Id.*

the complex of civil remedies (monetary compensation or restitution), must be implemented, and the owners of trademarks themselves may initiate lawsuits.[8]

So they did. The pioneer was Kayaba, a manufacturer of Japanese auto parts. Kayaba acknowledged that a legal entity imports Kayaba auto parts without the owner's consent, and demanded compensatory damages and the destruction of the goods. The Moscow *Arbitrazh* court again found in favour of the parallel import.[9] The reasoning of the court was that the main purpose of a trademark is to help the consumers to distinguish the goods of one producer from the goods of another. As the auto parts in question were original and were legally purchased in return for monetary consideration, their import and offer on the territory of Russian Federation is legal.[10]

However, this decision contradicts the legally binding norm which proclaims the national (territorial) principle of exhaustion, provided in Article 1484 of the Russian Civil Code. In accordance with that principle, a good may be imported on the territory of Russian Federation *subject to the owner's consent*, even if it has been being traded abroad for a long time.[11]

Disregarding the absence of judicial support, the Russian IP protectors tend to adopt the experienced views of Western specialists.

First, the owners of trademarks themselves, acting through their Russian representatives, if the trademark owner is a foreigner, organize associations, whose primary goal is to discuss achievements of Western legislators and executive officers in the sphere of IP protection. Producers of well-known goods and legal bureaus and agencies which specialize in IP protection are common members of such associations. Such a diversity of membership facilitates discussion of current problems from different perspectives and integrates opinions of both sides (producers and protectors) to a project in a form of an official note addressed to the State representatives.

Second, representatives of the Internal Affairs Department directly announce the possibility of European compensatory remedies introduction against consumers of goods of counterfeit origin in Russia. For example, Italy applies administrative punishment to customers who buy non-original goods in the amount of 10.000 Euros on average since 2005. Liability of individuals, who import counterfeit goods bought for personal usage has been introduced

8 *Id.*
9 A40-2250/09-51-27 from 26 June 2009.
10 <www.tks.ru/news/nearby/2010/04/14/0006>.
11 *Id.*

in France. The punishment for such violation varies from confiscation and fine to imprisonment.[12]

The statistics also support the improvement of the level of IP protection in Russia. According to one of the recent interviews of the Head of the Department of Export Control of Russian Federal Customs Service, the total amount of counterfeit goods imported into Russia decreased in 2009 in comparison to previous years.[13]

The owners of the goods themselves, taking into account the failure of Kayaba case, occupied themselves with the correction of mistakes. A German company, UVEX, initiated a lawsuit against the importer of UVEX original goods without its consent on the territory of Russian Federation. The owner demanded an order forbidding the importer to conduct any activities which are associated with the use of its trademark in terms of the Russian Civil Code, namely to place it on goods, labels and packing which are produced, offered for sale, sold, and/or demonstrated on exhibitions and fairs or are otherwise introduced into the commerce. UVEX also demanded compensatory damages in the amount of 100.000 rubles, but was silent on the point of goods confiscation and destruction. This claim was fundamentally different from the Kayaba claim in this final point. In accordance with the effective legislation in Russia, only counterfeit goods are subject to destruction. In this case, however, the plaintiff did not raise this claim, thus leaving the question of the origin of the goods aside and concentrating on the scope of the owner's IP rights in Russia. As a result, the court found in the owner's favor, stating specifically that Russia follows the principle of territorial exhaustion, meaning that even if the original goods were purchased from the owner abroad, their import into Russian Federation is subject to the owner's consent.[14]

3 Parallels Between the EU and the CIS

The EurAsEC Customs Union, which includes Russia, Belarus and Kazakhstan, in the summer of 2010 also recommends the enforcement of IP protection mechanisms in Russia.

The Customs Union seeks to enlarge the market outlet for the CIS participants and to harmonize their legislation. Since Russia, which seems to follow the Western model of IP rights protection more thoroughly than other members, may justly be considered one of the main participants of this union, there is a hope that its opinion will be respected and its behaviour taken as the model.

12 <www.e1.ru/news/spool/news_id-320581.html>.
13 <http://sinocom.ru/showthread.php?t=1205>.
14 <www.tks.ru/news/nearby/2010/04/14/0006>.

From my point of view the establishment of the Customs Union is one of the steps of EU and CIS convergence, which is evident for many reasons.

The CIS – is a regional international organization (agreement) invoked for regulation of cooperative relationships among the former members of USSR. Its main goals are:

1. Cooperation in political, economical, ecological, humanitarian, cultural and other spheres of human life.
2. Comprehensive development of Member States within the framework of a single economic territory.
3. Human rights and freedoms support.
4. Mutual judicial support and others.[15]

The European Union is an economic and political association of European Member States intended for regional integration. The standardized system of legislation, which operates in all Member States, allowed the creation of the single market which guarantees the free movement of people, goods, services and capital.[16]

Both the EU and CIS have common history, similar stages of economical, political, social and cultural development, and the rationales for these regional free trade areas are the same.

As already mentioned before, one of the main goals of the establishment of the EU was to create a single market without barriers and tariffs for the free movement of goods and services. At the time of the CIS establishment the creation of the single market was one of the main directions as well. Since 1991, the year of CIS establishment, the creation of Customs union seems to be the first adequate step towards this goal.

In conclusion, despite all the difficulties which IP protectors meet on their way Russia obviously moves closer to Western models of legal norms and their enforcement, which offers hope for stronger protection of IP rights.

15 <http://ru.wikipedia.org/wiki/%D0%A1%D1%82%D1%80%D0%B0%D0%BD%D1%8B_%D0%A1%D0%9D%D0%93>.

16 <http://ru.wikipedia.org/wiki/EU>.

12 Technological Development and Intellectual Property Rights

Kirill Smirnov

How does technological development change intellectual property laws and institutions and how does that change IP law? The IP regime, especially copyright, substantially changed and the number of available tools and institutions increased over last years.

Tangible property refers to physical objects that have dimensions and are limited by borders in material world (plot of land, house, table, etc). Intellectual property is an abstract category which is applied to information, which can be distributed in an indefinite number of copies without diminishing the existence of the first copy. The intellectual property right is based on a legally established monopoly of its creator (rights holder) to allow others to use his or her work. This monopoly aims to give the creator of work an incentive to share his work with society so that everyone could benefit from it. At the same time this monopoly is limited in time (*e.g.* in the US 20 years for patents, life period of the author + 95 years for copyright).

> "The principal justification for intellectual property derived from a broader economic problem: the inability of a competitive market to support an efficient level of innovation. In a competitive economy, profits will be driven to zero, not accounting for sunk costs such as research and development (R&D) or costs of authorship. From an *ex post* point of view, this is a good outcome, as it keeps prices low for consumers and avoids deadweight loss. But from an *ex ante* point of view, it produces a sub-optimal level of investment in R&D. Most firms would not invest in developing new technologies, and potential creators might not spend their time on creative works, if rivals could enter the market and dissipate the profit. Unlike tangible goods, knowledge and creative works are public goods in the sense that their use is nonrival [...]. One agent's use does not limit another agent's use. Indeed, in its natural state (cartooned in the digital age as 'bits want to be free'), knowledge is also 'nonexcludable.' That is, even if someone claims to own the knowledge, it is difficult to exclude others from using it. Intellectual property law is an attempt to solve that problem by legal means; it grants exclusive use of the protected knowledge or creative work to the creator. For other forms of property, exclusion is often accomplished by

> physical means, such as building a fence. Intellectual property is a legal device by which the inventor can control entry and exclude users from intangible assets".[1]

Intellectual property covers various objects. Here we will address objects that impact distribution of knowledge within the society. Mostly copyright. Trademarks are also very important IP institution, however it does not directly contain knowledge and has very different nature from patents and copyright. I will not address it in this chapter.

> "For purposes of exploring the economic dimensions of the intellectual property field, it is important to distinguish between two quite distinct functions. The principal objective of intellectual property law is the promotion of new and improved works – whether technological or expressive. This purpose encompasses patent, copyright, and trade secret law, as well as several more narrow protection systems (*e.g.*, mask works, database, design, and misappropriation). The other purpose of intellectual property law addresses a very different economic problem – ensuring the integrity of the marketplace. Trademark law and related bodies of unfair competition law respond to this concern"[2].

1 TRENDS IN IP REGULATION

Intellectual property protection as a legal institution developed over time. The key trend was the expansion of the number of objects subject to protection. While science and innovations developed, more and more new objects were becoming protected. From copyright, patents and trademark to new areas like industrial designs, plants. The driving force behind this expanding area of protected intellectual property rights is the growth of the economy and growth of businesses that build their success around protection of their IP rights. We will discuss how certain business models influence IP protection institutions.

Another trend in the development of IP protection was the extension of the period of protection. Mostly that has been happening in copyright protection.

> "The Copyright Act of 1976 extended the renewal term from 28 to 47 years for copyrights that were subsisting on January 1, 1978, or for pre 1978 copyrights restored under the Uruguay Round Agreements Act (URAA), making these

---

1 Peter S. Menell & Suzanne Scotchmer, *Intellectual Property, in Handbook of Law and Economics,* (2005), available at <http://papers.ssrn.com/sol3/papers.cfm?abstract_id=741424>.

2 *Id.*

works eligible for a total term of protection of 75 years. Public Law 105298, enacted on October 27, 1998, further extended the renewal term of copyrights still subsisting on that date by an additional 20 years, providing for a renewal term of 67 years and a total term of protection of 95 years".[3]

This extensions of the period of protection can be interpreted in different ways. As copyright industries develop, the larger part of copyrightable works are produced in the spheres of interest of major IP corporations (cinema production, record labels, etc.). These entities have more tools to lobby the extension of period for copyright protection and provide for themselves the ability to extract revenues over longer period of time.

Another argument may defend the extensions of terms on the grounds that nowadays marketing and distribution of copyrighted works requires more investment and it takes more time for those who invest to recover their expenses. This argument seems weak as we did not see that dramatic extensions of period of protection for patents while investments in patented innovations grew much higher than investments in marketing and distribution chains of music and cinema industries. Moreover, with the development of the Internet (*e.g.* myspace social network) many artists often employ much cheaper mechanisms of advertisement and distribution without turning to major corporations.

Protection of IP has also broadened geographically. New international treaties established grounds for international protection of different types of IP rights: the Berne convention for copyright, the Paris convention for patents, etc.

We may conclude that during last century IP rights protection has continued to embrace new objects that were not protected before. In some cases periods of protection were also developing and geographical area of protection also expanded. IP protection was growing along with industries built around intellectual property.

2 TECHNOLOGY AND IP RIGHTS

Developments in technology did not substantially change patent and trademark protection as institutions in general. The most notable changes happened in copyright industries. The development of digital technologies and then the internet easy copying and global distribution at virtually no cost were the most serious challenges to IP-related industries.

3 US Copyright Office, Circular 1, Copyright Basics 5-6. Available at <www.copyright.gov/circs/circ01.pdf>.

The international copyright treaties were amended to protect copyright in the internet environment.

A new 'making available' right was introduced. It is defined as an exclusive right for authors, performers and 'phonogram producers' to authorize or prohibit the dissemination of their works and other protected material through interactive networks such as the internet.[4] The existing international copyright protection framework was amended in 1996 by WIPO Copyright Treaty (WCT) that was adopted:

> "[r]ecognizing the need to introduce new international rules and clarify the interpretation of certain existing rules in order to provide adequate solutions to the questions raised by new economic, social, cultural and technological developments [and]the profound impact of the development and convergence of information and communication technologies on the creation and use of literary and artistic works".[5]

Article 11 of the WCT established that:

> "[c]ontracting Parties shall provide adequate legal protection and effective legal remedies against the circumvention of effective technological measures that are used by authors in connection with the exercise of their rights under this Treaty or the Berne Convention and that restrict acts, in respect of their works, which are not authorized by the authors concerned or permitted by law".[6]

In Russia, the WCT entered into force on 5 February 2009 while its key provisions have already been implemented in Part IV of Russian Civil Code and previously in Federal Law on Copyright and Related Rights.

The WCT was implemented in the 1990s and early 2000s by the DMCA in the United States and by Directives 91/250/EC addressing software copyright protection, Directive 96/9/EC on copyright protection of databases, Directive 2001/29/EC on 'technical protection measures' (TPM) that made illegal for users to circumvent the TPM in the EU.

---

4 *The WIPO Treaties: 'Making Available' Right*, (2003), available at <www.ifpi.org/content/library/wipo-treaties-making-available-right.pdf>.

5 World Intellectual Property Organization, *Copyright Treaty*, (1997), available at <www.wipo.int/treaties/en/ip/wct/trtdocs_wo033.html#P51_3806>.

6 *Id.*, Art. 11.

These developments demonstrate that copyright legislation is adapting to technology changes. As new technologies create tools for easier unauthorized distribution of protected works, legislative changes provide tools against it.

Legislative changes went even further; given the difficulty to identify and convict individual end user infringes of copyright in anonymous internet environment, some burden was laid on internet service providers (ISP). For example in US Digital Millennium Copyright Act established that the ISPs can benefit from a 'safe harbor' protection if they take down copyrighted material uploaded online by end-users upon receiving a notification from a rights holder.[7]

These examples show that copyright legislation transforms with development of technologies and new legal institutions were invented to protect IP in the digital environment.

3 MORE FLEXIBLE IP PROTECTION

As a response to developing digital technologies along with stronger IP regime, some new models of transferring IP rights are also being developed. The examples are the Free Software Foundation published GNU General Public License (GNU GPL)[8] and the Creative Commons licenses[9]. Contrary to the 'traditional IP regimes these licenses provide less strict regulation of IP rights and they are more focused on distribution of information for free, to foster common creativity rather than on financial benefits extracted from exclusive rights in intellectual property.

> Taking inspiration in part from the Free Software Foundation's GNU GPL, Creative Commons has developed a [w]eb application that helps people dedicate these creative works to the public domain – or retain their copyright while licensing them as free for certain uses, on certain conditions. Unlike the GNU GPL, Creative Commons licenses are not designed for software, but rather for other kinds of creative works: [w]ebsites, scholarship, music, film.[10]

7 17 U.S. C. § 512(c)

8 *GNU General Public License, version 3*, (2007), available at <www.gnu.org/copyleft/gpl.html>.

9 Creative Commons, *Licenses*, available at <http://creativecommons.org/about/licenses/>.

10 Miltiadis D. Lytras, Ambjörn Naeve, *Open Source for Knowledge and Learning Management: Strategies beyond Tools* 373, (2007).

These tools are similar to giving away real property for charitable purposes. However, we may expect a larger scale and number of application of flexible copyright regimes, as intangible objects can be duplicated without diminishing value of the initial object.

Comparing amendments addressing new technologies and giving tools to protect copyright in digital environment to the new forms of licenses allowing freer flow of works may lead us to conclude that there is no single trend in legal framework development: neither to create stronger, repressive IP protection regime, nor to distribute all copyrightable works for free. At the same time, the range of forms and variety of legal institutions substantially increased with the development of digital technologies. The choice of legal tools is defined by the business model. Traditional companies relying on strong IP protection strongly enforce their rights and lobby for ever increasing protection. At the same time, new competitive business models like Linux or new alternative ways of distributing music via social networks get a larger portion of market.

4 A Russian Perspective

As mentioned above, the Russian Federation has implemented in its Civil Code provisions established by WCT. At the same time, the Civil Code does not contain provisions that would enable more flexible regimes allowing authors or other rights holders to permit the use of their works for free or allowing them to make exceptions other than already established by law (*e.g.* 'fair use' provisions codified in Russian Law).

The Concept of Amendments to Russian Civil Legislation contained provisions aimed at creation of specific regimes similar to GPL and Creative Commons. It is highly desirable that these provisions would be implemented in amendments to IPR Chapter of Russian Civil Code. Such provisions would enable compatibility of Russian legislation with more flexible, 'weaker' forms of IP regimes, not only with stronger IP protection regimes.

From the perspective of law and economics, that would greatly benefit cash-strapped Russian educational system and start-ups. It would also better fit the nature of an emerging market business model, rather than the heavy IP protection favouring Western copyright giants.

13 Copyright v. Privacy Pursuing P2P

Maria Egorova

"You won't imprison everyone!"[1]

According to recent internet news,[2] the Members of Pirate Parties International[3] (PPI) presented an idea to transfer a torrent-tracker to an in-orbit satellite to exclude it from earth's laws.[4] There was a similar proposal earlier with regards to an aerostat, but the idea of an in-orbit satellite seemed to be more suitable to the PPI. Peter Sunde, the founder of the Pirate Bay torrent-tracker, similarly proposed working on "alternative internet" which will not be subject to ICANN[5] control and will be based on "P2P" technology.[6] The "Existence of centralized system which manages our information is unacceptable. We want internet to be free from censure"[7] – so say followers of Peter Sunde.

So, the pirates are, supposedly, ready for any extravagant measures to proceed with their "business". And what will be the reaction of the world's states?

Currently, state bodies of the vast majority of countries are concerned with the development of measures for preventing P2P pirating and ensuring copyright owners' right to protection. So, the European Union, the USA, and some other countries[8] since the year 2006 were

1 Phrase of a thief in a popular soviet film «Место встречи изменить нельзя» (1979).
2 <www.copyright.ru/news/main/>.
3 Pirate Parties International (PPI) is the political international of the Pirate Party movement. It was formally founded in 2010 at the PPI conference in Brussels, Belgium (<http://en.wikipedia.org/wiki/Pirate_Party#Pirate_Party_movement_worldwide>).
4 The undertaking with an in-orbit satellite will most likely fail because even on the orbit servers will need IP-addresses which may be blocked by a service provide at any time.
5 Internet Corporation for Assigned Names and Numbers international noncommercial organization established for regulation of issues related with distribution of IP-addresses and dealing with other Internet related issues.
6 P2P technology is based on the idea that users make a portion of their computer resources directly available to other network participants, without the need for central coordination by servers or stable hosts. (Rüdiger Schollmeier, A Definition of Peer-to-Peer Networking for the Classification of Peer-to-Peer Architectures and Applications, Proceedings of the First International Conference on Peer-to-Peer Computing, IEEE (2002)). Peers are both suppliers and consumers of resources, in contrast to the traditional client–server model where only servers supply, and clients consume (<http://en.wikipedia.org/wiki/Peer-to-peer>).
7 <http://internet.cnews.ru/news/top/index.shtml?2010/11/30/418245>.
8 The current negotiating parties of ACTA are a mix of developed and emerging economies: Australia, Canada, the European Union, Japan, Korea, Mexico, Morocco, New Zealand, Singapore, Switzerland and the United States. Although ACTA is now being negotiated amongst like-minded countries, it is hoped that major

negotiating an initiative to enter into an Anti-Counterfeiting Trade Agreement intended to establish international standards on enforcement of intellectual property rights. New legislation concerning this problem has been rapidly passed in many developed and emerging countries such as Russia, EU Member States, the USA, Japan, *et al.* Though different countries choose their own specific remedies and approaches to pursuing P2P practices, the basic direction of such activity is the same – to strengthen the enforcement campaign against Internet piracy.

So, news regarding P2P sharing problem looks like reports from a battle-field. In large part, it is related to the nature of the internet itself and the problem of necessity and frames of legal regulation. Though such issues are vastly discussed in the internet community as well as in the "real world", this chapter is not intended to proceed with considering all of the mentioned fundamental problems. Here we will discuss the immediate and seemingly clear problem of copyright infringement by means of P2P sharing, which is undoubtedly currently considered a huge global problem, entailing great damages for copyright owners.

Copyright infringement is reasonably considered a civil wrong by most countries. Hence, it must be prevented and punished like any other civil wrong. Internet in this sphere firstly became just one more tool for transferring of copyrighted objects. However, here, the legislators face the most intractable problems of pursuing copyright infringement: delocalisation.

Cases already heard in this sphere and measures taken by different countries have not yet given an adequate solution to this problem. So the issue is open and new measures have to be developed.

Pursuing P2P sharing faces certain difficult cornerstones. The most essential of them are:
- determining the subjects of liability,
- finding an adequate balance of privacy rights and intellectual property rights,
- finding proper legal measures and remedies which comply with fundamental rights and which would take into account technical specific of P2P sharing system.

This chapter proposes analysis of current concepts and modern initiatives with regards to P2P copyright infringement and provides proposals of possible measures in the framework of legal environment of democratic societies.

---

countries facing the same counterfeiting and piracy problems will eventually accede to it (<http://ec.europa.eu/trade/creating-opportunities/trade-topics/intellectual-property/anti-counterfeiting/>).

1 Analysis of Principal P2P Cases

First we shall examine three famous cases which were held in USA, European Union and Russia. All of them took different approaches to resolving P2P infringement problem. All the cases can be considered as a result of confrontation between pirates and states; all of them leaded to social dissonance and further discussion on adequacy of the measures applied and proposed steps on development of legal regulation of the internet.

Considering these three cases will be a starting point for our further analysis of legal measures on pursuing P2P copyright infringement.

2 *Grokster* case[9]

The *Grokster* case is one of the most important cases for P2P networks in the USA.

The facts of the case are quite common to P2P cases: a claim was brought against an owner of peer-to-peer file-sharing network (Grokster Ltd.) for copyright infringement through sharing of illegally downloaded files. Whether such downloads have substantially affected the retail sales of music, videos, and other works protected by copyright and the intellectual property laws is a matter of debate.[10]

The case was heard at all court instances – from the Los Angeles Federal Court to the US Supreme Court, and the final decision was against Grokster. Although the defendant managed to settle the claims with plaintiffs after the decision, this litigation actually lead to the end of the Grokster P2P network's existence.

If you now want to enter Grokster website, you will see the following warning:

> "The United States Supreme Court unanimously confirmed that using this service to trade copyrighted material is illegal. Copying copyrighted motion picture and music files using unauthorized peer-to-peer services is illegal and is prosecuted by copyright owners.
>
> There are legal services for downloading music and movies. This service is not one of them.

---

9 *MGM Studios, Inc. v. Grokster, Ltd.*

10 Oberholzer-Gee, Felix; Strumpf, Koleman (December 2004), "The Effect of File Sharing on Record Sales: An Empirical Analysis".

> YOUR IP ADDRESS IS XX.XX.XXX.XX AND HAS BEEN LOGGED. Don't think you can't get caught. You are not anonymous."[11]

Quite persuasive, is it not? So these are consequences of the *Grokster* case for an ordinary user. But what are the legal lessons of this case and its influence on development of doctrine in this sphere?

The most important points of the *Grokster* case were the choice of the liable subject – the owner of the P2P network, not just the individuals sharing files and the legal theories applied by the courts.

Grokster based its defense on the "Sony safe harbour"-theory that was established by the Supreme Court in *Sony v. Universal Studios*, 464 U.S. 417 (1984). The ruling in that case stated that, "...the sale of copying equipment, like the sale of other articles of commerce, does not constitute contributory infringement if the product is widely used for legitimate, unobjectionable purposes. Indeed, it need merely be capable of *substantial* non-infringing uses." (*Sony* 464 U.S. at 442).

The dispute between the plaintiff and defendant on the issue whether Sony safe harbor may be applied in this case was the question whether actual or potential non-infringing use is sufficient to fulfill the mentioned "substantial non-infringing uses" requirement. Grokster argued that it is; the plaintiffs argued that the non-infringing use must be the primary use, and not merely an incidental one.

The Court in this case based its reasoning on the position that a manufacturer of technological device which potentially can be used for infringement of others' rights may be protected by "Sony safe-harbor" only if non-infringing usage of such device is more commercially significant than the infringing use.

In one of the other cases regarding P2P networks (*Aimster* case) the 7th Circuit Court of Appeals held that, a manufacturer of technological device will enjoy the Sony safe-harbor only if "... it would have been disproportionately costly for him to eliminate or at least reduce substantially the infringing uses."

But in this case the Court took another position. The Court rejected Defendant's argument that the plaintiff should prove specific instances of infringement resulting from defendant's

11 <www.grokster.com/>.

acts, and stated that "Plaintiff need prove only that the Defendant distributed the product with the intent to encourage infringement."[12]

The other essential theory doctrine applied by the Court is an *inducement theory*. The inducement rule states that "one who distributes a device with the object of promoting its use to infringe copyright, as shown by clear expression or other affirmative steps taken to foster infringement, is liable for the resulting acts of infringement by third parties."[13]

The Court reasoned that Grokster's actions in this case evidenced "purposeful, culpable expression and conduct" by attempting to become an alternative to Napster P2P network;[14] also it refused to install filtering mechanisms to its software in order to decrease the infringing use; finally, the Court acknowledged an existence of correlation between the infringing use of Defendant's software and its revenue.

Hence, the *Grokster* case is a warning for other P2P networks, forcing them to exercise more careful supervision of possibly illegal downloading and to develop certain technical devices to prevent infringement.[15]

But many independent experts consider that the ruling in the *Grokster* case did not provide an adequate solution of P2P infringement for copyright owners. Surely, most of right holders expected that communication technologies that can be used for infringement should be per se prohibited without consideration of the actions and intentions of their creators. But the Court did not support such expectations.

Surely, the *Grokster* case provided certain directions for the right holders and enforcement bodies. On the other hand, it still did not resolve many essential issues: if the owner of P2P network exercised reasonable supervision and deleting of illegal materials but due to technical reasons some of them were still downloaded – whether he is still subject to liability? Can individuals be reasonably held liable for sharing (especially, taking into account, they may be citizens of different states); whether private data of individual infringers may be disclosed?

Some of these issues were raised in the next case we analyse.

12 2006 U.S. Dist. LEXIS 73714 at *58.

13 *Metro-Goldwyn-Mayer Studios, Inc. v. Grokster, Ltd.*, 545 U.S. (2005)

14 This P2P network was at that time subject of another litigation, and it was most likely it will cease to exist after the Court will held its decision.

15 Such programs are already used by Youtube.com and Google.com and some other websites.

3 *Promusicae v. Telefonica*[16]

In this case *Promusicae* (Spanish association of music producers) sued an internet provider Telefonica for its refusal to disclose personal data of individuals whom Promusicae suspected in copyright infringement by using Kazaa P2P network. Promusicae wished to sue their suspects.

The Spanish Court held that internet providers should not disclose personal data of users in civil cases because such disclosure is only permissible under Spanish law in criminal cases to safeguard public security and national defence. Promusicae appealed to the European Court of Justice.

Hence, the ECJ had to decide whether European law can be constructed in such a way, as to permit disclosure of personal information (protected under certain EU directives[17] and being a part of fundamental human rights) where such information is necessary to initiate civil proceedings for protection of owners' rights on the Internet.

The decision of the ECJ on the one hand confirmed that the service provider has no obligation to hand personal data over to Promusicae (in the context of a civil case). On the other hand, the ECJ held that EU law "does not preclude the possibility for the Member States of laying down an obligation to disclose personal data in the context of civil proceedings." However, it stated that when interpreting the EU law, the Member States should do so in such a way "which allows a fair balance to be struck between the various fundamental rights protected by the Community legal order" and that the measures taken in course of such interpretation should not be in conflict with "those fundamental rights or with the other general principles of Community law, such as the principle of proportionality".

Hence, some analysts consider this decision as providing a possibility of further implementing national laws permitting disclosure of personal data (as it was not clearly prohibited by ECJ decision). Others instead consider this decision a win of privacy over copyright

---

16 Case C-275/06, 2008 CELEX no 62006J0275 (29 January 2008).

17 Reference was made to interpretation of Directive 2000/31/EC of the European Parliament and of the Council of 8 June 2000 on certain legal aspects of information society services, in particular electronic commerce, in the Internal Market ('Directive on electronic commerce') (OJ 2000 L 178, p. 1), Directive 2001/29/EC of the European Parliament and of the Council of 22 May 2001 on the harmonisation of certain aspects of copyright and related rights in the information society (OJ 2001 L 167, p. 10), Directive 2004/48/EC of the European Parliament and of the Council of 29 April 2004 on the enforcement of intellectual property rights (OJ 2004 L 157, p. 45, and corrigendum, OJ 2004 L 195, p. 16), and Articles 17(2) and 47 of the Charter of Fundamental Rights of the European Union proclaimed in Nice on 7 December 2000 (OJ 2000 C 364, p. 1, 'the Charter').

and of infringers over right holders because this case rejected disclosure of personal data to Promusicae. The touchstone of "balance" mentioned by the Court did not make the situation clearer.

Therefore, the ruling left the issues somewhat open.

In any case, this decision became a basis for strengthening further enforcement campaigns against internet providers and owners of P2P sharing networks. Instead of trying to initiate civil proceedings against individual users which is difficult as a matter of fact and in law, as well as uneconomical and unreasonable it is easier to force service providers to monitor their web-content, to develop new filtering programs and to terminate infringers' access to such sites (see the three-tier graduated response recently adopted in the French Olivennes proposal).[18] This case may also promote increased lobbying for adoption criminal sanctions against copyright infringement.

This measures proposed by rights holders are understandable – millions of dollars of potential rights holders' revenue are lost to internet copyright infringement annually. But are such measures are adequate and effective?

In Russia there are copyright infringement is subject to penal sanction. But the volume of these crimes is still increasing despite the efforts of the enforcement bodies.

The following case shows the results of such enforcement campaign on example of one famous site.

4 TORRENTS.RU

On 18 February 2010 about 3 p.m. many Russian users were shocked by news that the major Russian torrent-tracker – torrents.ru – was blocked. It was done due to the order of an investigation committee who accused torrents in "violation of copyright law and illegal distribution of software that was developed by 1C and Autodesk firms".[19] A couple of days later torrents.ru moved to a .org domain zone and is now named rutracker.org.

The situation with Torrents.ru rapidly became one of the major discussion topics for citizens and legal experts. The public divided into two camps, but both consider the decision to

18 This initiative proposes terminating of internet access for copyright infringers on the internet (<http://news.bbc.co.uk/2/hi/technology/7110024.stm>).

19 26 February 2010, Suspicious of .Ru Zone "Official Russia" newspaper.

close Torrents.ru as a controversial one: "on one hand, many people claimed that it provided unique content that couldn't be found anywhere else and that content exchange is a new cultural phenomenon that should be recognized as an evolution of the information society. Some bloggers claimed that Torrents.ru is not responsible for the violations since it only provided tracks and did not distribute the content by itself. Other bloggers argued that Torrents.ru was distributing content illegally and those who oppose its closure just want to continue enjoying free and illegal access to information protected by the copyright law."[20]

One of the main issues in this case relates to procedural measures applied when closing torrents.ru. There was no court decision – just an order of an investigation committee. Lenta.ru news agency pointed out [RUS] that according to the law, RU-Center provider should have given torrents.ru one month to resolve the issue. However, it decided to close the site almost immediately because of the agreement that had been previously reached between the provider and the investigation committee.[21]

The owner of Torrents.ru said in an interview to "Echo Moskvy" radio station: "It was absolutely illegal. We will appeal against it, but in this case it's not the most important thing. The precedent is created. If you are an owner of domain name in .ru zone, you should know that it can be suspended at any moment by the order of an investigator."

One blogger with a nick serj-nickel wrote [RUS] a post that became one of the most popular ones regarding this issue and was re-posted by many other bloggers: "First, what is this 'freezing the delegation?' I can't understand – is there any decision of the court? I am not a lawyer, but from point of common sense, I think that you can close something so fast with so extreme measures only when it poses a threat to security. And what happened here? On February 16, someone wrote some paper and after two days everything is done. Everything is closed. Let's say that in Russia we have a bad corrupted unfair court, but in this case we had no any court at all".[22]

In addition, serj-nickel claimed that Torrents.ru was the most loyal Russian track torrent service in regard to copyright laws, since it promised to delete any track to content that violates copyright if the creator of content submits a request. Later, a public petition to the president, prime minister and the general prosecutor was placed on a petitions website. On behalf of the Russian Internet-community, the author of the petition wrote that the

20 *Id.*
21 Lenta.ru 26 February 2010.
22 <http://serj-nickel.livejournal.com/139844.html>.

investigation committee went beyond its authority: "The current criminal legislation does not include an option of "suspending delegation of domain". It contains the list of those measures impossible to be interpreted generally. Thus, the investigators who made this arbitrary decision obviously went beyond their powers and caused damages to more than four million users of the tracker.[23] The mentioned petition was signed by thousands people. But nothing was changed.

The mentioned decision once again proved the inefficiency of rapid and legally controversial measures in combating copyright infringement. Legislation has not developed enough; however, unreasonable strengthening of punishment leads mostly to unintended consequences rather than to establishing justice.

So, now infringers likely consider it easier and more efficient to move to another domain zone rather than to establish any reasonable dialog with the Russian authorities. That is surely not in the best interest of the state or of right holders.

5 Analysis of Recent Initiatives on Combating Online Piracy

The abovementioned cases gives us a sense of the complicated problems which face the State when developing legal regulation of the internet. It is obvious, that an adequate solution to these problems has not been yet given. So it is not surprising that most of the countries try to seek new schemes and approaches towards these issues.

This practice takes either or both of two paths – implementing new national legislation and establishing international norms and institutes.

6 Russia

New amendments have been recently proposed to the Civil Code of the Russian Federation proposing new measures on combating with internet infringement.

Firstly, on 14 October 2010, the Government of Russia has passed a Resolution on "Remuneration for free reproduction of soundtrack and audio-visual productions for personal purposes"[24] which established a special duty imposed on manufactures and

---

23 <http://Girus.ru> ("Civil initiative in Russia").

24 Постановление Правительства Российской Федерации от 14 октября 2010 г. N 829 г. Москва "О вознаграждении за свободное воспроизведение фонограмм и аудиовизуальных произведений в личных целях" (<www.rg.ru/2010/10/22/kompens-dok.html>).

importers of recording devices and virgin mediums (these devices include PCs, notebooks, mobile phones etc.). The amount charged is equal to 1% of market value of a unit of the device or virgin medium.

Also under consideration at the State Duma (Russia's Parliament) are some others proposals intended to combat copyright infringement. There is a law in draft on collecting of author's charge from communication operators for downloading of music and films.[25]

It should be mentioned that these proposals were rather negatively seen by citizens as well as by experts. The latter consider that established proposals will only entail increases of market prices but will not in any way affect the market for counterfeit products.

The second group of proposals is related to liability of internet providers and individual users for illegal content infringing copyright.

Russian norms on liability of internet providers are construed similarly to ones adopted in many western countries. Thus, ISPs shall not be liable for placement of illegal content if it did not know and should not have known that the content was illegal; upon receipt of relevant notice of infringement, provided there are due measures for eliminating consequences of infringement, to wit:the ISP should delete the illegal content within three days and "freeze" the domain or at least somehow limit access to the information upon receipt of an order from an enforcement body.

Proposals also include provisions on imposing fines for placement and downloading of "pirate" content. That will be approximately RUR 2,000-5,000 for individuals, RUR 250,000 for legal entities, and RUR 20,000-50,000 for state officials.[26]

One of the authors of this draft law, Mr. Milyavskiy, considers that torrent trackers should be invalidated as it is now technically impossible to monitor illegal files shared thereby.[27] That initiative will not be supported by state bodies considering the law in draft.

Proposals for decriminalizing or decreasing of punishment for some crimes related to copyright infringement are now also being considered.

---

25 <www.klerk.ru/law/news/180937/>.

26 <www.rosbalt.ru/2010/08/30/766607.html>.

27 <http://itua.info/keyword/442>.

Hence, the mentioned measures evidence the trend of establishing economic consequences of copyright infringement as opposed to criminal consequences. That seems rational and corresponds to international practice in this area, but it is still uncertain how these measures will be enforced (especially with relation to imposing fines on individuals) and how any obtained funds will be distributed between rights holders. It also seems that such measures will encourage disclosure of personal data which may entail a conflict between intellectual property rights and inviolability of private data.

The mentioned issues have not been yet reasonably resolved on the national level. Besides, as the torrents.ru case showed, infringers can easily change their location to foreign domain zone which does not fall under regulation of Russian authorities.

That is why international cooperation is so important in internet related issues.

7 Anti-Counterfeiting Trade Agreement (ACTA)

ACTA is a modern initiative of the USA, the EU and a few other countries intended to establish "new international legal framework that countries can join on a voluntary basis"[28] that should create "its own governing body outside existing international institutions such as the World Trade Organization (WTO), the World Intellectual Property Organization (WIPO) or the United Nations".[29] Negotiating countries described ACTA as a response "to the increase in global trade of counterfeit goods and pirated copyright protected works."[30]

ACTA shall be executed as a framework agreement; its provisions will require implementation legislation to have binding domestic legal effect. However, at least in theory, it is a big step forward for internet regulation.

Proposed drafts of the ACTA contain certain vitally important initiatives for pursuing online infringement. These are cooperation between the states, right owners, ISPs and other possible subjects; enforcement procedures, including criminal enforcement; list of measures necessary for implementation of the mentioned initiatives etc.

---

28 Ministry of Economic Development of New Zealand (2008). "On Anti-Counterfeiting Trade Agreement".

29 Pilieci, Vito (26 May 2008). "Copyright deal could toughen rules governing info on iPods, computers". Vancouver Sun, <www.canada.com/vancouversun/story.html?id=ae997868-220b-4dae-bf4f-47f6fc96ce5e&p=1>. Retrieved 27 May 2008.

30 *Id.*

Though, measures proposed by ACTA seem to be quite strict: they suppose the possibility of data disclosure at the request of enforcement bodies; criminal procedures and penalties applied in "cases of willful trademark counterfeiting or copyright or related rights piracy on commercial scale". Also during negotiating such measures as a "3 strikes scheme" were discussed, which would allow ISPs to disconnect an investigated infringer from internet access after sending three warnings; monitoring of users' activity, limiting access/speed of internet connection as a punitive measure for infringers etc were also discussed as possible remedies.

Negotiations regarding ACTA were taken under a veil of secrecy. This fact as well as the measures proposed by ACTA caused dissatisfaction of certain states as well as experts and general public.

As Nate Anderson with Ars Technica pointed out, "ACTA encourages service providers to collect and provide information about suspected infringers by giving them "safe harbor from certain legal threats". Similarly, it provides for criminalization of copyright infringement, granting law enforcement the powers to perform criminal investigation, arrests and pursue criminal citations or prosecution of suspects who may have infringed on copyright. It also allows criminal investigations and invasive searches to be performed against individuals for whom there is no probable cause, and in that regard weakens the presumption of innocence and allows what would in the past have been considered unlawful searches.[31]

There was even an open letter signed by many organizations who argue that "ACTA would create unduly harsh legal standards that do not reflect contemporary principles of democratic government, free market exchange, or civil liberties. Even though the precise terms of ACTA remain undecided, the negotiants' preliminary documents reveal many troubling aspects of the proposed agreement" such as removing "legal safeguards that protect Internet Service Providers from liability for the actions of their subscribers" in effect giving ISPs no option but to comply with privacy invasions. Further it says that "[ACTA] would also facilitate privacy violations by trademark and copyright holders against private citizens suspected of infringement activities without any sort of legal due process".[32]

It is not clear when ACTA will come into force and what will be its final redaction. Surely such agreement between major countries (taking into account that many other countries

31 Anderson, Nate (2008-06-02). "The real ACTA threat (it's not iPod-scanning border guards)", Ars Technica. Retrieved 14 June 2008.

32 Shaw, Aaron (April 2009). "The Problem with the Anti-Counterfeiting Trade Agreement (and what to do about it)", KEStudies 2.

are looking forward to join it – *e.g.*, Russia, India) will establish a new legal framework on internet regulation.

But the exact form of this framework and how it would correlate with fundamental principles of democratic societies are still at issue.

8 Proposals on Possible Measures

Having considered some modern initiatives regarding P2P sharing and internet copyright infringement as a whole it is possible to provide some hopefully adequate measures in this sphere.

First, it should be clear, that only a well developed set of measures taken by different subjects (states, ISPs, citizens themselves) can bring a desirable result.

Primarily it is a matter of establishing an adequate balance between private and commercial rights, as well as between state and international interests in this sphere.

The most frightening trend in combating internet copyright infringement is limiting privacy rights in order to punish the infringers. On the one hand, it has certain reasonable grounds, but due to possible unintended consequences as well as economic and legal inefficiency prudent policy analysts propose other possible solutions.

According to one security expert in his essay *The Value of Privacy*, "Privacy protects us from abuses by those in power, even if we're doing nothing wrong at the time of surveillance."[33]

Surely, privacy should not be treated as a shield for wrongdoers. But most infringements are made with no commercial gain, many of them are made by young people and long and controversial litigation proceedings in an uncertain legal framework rarely meets rights-holders' goal of monetizing their intellectual property. P2P networks will still exist – democratic societies cannot just make them illegal. So there always will be a certain share of infringements.

33 *The Value of Privacy* by Bruce Schneier.

Hence, it seems that two main directions for combating online infringement should be the development of technical measures for monitoring and eliminating of illegal content and economic measures to compensate right holders.

Technical developments must be reached in close cooperation (cooperation – not forced measures) between states and ISPs. Some sites already develop such technologies – Google, Youtube and others.

Economic measures may include certain duties imposed on recording devices and communication operators. A further step of such 'legalization' may lead to applying a special internet tax (such initiatives were recently discussed in the Netherlands). Implementation of such initiatives presents certain issues: how will these funds be distributed, whether it is fair to divide losses caused by infringers between all internet users etc. Surely, these issues shall be considered by experts, but it seems to be a fair price for not limiting private rights and protecting right holders' interests.

Alternatively, or in addition, a complex of state and commercial measures could be provided including demonopolization, measures on development of legal culture of citizens, etc. Most likely a balanced set of measures will be more efficient than pure attempts to disclose and punish all the wrongdoers by implementing relevant legislation based on common legal doctrines which are too hard to apply in modern world with rapidly developing technologies.

9 Conclusion

We have analysed the recent cases, theories and proposed measures on combating P2P infringement problem. It is obvious that this problem is complicated and sensitive. Until the mere existence of P2P networks will be considered illegal which is unlikely, given the basic principles of democratic societies: so long as technical measures do not enable monitoring all illegal content, P2P will exist.

Hence, to decrease the volume of illegal on-line sharing, new measures and approaches should be developed. Three main issues have to be resolved:

- finding an adequate balance of privacy rights and intellectual property rights – based on the principle of proportionality; (means-ends rational review with strict scrutiny for fundamental rights/suspect classes).

- establishing adequate legal and technical measures which would be in compliance with fundamental rights and which would take into account technical specific of P2P sharing system;
- due sharing of liability between different subjects (ISPs, P2P owners, individuals)
- providing adequate penalties as well as an enforcement procedure.

It seems that establishing of economic measures together with well considered enforcement procedures would be the most adequate solution. These best accord the interests of right owners (as they are interested in usage of there intellectual property objects together with obtaining benefit from such usage) and the interests of individuals (for which such measures may be less burdensome than limiting their privacy). Establishing measures of strict liability and criminal liability should suffice for cases of really "bad apples".

And last, but not least, harmonizing legislation and cooperation between states is also needed. Otherwise, the internet will still have "safe harbours" for pirates.

Until then remember – *you are not* anonymous !

Part IV
Corporate Law

14 No Blood from a Stone: Corporate Restructuring and Raiding Defense

Ilya Aleschev

1 Flying Over the Raider's Nest: Overview of Forced Takeovers in Modern Russia

1.1 *Hostile Takeovers in Russia – Defining and Distinguishing*

The topic of hostile takeovers and corporate raiding in Russia attracts a lot of attention in both legal and economic literature. However, regardless of the specific research issue or approach taken, almost every author venturing in this area starts from the same reservation – drawing a line between hostile takeovers and corporate raiding as they are traditionally understood in western law, and the uniquely Russian phenomena of "forced takeovers" ("strongarm tactics" – the exact terms may vary). The similar terminology is partly due to some common external features and partly due to lack of more convenient terms.

The traditional definition of a hostile takeover is "[t]he acquisition of ownership or control of corporation … typically accomplished by a purchase of shares or assets, a tender offer or a merger … that is resisted by the target corporation's board of directors."[1] Similar to that, a corporate raider is defined as "[a] person or business that attempts to take control of a corporation, against its wishes, by buying its stock and replacing its management."[2] Based on a market tools, these activities are generally considered positive to both target company shareholders and economy as a whole due to weeding out ineffective management and creating additional value due to synergy.[3]

The Russian market for corporate control, although only less than two decades old, has developed its own approach to acquisitions. Instead of relying on market methods, like buying free float shares off the market or making a tender offer, the typical takeover on

1 *Black's Law Dictionary*, 1493 (Bryan A. Garner ed., 8th ed., West 2004).
2 *Id.*, 365.
3 Olga Sergeeva, *Corporate Takeover in Russia* (MA in Economic and Legal Studies Short Thesis), 2009, <www.etd.ceu.hu/2009/sergeeva_olga.pdf>, pp. 4-5. See also: Kirill Tishchenko, Effective Defense Methods Against Hostile Takeovers And Raiders In Russia (Finance Master's thesis), 2009, <www.hsepubl.lib.hse.fi/FI/ethesis/pdf/12130/hse_ethesis_12130.pdf>, p. 10.

Russian market involves a mix of illegal and quasi-legal (formally legitimate, but aimed to reach illegal ends) methods with an end goal to acquire corporate control over target company or the assets it owns against the will of both a company management and its shareholders and for token or no consideration.

As one may notice, the key features that distinguish a "forced takeover" (as practiced in Russia) are that corporate control or assets are taken from their owners (1) against their will, (2) without adequate consideration and (3) by using means that are, even if formally legal, are illicit in essence.

A number of definitions provided by those who have studied this field may be useful to grasp a general understanding of this phenomena:

A hostile takeover in Russia means the redistribution of a company's ownership through a combination of legal, illegal, and illegitimate means, including forced bankruptcies, the use of administrative resources, raids by police, tax officers, or government inspectors, and even the violent seizure of documents, assets, offices, and places of business.[4]

In Russia a "hostile takeover" is not just a turn of phrase. Ruthless businessmen are employing armed thugs to intimidate their rivals and force them to hand over their companies – backed by corrupt policemen and courts.[5]

«Reiderstvo» differs greatly from US hostile takeover practice in that it relies on criminal methods such as fraud, blackmail, obstruction of justice, and actual and threatened physical violence.[6]

[C]orporate raiding will be defined as the seizure, or attempted seizure, of a business or a substantial part of its assets, through the corrupt reliance on a legal document, including, but not limited to, a court order, judicial decision, corporate resolution, corporate charter document, or state registration document.[7]

---

4 Alexander Settles, *Hostile Takeovers, Corporate Raiding, and Company Capture in Russia*, 2009, <www.cipe.org/publications/fs/pdf/083109.pdf>, p. 2.

5 Uwe Klussmann, *Russia's Very Hostile Takeovers*, Bloomberg Businessweek, 2007, <www.businessweek.com/globalbiz/content/aug2007/gb20070829_507498.htm>.

6 Thomas Firestone, *Criminal Corporate Raiding in Russia*, 2008, <http://heinonline.org/HOL/LandingPage?collection=journals&handle=hein.journals/intlyr42&div=68&id=&page=>, p. 1207.

7 Thomas Firestone, *Armed Injustice: Abuse Of The Law And Complex Crime In Post-Soviet Russia*, 2010, <http://findarticles.com/p/articles/mi_hb3262/is_4_38/ai_n55121897/?tag=content;col1>, p. 563.

Raiding in Russia is essentially different from corporate takeovers in developed countries. It is merely directed towards redistribution of existing property rights rather than achieving efficiency through putting the resources to better use.[8]

Hostile takeover is a transfer of assets ... conveyed by artificially initiated lawsuit, against owner's will and by using corrupt officials and judges, various methods of stealing shares and fraudulent schemes, as well as by construing unclear provisions in legislation.[9]

Studying corporate raids with relation to the criminal code of the Russian Federation, authors came to a conclusion that such raids always involve an aggregate of crimes. It is a complicated system invariably aimed to achieve one goal: to seize assets of a profit-making entity.[10]

[R]aiding may be defined as follows: it is an activity aimed to taking of other's assets against owner's will with minimum expenses by using criminal and legal offences with subsequent laundering title on these assets by reselling it to the good faith purchaser.[11] In this chapter terms "takeover" and "raiding" would be used to refer to the described above activities aimed to seizure of a corporate control or assets, unless expressly stated otherwise.

Having these definitions, it becomes clear that well established arguments in favor of "classic takeover" (putting more efficient management and inducing economy growth) are not very consistent with the essence of takeovers as they are practiced in Russia. Moreover, it is suggested that such raiding practices are in fact detrimental not only to target company management and shareholders, but also to the economy as a whole.

The arguments proposed are that, unlike "classic takeovers", it is not inefficient companies who face the most risk to become a raid target, but rather businesses that show a high level of corporate performance and possesses valuable assets.[12] Furthermore, facing a constant risk of the raider's attack, a company has to devote resources to protective measures that could be otherwise used in a business process to make profit a waste.[13] Redistribution of a corporate control in such a way does not create any additional value. The "fire sale" of

8 Sergeeva, p. 7.

9 Maria Usova, *Opposing Hostile Takeovers as a Step to Ecomomic Safety of Russia*, synopsis of a Ph.D. in Economics Thesis, 2010, <www.econsafety.ru/avtoref/usova.rtf>, p. 11.

10 Vladimir Aleshin, Evgeny Zholobov, *The Nature of Corporate Raid in the Sense of Penal Law*, Ugolovny Process, 2008, <www.skvlaw.ru/res/files/www/pdf/up08_42-45_Aleshin-Zholobov_eng.pdf>, p. 42.

11 Isaycheva E.A. *On Some Criticism of Corporat Raid in Russia*, Saratov State Academy of Law Herald, 2010, <www.sgap.ru/vestnik/files/04-2010.pdf>, p. 41.

12 Sergeeva, p. 18.

13 Sergeeva, p. 12.

assets and termination of target company business negatively effects society delayed wages to employees, unpaid debts to suppliers, strikes and, sometimes, even civil disorders In sum, the costs of raiders substantially exceed any social gains.[14]

As both the goal and methods of a Russian hostile takeover differs greatly from the "classic" one, the defensive measures differ as well. In practice, several anti-takeover measures, generally used in common-law countries, are either inapplicable or ineffective (counterattack by buying off raider company shares and poison pill), and some have proven only of limited efficiency (golden parachutes). Most authors' advice on how to protect one's business against a takeover centers on corporate governance and monitoring issues. Calls to amend legislation by eradicating the most dangerous loopholes are also common.

This chapter will focus on main methods employed by corporate raiders (historically and currently), target companies' weak spots that induce the takeover, and building a corporate structure as a protective measure to make corporate raiding less profitable and thus less probable.

Although most works in this area base their case study on few big-scale hostile takeovers (like Ilim Palp, Togliattiazot, Russneft, Smarts or Hermitage, not to say Yukos, which always stands apart for well known reasons), the current trend of raiding is to shift to small and medium business as targets. As large scale enterprises in most cases adopted at least some protective measures, small and medium enterprises (SME) are still mostly unprotected and, what is ever worse, unaware of the risks that are likely to come. Thus paper aims to outline solutions that may be useful to protecting such businesses against takeover.

1.2 *Predators' Evolution: Outline of Takeover Methods Development History*

Despite the fact that modern Russian history is quite short, there may be distinguished several periods when certain methods of takeover were most widespread.

In the early nineties due to privatization most Soviet-era enterprises were converted into AO (Joint Stock Companies), a legal entity form constructed after the common law public company, and the stock was greatly dispensed between employees. Other distinct features of that time were an extremely low level of law enforcement and a corresponding rise of organized crime, which not only racketeered businesses, but also substituted for state

14 Tishchenko, pp. 10-11.

authorities by providing protection and debt collection to the businesses, often demanding a share in profits.[15]

Ironically enough, taking control over business in this period (now often referred to as the "daring nineties") was most often made through buying shares from employees to accumulate stake large enough to remover management and to acquire operational control over company's assets – which sounds quite legitimate. The reality, unfortunately, was more ugly – the employees were misrepresented to sell their shares at unfairly low (or even token) price at best, if not under duress or physical pressure.

A more blatant method of "physical takeover" was also in use, in which the raider simply forged documents justifying his right on the corporate control (*e.g.* minutes on shareholders' meeting appointing CEO) and took over the target premises with support of mercenary securities and bailiffs (police mostly choose not to intervene). Once in control of the corporate documents, the raider quickly sold assets to entities controlled by him, and resold them subsequently.

Other methods distinct to this period were challenging privatization basing on the legal flaws that were unavoidable due to loosely drafted legislation and lack of experience to implement them, and subsequent re-privatization of business to the raider.[16]

These methods are almost not in use now, however, as there are very few companies left with the shares owned by employees, and the statute of limitations on privatization has expired.

The next period was from 1997 to 2002. Its key feature was a wide use of loopholes in bankruptcy legislation.[17] The most important of these were extremely low thresholds to be met to instigate bankruptcy proceeding[18] and the external officer appointment rules that may be summarized as "whoever strikes first rules the show".[19] Moreover, the external officer took over powers of all bankrupt's governance bodies (including the Board and the CEO), and that the creditors' meeting was free to accelerate bankruptcy proceeding to the asset sale stage.

---

15 See generally Vadim Volkov, *Who Is Strong When The State Is Weak: Violent Entrepreneurs In Post-Communist Russia,* 1998, <www.stanford.edu/group/Russia20/volumepdf/Volkov.pdf>.

16 Tishchenko, p. 26.

17 Isaycheva, p. 41.

18 Firestone, *Criminal Corporate Raiding in Russia*, p. 1210.

19 Sergeeva, p. 16.

As bankruptcy legislation underwent major redrafting in 2002, this method went into decline.[20] Not only thresholds on instigating bankruptcy proceedings were raised, but also the procedure itself was made more balanced, making it impossible to fast forward to the asset sale stage. What is even more important, much case law was generated and summarized by the Russian Supreme Commercial Court (although Russian courts decisions are not recognized as a law, guidelines issued by Supreme Courts' are binding). External officers were obliged to be members of a self-regulating organizations, and the appointment procedure was changed in attempt to avoid "puppet officers".

Although these amendments made "bankruptcy takeover" less attractive, it would be far too optimistic to say that it ceased to exist. Even now there are certain bad faith self-regulating organizations providing "sympathetic" external officers and the bankruptcy itself is still used as an element in takeover schemes, just not in a straightforward way.

Starting from 2002, decline of "bankruptcy takeover" forced raiders to switch to schemes exploiting flaws in corporate law[21] and in rules of civil procedure.

One of the most abused loopholes was the provision in RF Law on Joint Stock Companies stating that if a shareholders' meeting lacks a quorum, the adjourned meeting may have a quorum of 30%. The raider obtained a 30% stake in the target (or forged documents justifying its right thereto), and by applying various means (as the "empty envelope" tactic described above) ensured that the other shareholders would not show up. Having the initial meeting adjourned due to lack of quorum, the raider conveyed another meeting (also by itself), passing resolutions on CEO appointment, approval major transactions to sell key assets, transfer of a share register to the Registrar controlled by the raider and the like.[22]

In respect to the target companies incorporated as OOO (closely resembling LLC in common law) filing forged documents related to the sale of shares and nominating of a CEO to the State Register was a common practice. As tax authorities who keep the State Register are not entitled to review the filed documents on the merits, the amendments are automatically reflected in the Register, thus allowing the raider to impersonate himself as target company shareholder and/or CEO, *e.g.* to sell the assets.

20 Tishchenko, p. 24. See also Alexander Settles, Hostile Takeovers, Corporate Raiding, and Company Capture in Russia, 2009, <www.cipe.org/publications/fs/pdf/083109.pdf>, p. 3.

21 Settles, p. 3. See also Firestone, Criminal Corporate Raiding in Russia, p. 1212.

22 Tishchenko, p. 25.

Other methods commonly used were obtaining court ruling (usually under a bogus claim) on provisional measures in a form of injunction prohibiting the target's shareholders to vote their shares, or prohibiting legitimate CEO to obstruct "new CEO" activity, etc.

Nearly all of the loopholes described above were remedied by introducing relevant amendments to corporate and civil legislation in 2009 and 2010. Although it is yet too early to make any comments on whether these amendments reached their desired effect, one may predict that "corporate schemes" are facing the same decline that the "bankruptcy takeover" faced in 2002.

The current period demonstrates a rapid growth of forced takeovers made as extortions based on criminal cases artificially created against target business owners. Some believe that an unofficial beginning of this era was Yukos case in 2003-2004, when state-owned Rosneft ended up owning most of Yukos assets:

> "the first actual case of state takeover of the large privately-controlled business is associated with the Yukos assets expropriation. The tax authorities bankrupted this major oil company to settle tax debt for tax evasion. In December 2004, the Yukos' main production unit, Yuganskneftegaz, was sold to the state owned company Rosneft through the shell company Baikalfinansgroup."[23]

Others, however, believe that this period starts from 2005, when the formula "surrender your business in exchange of dropping criminal charges" was widely used.[24]

Using ambiguities in Russian legislation, police and security service officers (sometimes being corrupted by raiders, but more and more often acting as a raider themselves) either instigate criminal prosecution on an actual cause which is not usually prosecuted (under a selective implementation principle), or misconstrue legislative provisions to make up such a cause.

As defined by Thomas Firestone, "[c]ommissioned criminal prosecutions ('zakaznye dyela'), a term referring to (a) criminal cases 'commissioned' by third parties as a way of sabotaging business competitors and (b) criminal cases initiated by law enforcement for extortionate or other improper purposes, are probably the most clear-cut examples of criminal legal abuse in Russia."[25]

23 Tishchenko, p. 16.

24 Usova, p.13.

25 Firestone, *Armed Injustice*, p. 556.

Although there were attempts to remedy this situation, including legislation amendments banning pre-trial arrest on white collar crime (resulting in 22,5% drop in such arrests[26]), there are a lot of reports that courts and police find ways to circumvent these amendments.

According to the OECD report, there were 24 large and medium size companies taken over

> by the state in 2004-2006,[27] and there are sound grounds to believe that these figures are seriously underreported, as many SME takeovers never find their way to media. The general understanding of the current hostile takeover situation in Russian society is the same – a sociological poll on corporate raiding has shown that more than half respondents were sure that the State is a main raider, using both corporate means and force.[28]

To sum up, while there is substantial awareness to corporate raiding and there are serious attempts made to eradicate the same (*e.g.* legislation amendments aimed to cover loopholes and guidelines issued by Supreme Courts aimed to make caselaw more consistent not only with the letter of the law, but with its heart and soul as well), raiders adapt.

As laid out by Tishchenko, "in spite of the new introduction of various laws concerning corporate governance in Russia, predators find a way around the barriers, which have been built, often remaining within the boundaries of the law. As a result, government seems to be not really efficient at preventing raiders' from unethical and even illegal behavior. Therefore, substantial improvements have not been reached yet."[29]

Thus, acknowledging necessity of legislation amendments (which would most probably have their positive effect in a long-run scale), a more practical solution to a business owner would be making a review of the flaws in its business structure that make the takeover easier, cheaper and thus more probable to occur.

---

26 Editorial: Medvedev's Verdict, Vedomosti, 15 December 2010, 237 (2755).

27 Sergeeva, p. 10, citing Lucy Chernykhl. "Understanding State Takeovers in Russia" Working paper, preliminary draft, Bowling Green State University, 2008, p. 16.

28 L. Skidanova, Corporate Raid As a Social Phenomenon, 2009, <ftp://lib.herzen.spb.ru/text/IZV117_p1_8.pdf>, p. 311.

29 Tishchenko, p. 10.

2 Targets and Their Weak Spots: How to Get Raided

This section will provide a snapshot description of a typical Russian SME and will focus on the typical issues found in most such businesses that may be considered as creating or aggravating takeover risks, as well as outlining directions to mitigate them.

2.1 *How Typical Russian Small or Medium Business Is Structured*

While sole traders are used mostly by micro businesses (such as market or kiosk traders), the bulk of Russian SME is incorporated in a form of OOO, which more or less resembles the LLC. In some cases there are AO (JSC) involved, but these are mostly legacy companies created or acquired in the past, as currently newly incorporated companies in SME are almost always OOO, as AO involves additional compliance related to shares issue (and there are no benefits compensating it).

Typically there are one or several shareholders with stakes split in more or less equal way, with strong inclinations to round numbers, like 50 to 50 (which does not necessary clearly correspond with actual input into share capital or balance of powers). The shareholders typically hold management position in the company, like CEO, executive director and the like: "Unlike most of the Western companies, Russian ones are frequently characterized by the low level of separation of ownership and control, since managers often own a major block of shares in the companies that they run."[30]

Due to compliance and, especially, tax issues that legal entity tends to accumulate over time, it is a common practice to incorporate a new company once in a several years (most usually three years, an age thereafter a tax audit becomes more than likely) and, after transferring all the assets, employees and contracts to this new entity, to abandon an old one, sometimes with outstanding debts on taxes or contractual obligations left unpaid.

When the business grows, additional legal entities may be added, but corporate links (mother company owning shares in subsidiaries) are rare, as Russian tax legislation offers more favorable tax regimes to companies owned by natural persons. Thus several companies that form one business are either directly held by business owners, or when it is undesirable to disclose affiliation (*e.g.* when transfer pricing schemes are used), by entrusted persons like relatives or employees, with no legal means to enforce business owners' rights in case of abuse.

30 Sergeeva, p. 8, citing Alexander Radygin, Corporate governance, integration and reorganization: the contemporary trends of Russian corporate groups, Econ Change 39 [October 2007], p. 278.

Multiple companies forming one business rarely divide functions and are engaged in the same business activities in an interrelated way. The division is based on the level of compliance: most multi-entity businesses try to keep one "core" company free from compliance and tax issues as much as it is practically possible, transferring all potentially troublesome activity to "side companies", which eventually become expendable.

Occasionally mid-sized business may engage offshore corporate vehicles in its structure (in about 90% the jurisdiction is Cyprus, often supplemented by a BVI mother company), with primary goals being tax optimization and transferring money to a tax free jurisdiction (like BVI), as well as hiding business owners identities.

2.2 *Main Issues at Risk*

2.2.1 Corporate

Holding shares in the companies directly and availability of information on the business owners. Due to recent amendments into RF Law On LLC, that were introduced in 2009 and added a requirement that share transfer transactions shall be certified by a notary, filing forged documents to a state register has become practically inefficient takeover method, as it requires a corrupt notary public who could be easily tracked. Nonetheless the fact that data on shareholders is open to the public may still be considered as a certain risk, as raiders may use this data, for example, for extortion under an artificially created criminal case as described above.

Where AO's are engaged in the corporate structure, their share registers are often kept by the company itself, to avoid additional costs that would entail submitting the registers to the Registrar. However, as the share register is the sole document reflecting share ownership, if it falls into the wrong hands corporate control can be lost. One common example is a police search conducted under a criminal case initiated under a bogus cause – made solely to seize the share register and other corporate documents.

Having shares in certain companies held by entrusted persons is an even more grave risk. Whatever loyalties these persons may owe to the business owners now, things may change. Entrusted persons may be financially influenced, be subject to duress or there may be grounds to initiate criminal proceedings in their respect. One shall consider that as trust agreements are not acknowledged by Russian law, business owners do not have any option to formalize their relationships with entrusted persons.

Another loyalty-related issue is general failure to limit the CEO's powers in a company Charter. If the company's CEO is not a business owner himself but a hired manager (or when there are several business owners) it is only reasonable to relay certain issues to shareholders' approval, beyond those that are vested to shareholders' meeting by virtue of law. In reality, however, tailor-made charters are rare.

Finally, a common mistake is failing to monitor the State Register on Legal Entities data on any amendments related to one's companies. That allows raiders to gain time, raising their chances to successful takeover.

2.2.2 Assets and Real Property

Most SME business fail to designate a separate corporate vehicle for asset holding functions. Instead, the same entities that own real property, equipment and the like are engaged in operational activity, are parties to transaction with external counterparties, employ personnel etc. Thus, the key assets may be potentially seized under creditor's claims.

In many cases, the prior history of key assets is not flawless: there may be certain formalities not met with, transaction approvals not obtained, or other grounds for avoiding prior transaction. Failure to allocate recourses to clear these issues allows the raider to file a lawsuit (however frivolous it may be) to obtain a provisional measures like asset seizure or an injunction that may paralyze the target's business.

Another common issue is using land plots not in accordance with zoning, environmental issues or in violation of lease agreements terms and conditions. While normally government authorities would turn a blind eye to certain minor violations, once influenced by a raider they may become far more rigid, which may lead to audits, fines and even to land plot seizure.

Failure to monitor the State Register in Real Property is a general mistake as well, giving the raider enough time to resell the taken asset several times to protect it from recovery.

2.2.3 Compliance

While the statement that it is impossible to conduct business in Russia without breaching the law may look like an exaggeration, saying that it is impossible to conduct profitable business in Russia without breaching law would be most probably true. There are numerous regulations that are impractically costly or burdensome to comply with. For example, workplaces equipped with computers shall be organized in a way that displays shall be located at least two meters from one another.[31]

In reality this rule (as most of the number of similarly obscure rules) are not enforced. There is, however, administrative liability for beaching workplace safety regulations, providing either fine or suspension of company's operations up to ninety days.[32] It is up to state authorities whether to enforce the rule that is violated in most companies, and whether there would be a fine or a operations suspension. It is clear that such discretion gives grounds for corruption and extortion, and in certain cases compliance issues may give sufficient grounds for initiating criminal proceedings against business owners or officers.

Just two examples of the latter. In the Sofex case (also named "Chemists' case") an owner of a business dealing with certain solvent agent was criminally prosecuted and incarcerated because there was a criminal liability for dealing with "virulent" substances, and "[t]he absence of a statutory definition allowed the officers to rely on a list of allegedly 'virulent' substances that had been prepared by an outside expert who had no official status or legislative or administrative authority".[33]

As the *Wall Street Journal* lays out her story: "Ms. Yakovleva says her own problems with the law started in 2006, after she and her partner turned down an offer from an officer of the antidrug police to pay kickbacks on sales of diethyl ether, an industrial solvent that can also be used in illicit-drug production. About two weeks after they rejected the offer, she says, the antidrug police opened a criminal case into their company for selling the chemical without necessary licenses, using laws against 'illegal entrepreneurship' and money laundering."[34]

Another case (named "ketamine case") involves criminal prosecution against veterinarians for administering ketamine to pets due to contradictory provisions of Russian law prohibiting dealing with anesthetic ketamine in one act and authorizing it for veterinary anesthetic purposes in another.[35]

---

31 Sanitary Regulations (SanPin) No. 2.2.2/2.4.1340-03 as of 3 June 2003, Art. 9.1.

32 Russian Code of Administrative Offenses, Art. 5.27.

33 Firestone, Armed Injustice, p. 556.

34 Gregory L. White, Once-Jailed Russian Executive Pushes Law Changes, *Wall Street Journal*, 2009, <http://online.wsj.com/article/SB126212533991109359.html>.

35 Firestone, *Armed Injustice*, p. 558.

2.2.4 Debts

Russian businesses traditionally heavily depend on bank loan financing, as there are virtually no other ways to attract financing, especially for SMEs. Thus, banks typically hold mortgages on nearly all key company assets, as well as personal guarantees from business owners. Moreover, it is common for banks to insert acceleration clauses contingent on many circumstances, including those drafted in most discretionary way (like "decline of debtor's financial condition").

As a result, banks typically own their debtors, especially in current economy conditions. Since fall 2008, when the global crisis hit Russia, there were several waves of foreclosures and many banks (namely Sberbank and VTB) have even created subsidiaries for the sole purpose of managing seized assets (Sberbank-Capital and VTB-Capital, respectively). In many cases bank officers admitted to media that the only reason why banks do not foreclose is that they do not have resources to manage the seized asset.

In a situation like this a raider may approach officers of the bank holding liens on target business assets with a buyout proposal. The bank forecloses, evaluating seizes assets below their real market value, and sells them to the raider. According to Settles,

> "...creditors have become participants in raiding schemes involving the use of bank information regarding loans and deposits. Such schemes involve the raider working with mid-level bank management to identify borrowers that have been weakened by the crisis. Once a company refinances its line of credit, the bank has information about the financial position of that borrower. If the bank's management has a relationship with a raider, they can work together to take over the company's assets, while leaving the borrower with the debt."[36]

Most small and medium businesses are deprived on alternative means to attract financing, and are also not well enough structured, not having enough transparency and corporate governance levels to attract a White Knight.

2.2.5 Government Relations

Though quite important from a practical prospective, this risk is very hard to formalize. As the above overview of other risks shows, often too much depends on what approach certain government official will take. Considering the high level of corruption (as Transparency International placed Russia 147th out of 180 in the category of "highly corrupt"

36 Settles, p. 4.

countries[37]), it is hard to disagree that "none of these strategies is foolproof. Indeed, raiders have taken over companies with every one of the aforementioned defenses in place ... in the end, the only real preventative measure is to have very good political connections."[38]

3 Economy of a Raid

The idea that the role of protective measures is to make an attack cost so much that it would be inefficient to initiate it at all, is by no means new and is discussed at length in the literature on this subject.[39]

Considering, however, the obscene rate of return (estimated from 200% to 1000%[40]) it would be more realistic to suggest that the goal of protective measures is not to make an attack outright unprofitable, but rather to increase its cost significantly beyond the cost of an average attack on the comparable business, and thus induce the attacker to consider another, less protected target instead.

It should be noted, however, that information on costs and expenses related to takeover is not commonly available, that those sources that do exist may not be considered reliable. Furthermore, as the economy fluctuates and legislation changes, any figures that once were published may quickly become obsolete.

Nonetheless, this section will focus on typical takeover scenarios and costs behind them.

3.1 Forging Corporate or Transaction Documents and Registering Sale of Shares or Assets

As mentioned above, blatant forging of transactional documents related to target company shares or assets owned by the target company and subsequent submission of them to the relevant state register may be used to create a color of title good enough either to convey certain actions on behalf of a hijacked company (usually an asset sale) or to resell the taken asset several times to get bona fide purchaser protection.

---

37 <www.transparency.org/publications/gcr/gcr_2009>.

38 Brenden Carbonell, Dimitry Foux, Vera Krimnus, Ed Ma and Lisa Safyan, *Hostile Takeovers: Russian Style,* 2010, <http://knowledge.wharton.upenn.edu/article.cfm?articleid=2217>.

39 Tishchenko, p. 27.

40 Sergeeva, p. 7, citing Bunin, "Reiderstvo kak socialno-ekonomicheskiy I politicheskiy fenomen covremennoy Rossii" [Raiding as a socio-economic and political phenomenon of contemporary Russia], Research center of "Political Technologies" (May 2008), <www.politcom.ru/6192.html> [accessed April 2009].

This method was used in all its audacious simplicity quite recently by Vladimir Barsukov nicknamed Kumarin (now convicted and serving fourteen year imprisonment term) in raids that took place in St. Petersburg in 2009:

> "According to court documents from one recent case, a St. Petersburg organized crime boss, Vladimir Barsukov, a/k/a 'Kumarin,' and several of his associates were convicted of a raiding scheme in which they deposited false documents with the State Registry of Corporate Entities, purporting to transfer ownership of the target businesses to Kumarin's co-conspirators. This official registration then generated other official documents which were used as the pretext for the forcible takeover of the businesses. In some cases, officials at the State Registry were simply deceived into believing that the deposited documents were authentic. In other cases, they were bribed to accept documents that they knew to be false."[41]

In respect to amendments made to State Register on Legal Entities one shall consider that, due to recent legislation, transactions with shares in OOO (LLC) require certification by a notary, making forging more expensive.

This method is sometimes supported by a lawsuit initiated solely for the purpose of having the forged documents "confirmed" by a court decision:

> "[f]alsification includes the creation of fraudulent property ownership documentation, forgery of signatures and bribing of judges and governmental officials. This type of 'grey' raiding occurs, for instance, when raiders bribe a court to file a lawsuit against a targeted company. While the lawsuit may be fictitious, it can result in a legal 'arrest' of all outstanding shares of the company and deprive the executive board of its decision-making power. A company whose shares are "under arrest" cannot undertake significant business transactions or human resources decisions, or obtain financing."[42]

According to information that is publicly available, expenses related to altering a target company's corporate documents are estimated as "10,000 Euros and up" and for notarizing

41 Firestone, *Armed Injustice*, p. 564.
42 Carbonell, Foux *et al.*

documents "from 3,000 to 10,000 Euros".[43] Same figures are provided in two internet resources[44]. An estimate for expenses related to a corrupt judicial decision was "$35,000".[45]

3.2 *Abusing Bankruptcy Proceedings*

After amendments made to the bankruptcy legislation in 2002, it became much harder to misuse bankruptcy proceeding as a takeover mechanism: "all the raiders who formerly used the law on bankruptcy switched tactics and began to use loopholes in the corporate law."[46]

It is acknowledged, however, that despite these amendments certain loopholes in legislation are still used "as an instrument to so called hostile takeover of quite successful enterprises",[47] and the ratio of so-called "commissioned" bankruptcy proceedings is still high:

> "[a]ccording to the director of the Federal Service for Financial Recovery, 30 per cent of the 30,000 pending bankruptcy procedures are 'commissioned' (ordered) in order to change ownership and not to reestablish financial solvency."[48]

Typical bankruptcy takeover scenario looks something like this:

1. Accumulate target company debts. Buy them from creditors or forge documents. Forgery is sometimes backed up by litigation. Likewise, courts may be deceived or bribed to issue awards confirming bogus claims. Other fraudulent practices have also been used. For example: giving "notice" to the target by sending it an empty envelope; closing attacking company bank accounts to make it impossible to repay the debt.
2. Go bankrupt. Give no notice of bankruptcy to the target or other creditors. Convene creditors' meeting. Obtain the majority on the creditors committee, because other creditors do not attend due to lack of notice. Then, appoint a person fully controlled by the raider as an external officer.
3. Accelerate the bankruptcy proceeding. Now at the asset sale stage sell to an entity controlled by raider at a token consideration.

---

43 Firestone, *Criminal Corporate Raiding in Russia*, p. 1209.

44 See <www.abc-people.com/typework/economy/e-confl-3.htm> and <www.a-rsb.ru/index.php?go=News&in =view&id=133>.

45 Firestone, *Criminal Corporate Raiding in Russia*, p. 1216.

46 *Id.*, p. 1212.

47 Olga Selevich, Bankruptcy as a Property Redistribution Mechanism (synopsis of a Ph.D. in Economics Thesis), 2010, <http://sartraccc.ru/Disser/selevich.pdf>.

48 Sergeeva, p. 17, citing Alexander Radygin, "Corporate Governance, integration and reorganization: the contemporary trends of Russian corporate groups," Econ Change39 [October 2007], p. 283.

4. Protect assets (see below).

According to Firestone, two additional stages may be distinguished after asset sale stage: obtaining the court's decision and physical takeover: "[T]he raider obtains a judgment authorizing it to take the target company's assets. Finally, the raider 'enforces' the judgment and physically takes control of the company, usually through an armed assault."[49]

Regarding expenses related to "commissioned" bankruptcy proceeding there is information stating that they are estimated as 35-40 % of the target's value, out of which $2.5-3 million is used to bribe government officers.[50]

3.3 *Abusing Corporate Legislation*

As mentioned above, most takeover methods based on abuse of corporate legislation and civil procedure may be hard to implement these days, as the relevant loopholes were closed due to recent amendments introduced in 2009 and 2010.

Namely: adjourned shareholders meetings no longer enjoy 30% quorum (eradicating one of most widely used schemes[51]). There is a special procedure to convene shareholders meetings called by shareholders themselves. Corporate lawsuits may be heard only by a court of a region where the relevant company's registered office is located, etc. Even before that, the case law shifted towards more strict scrutiny of the grounds for granting preliminary measures like injunction.

As a result, schemes most commonly used in past, like filing "a lawsuit against the target, often in a remote location where the raider has influence over the local judiciary, and then obtain[ing] a judicial order authorizing seizure of some or all of the target's assets"[52] or "filing a frivolous lawsuit in order to obtain a court judgment temporarily restricting the voting power of other shares, thus giving the raiders a temporary majority, which they then use to change the board of directors"[53] and others are unlikely to be successful, at least in their present form.

---

49 Firestone, Criminal Corporate Raiding in Russia, p. 1216.

50 Ekaterina Kravchenko, Alexey Tikhonov, Half of Bankruptcy Proccedings in Russia are Commissioned by Competitors, 2003, <www.klerk.ru/law/articles/6601>.

51 Sergeeva, pp. 13-15.

52 Firestone, *Armed Injustice*, p. 564.

53 Firestone, Criminal Corporate Raiding in Russia, p. 1212.

On the other hand, corporate raiding schemes involving creating “a false power of attorney or other document authorizing him or a co-conspirator to enter into transactions on behalf of the target company and then transfers the target’s assets to himself or affiliated companies”, or “creation of a parallel shareholder register that falsely indicates a majority stake held by individuals and entities friendly to the raiders. This majority stake is then used to elect a new board of directors, which, in turn, transfers the target’s assets to companies controlled by the raider”[54] may still be successful, depending on the corporate governance and awareness levels inherent to target company.

In sum, due to the fact that the relevant amendments to legislation aimed to close the most abused loopholes have been introduced quite recently and there is no information on whether they were successful or not (as well as whether raiders adapted thereto or not), it is hard to evaluate this method.

Similarly to the previous method, there is open source information estimating expenses to corporate takeover as 30-50% of target’s market value.[55]

3.4 *Criminal Case: Extortion*

When it comes to criminal prosecution on artificially created grounds, little may be predicted. More common, however, are situations where the criminal case is based on certain compliance issues that the target company owners or officials actually have, either by construing ambiguous legislation or by applying the law selectively.

The former situation is similar to described above in the Sofex (or “Chemists’”) case, when lacuna or ambiguity in statutory provisions allow corrupt law enforcement officers to prosecute an activity that the business owners bona fide believed lawful. A variation of this method was attaching illegal entrepreneurship (RF Penal Code, Art. 171) and money laundering (RF Penal Code, Art. 174.1) charges to “use a paperwork violation in a company’s registration documents to charge the business owners with illegal entrepreneurship, declare all of the business’s proceeds illegal, and then threaten the owners and employees with aggravated money laundering (an offene which carries up to 15 years incarceration and a fine equal to the defendant’s total earnings).”[56]

---

54 *Id.*

55 Takeover as a Science, Dengi, No. 31(536) as of 8 August 2005, <www.kommersant.ru/doc.aspx?DocsID=599285>.

56 Firestone, *Armed Injustice*, p. 558.

The latter option, when the law is applied correctly but selectively, is an inevitable consequence of taking risks related to conducting business in Russia, where full compliance is virtually impossible, at least in terms of profit making.

Usually it happens this way: after the initial approach when the business owners receive "an offer they cannot refuse they either agree to sell their business to the interested party to reduce harassment, or they face a significant fine or prison term".[57] The owners then either agree and transfer a relevant stake in business to a nominal owner connected with relevant official, or, in the case they refuse, they are incarcerated under pre-trial arrest proceedings. While arrest is supposedly determined by the court, in reality judges rubber-stamp all the motions that prosecution produces. The share of acquittal verdicts is less than 1%.[58] Once incarcerated, conviction just about always follows. If the case really falls apart in court, judge typically sentences defendant to the time he actually served in a pre-trial arrest, to save embarrassing the prosecution.

As mentioned above, there were amendments aimed to limit amendments on white collar crime cases, but courts are reported to circumvent these amendments by arbitrary construing their wording.

There are a number of quotes reporting expenses related to a "commissioned" criminal prosecution initiated against undesired person: $50.000,[59] $20.000 to $50.000,[60] or "starting at $50.000 in Moscow and $20.000 in the regions outside Moscow".[61] It should also be noted that as corrupt and power abusive government officials become more and more involved in raiding activities, these costs may be inapplicable, as they themselves carry almost no expenses to initiate relevant proceedings.

3.5 *Hiding Taken Assets from Recovery*

As one may note from the above description of takeover methods, nearly all of them end with the key assets being taken under a dubious transaction which most probably will be voided in the near future. This is commonly referred to as "asset stripping".[62] Thus, the

57 Settles, pp. 4-5.

58 < www.pravo.ru/news/view/16783/>.

59 V. Parkhomov, Raiding as a New Threat to Russian Business' Safety, (2008). Available at <http://flk.isea.ru/statya2008_04parh.html>.

60 Jason Bush, Russia's Raiders, Spiegel Online, 2008, <www.spiegel.de/international/business/0,1518,558096,00.html>.

61 Firestone, *Criminal Corporate Raiding in Russia*, p. 1209.

62 Tishchenko, p. 4.

sale of assets by a target company to an entity controlled by a raider is by no means the end of the game.

The most common way to get away with what was taken is to convey the asset repeatedly via a chain of re-sales through several formally independent companies. The goal is to obtain protection granted by Russian law to the bona fide purchaser. "During the 'laundering' stage, the raider typically transfers the seized assets through a series of shell companies to an ostensible 'good faith purchaser,' exploiting provisions of Russian law which make recovery of misappropriated assets from a 'good faith purchaser' almost impossible. What this means, as a practical matter, is that even if a raiding victim succeeds in obtaining a court ruling voiding the transfer of his company's assets, he cannot recover the misappropriated assets. As the Chief of the Investigative Committee of the General Procuracy, Aleksander Bastrykhin, has written, 'after a raiding takeover, the property is laundered through a series of fictitious or offshore firms and eventually becomes the property of a good faith purchaser. Demanding it from such an entity is practically impossible.'"[63]

While costs related to re-selling the assets taken from a target company shall also be considered in total takeover costs, they are hard to estimate as the exact prices of incorporating and maintaining corporate vehicles may vary greatly.

4 Covering Your Assets: Building a Fortress Around a Business

The best defences are built before the attack starts. Yet, few business owners devote attention or resources to anti-takeover protection. At best, anti-takeover measures come as a second-tier goals to be reached as a side effect of a business restructuring aimed to attract an investor or prepare business for a sale. Many SMEs cannot afford any protective measures beyond most simple ones. Nonetheless, this section aims to outline directions for making major takeover methods more costly.

4.1 Corporate

Hide the business owner's identity by establishing a corporate structure using offshore vehicles and nominal shareholders, so that on Russian level it would be practically impossible to find out who controls the business.

63 Firestone, *Armed Injustice*, p. 566.

If there are several business owners, conclude a Shareholders' Agreement on off-shores providing therein clauses regulating share transfer restrictions and takeover situations

Centralize and formalize control over the business by implementing legally enforceable mechanisms to relay decisions made by business owner to the operational companies.

Amend Charters to cut CEO's powers to matters that shall be resolved on their level to procure desired balance between efficiency and safety from possible abuse of power.

If there any AO's involved, make sure that share register is kept with a trustworthy Registrar.

Keep corporate documents in a safe place other than premises owned or leased by the Company, where searches and seizures are likely to be conducted.

Monitor State Register on Legal Entities on a regular basis.

4.2 Assets

Conduct an extensive audit of all the key assets (real property, equipment, IP rights etc) and their legal history, and shall any critical risks be revealed, clear them out, *e.g.* by re-selling assets to another entity to enjoy bona fide purchaser protection.

Establish a corporate structure that designates separate formally unrelated vehicles for asset holding and operational activity (thus any risks that may arise out of the latter would not endanger assets).

Split the most valuable assets between separate legal entities, as it is assumed to "complicate and disorganize [the] aggressor's action".[64] Also consider setting a joint tenancy regime on most valued assets.

Encumber (*e.g.* mortgage) assets in favour of other companies, making them less attractive.

Monitor State Register on Real Property on a regular basis.

64 Tishchenko, p. 27.

4.3 Compliance

Conduct an extensive audit of business compliance issues and shall there be any that may entail serious consequences (like substantial fines, operation suspension or criminal charges), clear them out, if it is practicable

Screen business activity that generates the most dangerous compliance issues in a separate legal entity formally unrelated to the rest of the business.

Delegate powers that are related to personal liability for decisions taken to employees. For example if the head of the IT department is made formally responsible for handling software licenses, she shall take liability for pirated software on company computers that a police sweep may reveal.

Ensure that business owners are not personally involved in matters that may entail personal liability (*e.g.* no paper track and no direct orders beyond corporate governance procedures).

4.4 Mining the Business

Create interlocking debts between companies forming a business; base these debts on obligations that are hard to challenge (loans and promissory notes) and that are payable on demand.

Create mechanisms for rapid cash extraction from the operational companies and for transfer of the same to offshore vehicles.

Create a poison pill options for share buyout at non-market price by a reliable third party (or, which is more preferable, by a separate corporate vehicle controlled by business owner).

Ensure that the business may survive and operate for some time without direct supervision from business owner (*e.g.* by creating a board of directors and delegating it necessary powers).

Simultaneously, make it obvious to everyone that the business owner personally is the most key asset of the business and that the business will not survive a day without his or her participation.

Set up a trust owning shares of companies forming a business and insert into a trust deed clauses providing instructions in case of incarceration (putting a protector to supervise the trusts is also an option to consider)

5 Striking A Balance: Whether the Defence Pays off

Every defense has its price, and there are no ready answers whether it is practical to implement certain measures or not. Besides the actual costs related to designing and implementing new corporate business structure, one should consider maintenance costs to be borne by the business on a regular basis, as well as hidden costs resulting, for example, in the inability to benefit from a lenient tax regime or adapting to more complicated decision making procedures.

On the other hand, the positive effect of having defensive measures is not obvious, as the degree of lessening the takeover risk is hard to calculate (due to lack of statistical data). Even with the most sophisticated protective measures in place, absolute protection may not be guaranteed.

Despite, the fact that in reality many decisions on whether to implement defensive measures are inevitably intuitive, having one's own business at stake is a good incentive to at least consider the above measures.

15 *Societas Europae* and Russia-CIS: Article 7

Victoria Gulneva

1 Introduction

The establishment of single integrated market is the one of the primary objectives of the European Union.[1] As the EU Commission notes, harmonization of company law is important for the "creation of the Single Integrated Market for Financial Services and products"[2] and guarantees the freedom of establishment of the companies in the EU.[3] Any company in any Member State may do business in any other Member States. How does that apply by extension to Europe's Partnership Countries?

One of the steps in creating a Single Market through harmonization in company law area is the adoption of "pan-European form of company law",[4] the SE (*Societas Europae).*[5] The SE is created as a legal tool for companies conducting business in several Member States (MS) to operate "as a single company under EU law"[6] through offering to such companies the "reduction of administrative costs and [providing] a legal structure more conducive to carrying out activities within the Single Market as a whole",[7] "freedom of movement ... and more efficiency in the management".[8]

---

1 See Art. 3, para. 3 of the Treaty on European Union (Official Journal 115, 09 May 2008 P. 0017 - 0017) <http://eur-lex.europa.eu/LexUriServ/LexUriServ.do?uri=CELEX:12008M003:EN:HTML>.

2 See <http://ec.europa.eu/internal_market/company/index_en.htm>.

3 *Id.*

4 See Kirshner, Jodie A., A Third Way: Regional Restructuring and the Societas Europaea (2009). Available at SSRN: <http://ssrn.com/abstract=1443383>.

5 Council Regulation (EC) No 2157/2001 of 8 October 2001 on the Statute for a European Company (SE) [2001] O.J. L 294/1. [hereinafter SE Regulation]. See, also, Jan Andersson, *Model Business Corporation Act for Europe — The Alternative to Harmonization by Directives, or?*Scandinavian Studies in Law, 2004, 32. Available at: <www.scandinavianlaw.se/index.php/display>.

6 European Company Statute - Frequently Asked Questions, MEMO/10/592, Date: 19 November 2010 <http://europa.eu/rapid/pressReleasesAction.do?reference=MEMO/10/592&format=HTML&aged=0&language=EN&guiLanguage=en>.

7 *Id.*

8 Karol Linmondin, *The European Company (Societas Europaea) - A Successful Harmonisation of Corporate Governance in the European Union?*, 15 Bond L. Rev. Article 8., 26. (2003). Available at: <http://epublications.bond.edu.au/blr/vol15/iss1/8>.

The main privilege of the SE is mobility within the Community[9] as it may enjoy all the forms of mobility, *i.e.* “cross-border mergers, transfer of registered office, and fiscal neutrality for cross-border transactions”.[10]

However, Article 7 of the SE Regulation expressively requires that “the registered office of an SE shall be located within the Community, in the same MS as its head office. A MS may in addition impose on SEs registered in its territory the obligation of locating their head office and their registered office in the same place”.[11] Generally, this requirement is regarded as decreasing the integrated effect of the SE.[12]

This chapter analyses how Article 7 impacts the implementation of the SE, *i.e.* the transfer of registered office of SE as “freedom of choice to establish and reincorporate in another legislative regimes without any restrictions or high transaction costs is a fundamental precondition for the development of a “market-for-rules”’[13] and for the Single Integrated Market in general. The practice and legal problems arising from such requirement and their possible solution will also be investigated. This chapter also discloses how this limitation of freedom of SE affects Russian business and what conclusions shall be made by CIS countries in this regard.

2 PRACTICAL PROBLEMS OF ARTICLE 7

The necessity of the same location of place of incorporation and the head office involves both practical and legal problems.

According to the Report on the Application of the Statute for a European Company, a number of respondents found the requirement of Article 7 “an obstacle in practice”.[14] These practical obstacles may be divided into two categories: those that affect day-to-day life of the SE, and those that challenges the transfer of seat of SE.

9 Noëlle Lenoir, *The Societas Europaea (SE) in Europe: A promising start and an option with good prospects.* 4 Utrecht L. Rev. 15 (March 2008). Available at: <www.utrechtlawreview.org/index.php/ulr/issue/view/7>.

10 *Id.*, p. 17.

11 See *supra* note 5.

12 Maria Chetcuti Cauchi. *The European Company Statute: Freedom of movement of the Societas Europaea.* <www.chetcuticauchi.com/mcc/research/freedom-of-movement-european-company.htm> (last visited 14 February 2011).

13 Lorenzo Sasso, Societas Europaea: Between Harmonization and Regulatory Competition. *European Company Law*, Vol. 4, 2007, 6. Available at: <http://papers.ssrn.com/sol3/papers.cfm?abstract_id=1698232>.

14 The application of Council Regulation 2157/2001 of 8 October 2001 on the Statute for a European Company (SE), Report From The Commission To The European Parliament And The Council. Available at: <http://eur-lex.europa.eu/LexUriServ/LexUriServ.do?uri=CELEX:52010DC0676:EN:NOT>.

The first difficulty regards the challenges in decision-making process in the SE. The literal reading of Article 7 requires that all the management decisions shall be made by the board of directors when they are physically present in the Member State of the SE incorporation.

This makes it impossible for the SE management to take enjoy national regulations permitting "the board of directors or the management board of companies to be held through video-conferencing or telephone conferencing systems."[15]

Moreover, this involves extra time and extra costs for the SE because the board members, who may reside in different Member States, must travel to the Member State of SE incorporation for making business decision solely to obey the Article 7 requirement. In the modern business world fast decision-making is vital. It is indisputable that the physical necessity of management's presence at the office of incorporation limits the decision-making process, making the SE a less competitive form of legal entity rather than the form of legal entities established at the Member State level.

This obstacle may affect Russian businesses investing in the SE through Cypriot companies. The latest example is the Basic Element Group of Mr. Deripaska, who held 17% of Starbag SE through its Rusperia Trading Ltd. (Cyprus) and may appoint its representatives to the board of Starbag.[16] This may be limit Russian investment into the EU.

The second obstacle arising from Article 7 is connected with the freedom of transfer of registered office granted to SE under Article 8.[17] Article 7 greatly reduces the freedom of Article 8. "Article 7 seems to be paradoxical when compared to the freedom of establishment opportunity presented by Article 8. On the one hand, the SE is a company which has the advantage of transferring its registered office without the need to go through the process of winding up and creating a new legal person and on the other hand, its registered office can only move to another MS if and when the head office is also moved to that same MS."[18]

15 Commission Staff Working Document accompanying the Report (para. 3.2.2). <http://ec.europa.eu/internal_market/company/se/index_en.htm>.

16 See <www.strabag.com/databases/internet/_public/content.nsf/Navigation?OpenAgent &docid= 79E200B4108F278FC125736A0046758E&urldocid=9704F8C7EBBEB0ADC12577BD003CE9DB> and <www.russia-ic.com/news/show/11161/>.

17 See *supra* note 5.

18 See *supra* note 12.

Obviously, this also means additional costs and time.[19] Thus, the time necessary for transfer of the registered office takes in average from two to four months: one month – 8.3%, two months – 19,4%, three months– 13,89%, four months – 13,89%, six months – 11,1%, eight months – 8.3%, nine months – 2,78%.[20]

The only estimation of costs suffered due to transfer of registered office of the SE is € 19.108,33.[21] However, this information does not reflect how the costs for organization of meeting of the board change after the transfer of registered office of SE.

The movement of the board with the registered office also imposes additional costs and challenges to operating of SE. Thus, "redomiciling a head office can pose a threat to a company's public image".[22]

Providing the practical challenges set forth above, I cannot agree with <www.worker-participation.eu> which said that the requirement of Article 7 is not an obstacle in practice. Such conclusion was made by comparison of the number of SEs which transferred their office with the total amount of registered SEs. According to the latest research, 53 SE from 681 of established SE transferred their registered office.[23]

However, this message does not contain the full picture as it made the simple comparison only by correlation between the total numbers of SE transferring their seats with the number of established SEs. Moreover, the small percent of SEs which transferred their seat to the total number of established SE may not mean there is no problem. Instead, it may mean that such advantage of SE as freedom of transfer of seat is limited in its practical application.

Liquidated companies are used as illustrative examples of the Article 7 requirement which limits freedom of transfer of the corporate seat in practice.

19 Jérémie Duhamel Does the European company contribute to freedom of movement of companies? Should it? Are other approaches better? How can they be brought about? <www.juridix.net/eu_soc/movement_se.htm>.

20 See, Factsheet under <http://ec.europa.eu/internal_market/company/se/index_en.htm>.

21 *Id.*

22 See, Lucian Arye Bebchuck and Mark J. Roe, A Theory of Path Dependence in Corporate Ownership and Governance. 52 *Stan. L.Rev.* 127 (1999), citing in *supra* note 4 at p. 12.

23 See, Factsheet under <http://ec.europa.eu/internal_market/company/se/index_en.htm>.

The notable case is Narada Europe SE.[24] Narada Europe SE was created "to be able to move easily between European countries."[25] "Narada SE transferred its seats to the UK on 11-06-2007".[26] "It has four directors in a single-tier board: two are Chinese, and two are Norwegian."[27] In 2009 Narada decided to liquidate and on 2010 it was voluntary liquidated.[28] Under these facts we cannot exclude that the object of creation of SE was not achieved.

The case of Narada is a bad example for the prospects of Russia involvement in EU business environment. As a form of merger of "*Eltek*, a supplier of energy and transmissions systems to the telecommunication industry" and "a Chinese manufacturer of batteries for telecommunication, electronics and information equipment sectors", Narada is generally regarded as an example of cooperation of non-EU business EU business and the reason why SE may be interesting to non-EU business (Russia, India, China).[29]

Therefore, the empirical data evidence that requirement of Article 7 is an obstacle for practical use of SE within the Community and challenge the use of the SE as a form of cooperation of EU and non-EU business.

3 LEGAL PROBLEMS OF ARTICLE 7

Besides the practical obstacles, the requirements of Article 7 raise legal problems too, when examined closely. Article 7's requirement represents "a compromise between real seat theory and incorporation theory".[30] That is the source of the confused rationales of the law here. However, the close connection of the head office with the place of incorporation leads to the result that the real seat approach dominates in SE Regulation.[31]

Some scholars pointed out the unclear use of terms and definitions in the Regulation that challenges the application of real seat theory as well, even despite the incorporation approach. Thus, "doubts remain on the definition of head office (no definition is given in the regulation, should we consider the national cases law?). Moreover, is the real seat the

24 See <http://ecdb.worker-participation.eu/show_factsheets_details.php?se_id=51>.
25 See <www.seeurope-network.org/homepages/seeurope/.../sefactsheets052007.pdf>.
26 *Id.*
27 *Id.*
28 *Id.*
29 Lefevre Pelletier, *by Roland Montfort, Catherine Cathiard and Olivier Kodjo.* The European Company and the Directive 2005/56/EC on cross-border mergers: a view from France <www.imakenews.com/iln/e_article001007397.cfm?x=b11,0,w ≥.
30 *Supra* note 12.
31 Antonio Frada de Sousa. *Company's Cross-border Transfer of Seat in the EU after Cartesio.* Jean Monnet Working Papers No. 07/09, n. 199 (2009)at <http://centers.law.nyu.edu/jeanmonnet/papers/09/090701.html>.

same of the French 'siège réel', or the German 'Sitz'? On the same level, is the 'registered office', the 'siège statutaire'?"[32] All one can say is: "It is potentially problematic to try to decipher where the head office is located. Many times such location is quite unclear as a variety of processes in the administration of the company may be taking place in a variety of locations."[33]

The evidence of the dominance of real seat theory is that under Article 64 the sanction for breach of the unity of place of registration and the head office is liquidation.[34] From the approach of the Member States with incorporation theory, that sanction is too severe and odd because incorporation is the only connecting factor between the Member State and the legal entity and the location of the head office is irrelevant for legality of corporation.[35] The sanction for breach of Article 7 shows the importance of the real seat approach in SE regulation.[36]

Such severe requirements and support of real seat theory in SE Regulation contradicts the EC Treaty (former Articles 43, 48) and decisions made by the ECJ, especially *Überseering*.[37] In *Überseering* the ECJ held that "the freedom of establishment precludes Member States from denying such companies legal capacity and, as a consequence thereof, the capacity to bring legal proceedings before its national courts. ... In addition, the ECJ stated that the Member State has to recognize the legal capacity which the company enjoys under the law of its state of incorporation."[38] Therefore, the literal reading of *Überseering* permits companies registered in one Member State (*i.e.* supporting the incorporation theory) are free to transfer their place of incorporation and are fully recognized and have full legal capacity in the Member States (even those supporting the real seat theory).

However, the idea of *Überseering* does not apply to the SE. For the SE, legal capacity is restricted severely when the head office does not coincide with the place of incorporation.

As Wymeersh argued:

> "as far as the compatibility of these rules with freedom of establishment, as now interpreted by the ECJ is concerned, the exception to the treaty freedom

32 *Supra* note 19.
33 *Supra* note 12.
34 See, *supra* note 5.
35 See, *supra* note 12 and *supra* note 19.
36 *Supra* note 19.
37 See, *supra* note 15, and *supra* note 32.
38 Christoph Teichman, The European Company – A Challenge to Academics, Legislatures and Practitioners, <www.germanlawjournal.com/article.php?id=259>.

> will have to be assessed on the basis of the general good exception. Therefore, and as already mentioned above, the exception can be considered compatible to the extent that is relates to prudential measures, where for reasons of effectiveness of supervision, it can be deemed necessary that the company be located at its head office, and be subject to the jurisdiction of the state where its head office is located. But in other fields, such as the EEIG or the SE, the overall justification is not convincing."[39]

Nevertheless, some argue that such a contradiction is not so clear for the SE. Thus, "some scholars claim [to] try to avoid the problem when they say that the European Company does not fall under Article 43 EC As a counterargument, it has to be mentioned that the European Company fulfils the requirements of Article 43, 48 EC and it is not logical why the first form of a transborder company in Europe should not be entitled to benefit from the principles of the Treaty."[40]

Wymeersh in contrast states that "national companies benefit of a larger freedom of movement by the adoption of an 'apparent formation theory ' (if a company has apparently been formed under the jurisdiction of one legal system, all other Member States have to accept it on its territory)."[41] But it is quite strange "if the judicature finds the Treaty to prohibit Member States from laying down requirements for a company's establishment in another Member State, the Community legislator should be forbidden as well to require the concurrence of the head office and the registered office".[42]

Therefore, the main legal problem of the Article 7 requirement is that it contradicts the basic approach of the EU and rulings of ECJ.

---

39 Wymeersch, Eddy O, *The Transfer of the Company's Seat in European Company Law* ECGI – Law Working Paper No. 08/2003., 33. (March 2003). Available at SSRN: <http://ssrn.com/abstract=384802> or <doi:10.2139/ssrn.384802>.

40 Britta Kügler, The aftermath of Inspire Art -Applicability of the real seat theory and grounds for Justification, 2004 at <http://docs.google.com/viewer?a=v&q=cache:9s4wdMki-iYJ:lup.lub.lu.se/luur/download%3Ffunc%3DdownloadFile%26recordOId%3D1554814%26fileOId%3D1563452+real+seat+theory+SE&hl=ru&gl=ru&pid=bl&srcid=ADGEEShCrM_wgpYKle5PU_ZF6yw7IpfAM9CLJj69fTUjy3i1ocwI-iMpvgo3JJnE2vsmtUUcyRaY1YjO8z5TKVWmzSMsBL6OzKuhGL9U2X5M6yLPpfO-0ZuV24g0nPOzDPKaNNibyH5hS&sig=AHIEtbRSXrSOO3spG7Tol-dbNsJc5uRYHA>.

41 Citing in *supra* note 19.

42 *Supra* note 41.

4 Rethinking Article 7

The requirement of Article 7 and its impact on SE development should be rethought in the EU. The necessity of such rethinking is estimated upon the adoption of SE Regulation as "art. 69 require[s] the Commission to initiate a review of the Regulation within 5 years of its coming into force and one of the subjects specified for review is allowing the location of an SE's head office and registered office in different Member States."[43]

The study of the implementation of the SE by the EU Commission reported that the "significant developments have occurred that have changed the approach to the question of companies' seat. In particular, the jurisprudence of the European Court of Justice has opened the way for acceptance of the principle of separation of registered and head office in the European Union. Furthermore, according to some stakeholders the real seat principle is difficult to apply in practice in a modern world where the location of the headquarters of an international company, the place where the strategic decisions are taken, is not easy to determine. The principle where the applicable company law is determined by the law of the country of the SE's registered office is straightforward and easy to identify."[44]

The Report upholds the idea of separation of real seat of incorporation approaches.[45] Nevertheless, not everybody agrees. Thus,

> "stakeholders, *e.g.* some Member States and trade unions... fear that, *inter alia*, a possibility to separate the registered and the head office could make the fiscal control difficult to apply due to the lack of transparency of information about companies registered in other Member States. Some respondents to the public consultation mentioned a number of practical problems arising from the differences in national rules in the process of transferring the SE's registered office and from burdensome or unclear rules on the SE's internal organization".[46]

---

43 Carsten Frost. Transfer of Company Seat – An Upholding Story in Europe. <http://docs.google.com/viewer?a=v&q=cache:61x8jjKUqQ0J:www.victoria.ac.nz/law/documentation/VUWLR%2520PDFS/36%282%29/Frost.pdf+real+seat+theory+SE&hl=ru&gl=ru&pid=bl&srcid=ADGEESjmIMAAISgPBJXYx9gJt8d66GbZuZpsaftfo1Ub93xkKwkJONJGh4XXxA1CmU55qp3k9v7pqXK0Cgsj5WL3-ZHsSKIqzDGgDRrztLRiAnzWIS9ypnpBDM3Pn38Ynpr4tiRcVghW&sig=AHIEtbSMrDTY0GSSIdPVPJJXTZzQEoXclA>.

44 Report on the application of the Statute for a European Company (SE), available at: <http://ec.europa.eu/internal_market/company/se/index_en.htm>.

45 *Id.*

46 *Id.*

Some practitioners argue that "the SE Statute should offer more flexibility to the founders and shareholders on the internal organization of the SE, even if such flexibility is not available to national companies in the Member State of the SE's registration. This would also reduce the number of references to national legislation. However, as this would result in the SE being in direct competition with the national legal forms, doubt was expressed as to how much could be achieved politically on this issue."[47]

The example of applying Article 7 and possible amendments should be considered by Russia and other CIS states as well. Some scholars in Russia offered to use EU experience with SE implementation to develop a transnational corporate form for the CIS.[48] The idea is that permitting the establishment of transnational corporations will favor economic integration[49] and increase productivity by reducing transaction costs (multiple incorporation) and increasing legal certainty.

Absolutely upholding this approach, we should analyse whether such "Article 7 for CIS" may appear. The answer is "probably not". The battle between the incorporation theory and real seat theory will not be severe in the CIS. This is explained by the fact that the incorporation theory applies nearly uniformly in the CIS.[50] The only former Soviet Republics upholding the real seat theory are Ukraine[51] and Georgia.[52] We should however note the experience of Article 7's application in the cases of companies operating in Russia, Georgia and Ukraine.

Therefore, it shall be concluded that the strict requirement of Article 7 shall be mitigated in favour of achievement of the purposes of a Single Integrated Market; the place of

47 *Id.* [Internal citation omitted].

48 See Inshakova A.O. The Unification of Corporate Regulation in the European Union and the Community of Independent States. Synopsis of thesis for dissertation to doctorate degree. <http://docs.google.com/viewer?a=v&q=cache:imrvlqWvWuYJ:vak.ed.gov.ru/common/img/uploaded/files/vak/announcements/yuridicheskie/14-04-2008/InshakovaAO.pdf+%D0%BD%D0%B0%D0%B4%D0%BD%D0%B0%D1%86%D0%B8%D0%BE%D0%BD%D0%B0%D0%BB%D1%8C%D0%BD%D1%8B%D0%B5+%D0%BA%D0%BE%D0%BC%D0%BF%D0%B0%D0%BD%D0%B8%D0%B8+%D1%8E%D1%80%D0%B8%D0%B4%D0%B8%D1%87%D0%B5%D1%81%D0%BA%D0%B8%D0%B5+%D0%BB%D0%B8%D1%86%D0%B0+%D1%81%D0%BD%D0%B3&hl=ru&gl=ru&pid=bl&srcid=ADGEESjrS10Ok1f06PbFRwOwt_kiVKuvJ9D_IfucsrOe3r0wEGuBVg6k2yAI20sDvgaYIKovd_Fjr-4qvNH8Tv_cIAGgxn5O-6NeVNaBFVkC4b_OoLH34ylH5o5RiYyA-Gbhpmuylr2-&sig=AHIEt-bQr5BNBV9OBkjWRpESKYM_RsFuGcA>.

49 *Id.*

50 The theory of incorporation is applied in art. 1211 Model Civil Code of CIS (part 3). <www.iacis.ru/html/?id=22&pag=29&nid=1>.

51 Ruzakova O.A. Private International Law. 2005. <http://adhdportal.com/book_3391_chapter_15_Rozd%D1%96l_III.html>.

52 See Asoskov A.V. Legal Forms of Participation of Legal Entities in International Commerce. <www.modern-lib.ru/books/asoskov_anton_vladimirovich/pravovie_formi_uchastiya_yuridicheskih_lic_v_mezhdunarodnom_kommercheskom_oborote/>.

incorporation and head office should be separated. This approach will assist integration of Russian business into SE's as well. The lessons of this strict requirement shall be taken by CIS countries in case of creation of similar trans-national corporate entities like the SE in the CIS area.

Part V
Capital Markets

16 The Markets in Financial Instruments Directive (MiFID)

A Major Step to Harmonization of European Financial Markets

Lada Myasnikova

1 Implementation of MiFID and its Objectives

1.1 MiFID as a Key Element of the European Financial Services Plan

The Markets in Financial Instruments Directive[1] (2004/39/EC adopted on 21 April 2004) (further referred to as "MiFID") was intended to play a key role in the harmonization of the European financial markets. The MiFID was elaborated as a key element of the major economic development strategy – European Financial Services Action Plan ("FSAP"). "The objective of MiFID is to foster a fair, competitive, transparent, efficient, and integrated European financial market by providing e regulatory environment that (i) offers high-quality investor protection and (ii) allows for the creation of new markets and services. MiFID ... intended to create a fair, level playing field for the different types of trading platforms".[2]

A historical reference to the work standing behind the adoption of MiFID is presented in the article of Bob Penn "Markets in Financial Instruments Directive (MiFID): an Introduction":

> "MiFID was passed under the 'Lamfalussy process' for EU financial services legislation. "Lamfalussy" Directives are split into two levels – the 'Level 1' Directive which establishes the guiding principles of the legislation and 'Level 2' implementing measures. As Level 2, the Commission has proposed both a regulation ('Level 2 Regulation') and a directive ('Level 2 Directive') and it published drafts of these on 6 February 2006. These were prepared on the basis of advice provided by the Committee of European Securities Regulators

1 OJ L 145/1, 30 April 2004.

2 Hans Degryse, *Competition between financial markets in Europe: what can be expected from MiFID?*, 23 *Financ. Mark. Portf. Manag.*, p. 93, at p. 94 (2009).

> ('CESR'). On 30 June 2006, further drafts were published following their approval by the European Securities Committee ('ESC')".[3]

The FSAP was launched in 1999 to promote a fully integrated European capital market.[4] The main purpose of the FSAP was to provide the legal bedrock for EU financial markets' integration through uniform rules while providing a high level investor protection.[5] The FSAP accounts for the 42 measures aimed at strengthening financial service and securities regulation. Among the mentioned measures are the following key directives adopted after 2003: the Prospectus directive, the Transparency Directive, the Market Abuse Directive and the MiFID. The Prospectus Directive was introduced to adopt a European single passport system for prospectus of financial instrument; the Transparency and the Market Abuse Directives are designed to promote fair dissemination of investment information by issuers, and the purpose of the MiFID is to enable investment firms and exchanges to provide legal services throughout the EU Member States in the up-to-date regulatory framework.

1.2 The MiFID's Objectives

The main three objectives of the Financial Services Action Plan implemented in the MiFID are the following:

> "The three strategic objectives of the FSAP are to ensure a single market of wholesale financial services, to provide an open and secure retail market, and to establish state-of-the-art prudential rules and supervision".[6]

1.3 The Investment Services Directive as a "Draft" MiFID

Investment Services Directive (93/22/EEC) ("ISD") adopted in May 1993 is the basis for MiFID and which demanded improvement by implementation of the new up-to-date directive.

---

3 Bob Penn, 'Markets in Financial Instruments Directive (MiFID): An Introduction', 21 *Butterworths J. Intl. Banking & Fin. L.*, p. 338 (2006).

4 EC. Financial Service: Implementing the Framework for Financial Markets: Action Plan (Nov. 1999), available at <http://ec.europa.edu/internl_market/finances/docs/actionplan/index/action_en.pdf>.

5 Luca Enriques & Matteo Gatti, *Is There a Uniform EU Securities LAW After the Financial Services Action Plan?* (April 2007), available at <http://papers.ssrn.com/sol3/papers.cfm?abstract_id=982282>.

6 Bob Penn, 'Markets in Financial Instruments Directive (MiFID): An Introduction', 21 *Butterworths J. Intl. Banking & Fin. L.*, p.338 (2006).

The ISD provided a high-level of regulation of financial markets for the time it was introduced. However, further development proved that the existing framework required improvement. The essential principle of cross-border regulation of financial services imposed by the ISD is the so called "passport regime". "The ISD provides a high-level framework enabling firms engaging in certain activities (so-called investment firms) to establish branches, or provide services, across borders on the basis of their authorization in their Member State of incorporation ('home Member State') without the need for new authorizations in the Member States into which they do business ('host Member States')."[7] In return for the possibility to do business on the basis of authorizations in the "home Member State", the investment firms had to comply with the basic business requirements of the "host state" with respect to capitalization, organization, conduct of business rules etc.

1.4 ISD's Main Areas Improved by MiFID

The idea behind the European Union – to prevent war and reach peace and prosperity through integrated and harmonized markets[8] – is as relevant for regulation of financial markets as any other EU market and requires above all a harmonized European regulatory framework. The common regulatory framework should provide the same level of protection for investors throughout the Member States.

a. Accordingly, the first incentive for improvement of the ISD is the need to provide a common level of protection for investors among all the European Member States.
b. Another reason for regulatory improvement was the natural development of financial markets introducing into play new financial instruments – certain types of derivatives, based on credit, weather, emissions and other new types.
c. Development of alternative trading systems (as opposed to regulated stock exchanges) revealed the need to bring into conformity the rules protecting consumers interests and protecting free competition.
d. The "passport regime" requires the company to comply with sometimes numerous rules of Member States where the company conducts its business, also required modification in favour of uniform conduct of business rules.

7 *Id.*
8 Lectures on European Union Law, Prof. Eric Engle, Pericles Institute, Moscow 2010.

2 Important New Regulations Presented by MiFID

The MiFID takes the same approach as the ISD regarding permission to perform investment services throughout the territory of European Economic Area on the basis of home state authorization. However, the MiFID presents the following novelties in its regulation.

2.1 *Increased Scope of Regulation*

While the ISD's regulation was aimed at investment services, the MiFID included into the scope of the passport concept the *provision of investment advice* as a core rather than ancillary service. Other services covered by the new Directive include operating a multilateral trading facility, investment services and activities relating to commodity derivatives, credit derivatives and financial contracts for differences.

The main point of the new approach to regulation of cross-border investment services is that Member States may no longer impose their own conduct of business rules, and the rules of home Member State will apply. Thus the "passport regime" will give way to "country of origin regulation".

2.2 *Organisational Requirements*

The MiFID provides more thorough and detailed regulation of conflicts of interests taking place in the functioning of compliance and internal audit, holding client money and assets, outsourcing, continuity arrangements and record-keeping.

Article 13 of MiFID sets up a list of organisational requirements, including:
- establishment of adequate polices and procedures sufficient to ensure compliance of the firm with the directive (including personal account dealing rules);
- arrangements to deal with conflicts of interest ;
- continuity and regularity in performance of investment activities with proportionate systems, resources and procedures;
- taking reasonable steps to avoid undue additional operational risk when relying on a third party for the performance of critical operational functions (outsourcings);
- sound administrative and accounting procedures, internal control mechanisms and effective procedures for risk assessment;
- record-keeping for all services and transactions, in enough detail for the competent authority to monitor compliance;
- safeguarding of client money and assets.

The new detailed organisational requirements will cause substantive work on the part of investment firms and banks to improve their internal organisational policy and implement new procedures.

2.3 *Conduct of Business*

The rules of conduct of business are presented by the MiFID in greater detail and introduce the idea of "best execution" the mandatory obligation to provide best prices for client's orders. Article 21 of MiFID defines the best execution rule, stating in part (1) that: "Member States shall require that investment firms take all reasonable steps to obtain, when executing orders, the best possible result for their clients taking into account price, costs, speed, likelihood of execution and settlement, size, nature or any other consideration relevant to the execution of the order. Nevertheless, whenever there is a specific instruction from the client the investment firm shall execute the order following the specific instruction".

2.4 *Client Categorisation*

The MiFID distinguishes three categories of clients and imposes different client protection levels depending on their categorization: eligible counterparties, professional clients and retail clients. The directive provides for the possibility of changing the category both downwards – resulting in greater protection, and upwards – resulting in lower protection. The option of movement through categories is subject to discretion of the financial regulator in the Member State.

The eligible counterparties category includes (1) *per se* eligible counterparties: regulated entities, pension funds, certain own-account dealers, national governments, central banks and may include (2) other equivalent entities at the option of the individual Member State. The main feature of eligible counterparty category is that conduct of business obligations and best-execution obligations to not apply to investment firms when they enter into transactions with eligible counterparties in respect of any ancillary service directly related to those transactions (Article 24(1) of MiFID).

Professional clients are defined in the Annex II of MiFID as "clients who possess the experience, knowledge and expertise to make its own investment decisions and properly assess the risks that it incurs". Section I defines professional clients that are deemed to be covered by this client category. These are mostly institutional investors that do not need consumer client protection. Annex II of MiFID provides for the changing category possibilities: (1) opt-down and (2) opt-up. A client defined as a professional client by default may request to be treated as a retail client for certain transactions and therefore opt-down for greater investor protection. At the same time, clients not falling within the professional category may request to be treated as professional clients. Section II of Annex II sets forth the procedure to be followed to permit a client to opt-out to the status of professional. "In particular, the firm may opt a client up only if it has assessed the client's expertise and knowledge and is satisfied that the client is capable of making its own investment decisions and understanding the risks involved regarding the types of transactions and services envisaged."[9]

Retail clients are the clients not falling within the above named eligible counterparties or professional counterparties. The Directive contains the definition criteria as well as the procedural requirements in relation to the retail clients status.

Conduct of business requirements imposed by MiFID are set up in detail and are imposed on investment firms based on their category. A general obligation to act honestly, fairly and professionally in accordance with best interests of its clients is established by Article 19(1). In greater detail conduct of business rules are established by Articles 19-24 of MiFID, including obligation to disclose the existence and amount of payment to third party in relation to provision of services, requirement that all communications to clients should be fair, clear and not misleading, disclosure requirements, reporting requirements, best execution rule with respect to orders from both retail and professional clients.

2.5 Transparency Requirements

The MiFID imposes new pre-trade transparency requirements on multilateral trading facilities ("MTFs") and investment firms which deal for their own account systematically of exchange (systematic internalisers or "SIs"), and post-trade transparency requirements on MTFs and investment firms in respect of shares admitted to trade on a regulated market.

> "Transparency is the key issue of MiFID. It is driven by concerns about fragmentation. Fragmentation means the diffusion of liquidity in the market for a particular instrument across multiple trading venues (exchanges, trading sys-

9 Freshfields Bruckhaus Deringer, MiFID: Customer Classification, Suitability and Appropriateness, Briefing April 2006.

> tems and dealers). The concern results from the abolition of the concentration rule."[10]

The MiFID cancels concentration rule enabling competition between the different trading venues and costs of transactions.

> "The aim of the transparency requirements under MiFID is therefore to get the best of both worlds – the cheaper transaction costs associated with an open market for execution venues, and the liquidity and efficient price formation associated with a single market – by regulation".[11]

The MiFID obliges the execution venues to provide transparency on pricing. Pre-trade transparency requirements are supposed to make the price visible across the market. And the post-trade transparency rules will require disclosure after the transaction had been done, so that investors would be able to estimate the quality of execution in comparison with other service providers.

The MiFID accomplishes the goal of intermarket connections by means of enhancing the ability of investment firms to use the European single passport to conduct business throughout the European Union. This goal is accomplished by increased harmonization of national supervisory rules, recognition of MTFs as investment firms able to acquire and use single passport, and requirement placed upon clearing and settlement facilities to permit access to authorized forms.

3 THE IMPACT OF THE MIFID ON EUROPEAN FINANCIAL MARKETS

3.1 The Negative Reflections of the MiFID

The estimation of the results achieved by the MiFI Directive is different. Feedback is mostly positive. However, some skeptical opinions should be mentioned. For example Gary Wright in his article "MiFID: everything changes yet nothing really changes: a commercial view" expresses the opinion that MiFID had forced tight competition of major exchanges, not necessarily leading to best prices for investors. "It is very unlikely that investors have noticed any difference in price due to MiFID but at least the competition produced between

10 Bob Penn, 'Markets in Financial Instruments Directive (MiFID): An Introduction', 22 *Butterworths J. Intl. Banking & Fin. L.*, p. 155 (2007).
11 *Id*, at p. 156.

the new trading venues and the exchanges has caused the exchanges to rethink their prices and their services."[12] With respect to pre- and post-trade transparency rules introduced by MiFID, the market participants brought much debate pointing that the balance should be reached in offering transparency and at the same time allow market players to bring capital to financial markets and gain profit. "The problem comes in that, in the act of being fair and offering transparency, are you restricting the market of being able to have a reasonable chance of making profit? There needs to be balance in the transparency rules which enable fair market but give the opportunity to financial organizations using their own assets to put liquidity into the market to make a profit."[13]

With respect to trade reporting rules implemented by MiFID, although the new reporting system provides for thorough structure of order reports, at the end point it causes higher costs for investors:

> "This really should not be a problem for the market but unfortunately because of the creation of a more complex structure due to the many order/execution venues it has become difficult to produce a central solution. Indeed there is a number of new trade reporting systems which have now been introduced where once there was one. This added complexity and the inclusion of more systems and sources of reporting brings with it added costs. The costs arise initially within the market but will certainly be passed down the chain to the investor. The costs will not be highlighted but included within overall commission and other charges. Trade reporting now really does look like a cure worse than the illness!"[14]

Another important point dropped from the implementation process is delivery information about new benefits to investors. While the MiFID was initially designed to provide greater protection to investors, the mission to inform the investor of the new benefits was somehow omitted and left for the discretion of financial services firms. "BISS Research has found no campaigns to inform investors by any financial services firm. In fact there is still an enormous army of financial services professionals who still do not know what MiFID is and how it affects their business, let alone their clients"[15].

12 Gary Wright, 'MiFID: everything changes yet nothing really changes: a commercial view', 23 *Butterworths J. Intl. Banking & Fin. L.* p. 550, (2008).

13 *Id*, at p. 551.

14 *Id.*

15 *Id*, at p. 550.

3.2 *The Positive Effect of MiFID's Implication*

Among the most recognized achievements of MiFID are introduction of the new trading platforms removing the concentration rule and implementation of the best-execution rule. As the international market practice indicates, the co-existence of financial markets results in greater competition and thus cause further development of the market and increase of its quality. "MiIFD aims at providing a level playing field for trading by imposing uniform transparency requirements, removing the concentration rule, and allowing new trading platforms. MiIFD therefore provides opportunities for both suppliers and demanders of liquidity".[16] There are opposing insights at the effect of new transparency rules. "Indeed, although earlier studies showed negative effects of greater transparency, the most recent evidence suggests that greater transparency promotes liquidity. This reversal in results could be due to technology. Current technology allows investors to closely monitor the limit order book".[17]

The general positive effect of MiIFD should be recognized and credited to the merits of legislators. "The first results from MiFID are already apparent and quite positive – witness the introduction of Instinet Chi-X, Project Turquoise, and BATS and the reactions by incumbent exchanges... MiFID is a principles-based approach that leaves room for interpretation at the implementation stage. The market microstructure literature reveals that often even very minor changes can have important market-wide consequences. European supervisors and regulators should keep this bit of wisdom in mind and closely watch future developments".[18]

4 Any Sanctions for Late Implementation?

According to the intention of the legislators the MiFID should have been implemented throughout the Member States by the 1 November 2007. At that date a new comprehensive framework governing the execution of transactions in financial instruments should have been launched. The market participants should have been entitled for the reduced costs of securities trading on the integrated financial markets. However, at the fixed date the new Directive was still not implemented in some of the Member States. "Yet when the day came, some 13 of the 30 EEA states subject to MiFID were caught with some or all of their

16 Hans Degryse, 'Competition between financial markets in Europe: what can be expected from MiFID?', 23 *Financ. Mark. Portf. Manag.*, p. 93, at p. 101 (2009).

17 *Id.*

18 *Id.*

implementing legislation not yet in force or still being drafted".[19] Among the countries which did not manage to implement the MiFID timely were the Czech Republic, Poland and Spain. The legal consequences of such delay are based on the general obligation of EU Member States to implement Directives correctly according to the timetable specified.

The authorized body to bring infringement proceedings before the European Court of Justice (further – "ECJ") against a state which is in breach of its duty, is the European Commission according to the EC Treaty. Article 226 of the EC Treaty states that bringing the infringement action lie at the discretion of the European Commission:

> "If the Commission considers that a Member State has failed to fulfill an obligation under this Treaty, it shall deliver a reasoned opinion on the matter after giving the State concerned the opportunity to submit its observations.
>
> If the State concerned does not comply with the opinion within the period laid down by the Commission, the latter may bring the matter before the Court of Justice."[20]

The EC Treaty provides for the direct right of the Member State to request ECJ to start infringement proceedings:

> "A Member State which considers that another Member State has failed to fulfill an obligation under this Treaty may bring the matter before the Court of Justice".[21] (Former Art. 227)

However further the Treaty requires the Member State to refer to European Commission first:

> "Before a Member State brings an action against another Member State for an alleged infringement of an obligation under this Treaty, it shall bring the matter before the commission".[22]

The overview of the developments since the missing the deadline for implementation of the MiFID by the Member States is presented in the article "Of MiFID, EC Directives and

---

19 Jeremy Ison, Jeremy Kosky & Carlos Conceicao, 'Of MiFID, EC Directives and Compemsation', 23 *Butterworths J. Intl. Banking & Fin. L.*, p.139 (2008).

20 Official J. European Union, C 321 E/144, 29 December 2006.

21 Official J. European Union, C 321 E/145, 29 December 2006.

22 *Id.*

compensation" by J. Ison and co-authors: "In April 2007 the European Commission instituted infringement proceedings against 24 states that had missed the 31 January 2007 deadline for transposing MiFID into national law. (The gap between that deadline and 1 November was to give market participants time to adapt to the new rules). Proceedings commence with a pre-litigation stage, during which the Commission attempts to bring states into voluntary compliance. Once a state has fully transposed a Directive, proceedings against it are dropped: there is no scope for an action over a past default."[23]

While the Member State does not comply with its obligation to implement the EU legislation properly, it is exposed to financial sanctions by the ECJ. Former Article 228(2) of the EC Treaty reads:

"If the Member State concerned fails to take necessary measures to comply with the Court's judgment within the time limit laid down by the Commission, the latter may bring the case before the Court of Justice. In so doing it shall specify the amount of the lump sum or penalty payment to be paid by the Member State concerned which it considers appropriate in the circumstances.

If the Court of Justice finds that the Member State concerned has not complied with its judgment it may impose a lump sum or penalty on it".[24]

In the above referred article the authors present illustration of imposition penalty on the Member State: "As an illustration, for its failure to implement a Directive on waste disposal, Greece was ordered to pay €20 000 per day between judgment and compliance, plus costs (*Commission v. Greece* [2000] ECR I-5047)".[25] Further, the authors specifically point that complexity of the issues or need for consultation may not be considered as good defence as the court practice shows. Tempting as it might be in the context of MiFID, it is no defence for a Member State to point to the complexity of the issues (*Commission v. Belgium: Re Stock Exchange Listing Directives* [1987] ECR 761), or the need for wide consultation (*Commission v. Luxembourg* (*Re Head of Household Allowance*) [1982] ECR 2175), or the fact that other states have also failed to implement (*Ministere Public v. Blanquernon* [1990] ECR I-83).

23 Jeremy Ison, Jeremy Kosky & Carlos Conceicao, 'Of MiFID, EC Directives and Compemsation', 23 *Butterworths J. Intl. Banking & Fin. L.*, p. 139 (2008).

24 Official J. European Union, C 321 E/145, 29 December 2006.

25 Jeremy Ison, Jeremy Kosky & Carlos Conceicao, 'Of MiFID, EC Directives and Compemsation, 23 *Butterworths J. Intl. Banking & Fin. L.*, p. 139 (2008).

The issue of the right of the individual to claim reparation is considered by the ECJ in the case *Dillenkoffer v. Germany* [1996] ECR I-4845, where the court stated in the paragraphs 21-24 the conditions which must be met in order to enable individuals to recover damages:

> The rule of law infringed must have been intended to confer rights on individuals;
> The breach must have been serious;
> The actual cause should exist between the breach of obligation by the state and the damage of the individual.

Paragraph 26 of *Dillenkoffer* states that failure to transpose the Directive by the deadline would constitute a sufficiently serious breach of EU law.

> "Even if a financial institution could show that MiFID was intended to confer rights on individuals (*e.g.* the wider 'passporting' rights available to firms to offer services across borders), calculating loss and providing causation would be formidable challenge. Account would also be taken of any savings where the claimant had not (yet) incurred compliance costs of the new regime. The length in delay in implementation (with consequent loss of profit) will clearly be critical in any decision by a firm to take legal action."[26]

5 CONCLUSION

The recent Conference on the MIFID review and commodity and exotic derivatives held in September 2010 provided the venue for leading members of the European Commission to appraise the role of MiFID in regulation of financial markets and point out possible areas of the Directive which should be improved. Johathan Faull, Director General, DG Internal Market and Services, European Commission, underlined the vital role of MiFID in intensification of reform in the financial sector and named five areas where targeted modifications were needed: "increased organization, transparency and oversight of various market segments; continued progress towards a genuine single market for investment services; appropriate regulation to keep pace with increasing competition, fragmentation and speed; amendments to meet the new European supervisory structure; and finally, additional transparency and oversight measures in the commodity derivatives market".[27] Commissioner Michael Barnier (Internal Market and Services, European Commission)

26 *Id.*, p.140.

27 Conference on the MiFID review and commodity and exotic derivatives 20-21 September 2010 Summary, available at <http://ec.europa.eu/internal_market/securities/docs/isd/10-09-21-hearing-summary_en.pdf>.

noted the importance of MiFID and its success to date. "...however he also noted that since the original proposal was drafted, the financial world has witnessed deep changes which justify this review. Commissioner Barner stated that questions raised by the crisis must not remain unanswered and that he sought to fulfill four key objectives – increased accountability for financial actors; transparency for all; continuation of fair competition; and restoring confidence in the markets and financial intermediaries".[28]

The MiFID has played its role as a foundation of new reading venues, providing for more competition and thus leading to more liquid market. The following objectives were initially set up for MiFID, as Hans Degryse stated: "to foster a fair, competitive, transparent, efficient, and integrated European financial market by providing a regulatory environment that (i) offers high-quality investor protection and (ii) allows for the creation of new markets and services".[29] Mostly the named objectives were successfully reached; however, further development of European financial markets call for review and perfection of the Directive, which according to the statements of the European Commission may be expected in the near future.

28 *Id.*

29 Hans Degryse, 'Competition between financial markets in Europe: what can be expected from MiFID?', 23 *Financ. Mark. Portf. Manag.*, p. 93, at p. 94 (2009).

17 Insider Dealing and Market Manipulation

US, EU and Russian Federation Practice and Experience

Anna Voronova

1 Introduction

"Exploiting the natural variation of international data, [it could be found] that more stringent insider trading laws are generally associated with more dispersed equity ownership, greater stock price accuracy and greater stock market liquidity, controlling for various economic, legal and institutional factors."[1]

Increased and improved regulation of insider trading is both a cause and consequence of a sophisticated capital market featuring complex corporate shareholding structures and great stock market liquidity.[2] From 1990 to 2010 the world stock market survived several catastrophic events. The latest crisis (2008) showed everybody that information on this market is far from perfect. Even so-called "insiders" such as the Lehman Brothers have no idea in what exactly they are investing and how fast the price of its shares may fall.

In these circumstances, it seems that insider dealing's regulation is absolutely unnecessary. That conclusion may be too hasty. The greatest world financial crisis in history did not bring us to war, as it was in 20th century or earlier. Instead, it increased the number of new treaties about cooperation on different matters, such as transparency in banking sphere and so on, without war because the regulations were deemed by peoples as fair and honest

1 Laura Nyantung Beny, *Insider Trading Laws and Stock Markets Around the World: An Empirical Contribution to the Theoretical Law and Economics Debate*, <http://papers.ssrn.com/sol3/papers.cfm?abstract_id=193070&rec=1&srcabs=654703>.

2 For example, Eric Engle, 'Insider Trading in U.S. and E.U. Law: A Comparison', *European Business Law Review*, Vol. 26, pp. 465-490, 2010, available at: <http:// papers. ssrn.com/sol3/papers.cfm?abstract_id=1271868##>, states that insider dealing regulation is inefficient, because it prohibits or limits this process which is, in fact, the normal reaction of free market to information asymmetry. US regulations on the matter is very unclear (no clear definition of the "inside information", a lot of loopholes lived by the Supreme Court in determination of the term "insider"), and, following his logic, if the insider dealing field is unregulated, it works for the good of the public and financial markets, disseminating information without any restrictions. Following the logic of Laura N. Beny (see above), only "stringent insider trading laws" make the field work better.

for everybody. Insider dealing regulations constitute one piece of this quite balanced system, which worked, honestly speaking, rather well until the 2008 crisis. One of the causes of the 2008 crash was the appearance of overly sophisticated financial instruments, especially derived from the real estate credit market. These instruments were too sophisticated even for Wall Streets traders. The appearance of such instruments was a result of lack of necessary regulation which prohibit such instruments which are too far removed from reality and thus have a tendency to change reality at least on paper.My thesis is that insider dealing regulations is necessary in the structure of securities market regulations. I postulate that imposing the law on insider dealing, which is consistent with the rules in the US, the EU and Russia in 2010, is a good thing. This fact shows a trend to a global security market, in which more and more countries are becoming involved.

2 The US as a Pioneer in Regulation of Insider Dealing and Market Manipulation

2.1 Terms and Definitions – Insider, Insider Dealing; Brief Historical Overview and Current Rules

The prohibition of insider trading originally evolved in the United States as a matter of the state law fiduciary duties of corporate directors and officers. Even after securities regulation became a matter principally of federal concern, following the adoption of the Securities Act of 1933 and the Securities Exchange Act of 1934, federal law continued to largely ignore insider trading until the late 1960s. In the last four decades, however, federal prohibition of insider trading has emerged as a central feature of modern US securities regulation.[3]

For my short overview of US history of insider dealing regulation I would like to refer[4] to the Speech by SEC Staff: Insider Trading – A US Perspective on 16th International Symposium on Economic Crime, Jesus College, Cambridge, England, 19 September 1998.[5]

After the United States stock market crash of 1929, Congress enacted the Securities Act of 1933 and the Securities Exchange Act of 1934, aimed at controlling the abuses believed

3 Stephen M. Bainbridge, *An Overview of US Insider Trading Law: Lessons for the EU?*, Research Paper No. 05-5, UCLA School of Law (2004), <http://papers.ssrn.com/sol3/papers.cfm?abstract_id=654703>.

4 Also you may find a very good overview of this issue in Stephen J.Choi, A.c.Pritchard, *Securities Regulations: Essentials*, Wolters Kluwer, 2008, p. 149.

5 *Speech by SEC Staff: Insider Trading – A U.S. Perspective*, on 16th International Symposium on Economic Crime, Jesus College, Cambridge, England, 19 September 1998. Available in full at: <www.sec.gov/news/speech/speecharchive/1998/spch221.htm>.

to have contributed to the crash. The 1934 Act addressed insider trading directly through Section 16(b) and indirectly through Section 10(b).

Section 16(b) prohibits short-swing profits (profits realized in any period less than six months) by corporate insiders in their own corporation's stock, except in very limited circumstance. It applies only to directors or officers of the corporation and those holding greater than 10% of the stock and is designed to prevent insider trading by those most likely to be privy to important corporate information.

Section 10(b) of the Securities and Exchange Act of 1934 makes it unlawful for any person "to use or employ, in connection with the purchase or sale of any security registered on a national securities exchange or any security not so registered, any manipulative or deceptive device or contrivance in contravention of such rules and regulations as the [SEC] may prescribe." To implement Section 10(b), the SEC adopted Rule 10b-5, which provides, in relevant part:

> It shall be unlawful for any person, directly or indirectly ...,
> a. to employ any device, scheme, or artifice to defraud,
> b. to make any untrue statement of a material fact or omit to state a material fact necessary in order to make the statements made, in light of the circumstances under which they were made, not misleading, or
> c. to engage in any act, practice, or course of business which operates or would operate as a fraud or deceit upon any person, in connection with the purchase or sale of a security.[6]

These broad anti-fraud provisions make it unlawful to engage in fraud or misrepresentation in connection with the purchase or sale of a security.[7] While they do not speak expressly to insider trading, here is where the courts have exercised the authority that has led to the most important developments in insider trading law in the United States.

The breadth of the anti-fraud provisions leaves much room for interpretation and the flexibility to meet new schemes and contrivances head on. Moral imperatives have driven the development of insider trading law in the United States. And the development of insider trading law has not progressed with logical precision as the reach of the anti-fraud provisions to cover insider trading has expanded and contracted over time.

6 17 C.F.R. § 240.10b-5.
7 Section 17(a) of the Securities Act of 1933 reaches similar fraud in the initial offering or sale of a security.

The anti-fraud provisions were relatively easy to apply to the corporate insider who secretly traded in his own company's stock while in possession of inside information because such behavior fit within traditional notions of fraud. Far less clear was whether Section 10(b) and Rule 10b-5 prohibited insider trading by a corporate "outsider".[8]

During several decades the courts resolved several cases on insider trading which resulted in a set of rules for "outside" insiders.[9] The most famous and important from them are *SEC v. Texas Gulf Sulphur Co.*, 401 F.2d 833 (2d Cir. 1968), cert. denied, 394 U.S. 976 (1969), *Chiarella v. United States*, 445 U.S. 222 (1980), *United States v. Newman*, 664 F.2d 12 (2d Cir. 1981), aff'd after remand, 722 F.2d 729 (2d Cir. 1983), cert. denied, 464 U.S. 863 (1983), *Dirks v. SEC*(463 U.S. 646 (1983), *United States v. Carpenter*, 791 F.2d 1024 (2d Cir. 1986), aff'd 484 U.S. 19 (1987), *United States v. O'Hagan* 117 S. Ct. 2199 (1997).[10]

Through the rules and court decisions the term "inside information" was defined as "material non-public information" which, being known by reasonable investor, may influence his decisions to buy or to sell.

However, there is still a problem with the definition of the term "insider". Broadly speaking, it is a person who has a fiduciary duty to another person, whether natural or legal, from whom he receives insider information and tries to convert such information into a personal gain. In practice, it is sometimes impossible to determine whether a person has such a duty, or not, or what shall court do with a person, who do not have such a duty, but somehow receives such an information from the insider intentionally, occasionally, etc.

Nevertheless, US regulation of insider dealing has the longest history and the deepest analysis of the matter through the court decisions and SEC rules, commentaries and special instructions. That is why it was used by the EU for consolidating and updating of its own rules on insider dealing.

---

8 *Speech by SEC Staff: Insider Trading – A U.S. Perspective*, on 16th International Symposium on Economic Crime, Jesus College, Cambridge, England, 19 September 1998. Available in full at: <www.sec.gov/news/speech/speecharchive/1998/spch221.htm>.

9 *Id.*

10 For additional case law commentary see Kathleen F. Brickey, *Corporate and White Collar Crime. Cases and Materials*, 4th edition, Aspen Publishers, 2006, pp. 155, 168.

3 EU Insider Dealing Rules and Their Interaction and Coordination with US Regulations

The rest of the world's financial markets, with few exceptions, went almost unregulated until the 1980s. The first wide-ranging development outside the United States in efforts to ban insider trading was the European Community Directive Coordinating Regulations on Insider Trading, adopted on 13 November 1989 (the "EC Directive 1989"),[11] in order to create a single financial market in Europe. This Directive existed until new version of this Directive came into force – Directive 2003/6/EC of the European Parliament and of the Council of 28 January 2003 on insider dealing and market manipulation (market abuse) (the "Directive 2003").

Main definitions (like "insider information") were improved and clarified in accordance with previous European case law; new definitions and technical provisions (like "financial instruments") were introduced in order to meet needs of developed financial markets; several gaps, determined by the courts during the existence of first Directive 1989 were filled; and now Directive 2003 also covers market manipulation.

In comparison with the US regulations EU rules have the same goals: protection of the integrity of the market, of investors, and of investor's confidence in financial markets. A special goal for the EU also exists: to establish a minimum standard of insider dealing regulation for the Member States of the Union.

Definition of the term "insider information" in EU has the same features as its definition in the US: information of "precise nature", which non-public.[12] However, definition of

11 Council Directive 89/592 Coordinating Regulations on Insider Trading, 1 Common Mkt. Rep. (CCH) 1761 ("Directive 1989").

12 Art. 1 of the Directive 2003/6/EC of the European Parliament and of the Council of 28 January 2003 on insider dealing and market manipulation (market abuse) (Available at: <http://eur-lex.europa.eu/LexUriServ/LexUriServ.do?uri=OJ:L:2003:096:0016:0016:EN:PDF>):
"Inside information" shall mean information of a *precise nature* which has not been made public, relating, directly or indirectly, to one or more issuers of financial instruments or to one or more financial instruments and which, if it were made public, would be likely to have a significant effect on the prices of those financial instruments or on the price of related derivative financial instruments.
In relation to derivatives on commodities, "inside information" shall mean information of a precise nature which has not been made public, relating, directly or indirectly, to one or more such derivatives and which users of markets on which such derivatives are traded would expect to receive in accordance with accepted market practices on those markets.
For persons charged with the execution of orders concerning financial instruments, "inside information" shall also mean information conveyed by a client and related to the client's pending orders, which is of a precise nature, which relates directly or indirectly to one or more issuers of financial instruments or to one or more financial instruments, and which, if it were made public, would be likely to have a significant effect on the prices of those financial instruments or on the price of related derivative financial instruments.

insider does not demand the person have a fiduciary duty to the source of information, unlike the US (Arts. 2 and 4 of the 2003 Directive).[13] The "insider" just shall know or ought to know that information is "inside".

Without any doubts, European legislation was influenced by American rules. Nevertheless, European legislation is a little bit more "up to date", because of 2003 consolidation and renovation. American legislators leaft all loopholes to the courts, which prefer to decide cases on a "case-by-case" basis, without addressing universal rules for insider dealing, whereas united Europe tries to introduce minimal common universal standards within its borders. These facts show us the usual difference between common law and civilianist law countries, which are two ways to address a given legal issue. In the next part of my article I will discuss the "Russian way" of addressing insider dealing issues.

4 Russian Rules on Insider Trading and Market Manipulation

For the first time in the history of the Russian Federation, Federal law 224-FZ dated 27 July 2010 "About countermeasures against illegal use of insider information and market manipulation"[14] (hereinafter – the "Law") has been enacted. The Law is in force as of January 2011. The bill of this Law has been discussed and drafted for the period of almost ten years before it became a reality in the Russian legal system; it became a reality only after several years of intensive growth and the subsequent crash of Russian stock market in 2008.

---

13 Art. 2 of the Directive 2003/6/EC of the European Parliament and of the Council of 28 January 2003 on insider dealing and market manipulation (market abuse) provides:
Member States shall prohibit *any person referred* to in the second subparagraph who possesses inside information from using that information by acquiring or disposing of, or by trying to acquire or dispose of, for his own account or for the account of a third party, either directly or indirectly, financial instruments to which that information relates. The first subparagraph shall apply to any person who possesses that information:
(a) by virtue of his membership of the administrative, management or supervisory bodies of the issuer; or
(b) by virtue of his holding in the capital of the issuer; or
(c) by virtue of his having access to the information through the exercise of his employment, profession or duties; or
(d) by virtue of his criminal activities.
And Art. 4 states that "Member States shall ensure that Arts. 2 and 3 also apply to any person, other than the persons referred to in those Articles, *who possesses inside information while that person knows, or ought to have known, that it is inside information.*"

14 Российская Федерацияфедеральный Законо Противодействиинеправомерному Использованию Инсайдерской Информациии Манипулированию Рынком И О Внесении Изменений В Отдельныезаконодательные Акты Российской Федерации (Federal law 224-FZ dated 27 July 2010 "About countermeasures against illegal use of insider information and market manipulation"). Available in Russian at: <http://base.consultant.ru/cons/cgi/online.cgi?req=doc;base=LAW;n=103037;div=LAW;mb=LAW;opt=1;ts=DB5E93EF4DF94351C70AA7AB1ACE6DED>.

The purposes of the law set out in its Article 1 defined as next: "*provision of fair price formation for financial instruments, foreign currency and (or) goods, provision of investors' equality and investors' confidence building, and also provision of preclusion of market abuse in a forms of illegal use of insider information and (or) market manipulation*".

This definition looks similar to the US and EU purposes of establishing of rules on insider dealing. However, there are no ideas about market integrity and investor protection. Instead, the Russian law states that fair price formation shall be provided, not investors security; equality of investors shall be guaranteed, not the protection of them; and inside dealing rules cover currency and goods pricing. In such mismatches I see, next, three points:

1) Possibly, the Russian legislators will try to find their "own ways" to address any problem. The problem of insider dealing has almost one hundred years of history in at least one country – the United States. This is reflected in the recent codification of all experience in the field in the EU Directive 2003. However, the new Russian law seems almost unfamiliar with foreign practice or voluntary ignoring it without any justification (as shown below).

2) Several provisions of the law provide exceptions from regulation, for example, Article 1, p. 3, exempts the Central Bank, Government and municipal authorities; that clearly shows that legislators still deem the law as an "instrument of the ruling class", not as a neutral instrument for solving arguments.[15] This also shows that legislators gave some preferences to the governmental bodies. This explanation was provided: the Central Bank (and persons acting on its behalf) is not subject to the provisions of the law when the Bank undertakes transactions with financial instruments and (or) foreign currency "for the purposes of implementation by Central Bank an unitary state monetary and credit policy, and of ruble protection and stabilization". However, that explanation is too vague and does not contain the prohibition of inside information use in cases where such use could result in substantial harm to ordinary investors. It also does not contain an obligation to cover the damages incurred by ordinary investors because of the Central Bank or its agents' transactions. Concerning the Government and municipal authorities, it is clear that their exclusion from the scope of the Law was made for the purposes of state or municipal' debt management. The justification also seems too vague, and no measures to prevent or mitigate the harm from the state agents were established. By such provisions the State reserves a right for itself to trade on inside information. Perhaps the State should have such a right, but which measures would prevent the State from using such rights against private interests?

15 Firestone, Thomas, 'Armed Injustice: Abuse of the Law and Complex Crime in Post-Soviet Russia', *Denv.J.Int'l L.& Pol'y*, Vol. 38:4, pp. 555, 572.

An obvious example: approval from the government FFMS[16] is required for several types of deals, such as mergers and acquisitions. In essence, the Government acts through the FFMS. The FFMS is an agent of the Government. Through intrastate informational channels, information about the merger/acquisition comes into possession of the Government. The government may now legally trade on the basis of that information without any restrictions or refuse to permit the the merger/acquisition. That seems unfair.

3) Several important issues, like a list of information, which could be recognized as inside information, were left to the discretion of FFMS (for the whole market) or state or municipal bodies or their agents – who, under the law of the Russian Federation, have the authority to invest temporarily surplus funds into financial instruments. It makes the law at the current moment unenforceable *de facto*. It usually takes up to two years to receive necessary acts from the Federal Service, and also, at least a couple of years to build some practice and understanding on the market and an eternity to fill the loopholes.

The official date when the law became effective is January 2011. The main highlights of this act follow.

The Scope of the new law main rules and provision which would constitute a new regime of insider dealing in Russia.

The new law:
- defines the term "insider information";
- lists actions which could be deemed as "market manipulation" and defines "market manipulation"; see, Article 185.3 of Criminal Code of Russian Federation;
- lists legal and natural persons which could be deemed as "insiders" (no definition) and their obligations arising from this status;
- directly prohibits transfer of insider information' to third persons and prohibits use of insider information in transactions with financial instruments, securities and goods;
- provides for criminal and administrative liability for the illegal use of insider information and market manipulation.

4.1 *Main Terms and Definitions*

Insider information is defined as a "Precise and concrete information which was not made publicly available or disseminated (including data which constitutes commercial, official, bank secret, postal money order secret (in part of postal money transfers) and other data

16 Federal Financial Market Service (FFMS) – Federal'naya Slugba po Finansovym Rynkam (FSFM).

protected by law), and dissemination or disclosure of which may significantly influence the prices of financial instruments, foreign currency and (or) goods and *which related to the information, included in corresponding list of insider information.*"

The last part of this definition refers to the FFMS regulations or to the internal regulations of the bodies defined in Article 3 of the law which do not exist yet.

Market manipulation is defined as intentional dissemination through the mass media, including electronic, informational, telecommunication public networks (including Internet) of information which is known to be false, or commiting of transactions with financial instruments, foreign currency and (or) goods or commitment of other intended actions which is prohibited by legislation on illegal use of insider information and market manipulation in matters of the Russian Federation, if as a result of such actions price, demand or supply of financial instrument, foreign currency or good became out of the level, which could be formed without the above mentioned actions, and such actions resulted in significant damage for citizens, legal entities or State, or resulted in excessive revenue or in avoidance of significant damages for violator.

Insiders. The Russian legislator choose a quite strange way how to define who is an insider. He made a list of them and included in this list:

- issuers and management companies;
- legal entities which have dominant position in the market in accordance with Federal law No. 135-FZ dated 26 July 2006 ("Competition Law");
- trade organizers, clearing organizations, depositories and credit organizations which settle accounts for clients' operations through the trade organizers;
- professional participants of stock market and other persons which carry out clients' operations with financial instruments, foreign currency and (or) goods on the basis of insider information obtained from the clients;
- persons who may obtain information from the abovementioned persons on the basis of the concluded agreements, including auditors (auditors' organizations), appraisers, professional participants of stock market, credit organizations and insurance companies;
- persons owning 25% of the issued stock of the company' and other persons, who have access to the insider information because of direct authorization by provision of Russian law;
- members of the Board of Directors, CEO (including managing companies, managing or temporary administrators), members of auditing committee;
- persons who have an access to the information about directing of mandatory, voluntary or competitive offer for stock purchase in accordance with Russian Federation legislation

about stock companies, including persons who directed such offers, credit organization which provided bank guarantee, appraiser;
- federal executive authorities, subject's of the Russian Federation' executive authorities, local authorities and other state bodies which under the law of Russian Federation authorized to invest temporarily surplus funds into financial instruments, Bank of Russia;
- heads of the above mentioned authorities, employers of the Bank of Russia, members of National banking council;
- informational agencies which provide mandatory disclosure or dissemination of information for persons defined in 1-4, 9 paragraph of this Article, Bank of Russia;
- rating agencies which give ratings for persons defined in 1-4, and also for securities;
- natural persons who have access to insider information on the basis of employment contracts or on the basis of the civil contracts.

All these insiders could be divided into three categories: financial intermediaries and consultants, governmental bodies, and "real insiders".[17] There is no discussion about fiduciary duty to the source of information. There is also no discussion about so called tippees of different kinds, just a list of insiders. My guess that it is not enough for insider dealing matter regulation, because the question "who is an insider", which is the key question for such regulation, was not answered very well, and even the logic of the legislator is not clear for addressees of this law.

4.2 *Restrictions for Insider Information Use*

Article 6 of the law "About countermeasures against illegal use of insider information and market manipulation" prohibits any person from using of insider information:
- for making transactions with financial instruments, foreign currency and (or) goods, which insider information is about, on his own behalf or on behalf of any third person, excluding operations in the framework of previously agreed deals, which were agreed before the insider information became known to the such person;
- by transmitting such information to any third person, excluding cases where such information transmitted to a person, listed in the list of insiders, in connection with his obligations fulfilment under the laws, employment contract or in accordance with contract' obligations;

17 There is another classification of the subjects of this law, given by Russian lawyer I.Goryachev in his article, available in Russian at: <http://lawfirm.ru/article/index.php?id=798>. Goryachev divided insiders into five groups: trade participants, corporate subjects, natural persons, representatives of the Government, information and rating agencies.

- by giving recommendations to any third persons, obliging or stimulating them by any way to purchase or sell financial instruments, foreign currency and (or) goods.

4.3 *Liability for the Violations of the Law*

Two types of liability provided by the new law for insider dealing and market manipulation are:

1. Criminal liability[18] in the form of fine and imprisonment (maximum term of imprisonment is seven years).
2. Administrative liability for natural persons (maximum fine is app. $170) and government officers (maximum fine is app. $1.700) and for legal entities in the amount of no less than app. $17.000 in cases when excessive revenue was made or losses were avoided.

Also, if the violator has a special license for its activity on stock markets (such as broker or dealer license), such license could be cancelled and a person prohibited from the activity in the field for some period.

Commentaries of Russian Lawyers About the Future Use of the New Law

There are not too many commentaries on the matter yet, because the list of insider information is not published by the FFMS. Nor have any lists of insiders in financial institutions been drafted. The law enters into in force until January 2011. There are only rare thoughts that it is positive sign of Russian stock market development and some critique.

For example, Pepelyaev Group (one of the leading Russian law firms) pointed out[19] that law does not contain any provision that may prevent Russian government officers from making statements which influence stock prices of several issuers, what happened very often (here we do not take into account official macroeconomic statements). Also they noted that it is interesting that provisions about criminal liability will be in force only three years after the law's implementation. That means that criminal liability will be a reality only after January 2014. It shows that legislators do not expect very rapid compliance by market participants with this law. The questions whether deals concluded on the basis of insider information should be voided (or voidable) has not been decided. In the Russian reality, such a strict prohibition might bring about a collapse of the stock market. On the other hand, the violator could pay a fine and continue to violate the rules. Taking into

18 In Russia criminal liability exists only for natural persons.

19 Pepelyaev Group, *Illegal Use of Insider Information*, available in Russian at: <http://lawfirm.ru/article/index.php?id=777>.

account the volume of funds which are involved in the stock market, fines, only, will not change the situation.

5 Conclusion

Without any doubt, implementation of the law on insider dealing and market manipulation is a good sign. The government is at least trying to regulate the field. Implementation of such rules will bring us closer to the internationally recognized standards of insider dealing regulations, and to the possibility of closer cooperation with the International Organization of Securities Commissions (IOSCO) and the financial authorities and regulators of other countries.

Nevertheless, even a brief analysis shows that rules are very vague. Several questions were not well resolved. One of the main definitions – insider – was defined through the list of persons. Some issues were not addressed at all such as the liability of government officers responsibility. Effective exemptions for state and municipal financial bodies were given without any logic or limitations.

I would like to attribute such defects to the transition condition of my country and will wait for practice developments which, without any doubts, will raise unaddressed or unsolved questions sooner or later.

Part VI
Taxation

18 Thin Capitalization and Deduction of Interest Paid on Foreign Loans

A Veiled Threat to Foreign Investors?

Dariya Lulakova Aydyn

1 Introduction

The international economic environment, is highly turbulent and subject to constant changes and presents modern companies with a growing number of quite sophisticated challenges. Raising capital and reducing costs in this world of changes are the most vital and pressing of them. And, naturally, the rules become more complicated for the market players when the economic and legal systems of two or even more countries are in concern, which is not so unusual for an interdependent and continuously globalising economy of nowadays.

Generally, "companies seek financing either through equity (privately-held stakes or public share placements) or through loan facilities. The latter offers significant tax advantages, as interest payments are tax-deductible expenses in most countries – including [...] Russia. However, in [case] a company in Russia seeks debt financing from its owners, thin capitalization rules can prove highly problematic from the standpoint of Russian tax legislation".[1]

The thin capitalization rule was introduced into the Russian Tax Code (the Tax Code) in 2002.[2] "This special rule for tax treatment of interest paid on loans was introduced as a means of fighting [abusive] tax minimization".[3] Since then, the broad and ambiguous phrasing of the statute has been subject to a wide range of interpretations by both state authorities and taxpayers.

1 Olga Sorokina, *Thin Capitalization and Controlled Debt: Taxation and Legal Issues in Russia* (3 December 2008) (available at <www.acg.ru/english/news2.phtml?m=3710>) (accessed 18 December 2010).

2 Introduced by Federal law N-57-FZ, §74, 29 May 2002. See <www.consultant.ru/online/base/?req=doc;base=LAW;n=90080;p=3#p792> (Russian text, last accessed 18 December 2010).

3 Stepan Guzey, Andrey Tsyb, *Thin Capitalization – International Experience and Russian Practic*, p. 1 (July 2009) (available at <www.legal500.com/assets/images/stories/thin_capitalization_in_russia.pdf>).

Some of the most intense disputes, naturally, end up probated in court. And while the latest decisions of the higher level courts prove to rule in favour of the taxpayers, the lower level courts tend to support much less favourable, but even more strict positions of the tax authorities. Moreover, the Tax Code itself is subject to continuous amendments and additions.

Are these all naturally evolutional and positive changes of Russian economy and legislation – or veiled threats for foreign investment business? This chapter looks into these questions one by one.

2 Legislative Framework

The rule of thin capitalization is provided by the laws of many countries. "The national laws of many EU Member states include provisions according to which an infra-group cross-border interest payment may be treated as non-deductible dividend in a thin capitalisation situation."[4] "In Germany, for example, the thin capitalization rule has been known for long as a way to tackle tax dodgers .... France is one of the few countries where interest expenses borne in connection with the acquisition of shares or financing (also by the "related parties") are tax deductible[5] .... The mechanism for enforcing the thin capitalization rule may be found in UK laws, too."[6] And these rules are subject to constant amendments: the major changes took place in European tax legislation in 2002-2006 in response to the judgment of a famous *Lankhorst-Hohorst* case.[7] Russia is not the first and not the only country applying the thin capitalisation rule and trying to remodel it in order to improve the efficiency of its application.

4 M. Helminen, *EU tax law: direct taxation*, 87 (IBFD 2009) (available at: <http://books.google.ru/books?id=JDLGMplAoU8C &pg=PA87&dq=thin+capitalization+eu&hl=ru&ei=BRoNTZvIDc2VOrqwhaEJ&sa=X&oi=book_result&ct=result&resnum=3&ved=0CDMQ6AEwAg#v=onepage&q=thin%20capitalization%20eu&f=false>).

5 See also Catherine Charpentier, Nadune Gelli, *French Thin Capitalisation Rules* (Feb. 2008)(available at <www.ashurst.com/page.aspx?id_content=2407>).

6 See Guzey, Tsyb, *Thin Capitalization – International Experience and Russian Practice.*

7 See generally Case C-324/00 *Lankhorst-Hohorst* [2002] ECR 1-11779, B.J.M. Terra, Peter Jacob Wattèl, *European Tax Law*, 584 (Kluver 2008). Available at: <http://books.google.ru>; Helminen, *EU Tax Law: Direct Taxation*; see also Claire Guionnet-Moalic, *New French Thin Capitalisation Rules: Limitations on Interest Paid, Tax Planning International Review*, BNA (Feb. 2006) (available at: <www.hugheshubbard.com/files/Publication/f0ef2ae1-d745-49e0-b47c-a8980dd98e7f/Presentation/PublicationAttachment/4b4701a2-bbff-429d-a013-a8f5aa8c0e8a/Article_New_French_Thin_Capitalisation_Rules.pdf>); HM Revenue & Customs, *NTM561000 – Thin capitalisation: FA2004 legislation – main changes to the thin capitalisation legislation*, <www.hmrc.gov.uk/manuals/intmanual/INTM561000.htm> or John Neighbour, Daniel Head and Trevor Danks (KPMG UK), *HMRC's Updated Thin Capitalisation Guidance*, <http://rd.kpmg.co.uk/WhatWeDo/20491.htm> (accessed 18 December 2010).

Currently, the Russian thin capitalisation rule is provided in Article 269(2) of the Tax Code and it is applied to the interest payments on so-called "controlled debts".[8] Namely, in case the amount of the "controlled debt" of a Russian borrowing company is three times larger than its equity, "then the interest on such "controlled debt" cannot be deducted in full.[9] "The excess interest is considered a dividend, which is non-deductible for profits tax purposes and generally is subject to withholding tax of 15% or lower rate under an applicable [Double Taxation Treaty]."[10] "Therefore, the key question in any group financing is whether the debt can be viewed as [a] 'controlled debt'."[11]

> "According to Article 269(2), 'controlled debt' of a Russian company exists in the following three situations:
>
> 1) A Russian company has an outstanding debt to a foreign company which, directly or indirectly, owns more than 20 percent of the charter capital in the Russian company;

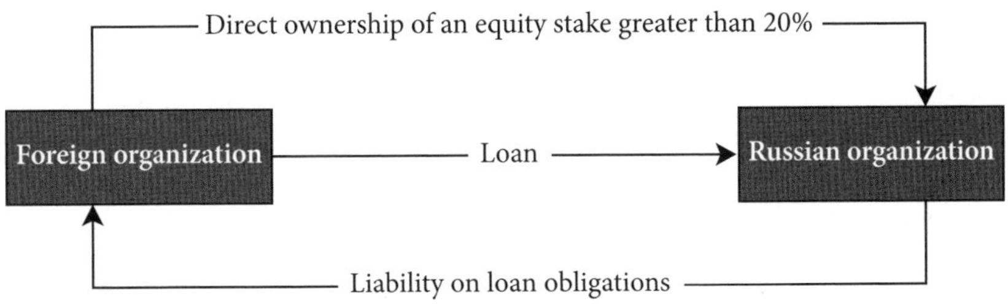

> 2) A Russian company has an outstanding debt to another Russian company, which is an affiliate of a foreign company which, directly or indirectly, owns more than 20 percent of the charter capital in the first Russian company;

Indirect ownership of an equity stake greater than 20%

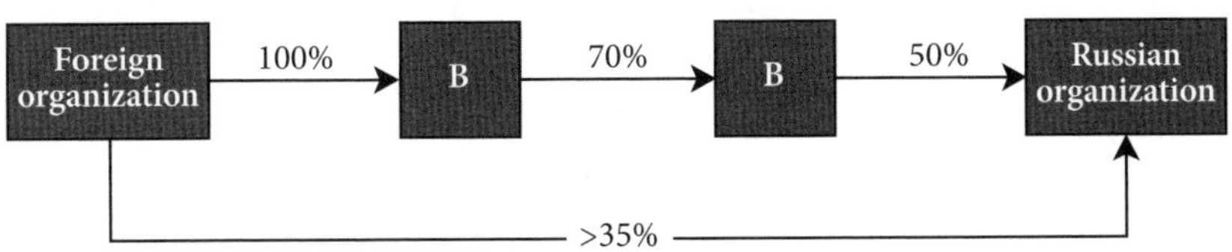

8 See Article 269 (Russian text) (available at <www.consultant.ru/popular/nalog2/3_4.html#p6379> (current at 18 December 2010), etc.

9 Anna Lesova, Judith Harger, *New Ruling on Russian "Thin Capital" Limitations for Loans, Russian Law News (Dewey & LeBoeuf LLP)* (Oct. 2010) (available at <www.russianlaws.com/newsdetail.aspx?news=7215>).

10 KPMG, *Doing Business in Russia* (2008) (available at <www.kpmg.ru/russian/supl/library/taxlegal/Doing_business_in_Russia.pdf>).

11 *Supra*, see also *id.*

3) A Russian company has an outstanding debt under a loan which is secured by a foreign legal entity, which, directly or indirectly, owns more than 20 percent of the charter capital in that Russian legal entity, or by a Russian affiliate of such foreign legal entity."[12]

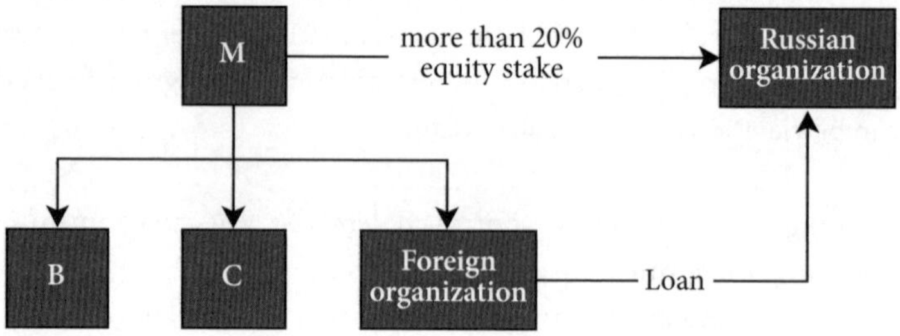

3 Court Decisions Preventing Further Strictening of the Official State Authorities' Position

3.1 Significance of the Court Decisions for Tax Regulation Sphere in Russia

"Although Russia is not a common law jurisdiction, the role of case law in the resolution of tax disputes has increased significantly over the last decade. In the absence of any statutory general anti-avoidance rules, in tax disputes the courts frequently invoke various fiscal realism case law doctrines introduced by the highest courts of the Russian Federation, such as the 'bona fide' concept, 'unjustified tax benefit,' 'business purpose' or a 'substance over form' principle. In 2006, the Presidium of the Supreme Arbitrazh Court adopted a resolution that effectively gives precedence to 'substance' over 'form,' and introduces a test for determining whether the companies involved in a transaction have legitimate business goals or are using a purely tax-driven structure aimed at avoiding Russian taxes." Some examples of the most famous court decisions given below perfectly illustrate the current ambiguity of the thin capitalisation rule application in Russia.[13]

12 *Id.*

13 Lesova, Harger, *New Ruling on Russian "Thin Capital" Limitations for Loans, Russian Law News (Dewey & LeBoeuf LLP).*

3.2 *Taxpayers vs. Authorities – A Classic Deadlock. Who Is to Cut the Tie?*

According to the taxpayers position, the text of the law described in the preceding section of the article implies that "[t]his definition is exhaustive. Therefore, it appears [for example] that a debt owed to a foreign sister company of the Russian borrower cannot be viewed as 'controlled debt' and consequently does not fall within the scope of the Russian thin capitalisation rule."[14] However, it seems that in the recent years the Russian tax authorities have been determined to broaden the application of the "thin capitalisation" rule.[15]

"The Russian authorities are slowly but steadily beginning to scrutinize loans received from foreign sister companies, which, in the past, have been the most common way of arranging inter-company funding into Russian subsidiaries. The fact that article 269 does not specifically include such loans within the purview of the thin capitalization rules may not be a guarantee that the rules will not be invoked."[16]

"A literal reading of [the A]rticle 269, section 2, suggests that loans received from foreign sister companies are not covered by the thin capitalization rules and, to date, the Russian tax authorities generally have accepted this interpretation. However, in a recently announced decision [of the *MirLand* case (later overturned)[17]], the Russian Arbitrazh Court of Appeal upheld the decision of a lower court that recognized the debt of a Russian company to a foreign sister company as controlled debt. The case started with the Russian tax authorities challenging the deduction of interest on a loan obtained by a Russian company from its foreign sister company."[18]

"The tax authorities took the position that the funds provided to the Russian company actually belonged to the foreign parent company, which raised the funds through an IPO and subsequently distributed them among its subsidiaries. The Arbitrazh Court of Appeal followed the "substance over form" approach, establishing an affiliation between the parent company, the lender and the borrower and concluding that the funds received by the Russian company de facto originated from the parent company, even though they were

---

14 *Id.*

15 To be discussed in more detail above. See also *Russia Tax: Thin cap rules may be applied to foreign sister companies* (July 2010) (available at <www.taxrates.cc/html/07f-russia-thin-cap-rules.html>).

16 Andrey Ganin, Shereen Chirambo (Deloitte Tax LLP), *Russia Tax: Thin Cap Rules May Be Applied To Foreign Sister Companies* (16 July 2010) (available at <http://newsletters.usdbriefs.com/2010/Tax/WTA/a100716_4.pdf> and <www.taxrates.cc/html/07f-russia-thin-cap-rules.html>).

17 Lesova, Harger, *New Ruling on Russian "Thin Capital" Limitations for Loans, Russian Law News (Dewey & LeBoeuf LLP).*

18 *Supra* at 1.

technically provided to the Russian company under a loan agreement with the foreign sister company. The Russian company's debt was actually with the parent company and, therefore, should be treated as controlled debt. This conclusion indirectly supports a previous position taken by the Russian Ministry of Finance in private clarifications, in which the Ministry stated that a court may decide to establish an affiliation between parties on grounds beyond those set forth in the Tax Code (*i.e.* when there is a direct or an indirect participation of less than 20%) and apply these conclusions for purposes of the thin capitalization rules."[19]

[Thus, the above] ruling was one of the signals to the market players that "loans issued by foreign sister companies to Russian borrowers could now be treated as being subject to restrictions under the thin capitalization rules, thus creating new tax risks for foreign companies investing into Russia."[20]

3.3 *Recent Decision of the Federal Arbitrazh Court Turns the Picture in Favour of the Taxpayers*

"The above [mentioned] decision [of the Russian Arbitrazh Court of Appeal] contradicts several other decisions in which the courts followed the literal interpretation of article 269 of the Tax Code and resolved the cases in favor of the Russian taxpayers, thereby refusing to consider the loans as controlled debt."[21]

Most "[f]ortunately for taxpayers, in July 2010, the Federal Arbitrazh Court confirmed that the thin capitalisation rules are not subject to such a broad interpretation, and should be applied only in cases explicitly referred to in the Tax Code (*i.e.*, the three scenarios mentioned above). The Court stated that on the facts of the case the Hungarian sister financing company could not be viewed as a direct or indirect shareholder of the Russian borrower, as this would contradict the provisions of Russian law. As a result, the Court decided that the loan received by the Russian borrower from the Hungarian sister company was not a "controlled debt", and the interest expense accrued in Russia was fully deductible for the purposes of computing the taxable profits of the Russian company."[22]

---

19 *Id.*
20 *Id.*
21 *Id.*
22 Lesova, Harger, *New Ruling on Russian "Thin Capital" Limitations for Loans.*

"The continuing attempts of the tax authorities to challenge loans from foreign sister companies are consistent with earlier clarifications issued by the Ministry of Finance[23] with respect to the scope of the thin capitalisation rule. Despite the judgment in the [2010] *MirLand* case in favour of the taxpayer, there could be more appeals to the Courts on the same point, but with a different outcome. It is also possible that the Russian thin capitalisation rule could be expressly amended in the future to apply to loans provided by *any* foreign affiliated party."[24]

3.4 *Other Examples of Courts Ruling in Favour of Taxpayers: Possible Application of Double Taxation Treaties (DDT)*

There are other examples of the recent court decisions that ruled in favour of the taxpayers, some of them explicitly imply a possibility of non-application of the thin capitalisation rule in light of special provisions of Double Taxation Treaties.

"Until recently, Russian thin capitalization rules were not applied only if such special conditions [had been] provided in a double taxation treaty between Russia and the state in which the lending company is resident (*e.g.* Russia has treaties with Germany and the Netherlands).

Russian courts have always supported taxpayers and confirmed their right to recognize interest paid to German and Dutch creditors as expenses without any limitations, as application of the thin capitalization rules in this event would have contradicted the international treaties that have priority over the Russian tax legislation.

However, much to the regret of taxpayers, only a limited number of international treaties expressly provide for the possibility to recognize interest for tax purposes without any limitations."[25]

---

23 See generally, Russian Ministry of Finance, *Russian Tax Policy Guidelines for 2010 and target period of 2011-2012and Russian Tax Policy Guidelines for 2011 and target period of 2012-2013* (available at <www1.minfin.ru/ru/tax%5Frelations/policy/>) (accessed 18 December 2010).

24 *Supra.*

25 Oxana Kovaleva, *Russian Thin Capitalization Rules in Light of Double Taxation Treaties: Trends in Court Practice*, The Moscow Times (09 February 2010) (available at: <www.themoscowtimes.com/business/business_for_business/article/russian-thin-capitalization-rules-in-light-of-double-taxation-treaties-trends-in-court-practice/399283.html>).

"On 14 May 2010 the Russian Ministry of Finance provided further clarifications with regards to excessive interest payments via a new circular.[26] According to the clarifications an amount of interest paid by a Russian Company to its foreign parent (or domestic company affiliated to the parent Company) may be re-classified as dividends. This re-classification would apply when a Russian Company exceeds the debt to equity ratio provided under the relevant Russian legislation. In such cases, the amount of interest in excess of the permissible ratio is considered a non-deductible expense and accordingly re-classified as dividends."[27]

"In view of the above, precedents established by commercial arbitration courts of the Moscow region and Northwestern circuit [...] are invaluable for taxpayers. In these cases, when assessing the lawfulness of nonapplication of the Russian thin capitalization rules, courts have for the first time referred to the provisions on nondiscrimination provided in the international treaties with Cyprus and Finland."[28]

The first, the *AEK* case,[29] concerned a loan granted by a Finnish company to its Russian 96.4% subsidiary. The second, the *Field Invest* case, dealt with parent-subsidiary debt financing from Cyprus.[30] Both the 1996 Finland-Russia tax treaty and the 1998 Cyprus-Russia tax treaty do not contain special provisions enhancing the deductibility of interest. Nevertheless, the non-discrimination and the 'autonomous interpretation' arguments were enough for the courts to overturn the assessments issued by the tax authorities."[31]

"The courts have [ruled] that the Russian thin capitalization rules would not apply pursuant to the Russia-Cyprus Double Tax Treaty and the treaty concluded between Russia and Finland. The courts followed the assumption that interest paid by a Russian taxpayer to a foreign creditor is recognizable for tax purposes on the same terms as interest paid to Russian creditors.

Also, courts noted that Russian companies whose capital is owned or controlled by a foreign entity are not subject to a tax burden different from that of similar Russian companies."[32]

26 See Letter of the Russian Ministry of Finance N 03-08-05 dated 14 May 2010 (Russian text) available at <www.consultant.ru/online/base/?req=doc;base=QUEST;n=80961>).

27 Mr. Charles Savva (Savva and associates Ltd.), *September 2010 Newsletter- New Developments in Russia Regarding Cyprus Structures* (September 2010) (available at http://savvacyprus.com/74.html).

28 Kovaleva, *Russian Thin Capitalization Rules in Light of Double Taxation Treaties: Trends in Court Practice.*

29 Decision of the North-Western District Arbitrazh Court, No. A26-6967/2008, 23 September 2009.

30 Decision of the Federal Moscow District Arbitrazh Court, No. KA-A40/9453-09-2, 23 September 2009.

31 Boris Bruk, *Russian Thin Capitalization Rules: Are They Compatible with Russian Tax Treaties?* European Taxation, 506, 507 (November 2010) (available at <www.salans.com/~/media/Assets/Salans/Publications/2010/20101101-Russian%20Thin%20Capitalization%20Rules.ashx>).

32 Kovaleva, *Russian Thin Capitalization Rules in Light of Double Taxation Treaties: Trends in Court Practice.*

"The decision[s] appeared to provide a solid foundation for relief from discriminatory thin capitalization provisions."[33]

3.5 *Other Examples of Tax Authorities and Judicial Branch Confrontation*

The optimistic examples of the cases discussed above may not, however, be considered a strong trend of heroic courts tending to rule just in favour of the taxpayers as opposed to the vicious and narrow-minded Russian tax authorities. Just an opposite situation may occur in the Russian practice, where the Resolution of the Supreme Arbitrazh Court would provoke a burst of indignation among both taxpayers and banks, and be neutralized by the position of the financial bodies.

Namely, a case decided by the Supreme Arbitrazh Court in the late 2009 a involved an allegedly unlawful deduction by a taxpayer in the years 2005-2006 of an interest on a loan that had to be paid in 2010-2014 after the main loan sum had been returned to the lender by the end of year 2010. "Such loan conditions, in fact, differ from standard business practice where payment of the principal debt and interest do not have significant time differences. However, without straight or indirect reference to illegal tax optimization, the Supreme Arbitrazh Court stated that since under the condition of the loan agreement payment must be arranged for the period from April 1, 2010 to Nov. 1, 2010, the company has no obligations on debt repayment until that period, which means that it has no [deductions] to be included into the tax base when computing income tax."[34] Subsequently, the Federal Tax Service specified in an official letter, No. 3-2-06/22, dated 17 March 2010 "the necessity of accounting for interest under loan agreements during the whole period of the contract regardless of the contract conditions relating to the date of payments under the loan agreement. Such an approach, according to the Federal Tax Service, fits the general format for acknowledgement of income and expenses for taxation under an accrual method, according to which income and expenses are recognized in the accounting period to which they refer, independent of the actual date of payment."[35]

As some of the experts clarify, this was relief for taxpayers, mostly, "because of the financial crisis, not all debtors could repay their loan interest in the agreed time. This is why interest payments moved away from the repayment period, not as a result of active tax optimization

33 *Supra.*

34 Alexei A. Yakovlev, *Interest on Credit in the Income Tax Structure: Tax Risks to Be Considered*, The Moscow Times (26 May 2010) (available at <www.themoscowtimes.com/business/business_for_business/article/interest-on-credit-in-the-income-tax-structure-tax-risks-to-be-considered/406820.html>). See also Supreme Arbitrazh Court Resolution No. 11200/09 (24 November 2009).

35 *Id.*

but because of objective conditions. Moreover, in the crisis and post-crisis periods, a practice for the refinancing of debt became widespread in business and banking where the new credit repays the earlier loan and the repayment period for interest payment is postponed. As for the legal position of the panel of the Supreme Arbitrazh Court in Resolution No. 11200/09, dated 24 November 2009, it could either cause considerable problems with the loans granted earlier or lead to credit reduction in the recovering Russian economy. Application of this legal position to all tax litigation cases involving taxpayer companies, where the question of the tax basis reduction on loan agreements is considered, could be a reality since the legal positions of the panel of the Supreme Arbitrazh Court were legalized as obligatory precedents by Resolution No. 17, dated 12 December 2007."[36]

4 Latest Amendments of the Laws Concerning Loan Interest Deductability Are Aimed to Respond the Current Economic Situation

"The [current] economicpolicy of the Russian authorities is targeted at meeting the consequences of the crisis. The Central Bank has already reduced the refinancing rate several times during 2010 to stimulate Russian economic and financial recovery. These measures are directed at making credit resources accessible and are meant to improve the crediting process. The reduction of real bank rates is progressing at a slow pace, although the credit market is becoming more active."[37]

"During the last years the maximum deductible interest rate has changed to let Russian companies deduct interests in big lots during the crisis, when the interest rates at the loan market had grown. However, recently the maximum deductible interest rate has returned to its previous level (except for the interests in roubles occurred prior to November 1, 2009)."[38]

---

36 *Id.*

37 *Id.*, see also Alexander Anichkin, Dmitry Tolkachev, *Clifford Chance, Client briefing. Changes to Interest Deductibility Rates and Other Amendments to Russian Tax Regulations*, 2 (2010) (available at <www.cliffordchance.com/publicationviews/publications/2010/08/changes_to_interestdeductibilityratesandothe0.html>).

38 The maximum rate of CBR multiplied by two applies to the interests in roubles occurred prior to 1 November 2009 – see generally, Federal Law of Russian Federation FZ-229 Article 2 (23*)*, Rossiyskaya Gazeta (2 Augustus 2010) (Russian text available at <www.consultant.ru/online/base/?req=doc;base=LAW;n=103118;p=2>) (accessed 18 December 2010), see also Alexander Anichkin, Dmitry Tolkachev, *Clifford Chance: Client briefing. Changes to Interest Deductibility Rates and Other Amendments to Russian Tax Regulations*, 2 (2010) (available at <www.cliffordchance.com/publicationviews/publications/2010/08/changes_to_interestdeductibilityratesandothe0.html>).

Federal Law No. 229-FZ (27 July 2010 the "Law")[39] "introduced certain changes into Russian tax legislation, including a change in the threshold of deductible interest on loans denominated in foreign currency. The Law generally enter[ed] into force on 2 September 2010, but the lower thresholds discussed below will become effective only in 2011-2012."[40]

In detail the picture looks like this. "Under art. 269 (1) of the Russian Tax Code, as a general rule interest on loans and other borrowings in Russia is subject to limitations on profits tax deductibility and must be charged at a rate which is not more than 20% above the average rate charged for comparable loans made in the same quarter. In the absence of comparable data or at the taxpayer's choice, the maximum rate is as follows:

α) [...] the refinancing rate of the Russian Central Bank [(CBRR)] at the date the loan is provided, multiplied by 1,1 [for **ruble loans**]; and

β) 15% for **foreign currency** loans.

However, these rules had been suspended for the period from *1 September 2009 to 31 December 2009*:

χ) a maximum rate of the refinancing rate of the Central Bank multiplied by 2 for **ruble loans** and

δ) a maximum rate of 22% for **foreign currency** loans applied.

Further, state legislative authorities have iteratively suspended the relevant provision of Article 269 (1) and have established that during the period from *1 January 2010 to 30 June 2010*:

ε) a maximum rate of the refinancing rate of the Central Bank multiplied by 2 for **rouble loans** and

φ) a maximum rate of 15% for **foreign currency** loans shall apply for interest expenses on debt obligations arising *before 1 November 2009*.[41]

The new changes followed in 2010 (implemented by 229-FZ):

---

39 Federal Law No. 229-FZ.

40 Dmitri V. Nikiforov, Evgeny V. Smirnov, Anna S. Dulova, *Debevoise and Plimpton LLP. Russia: Reduced Interest Deductions on Foreign Currency Loans in 2011 and 2012*, 26 (August 2010) (available at <www.debevoise.com/files/Publication/40f8eaaa-a742-4abf-b798-c5ecf95eecce/Presentation/PublicationAttachment/06ed5631-53e2-4e33-83ea-d3e65b6a2707/RussiaReducedInterestDeductionsonForeignCurrencyLoansin2011and2012.pdf>) See also Anichkin, Tolkachev, *Clifford Chance: Client briefing. Changes to Interest Deductibility Rates and Other Amendments to Russian Tax Regulations.*

41 Dominique Tissot, Anastasia Prozor, *CMS: Russia Tax outlook, #9December 2009 – January 2010, Major Amendments to Russian Tax Legislation Coming into Force in 2010* (available at <www.cmslegal.ru/Hubbard.FileSystem/files/Publication/6c8c0920-0750-4757-8cfc-014c4b28afc4/Presentation/PublicationAttachment/76b3dd9f-a6c0-421c-a457-02c4baa9774b/CMS%20Tax%20Outlook_Dec%20Jan%202010.pdf>).

- "the amendments anew the temporary increase the maximum rate of the interest of loans denominated in *roubles up to CBRR multiplied by 1.8*, that makes loans (or credits) in roubles more attractive due to considerable recession of the CBRR in last period. If we consider the current refinancing rate of 7.75% to be a base, then a deduction would be possible at a rate about 13.95% (7.75% x 1.8) for all interests accrued with regards to loans or credits in roubles for the period starting 1 January 2010 to 31 December 2012. Thus, in contrast with the foreign currency loans the amendments gave retroactive effect to the rules of interest deductibility of loans denominated in roubles."[42]
- As to the *loans in foreign currency*, within the same period starting 1 January 2010 to 31 December 2012 the maximum deductibility rate is going to be temporary reduced. "[W]ith regards to the current CBRR of 7.75%, only an amount of interests corresponding to the *maximum rate of 6.2%* (7.75%*0.8) would be acceptable for deduction. It is also worth mentioning that the latest amendments apply to any interest accrued in 2011 - 2012 with regards to the loans denominated in foreign currency with no regards to the date of the loan allotment."[43]

It is believed that: "[t]hese new rules represent a temporary concession and the thresholds on loans will most likely be returned to the original rates fixed in art. 269 (1) as soon as the country emerges out of recession."[44] The tax experts further note that:

- new rules may influence the effectiveness of the intergoup financing including those that are partly aimed to the repatriation of profits. Thus, the loans structure (including the inner group loans) may require re-examination in view of the Amendments (including, for example, substitution of the loans denominated in foreign currency for ruble-denominated loans).[45]
- the maximum deductible interes rates decline may also create a certain competitive advantage for Russian banks, ready to provide provisions or securities (обеспечение) in roubles.[46]

---

42 Anichkin, Tolkachev, *Clifford Chance: Client briefing Changes to Interest Deductibility Rates and Other Amendments to Russian Tax Regulations*, 2 (2010).

43 *Id.*

44 Tissot, Prozor, *CMS: Russia Tax outlook, #9December 2009 – January 2010, Major Amendments to Russian Tax Legislation Coming into Force in 2010.*

45 *Supra.*

46 *Id.*

5 CONCLUSION

The continuing attempts of the tax authorities to challenge loans from foreign companies with respect to the scope of the thin capitalisation rule are consistent with the policies declared by the Ministry of Finance.[47] The plans namely include amending of the thin capitalisation rule applied to loans provided by foreign affiliated parties and the rules of determining affiliation.

At the same time the current attempts of the courts to defend the position of the taxpayers as opposed to the narrowing approach of the tax authorities are promising, but not yet reassuring. Courts of the lower instances, especially in the Oblasts (regions), tend to support the official authorities and the decisions of the higher level courts are not always predictable and may produce different results.

There are also temporary amendments taking place in the Russian tax legislation, presumably aimed to help the Russian market overcome the economic crisis. These may be also regarded as attempts of the legislators to develop and test the possible mechanisms that could be applied to changing of some of the positions of the law itself on a temporary basis.

It is obvious that the Russian legal system, especially its tax system, is still stumbling through "adolescence", with gains and setbacks that are natural for such times. But however natural, opportune and timely certain changes and rapid progress in initial results may seem or claim to be, the lack of experience may sometimes also cause considerable turbulence and unpredictability; it is always easier to make great initial progress when starting from "zero".

Thus, with regards to the above mentioned trends and the on-going changes of the Russian realities in the sphere of tax regulation of "controlled debts" received from affiliated bodies, thin capitalisation rules, and foreign loan interest deductibility, international investors operating in Russia should be advised to regularly and carefully "re-examine the business functions and substance of companies involved in financing their Russian projects, to ensure that their involvement cannot be viewed as artificial or solely aimed at tax avoidance."[48] Generally, advice from a competent consultant specialized both in Russian and international tax legislation is needed when drafting a new loan agreement within the group.

47 See generally, Russian Ministry of Finance, *Russian Tax Policy Guidelines for 2010 and target period of 2011-2012and Russian Tax Policy Guidelines for 2011 and target period of 2012-2013* (available at <www1.minfin.ru/ru/tax%5Frelations/policy/>) (accessed 18 December 2010).

48 *Supra.*

19 Interest Deduction Limitations in Russia

Types, Methods of Avoidance and Practical Issues

Julia Ivanetz

For many years, debt financing has been one of the most common forms of funding Russian companies by foreign companies. From the tax perspective, financing by loans is more favourable to Russian recipients than financing by equity investment. The reason is that, unlike dividends, interest payments are tax deductible and may reduce the taxpayer's taxable income.

Understandably, debt financing has become an increasingly popular tax minimization feature, particularly in the sphere of international tax planning. To limit abusive tax planning, Russian legislators introduced two types of anti-avoidance rules, both set forth in article 269 of the Tax code of Russian Federation.

1 General Limitation

The first of the above-mentioned rules can be called general limitation and it is partially based on the arm's length principle. This rule generally conditions interest deduction by the average amount of interest paid to Russian companies in the same quarter on similar loans. The term "similar" as applied to loans means: a) issued in the same currency, b) on the same period, c) to similar amount and d) with the same security. If the above mentioned conditions are satisfied, interest payments are deductible, provided they do not deviate from the average amount of interest as mentioned above for more that 20%.

This rule seems rather generous (a 20% allowable deviation from the general interest amount is an unprecedentedly user-friendly condition). However, it can rarely be used in real life. Indeed, to apply this rule, the debtor company should have several Russian loans issued on similar conditions in the same quarter. The majority of Russian debtors do not qualify for these terms.

For those who do not qualify (or simply prefer to be treated differently), the alternative interest deduction model is available. It imposes a fixed limitation for the deduction of interest amount. This amount has been changing from year to year.

"Under the rules applicable in 2010, any interest on a foreign currency loan accrued at a rate not exceeding 15% per annum generally may be deducted for tax purposes. The rate on a rouble-denominated loan is the refinancing rate of the Russian Central Bank (CBR) multiplied by 1.8 (*i.e.* 13.95% per annum).

The recent amendments provide that, for the period from 1 January 2011 to 31 December 2012, a new threshold of 0.8 times the CBR will be applicable to foreign currency loans (the law is silent on what rules will apply after 2012). With the current CBR set at 7.75%, the new threshold for the deductibility of interest will be 6.2% (0.8 x 7.75%), rather than 15%. The rules governing the deductibility of interest on loans in roubles will remain unchanged."[1]

Figure 18.1 summarizes the interest deductibility limitations in Russia for the past two years:[2]

Figure 18.1

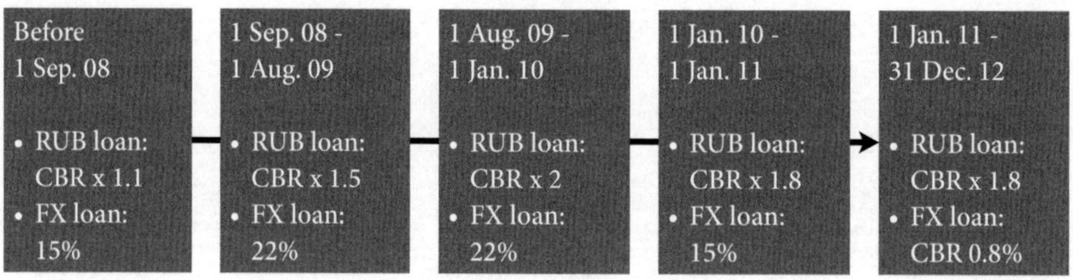

Figure 18.2 shows the dynamics of CBR interest rates changes for the period 2008 to 2010:

1 <www.deloitte.com/view/en_PG/pg/insights-ideas/itbg/390b206a2d18a210Vgn-VCM2000001b56f00aRCRD.htm>.

2 *Id.*

Figure 18.2

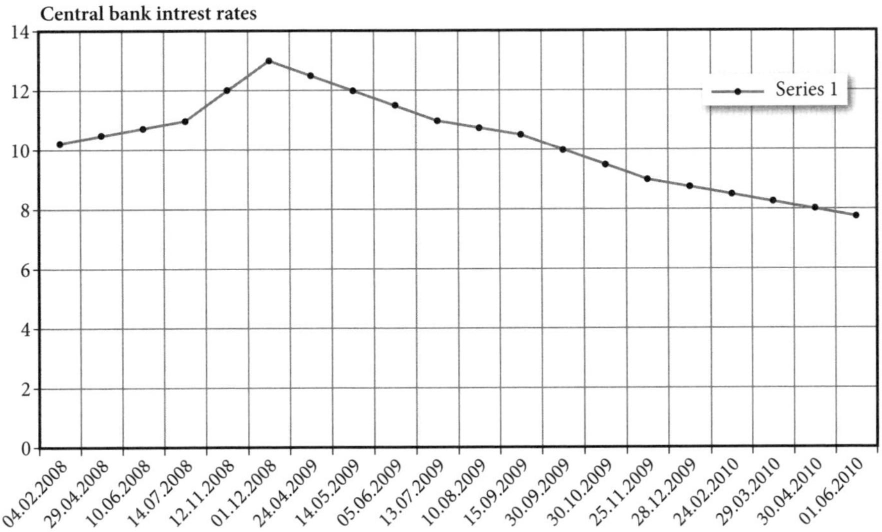

All these changes reflect the Russian government's intent to encourage the use of Russian currency in transnational loan transactions.

So, now foreign lenders might be highly interested in re-examining their Russian financing structures to avoid the negative effect of the new rules.

What are the possible solutions?

a. switching to the first mentioned deduction rule (*i.e.* applying the deduction limit equivalent to the aggregate amount of interest paid to Russian lenders on similar loans);
b. converting into rouble-denominated loan;
c. treaty shopping.

The last mentioned mechanism (treaty shopping) deserves detailed discussion. The basic point here is that Russian double tax treaties generally contain provisions which allow reversing the negative tax implications resulting from the application of domestic interest deduction limitation rules.

One such provision prohibits the application of limitations to the deduction of interest. This provision is very rarely contained in Russian double tax treaties, however it is included in the Russia-Germany DTA and in some other treaties, like the one with Belgium, Great Britain, Netherlands and some other countries. In the German treaty, this provision is set forth in the most unambiguous form. In other treaties the formulations of similar provisions are much more doubtful. This may cause difficulties when referring to these provisions in court.

The other provision allowing reversing the Russian domestic tax law limitations is the non-discrimination clause. However, despite the fact that non-discrimination clause has been in many cases successfully used to reverse Russian thin capitalization provisions (which will be discussed further), there is not yet any clear taxpayer-favourable practice in terms of general limitations. To the contrary, in the *Field Invest* case,[3] in which the court held in favour of the taxpayer and reversed Russian thin cap rules, it implied in obiter dictum that tax treaty protection is not absolute and a treaty cannot override general statutory limitations regarding the deductibility of interest.

So, the Russian general limitation rule implies either the arm's length principle (conditioning the interest deduction by average amount of interest paid to Russian companies in the same quarter on similar loans) or a fixed limit on the deductible amount. Since 2011 the fixed limit on foreign-currency loans will be reduced. However there are a few ways to avoid the negative impact of these statutory limitations.

2 Thin Capitalization Rules

In addition to the general limitations on the deductibility of interest, the Russian thin capitalization rules affect the deductibility of interest if:

(1)(a) debt financing is provided by a foreign legal entity that directly or indirectly owns more than 20% of the Russian entity financed; or

(b) debt financing is provided by a Russian affiliate of such foreign entity; or

(c) debt financing is provided by another person but repayment of the loan is guaranteed or secured in another way by such foreign entity or its Russian affiliate (such a debt is defined as a "controlled debt");

and

(2) In any of the above scenarios the controlled debt to equity ratio of the borrower exceeds 3:1 as of the last date of each reporting (tax) period.[4]

3 Decision of the Federal Moscow District Arbitrazh Court, No. KA-A40/9453-09-2, 23 September 2009.

4 Boris Bruk, *Russian Thin Capitalization Rules: Are they compatible with Russian Tax Treaties?*, European Taxation, 507(November 2010).

The excess interest (*i.e.* amount of interest on the controlled debt exceeding the 3:1 ratio) is considered a dividend, which is non-deductible for profits tax purposes and generally is subject to withholding tax at the standard rate: 15% (which can be reduced by double tax treaty, but, unlike interest payments, is never eliminated).

Russian thin cap rules can be avoided relatively easily and in many different ways.

1. First of all, as follows from the formulation of the law, Russian thin cap limitations do not apply to "foreign sister" financing; in other words, where a Russian borrower takes a loan from a foreign subsidiary of its own foreign parent company. Such structures are widely used in order to finance investments in the Russian market in the most tax efficient way.

However, this year, the tax authorities challenged a financing structure of this kind which had been put in place by an international investment group, deploying a "substance over form" argument in support of their position.[5]

Although Russia is not a common law jurisdiction, the role of case law in the resolution of tax disputes has increased significantly over the last decade. In the absence of any statutory general anti-avoidance rules, in tax disputes the courts happen to invoke various case law doctrines introduced by the highest courts of the Russian Federation, such as the "bona fide" concept, "unjustified tax benefit," "business purpose" or a "substance over form" principle. In 2006, the Presidium of the Supreme Arbitrazh Court adopted a resolution[6] that effectively gives precedence to "substance" over "form," and introduces a test for determining whether the companies involved in a transaction have legitimate business goals or are using a purely tax-driven structure aimed at avoiding Russian taxes.[7]

Nevertheless, until recently, the above concepts were not broadly applied in resolving tax disputes concerning thin capitalisation. The situation changed in 2010 with the *MirLand* case[8] outlined below.

The case relates to an international real estate investment and development group based in Israel. In 2004, it established a Cyprus domiciled holding company whose sole function was to hold the Russian real estate business. It had a Russian direct subsidiary. The Russian

5 <www.russianlaws.com/newsdetail.aspx?news=7215>.

6 Resolution of the Plenum of the Supreme Arbitrazh Court of Russian Federation No. 53 of 12.10.06 "On estimating the reasonableness of tax benefits by Russian arbitrazh courts".

7 <www.russianlaws.com/newsdetail.aspx?news=7215>.

8 Decision of the Federal Moscow District Arbitrazh Court, No. A40-107003/09-114-785, 13.07.2010.

subsidiary was debt-financed by its Hungarian sister company, *i.e.*, another subsidiary of the Cyprus holding company. Based on the literal wording of the law, such a structure is not captured by the Russian thin capitalisation rule, as only direct or indirect equity participation in the Russian borrower creates a "controlled debt", which is a pre-condition to the rule applying (as explained above).

Nonetheless, the investigating authority took the position that the funds provided to the Russian subsidiary (borrower) by the Hungarian sister company in fact belonged to the Cyprus holding company, as the money was raised through an IPO of the holding company on the London Stock Exchange. The tax authority regarded the legal route by which the IPO proceeds were applied towards the financing of the Russian business, namely via back-to-back loans through the Hungarian affiliate, as a mere technicality, on the basis that the funds being lent to Russia ultimately belonged to the Cyprus holding company. Referring to the official corporate website of the holding company, the tax authority cited the fact that the group was described as having been created in order to carry out real estate investment projects in Russia. The tax authority concluded that the Cyprus holding company determined the objectives for all group members, and that they were devoting their efforts towards achieving the goals set by their Cyprus parent and utilising within the group the funds obtained by the Cyprus holding company. On that basis, as the Cyprus holding company was the sole shareholder of both the Russian borrower and the Hungarian lender, the Russian borrower's debt under the loan from the Hungarian financing company was a "controlled debt" within the meaning of the thin capitalisation rule.[9]

The trial and appellate courts supported the "substance over form" approach of the tax authority. This created uncertainty for the business community regarding the tax treatment of existing and future investments financed in the same way.

Fortunately for taxpayers, in July 2010, the Federal Arbitrazh Court confirmed that the thin capitalisation rules are not subject to such a broad interpretation, and should be applied only in cases explicitly referred to in the Tax Code (*i.e.*, the three scenarios mentioned above). The Court stated that on the facts of the case the Hungarian sister financing company could not be viewed as a direct or indirect shareholder of the Russian borrower, as this would contradict the provisions of Russian law. As a result, the Court decided that the loan received by the Russian borrower from the Hungarian sister company was not a "controlled debt", and the interest expense accrued in Russia was fully deductible for the purposes of computing the taxable profits of the Russian company.

9 <www.russianlaws.com/newsdetail.aspx?news=7215>.

This court decision takes the view that the thin capitalisation rule should be interpreted strictly, in accordance with the wording of the Tax Code, and that there is no scope for widening the application of its provisions.[10]

This judgment demonstrates the domination of formalistic approach in interpreting Russian tax law norms by Russian courts. Anti-avoidance court doctrines are still very weak in Russia, and probably will not be widely applied by courts unless included in tax legislation.

2. The second way to avoid Russian thin cap rules is using the above mentioned double tax treaty provisions.

One of such provisions is the one which prohibits the application of limitations to deduction of interest. This provision is very rarely contained in Russian double tax treaties, however it is included in the Russia- Germany DTA and in some other treaties, like the one with Belgium, Great Britain, Netherlands and some other countries.

This provision as specified in Russia-Germany DTA has the most distinct form (compared to similar provisions in other DTAs), and is thus easily enforceable. Notably, para. 3 of the Protocol to the tax treaty provides for unlimited interest deductibility. The court in *Ferrotek* case[11] confirmed that such provision prevails over any Russian domestic tax law norms. Besides, the court mentioned that the definitions of the treaty should apply autonomously (without regard to Russian domestic tax law).

The *Ferrotek* case was soon followed by another, similar case involving double tax treaty between Russia and Netherlands (*Swedwood Tikhvin*[12]). In that case the taxpayer raised two arguments: one relating to the provision of the Protokol to Russia-Netherlands tax treaty which is kind of similar to the above-mentioned Protokol to Russia-Germany DTA (although set forth in a vaguer form) and the second one – relating to non-discrimination clause. The court again found in favor of the taxpayer and stated that the treaty provisions override Russian interest deduction limitations.

The other provision allowing reversal of Russian domestic tax law limitations is the non-discrimination clause. Perhaps for the first time the non-discrimination provisions of tax treaty were given true legal weight[13] in the above mentioned *Swedwood Tikhvin* case. In

10 *Id.*

11 Decision of the Federal Moscow District Arbitrazh Court, No. KA-A40/6616-05, 25 February 2005.

12 Decision of the Federal North-Western District Arbitrazh Court No. A56-19578/2006, 9 April 2007.

13 Boris Bruk, *Russian Thin Capitalization Rules: Are they compatible with Russian Tax Treaties?*, European Taxation, 507(November 2010).

that case, the court compared the situations where the lendee was a Russian resident and where the lender was the resident of the treaty state. As it found that the treaty country resident was treated less favourably than how a Russian resident would be treated in similar situation, it held that the treaty country resident was discriminated against. Thus, the court disallowed the limitation on deduction of interest paid to the Netherlands company.

This decision very soon was followed by another two court decisions that, coincidentally, were issued on the same day:

> The first, the AEK case,[14] concerned a loan granted by a Finnish company to its Russian 96.4% subsidiary. The second, the *Field Invest* case, dealt with parent-subsidiary debt financing from Cyprus.[15] Both the 1996 Finland–Russia tax treaty and the 1998 Cyprus–Russia tax treaty do not contain special provisions enhancing the deductibility of interest. Nevertheless, the non-discrimination and the "autonomous interpretation" arguments were enough for the courts to overturn the assessments issued by the tax authorities. The decision appeared to provide a solid foundation for relief from discriminatory Russian tax law provisions.[16]

Based on the above, I can draw out several basic points which could be useful to taxpayers, and other points which could be useful to the government.

From the taxpayer's perspective, interest deduction limitations should be observed when developing cross-border debt financing structures. From the 1 January 2011, foreign currency loans will be treated less favourably than in 2010 in terms of general interest deduction limitations.

Double tax treaty provisions can be used as a very helpful tool in reversing negative tax consequences of Russian limitation rules. For general limitations, the court practice is relatively instable, although the chance of winning the case based on the German treaty is relatively high. For thin cap rules, conversely, the taxpayers' position in court is relatively strong.

14 Decision of the North-Western District Arbitrazh Court, No. A26-6967/2008, 23 September 2009.

15 Decision of the Federal Moscow District Arbitrazh Court, No. KA-A40/9453-09-2, 23 September 2009.

16 Boris Bruk, *Russian Thin Capitalization Rules: Are they compatible with Russian Tax Treaties?*, European Taxation, 507(November 2010).

"Sister company" avoidance tactics can still be successfully used, while the courts prefer to stick to the wording of the Tax Code provisions rather than apply anti-avoidance precedent-related doctrines.

From the government's perspective, the great number of avoidance mechanisms might be a subject to think about. The "sister company" scheme is based on a long-standing and widely abused loophole. As of today, I have not heard about any initiatives to change the law.

The 20% deviation from arm's length amount of interest allowable under general limitation rule is unprecedented in generousity and opens up many opportunities to tax abuse. Such a deviation seems inadequate and should be outlawed.

The codification of anti-avoidance court doctrines is the precondition of their enforcement. In a country such as Russia where courts take the literal text of the law very seriously and do not deviate from it court created doctrines, if existing at all, will never operate effectively. The only way to empower courts is is to include anti-avoidance provisions into statutory law.

Double tax treaties which contain conditions which enable taxpayers to escape from national anti-avoidance rules are destructive and should be re-negotiated.

Tax avoidance mechanisms in Russia are numerous, widely applied and extremely easy to obtain. This is the result of weak, ineffective national laws to suppress tax avoidance and from the narrow formalistic approach taken by the courts.

20 Double Taxation Between the EU and Russia

N. Maslennikova

1 Russia Seeks to Form a Single European Jurisdiction for Business Incorporation and Taxation Issues

The possibility of ratifying the Protocol on amendments to the Double Taxation Treaty concluded between Russia and Cyprus by both countries forces Russian companies and the owners of real estate located in Russia to seek other jurisdictions that have more convenient legislation in taxation and rules of incorporation. The minimum share requirements and the low rate of taxes are the main points that Russian companies take into account.

In order to be more transparent, most Russian companies look to jurisdictions, which require the full disclosure of the shareholders, directors and business activities.

To understand whether one or the other European jurisdictions is convenient to the purpose pursued by the Russian companies in incorporating the new company, it is necessary to analyse the general provisions of European law regarding the incorporation of the companies in one of the member State and its taxation with anti-avoidance tax rules.

The main source of European Union law is the Treaty on the functioning of the European Union (hereinafter referred to as the "Treaty").

In accordance with the provisions of the Treaty with the purpose of establishing the single market, all citizens of the European Union (hereinafter referred to as the "EU") are guaranteed four basic freedoms: the free movement of goods, services, persons and capital. The freedom of establishment is within the framework of the free movement of persons.[1] The European Court of Justice (hereinafter referred to as the "ECJ") recognized the direct effect of the Treaty' provisions regarding to the freedom of establishment.[2]

1 Art. 43 of the Treaty.

2 Case 33/74 *Van Binsbergen v. Bestuur van de Bedrijfsverenigning voor de Metaalnijverheid*, 1974, ECR 1299.

Under Article 48 of the Treaty, companies, corporations and any other legal entities, which were established in accordance with the national law of the Member States, whose registered place of business and management is in the EU are considered as fiscal persons who are the citizens of the Member States. Only entities that have their business aim to receive profit are considered within the scope of Article 43 of the Treaty.

According to the Article 1 of the Brussels Treaty of 1968,[3] the entities, established under the national law of one of the participants of the Brussels Treaty, and having the registered addresses in the territory of applicability of this Brussels Treaty, shall be recognized as established under the law of the Treaty' participants. Thus, the Brussels Treaty gave preference to the principle of incorporation, well known to the Netherlands, Great Britain and Ireland. This theory of corporate citizenship/residence is generally known as the "place of incorporation theory".

Under the principle of incorporation, the law applicable to the entities is the law where the company was established (incorporated). Usually, its a law of place of incorporation or registration of the company. But this principle has some shortcomings. For example, it allows abuse of process (formal legal manipulations with no correspondence to factual reality) by creation of shelf companies ("shells"), which are established only for the registration of business correspondence. Often, shells are abused for tax evasion and money laundering. Therefore, in Germany and France, for instance, courts determine the nationality of the enterprise entity by the real and effective place of administration. This is usually known as "the real seat theory". The "real seat" can differ from the place of incorporation or registration of its Article of Association. The "real seat theory" focuses on the place which is the administrative centre of the company (management).

Under Article 4 of the Brussels Treaty, State-participants can stipulate the mandatory use of its local interim legislation to the companies that have their administrative centre of business at their territory, but the registered place of incorporation is in the territory of other State-participate of the Treaty. The provision that restricts the principle of incorporation was one of the reasons pursuant to which the Brussels Treaty has not come into effect yet.[4]

The incorporation of a legal entity in the Member State other than the State where it was initially incorporated, is made in the forms of initial and secondary incorporation. Pursuant

3 Brussels Convention on Jurisdiction and the Enforcement of Judgments in Civil and Commercial Matters 1968.

4 According to Art. 14 of the Brussels Treaty to come into force all States-participant have to ratify the Treaty, But the Netherlands, for example, being the participant of the Treaty does not ratify it yet.

to Article 43 of the Treaty, restrictions of the freedom of establishment and economic activity of the citizens of any Member States in the territory of other Member State must be eliminated. Other restrictions in respect of establishment of the agencies, branches or subsidiaries by the citizens of the member State, who establish themselves in the territory of the other Member State must also be eliminated.

In the case of initial establishment, the company is striving to subject its activities to the law of a Member State, other than that where it was created. This raises problems similar to those that occur in the mutual recognition of legal status. For instance, under the law of France the legal address, the real one, and the administration management have to be in France. Transfer of location of the central administrative management outside of the France (or a state following the French model) presupposes the elimination of the company with all consequences in the field of taxation and the establishment of a new entity under the laws of the host country (*e.g.* realization events). However, in other states, for example, in Britain and the Netherlands, the transfer of the location of the central administration of a company incorporated in accordance with their legislation, to another Member State does not entail loss of the corporate existence under, respectively, English or Dutch law, at least so long as the company's registered address remains in the UK (or, respectively, Holland).

In this regard, the ECJ considered the case concerning the possibility of preservation of the initial incorporation of the status of State institutions in the event of the location of the central administration to another Member State.[5] The company *Daily Mail*, incorporated under the law of Great Britain, intended to locate their directors and central administration to the Netherlands yet while maintaining its status as a British company. The operation was permitted by law, both in the UK and Holland. However, under the laws of England, companies are taxable at the location of the fiscal residence of the company, and under such law is considered the location of the management (Directors). Thus, such a transfer was motivated by tax avoidance. To avoid similar situations, the UK passed a law in 1970 on income tax and the taxation of subordinate companies, subjecting such transfers to compulsory prior permission by the UK. The company believes that provision of the law was incompatible with the principle of freedom of establishment under the EC Treaty.

The ECJ pointed out that the transaction only concerned removal of a British company outside of Britain – and not a hindrance to foreign establishments seeking to do business in Britain. Thus, a permit is necessary only when the company while retaining their legal

5 *Daily Mail*, N 81/87, 27 September1988.

status and British nationality, wants to move the location of the board outside the United Kingdom.

The ECJ ruled that Articles 43 and 45 should not be interpreted as conferring the right to national companies to transfer the location of the central administration and board in another Member State, while retaining the status of the State under whose laws it was created. The rationale was that significant differences in national legislation among the EU Member States justify such a decision, as do the absence of any Convention concluded pursuant to Article 293 of the Treaty. Article 293 which provides for the concluding the Conventions, including the preservation of the status of legal person in case of transferring the seat of the company from one country to another. The absence of such a convention was also a justification of the Court's ruling.

Article 43 ECT, as part of a secondary (re)incorporation, provides for the opening of agencies, branches or subsidiaries. However, Article 43 only governs the opening of secondary institutions companies *within* the EU – and Russia is currently not an EU Member State.

However in accordance with Article 48, the incorporation of a company in one of the EU Member States, even if its real seat is in fact outside the EU, entails the right of the Company to open secondary institutions within the EU subject to an effective and sustained communication with the economy of any EU Member State. This provision does not mean that a company incorporated in a third country, cannot open its secondary institution in the territory of EU Member States. *Centros*[6] was a company registered in England and Wales in 1992. In the *Centros* case, the Department of Commerce in Denmark refused to register Centros's branch in Denmark. The basis was the fact that the company Centros, which is not conducting business in the United Kingdom, registered in the UK in order to circumvent more stringent corporate regulation under Danish law. In fact, the Centros company had the intention to establish Denmark as its primary and not secondary, but place of business.

Centros also referred to Articles 43 and 48 of the EC Treaty, which guaranteed the right of the company, established within the territory of the EU in accordance with the laws of one of the EU Member States, the right of establishment of secondary enterprises on the territory of any other EU Member State.

6 *Centros Ltd c. Erhvervsog Selskabsstyrelsen*, No. C-212/97, 9 August 1999.

The ECJ ruled that, firstly, the refusal to register the branch office, established in accordance with the legislation of one Member State, contradicts the meaning of Articles 43 and 48 of the Treaty, despite the fact that the primary purpose of incorporation was the intention of opening a branch in another state, where in the future should be the main business of the company.

Secondly, the ECJ recognized the right of the Member States to accept, under certain circumstances, measures against the use of EU citizens guaranteed to them by the constitutive acts of human rights and freedoms in order to circumvent national laws or to commit illegal acts.

Thus, the ECJ extended the notion of freedom of establishment, pointing out that the establishment of a primary or secondary business for profit in one of the Member States may not be a ground for deprivation of the right of freedom of establishment.

Article 42 of the EC Treaty considered by the ECJ as a guarantee of the principle of equality in relation to national companies and companies from other Member States. This principle includes not only the elimination of restrictions based on nationality, but also any other form of discrimination, which employ different criteria, leading to similar results. Hence, it includes direct or indirect discrimination.

But, for example, in *Futura*[7] case the Court said that restriction on freedom of establishment is possible, if the subsidiary's establishment was for tax evasion.

In *Laerstate BV v. HMRC*[8] the British Court of First Instance considered the possibility of recognition of the Dutch company tax resident in the UK on the grounds that the management and control were carried out by the British resident. In reaching its decision, the court took into account not only the way in which documents were furnished the company, but all the facts of the case. The court found the company a tax resident of the UK, which entailed application of the British-Dutch double taxation avoidance agreement, and resulted in the obligation to pay UK tax on profits.

In Britain, the issue of corporate tax residency is often not so simple as in Russia. In contrast to Russia, where the residency of legal persons is determined only by territorial criteria (*i.e.*, place of registration), in the UK there is a second criterion for determining the residence – place of management and control. This means that if the organization is not reg-

7 C-250/95, *Futura Participations SA Singer v. Administration des Contribution.*
8 *Laerstate BV v. HMRC*, UKFTT 162 (2009).

istered in the UK, it may nevertheless be recognized as a British tax resident if it is determined that its command control center is in the UK.

The common law concept, introduced by judicial decision in the case of *De Beers Consolidated Mines Ltd v. Howe* (1905) is "management and control". Since *De Beers*, the British courts have modified and developed this concept, detailing the meaning of governance and control more and more. The most recent of judicial precedents in the matter involve a Dutch company, the sole member of which was a German citizen (Mr. Bock). He was also one of its two directors. The second director was a Dutch citizen (Mr. Trapman). In 1992, the Dutch company acquired shares, which in 1996 sold at a profit.

Some time after the purchase of shares by Mr. Bock became a British tax resident. Shortly before the sale of shares he resigned from his post as director of the Dutch company, retaining 100% participation in its capital, and as subsequently claimed the tax authorities, de facto control over it. The British tax authorities recognized the Dutch company as a tax resident of the UK. According to them, during the entire period (*i.e.* from 1992 to 1996), the company was actually run by the British tax resident (Mr. Bok). As a Director, he made the major management decisions; resigned, and retained control of the company, while the Dutch director was acting on his instructions.

Recognizing the Dutch company as a tax resident of the UK, British tax authorities accrued to her British tax profits from sale of shares. In addition, they banned a Dutch company from using the agreement on avoidance of double taxation on certain payments from the UK to Holland, justifying this by saying that the Dutch company is not really taxable in the Netherlands (and thus is tax resident in the UK).

The Court considered the arguments of the tax authorities more persuasive and found the dominant CEO and controlling shareholder a British resident, while the Dutch Director was largely secondary. The Court recognized that Dutch company was managed and monitored from the UK, and therefore can be recognized as the British tax resident.

Most EU Member States have elaborated anti-avoidance legislation – rules aimed to combating tax evasion. The anti-avoidance rule may be based on written or unwritten legal principles, domestic law, international tax treaties, on a doctrine of the predominance of substance over form (substance over form) and/or a on business purpose. There are of course many other anti-avoidance rules in use throughout the world. These include anti-offshore rules (anti-tax haven rules), re-qualification of the transaction with the exception of extra steps, such as sales through off-shores (step transactions, arm's length principle). Any of these doctrines raises many questions. For example, one of the contentious issues mentioned above is the place of company management (place of effective/administrative management).

Austria and Spain, along with some European countries, have developed and put into practice the most powerful anti-avoidance doctrines. Russian-European holding companies located in one of these countries should be particularly careful to plan their operations, particularly in the payment and receipt of passive income (dividends, interest, royalties) from those countries or in those countries.

In Austria, there are strong rules of anti-avoidance, opposing tax evasion. Among these rules are: the principle of the predominance of substance over form; the right of tax authorities to reject transactions or structures selected solely for the purpose of tax evasion or avoidance. The question whether the fiscal objective of avoidant structures must be the sole or predominant one remains an open question internationally in the field of double-taxation. The US Supreme Court applies the doctrine of economic substance and emphasizes the priority of tax purposes – the avoidance purposes need not be unique there. In contrast, various Austrian tax laws establish specific rules, such as: the rule of "actual place of management", the rules against tax evasion in the application of the regime release received dividends from taxation (participation exemption); such treatment shall not apply when receiving dividends from passive companies registered in low tax jurisdictions – those jurisdictions having an effective tax rate of less than 15% (calculated according to Austrian rules). A similar rule applies in Russia as to the controlled foreign company (CFC). In respect of offshore investment funds, the CFC income controlled entity should be included in the profits of the company that controls it.

When incorporating companies in EU, it is essential to think of the holding structure as a whole. National law cannot contradict EU law. However, taxation is generally the province of the Member States – albeit, subject to general principles of EU law and EU Directives and Regulations. So far as Russia does not intend to be the part of the EU and continues to negotiate amendments to the Double Taxation Treaties concluded with the Member States individually (bilateralism) with the purpose to strengthen the provisions of exchange and disclosure of information, the analysis of each jurisdiction in the EU that is more suitable for the purposes of Russian business, especially owners of real estate, remains a topical issue.

21 Controlling the Offshore in Russia: Local Rules Needed

Vladimir Kokorin

This chapter identifies some local gaps through which money can (and does) flow out of the Russian economy, and what can law do to address the issues that Russia has to face as regards the offshore mechanisms that create such gaps. Money is essentially being stolen by corporate entities to benefit their seemingly independent owners, whose names will never be revealed, unless young Russian capitalism is regulated the right way.

It has never been a secret (in fact, it is commonplace) that offshore jurisdictions were (and are) used by wealthy individuals as tax and identity shelters. That is especially so in Russia, where corruption has historically been sky-high[1] and keeping your wealth out in the light may cost you dearly.

The legal system of the state functions to help the state and its people reach their goals.[2] One of these goals is creation of a transparent regulatory system as regards corporate governance. That would ensure promotion of the state interests worldwide, and not to the least extent as regards successful cooperation with international financial and corporate security organizations.

While the Russian administrative regulation system is still heavily focused on governing domestic matters, the beginning of this millennium has shown certain positive developments in the area of anti-money laundering and tax evasion. The OECD and FATF[3] were effective at securing financial transparency and stability globally by, inter alia, trying to (i) evaluate

1 The latest Transparency International Corruption Perceptions Index has Russia sharing 154th place (along with Cambodia and Kenya) out of 178 in total (See *Corruption Perceptions Index 2010 Results* at <www.transparency.org/policy_research/surveys_indices/cpi/2010/results>).

2 S.S. Alexeev, *Theory of State and Law*, textbook, 2004 (<www.lawbook.by.ru/theory/Alexeev/29.shtml>).

3 Organization for Economic Co-operation and Development and Financial Action Task Force. While we should not overestimate the altruism of OECD (it was initially created as OEEC by US in 1947 as part of the Marshall Plan (see <www.oecd.org/pages/0,3417,en_36734052_36761863_1_1_1_1_1,00.html>) and was basically intended to promote the post-war US financial interests), its achievements as regards development of the global economy and countering the transnational crime are self-talking. See <www.oecd.org> for details. Financial Action Task Force (FATF) was established by the G-7 summit in 1989 to fight the outrageous organized crime in banking and financial sectors (<www.fatf-gafi.org/pages/0,3417,en_32250379_32236836_1_1_1_1_1,00.html>).

every country's financial regulation system's functionality (and vulnerability) and (ii) to persuade them to take account of forty Recommendations.[4] So, in 2001 the anti-money laundering agency was established in Russia,[5] and the law on anti-money laundering (the AML Law) was passed. Special regulations were put in a force, whereby all banks and financial organizations had to establish and maintain control systems aimed at identifying and reporting all suspicious transactions.[6]

However, monitoring the financial sector cannot be the exhaustive measure for ensuring the legality of all money flows. For example, multi-million advisory service agreements are not extraordinary in Russian business these days. In contrast, back in the nineties, such contracts were the primary means for the fraudulent export of money. The state cannot afford to undermine business operations by trying to investigate every deal that might fit in the officially "suspicious" category. Moreover, the Russian Federation does not have sufficient resources to investigate each and every possible instance of fraud. A "big fish" and "deterrence" strategy is the correct response to limited state resources.

The economic security of Russia is directly dependent on the regulatory efficiency of the administrative sector. Much more must be done by the legislator to match the flexibility of the common law instruments in this field. Capital keeps flowing out. Mr. Kudrin, the Russian Minister for Finance, reported the USD 52 billion outflow in 2010.[7] This, despite certainly being the consequence of the 2008 crisis, resembles the 1990s where the rush of privatization provoked massive capital outflow.[8]

One simple question arises immediately – where are all the money flowing to? The answer is just as straight and simple – to offshores.

What are "offshores"? That is easier asked than answered. I define an "offshore" as a legal entity with special legal status that allows such entity to (i) maintain the level of its tax at a perfect minimum, (ii) have no tax or other reports or returns filed anywhere, and also gives such entity the benefit of a certain confidentiality of ownership (perhaps subject to

---

4 See *FATF 40 Recommendations.* <www.fatf-gafi.org/document/28/0,3746,en_32250379_32236920_33658140_1_1_1_1,00.html>.

5 See the *President's Decree of November 11, 2001 "On the authorized authority to counter the money laundering".* Collection of the Legislation of the Russian Federation, 14 April 2001, # 45, p. 3418.

6 See, primarily, the *Federal Law of the Russian Federation "On countering the money-laundering and terrorism financing".* The collection of the legislation of the Russian Federation. 2001, No 33 (Part 1), p. 3418.

7 See RBC Economics: <http://top.rbc.ru/economics/03/02/2010/367594.shtml>.

8 A.N. Generalov. *Tax planning in Russianenterprises in the system of anti-money laundering.* Dissertation, 2006 (<www.dissercat.com/content/nalogovoe-planirovanie-rossiiskikh-predpriyatii-v-sisteme-protivo deistviya-otmyvaniyu-nezako>).

administrative restrictions).[9] I will not venture deep into where and how such status is awarded, but will explain the basics below.

If you look at the corporate and tax laws of the most prominent and hardcore offshore jurisdictions (*e.g.* BVI. Panama, Bahamas, Seychelles, Belize, etc.), you will probably notice that for the company incorporated in an offshore jurisdiction to enjoy the tax benefits, has to abstain from doing business (i) in the territory of such jurisdiction and (ii) with the residents of such jurisdiction. This is the crucial point of all the offshore phenomenon – the government of the jurisdiction effectively waives its right to (i) control the activity of the legal entity incorporated in such jurisdiction and (ii) receive part of its income as a tax. This looks barely legal at a first glance: in essence, the government is paid to close their eyes. However, we will not investigate the nature and basics of the offshore industry here.

It is a general perception in Russia that offshore companies are used, primarily, to:

1. facilitate tax savings;
2. procure the confidentiality of transactions and cash-flow;
3. serve as transmission units in anti-money laundering schemes;
4. secure the property from claims of third parties and governments.[10]

This perception is so close to the truth as to suffice for as an accurate enough description for this chapter. It is clear from the above that offshore companies can be used for criminal purposes, namely:

1. legalization of proceeds of crime;
2. tax evasion;
3. concealing information about illicit transactions and money flow.[11]

Ever after the Naples Declaration[12] UN, Interpol, OECD, FATF, EU, CE and many other international and supranational bodies and associations have been ceaselessly fighting transnational financial crimes. FATF has published its 40 Recommendations in 1990, and later (which is more important for the purpose of this chapter) – the Report on money-

9 See V.A. Kokorin, *Administrative regulation of offshore mechanisms: the international experience.* Dissertation, 2007. This definition is slightly modified though, and it should be noted that the "ownership confidentiality" part is not attributive to an offshore entity itself, but rather is related to the nominee shareholding and directorship options, as well as trusts, whereby the beneficiary owners can remain concealed (often abusively). That will be discussed below.

10 *Id.*

11 *Id.*

12 *Naples Political Declaration and Global Action Plan against Organized Transnational Crime.* A/RES/49/159, UN 94th plenary meeting, 23 December 1994. This is not to say that the transnational crime had not been fought against before, but the Naples Declaration was an official war declared on organized transnational criminals.

laundering (1999). The research that was in the base of the Report noted, amongst other, the following key points:

- many offshore centres and so-called non-cooperative countries and territories fail to provide the necessary information and legal aid;
- new payment technologies have security gaps. The rapid development of smart-cards, internet-payments and electronic cash can make these instruments effective money-laundering tools – even more so when they are supported by corporate mechanisms;
- professional service providers (lawyers, accountants, auditors) are tending to become more involved in transnational criminal schemes;
- and thus recommends implementation of the suspicious transaction reporting procedures as ordinary procedures by banks and other financial institutions coupled with increasing the investigative efforts of national financial task forces to facilitate search and identification of new money-laundering techniques.

For Russia, the most important point is the emergence of the concept of "non-cooperative countries and territories" (NCCTs) that was further developed and given the independent life in the so-called FATF NCCT Report (this explains why Russia was so extremely fast in passing and implementing the anti-money-laundering legislation).[13] The NCCT Report, published in February 2000, contained 25 auxiliary criteria to identify national rules and procedures non-compliant with international standards for countering the money-laundering. Right after the NCCT Report, in June 2000, FATF published the first NCCT Review, which was basically a list of NCCTs. Russia was there falling under 10 of the 25 criteria set in the NCCT Report.[14] Rapidly implementing relevant legislative measures, Russia managed to clear its way out of the NCCT list by October 2000. To say, the last NCCT (which was Burma-Myanmar) was crossed off of the list in 2006, and since then no country has re-entered it. The NCCT reports were annual, and the last report was published in 2007, concluding the NCCT monitoring process. After such conclusion FATF established the International Co-operation Review Group (ICRG) that:

> "...has analysed high-risk jurisdictions and recommended specific action to address the [money-laundering and terrorism financing] risks emanating from them. Throughout 2008 and 2009, the FATF issued a series of public statements expressing concerns about the significant deficiencies in the [anti-money-laundering and counter-terrorism-financing] [(AML/CFT)]regimes of a

13 The Financial Action Task Force on Money Laundering. *Report on non-cooperative countries and territories.* Paris: FATF Secretariat, Organization for Economic Co-operation and Development. 2000.

14 The Financial Action Task Force on Money Laundering. *Review to identify non-cooperative countries and territories: Increasing the worldwide effectiveness of ant-money laundering measures.* Paris: FATF Secretariat, Organization for Economic Co-operation and Development. 2000.

> number of jurisdictions";[15] "Based upon the results of this process, the FATF issued two public documents in February 2010 — the "Public Statement" and "Improving Global AML/CFT Compliance: Ongoing process." Both documents were updated in June and October 2010 ... The October 2010 Public Statement reaffirmed the FATF's 25 February 2009 Public Statement...".[16]

However, Russia was never mentioned in the post-NCCT FATF documents, which is a pretty remarkable achievement.

So, Russia is now considered a jurisdiction with a high level of (AML/CFT) protection. That's good news; or is it?

The ease and rapidity with which companies in certain jurisdictions can be set-up and dissolved or struck off not only facilitates legitimate processes (venture financing, tax planning, mergers and acquisitions), but also helps to conceal the tracks and beneficiaries of funds. In the NCCT Report, FATF specifically mentioned that shelf companies and nominees, widely used in offshore jurisdictions, are frequent tools for legalizing crime proceeds – and so the ability of the regulatory bodies to obtain and share the information on identity of the companies and their ultimate owners is a key point in the area of regulating the offshore industry.[17]

In November 2006 FATF published the report on misuse of corporate tools, including trust and company service providers.[18] In short, the basic idea of the report was that the primary purpose of misuse of offshore companies is the concealment of the ultimate beneficiary of the money. Often corporate structures involve cascades of legal entities established in different jurisdictions which are only used to hide the beneficiary and run illicit schemes. Complex structures may create the "sham" of legitimacy, where attracting the capital becomes easier but suffering liability – more remote. FATF have described in their reports cases where trust-involving[19] holding groups were used as fraudulent instruments to attract funds (insurance, pensions, etc.), which were then dispersed over the branchy

---

15 FATF-GAFI webpage, section for High-risk and Non-cooperative jurisdictions (<www.fatf-gafi.org/pages/0,3417,en_32250379_32236992_1_1_1_1_1,00.html>).

16 *Id.*

17 Kokorin, *supra* at p. 105.

18 The Financial Action Task Force on Money Laundering. The misuse of corporate vehicles, including trust and company service providers. Paris: FATF Secretariat, Organization for Economic Co-operation and Development. 2006.

19 By "trust" I mean the legal concept of owning a property in someone's name.

structure only to concentrate on the offshore bank account of the then-unknown individuals.[20]

Based on the foregoing, it is safe to say that the primary vulnerable spot in administrative regulation is the option to use nominee shareholders, as well the possibility for the company to function with no shareholders at all. Yes, the common law system recognizes the concept of beneficiarl owners as opposed to registered owners – however, Russia does not have such distinction (at least not clearly and not exactly officially). This means that tracing the ownership of funds in the corporate circuit is immensely complicated, if not impossible. It seems prudent to me to introduce mandatory disclosure of company beneficiaries at the company registration stage.[21]

Professional service providers (corporate service providers, lawyers, notaries, accountants, auditors), as a rule, are always involved in the process of establishing and managing corporate mechanisms. Therefore, controlling their activity and using their own tools of collecting, storing and sharing information is crucial for the legal system. However, Russian law does not require any of the mentioned professionals to perform thorough know-your-customer or due diligence checks when establishing client relationships and transacting with clients, which means (at least…) that the information that could be collected by these useful people merely gets lost.[22]

The time is ripe in Russia (and has been – probably since the NCCT initiative concluded in 2007) for special legislation that would, inter alia:

20 Kokorin, *supra* at p. 106.

21 I need to note that there are beneficiary identity disclosure requirements in Russian antitrust law (See the *Order of the Ministry of the Russian Federation for the antimonopoly policy and entrepreneur support of 13.08.1999 No 276 "On approval of the Regulation on the manner of antimonopoly filings and notices in conformity with sections 17 and 18 of the Law of the Russian Federation "On competition and limitation of the monopolistic activity in the goods markets"*. Rossijskaya Gazeta, # 92-93, 16 May 2000; *Federal Law of the Russian Federation of 26.07.2006 # 135-FZ "On protection of competition"*. The collection of the legislation of the Russian Federation. 31 July 2006 # 31, p. 3434). More strange it is to me then that similar requirements are still not implemented in the company registration area. Some might say that it is useless – since the company shares can be sold to virtually anyone and the beneficiaries may change rapidly – but I would not agree, because (i) the control over transfers of the equity interests is pretty tight, and (ii) introducing strict rules for beneficiary identity disclosure in other areas (depositories, auditors, stock brokers, etc.) may give a huge boost to increasing AML/CFT security in Russia.

22 The professional responsibility issues have long been a difficulty for the Russian professional society, but it's a sad fact that there is no developed system of professional responsibility – but that is, unfortunately, not the purpose of this chapter. To be just, some information collection requirements are imposed on advocates, lawyers, and accountants (by the AML Law) – they need to identify the persons they serve (names and addresses, ID document details for individuals, and names, registered numbers, addresses for legal entities) and "undertake reasonable … measures to identify beneficiaries". Since the term "reasonable" is very vague and broad in Russian civil interpretive jurisprudence, this requirement seems as good as none.

- fix the criteria for identifying the corporate gaps and loopholes as regards the creation and management of corporate entities;
- introduce the institute of professional intermediaries to be responsible for the accuracy, authenticity and completeness of the information that has to be provided and maintained in the course of creating and servicing legal entities;
- establish transparent and comprehensive rules for piercing the corporate veil and holding liable the persons involved in crimes committed through corporate mechanisms.

Absent such legislation, Russians can only enjoy being out of the FATF "black list" to a certain extent (and much was indeed done to that end). However, the money will keep flowing out. Only sewing all the holes in the pocket can stop the outflow – and the biggest holes are still yet to be sewn.

22 Russia v. Charity and Non-Profit Organizations?

Ekaterina Pritchina

1 Introduction

As a corporate lawyer engaged mainly in Mergers and Acquisitions deals and investor support I was not too much concerned about the nonprofit, nongovernmental and charity organizations conditions in Russia. Of course, I was aware of the main laws and regulations in this sphere, and even what the norms say. But the whole picture of the real life of such organizations in Russia I have got only starting work on *pro-bono* matters with the Moscow branch office of a foreign non-profit corporation. Honestly, I was shocked by what I found through my research in this area.

Now I can directly say: contemporary Russian policy states – we do not want charity and non-profit organizations, especially with foreign funding.

The activity of these organizations is almost paralyzed by the tax, legal and administrative norms and regulations which seek to stop illegal businesses from working under the cover of charity and non-commercial activities. Ironically, these barriers lead only to this: that charity and non-profit organizations in Russia are compelled to act using the loopholes, evading the regulations and even committing fraud (making misstatements etc.) with respect to the Russian authorities, in order to conduct their ordinary activity.

The present legislation and the political ideas behind it bar the development of Russian civil society as well as economic growth and business social responsibility in Russia.

In this chapter I will develop the above thesis using contemporary Russian legislation, articles of foreign and Russian authorities, as well as practical examples from my *pro-bono* work.

In the first part of this chapter I will outline the general issues of legal status of non-profit and charity organizations in Russia. The second part contains the comments concerning to the practical issues and legal and tax implications of charities and non-profit organizations activity in Russia, including compliance of certain types of such organizations activities with Russian law.

2 General Issues of Legal Status of Non-Profit and Charity Organizations in Russia

In his 2004 Address of the President of Russian Federation to the Federal Assembly Vladimir Putin admitted the role of non-profit organizations in Russian civil society development, and at the same time he stated that "not all organizations are orientated toward standing up for the real interests of the people. The priority for some is to receive financing from influential foreign organizations. Others serve dubious group and commercial interests".[1]

This completely reflects the current Russian two-faced policy and legislation relating to the charity and non-profit (non-commercial) organizations. As a result, the position and regulation of non-profit organizations in Russia is really confusing. Current Russian tax law prevents non-profit organizations from developing financial autonomy and also prevents charity and donation itself by minimizing (almost eliminating) the tax privileged regime for such activity.[2]

Tax-exempt status in Russia is not automatic for non-profit and charitable organizations. Some organizations might receive exemptions from profit taxes on certain income sources, but there are no "blanket exemptions" for any organisations.[3] This is completely different from the US regulation. The concept of charitable status in Russia is not inherently linked to tax benefits.[4]

A non-commercial (non-profit) organization is one which does not have profit-making as the main objective of its activity and which does not distribute earned profits among the participants (Art. 2 of the Federal Law N 7-FZ "On non-commercial organizations", dated 12 January 1996 – hereinafter "the NCO Law").[5]

---

1 Leslie Lutz, *Economic Constraints, Political Motives: Contemporary Russian Nonprofit Tax Law*, The International Journal of Not-for-Profit Law, available at <www.icnl.org/knowledge/ijnl/vol7iss3/art_4.htm>, citing President Vladimir Putin, "Послание Федеральному Собранию Российской Федерации", Moscow, Russia, 26 May 2004, available at <www.president.kremlin.ru/text/appears/2004/05/71501.shtml>

2 See also Lutz, *id.*

3 *Id.*, citing *The Survey of Tax Laws Affecting NGOs in the Newly Independent States*, International Center for Not-for-Profit Law, available at <www.icnl.org/tools/default.htm>.

4 *Id.*, citing David Moore, "The Fiscal Framework for Corporate Philanthropy in CEE and NIS," International Journal of Not-for-Profit Law vol. 6, no. 2 (2004) [electronic journal], available at <www.icnl.org>.

5 As amended by the Federal Law N 164-FZ on 22.07.2010, coming into force on 1 January 2011, available at <http://base.consultant.ru/cons/cgi/online.cgi?req=doc;base=LAW;n=100256;fld=134;dst=4294967295;

Non-profit organizations "may be created for achieving social, charitable, cultural, educational, scientific and managerial goals, for the purposes of protecting the health of citizens, developing the physical culture and sports, satisfying the spiritual and other non-material requirements of citizens, protecting the rights and legitimate interests of citizens and organizations, settling disputes and conflicts, rendering legal aid, and also for any other purposes directed towards the achievement of public weal".[6] Non-profit organizations may be created in the form of social or religious organizations, non-profit partnerships, institutions, autonomous non-profit organizations, social, charitable and any other funds, associations and unions, and also in any other forms stipulated by the federal laws.

Under Article 1 of the Federal Law "On charities and charitable organizations" N 135-FZ, dated 11 August 1995 (hereinafter "the Charities Law")[7], charity is a voluntary activity of citizens and legal entities without seeking for profit or on free-of-charge (non-payment or discount conditions) transferring citizens or legal entities property, including money, works and services and other support.

According to Article 5 of the Charities Law charity providers are persons, who provide charitable donations, particularly, transferring property ownership, including money and/or intellectual property objects, non-profit or free-of-charge (non-payment or discount conditions).

According to clause 1 of Article 582 of the Civil Code of the Russian Federation (hereinafter "the Civil Code")[8] charitable donation is a donation of property or interest (right) for purposes of common well-being to charitable, religious and other analogical organizations.

Thus, donation can be as by a purchasing of property as well as money transferring. Cash donation is allowed only by natural persons. Legal entities should donate only non-cashitems. The fact of property or money donation should be recorded in an agreement of donation.

The Resolution of the Moscow Administration of the Federal Tax Services N 20-12/46404, dated 30 June 2005, "On taxation"[9] clarifies the taxation of donated property.

from=100204-65>.

6 Art. 2, Federal Law No. 7-FZ Federal Law No. 7-Fz Of January 12, 1996 On Nonprofit Organizations. Available at <http://legislationline.org/documents/action/popup/id/4378>.

7 Available at <http://base.consultant.ru/cons/cgi/online.cgi?req=doc;base=LAW;n=83421;div=LAW;mb=LAW;opt=1;ts=99961FCBCB882CB7D915B64DCAC7EC6A>.

8 Available at <http://base.consultant.ru/cons/cgi/online.cgi?req=doc;base=LAW;n=89528;fld=134;dst=4294967295>.

9 Available at <http://base.consultant.ru/cons/cgi/online.cgi?req=doc;base=MLAW;n=65292;div=LAW;

According to Article 26 of the NCO Law, the sources for non-profit organization property formation, among others, are regular and simultaneous proceeds from settlers (participants, members), voluntary property contributions and donations.

The charitable organization shall be a non-governmental (non-state and non-municipal) non-profit organization, set up to realize the goals stipulated by the Federal Law by way of performing charitable activity in the interest of a society as a whole or of the individual categories of persons (Art. 6 of the Charities Law).

According to Article 21 of the Charities Law, participants in charitable activity shall have the right to engage in international charitable activity in conformity with the Russian legislation and international treaties of the Russian Federation.

International charitable activity shall be performed by participating in international charity projects and in the work of international charitable organizations, by interacting with foreign partners in the corresponding sphere of charitable activity, and also in any other form accepted in the international practices and not contradicting the legislation of the Russian Federation or the norms and the principles of international law.

A charitable organization has the right to accept charity donations from foreign citizens, stateless persons, and also from foreign and international organizations. These donations shall be used in conformity with the procedure, stipulated by the Charities Law.

Article 12 of the Charities Law stipulates that a charitable organization shall have the right to perform charitable activity, aimed at achieving the goals for the sake of which it was set up, and also the charitable activity aimed at achieving the goals, stated by Russian Federal Law.

A charitable organization shall have the right to be engaged in activity involved in attracting resources and in conducting extra-realization (non-sale) operations.

A charitable organization shall have the right to engage in business activities only to achieve the goals, for the sake of which it was set up and which correspond to these goals.

The sources of the charitable organization property formation may be the following (according to the Art. 15 of the Charities Law):

- the contributions, made by the founders of the charitable organization;

---

mb=LAW;opt=1;ts=5D75E7DE48CC29D51BB3DC05270714AA>.

- the membership dues (for the charitable organizations, based on the membership);
- the charity donations, including those of the goal-oriented nature (charity grants), made by the citizens and by the legal entities in the monetary form or in kind;
- the non-operating revenues, including the revenues from securities;
- the incomes from the activity, involved in attracting the resources (conducting campaigns to attract philanthropists and volunteers, including the organization of entertainment, cultural, sports and other massive events, launching campaigns to collect charity donations, holding lotteries and auctions in conformity with the legislation of the Russian Federation and selling the property and the donations, given by the philanthropists, in accordance with their wishes);
- the incomes from business activity, permitted by the legislation;
- the incomes from the activity of economic companies, set up by the charitable organization;
- the labour of volunteers;
- other sources, not forbidden by law.

A charitable organization may possess, by ownership or other property right: buildings and structures, equipment, monetary means, securities and the information resources, and also other property, unless otherwise stipulated by the federal laws as well as the results of intellectual activity.

A charitable organization may make any transactions with respect to the property it possesses by the right of ownership or by a different kind of the real right, which do not contradict the legislation of the Russian Federation, the rules of this organization and the philanthropist's wishes (clauses 1 and 2 of the Art. 16 of the Charities Law).

Clause 3 of the Article. 16 of the Charities Law states that charitable organization shall not use over 20% of the funds, which this organization spends in the course of the fiscal year for the remuneration of the labour of the administrative-managerial personnel. This restriction shall not cover the remuneration of the labor of the persons, participating in charity programs.

Unless otherwise stipulated by the philanthropist or by the charity program, not less than 80% of a charitable donation, made in monetary form, shall be used for charitable purposes in the course of a year from the moment when this donation is received by the charitable organization. Charitable donations, made in kind, shall be directed towards charitable purposes in the course of one year from the moment of their receipt, unless otherwise decreed by the philanthropist or by the charity program (sub clause 4 of the Art. 16 of the Charities Law).

Article 17 of the Charities Law provides the requirements for the charity programs. A charity program shall be a complex of measures, approved by higher management body of a charitable organization and aimed at carrying out the concrete tasks, corresponding to the constituent goals of this organization.

The charity program shall include an estimate of the supposed anticipated revenues and of the planned expenditures (including the remuneration of labor for the persons, participating in the implementation of the charity program), and shall fix the stages and the term of its implementation.

At least 80% of income from extra-realization operations, from proceeds of the economic companies set up by the charitable organization, and of the earnings from permitted business activity, which have accrued in the course of the fiscal year shall be used to finance the charitable program (including outlays for material, technical, organizational and other provisions, for the remuneration of labor for the persons participating in the implementation of the charity program, as well as other expenses related to the implementation of the charity programs) shall be used by the charity operations. During the implementation of the long-term charity programs, the incoming means shall be used within the term fixed by those programs.

Article 19 of the Charities Law provides that the charitable organization shall conduct accounting and reporting in conformity with the procedures provided by the legislation of the Russian Federation.

The Ministry of Justice of the Russian Federation is the body that renders the decisions on state registration of a charitable organization and shall control the compliance of charitable organization activity with the goals, for the sake of which it has been established.

Clause 2 of Article 19 of the Charities Law states that the charitable organization shall annually report to the supervising body on its activity, containing the following information:
- The financial and economic activity, confirming the observance of the stipulations of the present Federal Law for the use of the property and for spending the means of the charitable organization;
- The personnel composition of the higher management body of the charitable organization;
- The composition and the content of the charity programs of the charitable organization (the list and the description of the said programs);
- The content and the results of the activity of the charitable organization;

- Any violations of the requirements of the present Federal Law, revealed as a result of the check-ups launched by the taxation bodies, and the measures which have been taken to eliminate those violations.

The annual report shall be filed with the supervising body that has rendered a decision on state registration within the same term as an annual report on the financial and economic activities, submitted to taxation bodies.

The charitable organization shall provide for open access, including the mass media, to its annual reports (sub clause 5 of the Art. 19 of the Charities Law). The expenses for annual report publishing are charity purpose expenses.

The information on the amounts and on the structure of the incomes of the charitable organization, as well as the information on the size of its property, its expenditures, the number of its workers, the remuneration of their labour and the drawing in of volunteers shall not be made a commercial secret.

The tax authorities shall exert control over the sources of the charitable organizations' incomes, the amounts of received sums, and their payment of taxes in conformity with the tax legislation.

Under sub clause 1 of clause 2 of Article 251 of the Tax Code of the Russian Federation (hereinafter "the Tax Code")[10] money and property donated to non-profit organizations for charitable purposes should not be accounted for taxation purposes to the charitable organization, provided that the charity conforms to certain conditions.

On the basis of sub clause 1 of clause 2 of Article 251 of the Tax Code, the charitable organization which has received money or property for charitable purposes does not consider them at the accounting of its tax base if certain conditions are complied with. Such conditions concern:

1. The organizations which have received charitable payments are obliged to keep separate tax accounts of such incomes and their expenses, as well as the sums of incomes and expenses from the activity connected with manufacture and (or) realization of the goods, works, services, property rights, and incomes and expenses from non-realization operations. The requirement to keep separate accounts arises not only for those non-commercial organizations which have no incomes of realization existing only at the

10 Available at <http://base.consultant.ru/cons/cgi/online.cgi?req=doc;base=LAW;n=106436;fld=134;dst=4294967295>.

expense of special-purpose financing and (or) purpose receipts (charitable payments); it also arises for those which are recognized as such from the profit taxation point of view. In the absence of maintenance of separate accounts in organizations which have received purpose financing (purpose receipts), the specified sums are considered as subject to the taxation from the date of their receipt (sub clause 1 of clause 2 of Art. 251 of the Tax Code of the Russian Federation).

2. The property received should correspond to the requirements of the Tax Code of the Russian Federation, and also some other conditions should be complied with. Otherwise, sums of charitable payments are included in the structure of non-realization revenues (and are considered in profit tax calculation accordingly).
3. Funds of a charitable payment should be used only according to a special-purpose designation. Such a norm is directly provided by the clause 14 of Art. 250 of the Tax Code of the Russian Federation, according to which the non-realization revenues includes property received charitably (including in the form of the charitable help, donations), special-purpose receipts (whether in the form of special-purpose financing or not), and not used as a special-purpose designation admits. When special-purpose funds are not spent as they were assigned, they are subject to inclusion in the structure of non-realization revenues during the moment when the addressee of property (including monetary resources) actually used the specified property not on a special-purpose designation or has broken the conditions on which they were given (sub clause 9 of clause 4 of Art. 271 of the Tax Code of the Russian Federation).

According to the Charities Law such operations are released from VAT taxation on the basis of sub clause 12 of clause 3 of Article 149 of the Tax Code of the Russian Federation. Transfer of goods (including works and services) specified in this sub clause are exempt from VAT only if listed by the taxing authority as exempt and documented by the taxpayer in official representations to the tax bodies. In order to exempt these operations from taxation the taxpayer should file the following documents with the tax body:

- The contract (agreement) of the taxpayer with the addressee of the charitable help on gratuitous transfer of the goods (performance of works, rendering of services) within the framework of charities rendering;
- Copies of the documents confirming the account by the addressee of the charitable help of gratuitously received goods (the executed works, the rendered services);
- Certificates or other documents conforming the special-purpose use of received (executed, rendered) within the framework of charities of the goods (works, services);
- The document confirming actual reception of the goods (works, services) by the addressee – the physical person.

The following cannot be considered charitable activities:

- Direction of monetary and other material founds, and also rendering assistance in other forms to commercial organizations.
- Support of political parties, movements, groups and campaigns.

Thus, in the case of a gratuitous transfer by a public association of any goods (including work and services) to a commercial organization or to a physical person, except to charities, the association donation is subject to the Value Added Tax.

According to sub clause 12 of the clause 3 of Article 149 the gratuitous transfer of the goods (performance of works, rendering of services) within the framework of charities according to the Charities Law, with the exception of excisable goods, is exempted from the taxation by the tax to the added cost (value added tax: VAT). Therefore, distribution of the humanitarian help would not be taxed by VAT.

At distribution of humanitarian help among physical persons, it is not necessary to withhold the tax on such distributions to incomes of physical persons according to sub clause 8 clause 1 of Article 217 of the Tax Codes.

The responsibility of the Charitable Organization is stipulated by Article 20 of the Charities Law. In the cases of violating the Law, the charitable organization shall bear responsibility according to Russian legislation. If the charitable organization performs actions, contradicting its set goals and also the Law, the body which registered the organization shall send it a warning in written form, which the charitable organization may appeal in the court. In case of repeated warnings, the charitable organization may be liquidated.

All the funds earned by the charity organization in performing business activities in violation of Article 12 of the Charities Law, shall be withdrawn into the revenue of the local budget by the place of location of the charitable organization, and shall be liable to the use for charitable purposes in conformity with the procedure defined by the municipal bodies for the social protection.

3 Problematic Issues of Charitable Non-Profit Organization Activity in Russia

3.1 *Operating Expenses and Use of Donated Property*

In order to for the transfer of money or property to be recognized as charitable (and non-taxable), it should be in conformity with the purposes determined by Article 2 of Charities

Law. Charitable purposes include provision of public health services, science, education, art, support of religious organizations, low-income groups of people, and support for victims of natural disasters.

The Law also provides that donations to the charity or non-profit organization of property shall be used strictly for the purposes stipulated in the organization's charter. The tax authorities do not tend to deem the organization's operational activity (admin, overhead) as a "purposeful" and "charter activity".

Thus, *e.g.*, I faced the problem of an old used car which was donated to a charity (the "vehicle").

The vehicle is actually used by the Director of the organization for both business and personal purposes (including trips to the church, getting to the office and back home, to drive the children to school, shopping etc.). The car was registered at the legal address of the organization in Moscow (which is only nominal – not real – as is usually the case in Russia). Actually, the vehicle is parked at night at the territory around the dwelling house of the Director's residence. The parking rent (bailment) is paid by the Director personally in cash, and such payment are not accounted. All vehicle transit expenses have been accounted for with a regard to the first address.

Of course, the organization would like to do all things officially; the expenses regarding the maintenance of the car (parking payments, fuel cost, repair etc.) is considered as purposeful expenses and have no tax consequences. At the first glance, this is a normal situation. and a Director's employment agreement can provide him with a corporation car.

But remember that you are in Russia – this car is donated to the charity organization. According to my practical experience in the present situation, the tax authorities during the inspection would deem that vehicle was used for personal purposes, rather than for organization charter activity (*i.e.* a charitable purpose).

In the case of non-charter use of donated property, the tax authorities are entitled to charge the donated vehicle cost with VAT at the rate of 18%, profit tax at the rate of 20% and personal income tax of the Director at the rate of 13%, and also they can impose fines and penalties.

The only way to avoid the tax authority's accusation of misuse of charitable property by the organization and Director for the non-purposeful use of the vehicle is to conceal the use of the vehicle for personal purposes in accounting and before the tax authorities – even though a "company car" is usually part of a compensation package (and so the use of the vehicle is not a misuse). But in practice, the use of the vehicle and all the trips should be included into the current charitable projects (programs, registered with the Ministry of Justice) and with filling of the special route cards (travel orders) accordingly.

Each trip should be recorded in accord with the kilometric area in the route card (the Decree of Ministry of Transport N 152 dated 18 September 2008) and other requisite requirements.

Use of route cards with indication of the trips' purposes as primary documents in accounting is necessary for correct write-off (accounting) of fuels and lubricants, otherwise it is not possible to claim that vehicle was used in accordance with the authorized purposes.

The certain quantity of gasoline for certain kilometres is paid for the known price specified in the check.

The Letter of the Ministry of Finance (the Department of a tax and customs-tariff policy) N 03-03-04/1/129 dated 20 February 2006 contains the following interpretations and explanations on the matter of documentary confirmation of the expenses connected with the maintenance of vehicles (cars), used by employees for performance of official duties by them.

According to clause 1 of Article 252 of the Tax Code for tax purposes the profit tax of the organizations expenses admits the proved and documentary confirmed expenses (and losses in the cases provided by Article. 265 of the Tax Code) carried out (suffered) by the tax payer.

The proved expenses are understood as economically defensible expenses the estimation of which is expressed in monetary form.

Documentary confirmed expenses are understood as the expenses confirmed with documents, issued according to the legislation of the Russian Federation. Any expenses are admitted as such, provided that they are made for realization of the profit activity.

On the basis of clause 1 of Article 11 of the Tax Code institutes, concepts and terms of civil, family and other branches of the legislation of the Russian Federation, used in the Code, are applied in that sense they are used in these branches of the legislation.

According to Article 9 of the Federal law N 129-FZ "On accounting" dated 21 November 1996[11] primary (initial) accounting documents are accepted if they are drafted under the form from the albums of unified forms of the primary accounting documentation, and the documents, which form is not provided in these albums, should contain the specified obligatory requisites.

Form N 3 "The vehicle route card", approved by the Decision of Goskomstat of Russia N 78 dated 28 November 1997 as a part of the complete set of the unified forms of the primary accounting documentation on the account of works in motor transportation services, extends to all legal entities who are operating vehicles (cargo, automobile, including office cars, specialized vehicles and taxis), and has a binding character for the motor transportation organizations.

As to other organizations, they can draft the form of the route card or other document confirming the expenses made in the form of fuels and lubricants in which all requisites provided by clause 2 of Article of 9 of the Federal law "On accounting" should be reflected. Thus, primary documents should be constituted with such regularity that allows proving expenses made validily on the basis of such documents.

The monthly drawing up of the route card allows organizing the account of hours worked, the fuels and lubricants consumed; the route card, constituted with such periodicity, can confirm the above-named expenses of the tax payer.

Thus, you can see that this documentation process and risk of accusation of fraud is a real nightmare for charity or non-profit organizations, which often cannot afford even a part-time accountant. The regulations itself force organizations to make false statements in accounting. Charities and non-profit organizations often ask their donors not to provide property in the form of donation in order to make their life easier: they think it is easier and less risky to simply make a purchasing agreement with nominal property price and pay taxes.

3.2 *Organization's Staff Salaries*

Another of the problems facing charities is their staffing. This is especially true, when some of the charity's staff are foreigners. Most of the charitable organization's staff are not officially employed at all. Some act on the basis of volunteer agreements. It is obvious, that

11 Available at: <http://base.consultant.ru/cons/cgi/online.cgi?req=doc;base=LAW;n=105200;div=LAW;mb=LAW;opt=1;ts=1DC3CFC79D8DFDF17EB53B5AED1B5FC7>.

organizations would like to employ staff and pay salary officially in compliance with the Russian legislation. As we can see, this is almost impossible.

According to Article 22 of the Charities Law, foreign citizens, stateless persons, and foreign and international organizations are entitled to participate in charitable activity on the territory of the Russian Federation in conformity with the law.

Clause 3 of Article 16 of the Charities Law states that charitable organizations shall not use for the remuneration of the labour of their administrative-managerial personnel over 20% of the funds, which this organization spends in the course of the fiscal year. This restriction shall not cover the remuneration of the labor of the persons, participating in charity programs.

In case of official employment of personnel, the charitable organization should pay salary taxes.

Unified Social Tax (ESN) should be paid over the actually paid out amounts to the personnel: at the rate of 26% in 2010, and at the rate of 34% since 2011 from base salary not exceeding RUB 450 000 per year.

And income tax should be withhold from the pay-out amounts at the rate of 30% for non-residents, who live in Russia less than 183 days within a year, and at the rate of 13% for residents.

The tax authorities tend to consider (referring to clause 2 of Art. 251 and clause 2 of Art. 321.1 of the Tax Code of RF) the sums of donations received by a charity or non-profit organization on the basis of contracts on donation (even with definition of their target use – for salary payments), as subject to inclusion in structure of its profit at the profit tax calculation.

Furthermore, the employment of foreigners in Russia is subject to the special regulation (prior application, approval, limits, quotation, work permits, visas etc.) of the Federal Migration Service and Russian Government[12] and it is very costly both in terms of money and time to comply with all the requirements.

12 See, *e.g.* Government Decrees at <http://base.consultant.ru/cons/cgi/online.cgi?req=doc;base=LAW;n=106927;div=LAW;mb=LAW;opt=1;ts=C540B75F93277DE580AC021FDECDF115>.

3.3 *Charity – Soup Kitchens and Distribution of Donated Clothes*

Charitable organizations' worldwide usual activity is running soup kitchens and gathering and distributing donated clothes for elderly people, single mothers and children, the homeless, and other people in need. In Russia this ordinary charitable organizations activity has almost stopped due to administrative norms.

To organize soup kitchens, the organization must first have registered with the Ministry of Justice's charity program, where such soup kitchen shall be indicated with budget; it shall obtain several permits from the authorities and comply with very strict requirements on sanitary norms.[13] And that is is not all. There are also tax regulations.

Thus, several soup kitchens running in Moscow by the charity organization I was working with serve hot meals through the local "*stolovaya*", or cafeterias, to elderly Russian pensioners and low-income families. Distribution of meals among pensioners is made by volunteers. Payments for dinners are made by this organization directly to the *stolovaya* management by cash. The directors of *stolovaya* would agree to receive funds officially by bank account transfer only in case of increase in meal price. The question was, how to run the soup kitchens officially and make payments for the meals through the organization's bank account? And the issue was not only in the 20% increase in the cost of meals.

According to sub clause 3 of clause 8 of Article 217 of the Tax Code, only one-time paid sums (including in the form of material support) of physical persons' income in the form of humanitarian help (assistance) and also in the form of charitable support rendered by duly registered Russian and foreign charitable organizations (funds, associations) according to the charities legislation, are exempted from taxation. These provisions are applied also to incomes in natural form (*in natura, i.e.* in kind).

Thus, in the case that provided meals are not a one-time support for a person, according to sub clause 3 of clause 8 of Article 217 of the Tax Code, the organization shall withhold the income tax from the cost of meal (as a tax agent).

In order for the transfer of money or property to be recognized as charitable, it should be in conformity with the purposes determined by Article 2 of Charities Law: public health services, science, education, art, support of the religious organizations and low-income groups, of people or victims of acts of nature.

---

13 This is a normal practice in Russia when soup kitchens are dispersed by OMON and militia grabs migrants and homeless people. Now volunteers try to feed people secretly. See *e.g.*, Aleksandra Krylenko, *One Hundred People Want To Eat*, available at <www.miloserdie.ru/print/4/19/9707>.

The Executive Order of the Government of the Russian Federation "On establishing a living wage per capita and on the basic socially-demographic groups of the population as a whole across the Russian Federation for the 2d quarter of 2010" N 763, dated 28 September 2010[14] states that according to clause 2 of Art. 4 of the Federal law "On the living wage in the Russian Federation" the per capita living wage size for the 2d quarter of 2010 is established as RUB 5198, for able-bodied population RUB 6070, pensioners RUB 4475, children – RUB 5423.

The living wage minimum is intended to be an estimation of a standard of living of the population at social policy realization in the country. It is applied to a rationale established on the federal level of the minimum wage rate, sizes of scholarships, allowances and other social payments. In statistics, scientific researches, and forecasts the living wage indicator is considered as the poverty threshold.

Only people who have income less than the indicated norm, which is confirmed by documentation can be recognized as a low-income persons for purposes.

However, the income tax should be withheld by the charitable organization in any case, so long as such support is not one-time. Otherwise, charitable organizations should prove before the tax authorities the "one-time" condition of support, *e.g.* to provide the tax authorities with the list of persons who get the support obtaining the signatures of charity event participants (donation receivers) for provided meals.

It is also necessary to obtain a reference from the authorities ("spravka") on the level of income of these persons (donation receivers) and their families, to confirm that such level is less than living wage.

Thus, we can see that in compliance with these requirements, charitable organizations are forbidden from feeding homeless people, non-citizens (like foreign students and young people from African states we often see working in Moscow streets), refugees, people with occasional employment, etc. And this organizations need a large staff of accounting and administrative people to make records properly (and expanses for their salaries also). It is also obvious that donee, *e.g.* the elderly Russian pensioner ("*babushka*"), would not be very happy to obtain and bring a spravka about her income for the first time to have dinner (which cost is about RUR 50-70) and to pay the income tax for the next times and bring

14 Available at <http://base.consultant.ru/cons/cgi/online.cgi?req=doc;base=LAW;n=105352;div=LAW;mb=LAW;opt=1;ts=7417DF6AEC3061C33E8EF1A3C74DCFA3>.

the passport for registration in the list provide her the signature for having the meal. Imagine the poor volunteer telling a hungry *babushka* all these legal facts.

The same situation holds for with donated clothes distribution – it is currently almost entirely stopped and where it exist is run mostly illegally. There are strict sanitary norms regarding the premises for clothes storage and a requirement for several permits to maintain such premises. There also is a requirement that the donated clothes should be dry-cleaned (receipt from dry-cleaner needed) or the organization shall have special equipment for clothes cleansing and permits to do it on its own or organize cleaning through the outside organization.[15] People usually do not want to spend additional money to donate used clothes, and other ways are too expensive for charity organizations in Russia. Then, the same tax norms requirements as in the soup kitchens situation (as discussed above – sub clause 3 of clause 8 of Art 217 of the Tax Code) apply here to clothes' donation. Many charity organizations simply quit[16] but some still organize clothes donation – in fact running it illegally.[17]

3.4 *Education Programs and Stipend Fund (Scholarships)*

Non-profit organizations often run educational services to needy people who can help them to adapt to surrounding circumstances (like language and computer classes) and also distribute stipend funds to the attendees.

Under the Russian law, educational services can be provided only by the certified organizations with the license and staff of professional tutors (teachers, professors). Only such organizations are entitled to issue official diplomas.

Thus, charitable organization are allowed to provide only "general training" services rather than "educational" services without which would issue official educational documents issuing (diplomas).

Even in this case, such organizations should withhold and pay all taxes on students' imputed income (*e.g.*, scholarships) as well as such free-of-charge services as are deemed by the tax authorities as income. Also, tutors' salary taxes should be withheld from tutor's salaries

15 See, *e.g.* publication at <www.vppress.ru/stories/2238>.
16 See, *e.g.*, publication at <http://rdumu.wordpress.com/2009/10/15/v-sobornoj-mecheti-otkazalis-ot-sbora-isporchennyx-veshhej-dlya-blagotvoritelnoj-razdachi/>.
17 See, *e.g.*, publication at <www.vppress.ru/stories/2238>.

and paid 34% over the amounts paid and 13% from salaries (clause 21 of Art. 217 of the Tax Code).

Clause 11 of Article 217 of the Tax Code stipulates the taxation of charity funds scholarships, but in case there is the charity organization rather than fund, this rule cannot be applied. Thus, full taxes should be paid.

3.5 *Medical Care and Medications*

Another ordinary charitable and non-profit organizations' activity (worldwide) is providing disadvantaged individuals with medical consultations, health care and subsidized prescription medication for diseases and illnesses.

Often, such organizations engage volunteers and migrants with medical education. However, in Russia medical care services can be provided only by licensed medical organizations with professional certified medical staff and under the official agreement on medical services (according to the Executive Order of the Government of the Russian Federation, dated 22 January 2007 N 30; The Decree of Ministry of Public Health Care of the Russian Federation, dated 10 May 2007 N 323). Medication distribution shall be conducted only by pharmacy a licensed pharmacy organization.

Thus, these activities of charitable and nonprofit organizations can be qualified as – illegal entrepreneurial (business) activity, which must seem astonishing to foreign eyes.

Furthermore, organizations should withhold and pay the income tax for each recipient of medications and medical services according to the clause 28 of Article 217 of the Tax Code and fulfil other requirements as discussed above relating to the soup kitchens and clothes donation activities.

Some of the people in need of medical care are homeless, some are migrants who do not have visas and permits to stay in Russia and other similar problems; and they simply cannot go to state medical organizations, even in case of emergency need because they afraid of being pursued by the state authorities. They also cannot report violence and bodily harm because of these reasons. Obviously, medical care to such people cannot be reported in compliance with regulations.

Thus, charities organizations sometimes act directly illegally (knowingly or not) by providing medical help to certain indigent people.

4 Conclusion

At the present time, Russian law and tax regulations are completely unfriendly to non-profit and charity organizations. There are a lot of administrative norms and regulations that non-commercial organizations should comply with. The time and money required (including taxes and accounting) to make the activity of charity non-commercial organizations completely in compliance with the laws' requirements would paralyze any charitable activity at all in Russia.

Furthermore, the lack of tax deductions for charitable donation leads to weak financial support for such organizations and their programs. That, in turn, leads to a weak Russian civil society and business responsibility,[18] especially in the country's transition period. The result? Real and needless economic hardship for millions of people. While many Russians are wealthy, many more are not, and many are even outright impoverished. Russia definitely needs to change its policy toward non-commercial organizations and charities. It is a matter of national survival.

18 See Leslie Lutz, *Economic Constraints, Political Motives: Contemporary Russian Nonprofit Tax Law*, The International Journal of Not-for-Profit Law, available at <www.icnl.org/knowledge/ijnl/vol7iss3/art_4.htm>.

23 A Taxing Question for Human Rights

The European Court of Human Rights, the Value Added Tax, and the Russian Federation

Vladimir Gritsenko

1 Introduction

On 12 October 2006 the Plenum of the High Arbitrazh Court of the Russian Federation (HACtRF Plenum) issued prominent guidelines regarding some aspects of tax benefits, including VAT refunds: tax authorities may no longer disallow the VAT refund for the customer merely on the grounds that the latter did not select its business partner with due prudence.[1] Unsuspecting and non-interrelated Russian taxpayers should not bear the tax risk of doing business with bad faith partners who are not complying with tax obligations.

In this respect, the legal position of the High Arbitrazh Court of the RF (HACtRF) complies with the European Court of Human Rights (ECtHR) conclusion reached later on 22 January 2009 in *Bulves AD v. Bulgaria.*[2]

Were the rulings of the ECtHR and the guidelines issued by the HACtRF Plenum based on the same considerations? Does *Bulves* affects outcome of the cases tried later in Arbitrage Courts of Russian Federation? This chapter attempts to reveal interrelations between the prominent (from the Russian point of view) ECtHR judgment in *Bulves* and the position of HACtRF proclaimed in Resolution No. 53.

In order to start the analysis it is important to understand a legal background of interrelations between Russia and ECtHR.

---

1 See Section 10 of Plenum Resolution of High Arbitrazh Court of the RF "On Arbitrage Courts' Assessment of Reasonability of Tax Benefit to Be Receipt by the Taxpayer", 12 October 2006 No. 53 in Vestn. VAS [Herald of High Arbitrazh Court of the RF] No. 12 [monthly] (hereinafter "Resolution No. 53") available at: <www.arbitr.ru/?id_sec=353&id_doc=1240&id_src=47A46C7D005349FA240CB7C9341F70EC&p=-1>.

2 *Bulves AD v. Bulgaria* (3991/03) [2009] S.T.C. 1193 (ECHR) available at: <http://cmiskp.echr.coe.int/tkp197/view.asp?item=1&portal=hbkm&action=html&highlight=Bulves&sessionid=61311740&skin=hudoc-en>.

2 Russia Joins the ECHR

"The European Convention of Human Rights and Fundamental Freedoms (ECHR) is often portrayed as one of the most successful regimes for the protection of human rights in the world today, and its judicial control body, the ECtHR, as an international tribunal rivaled in effectiveness only by its European sibling, the European Court of Justice (ECJ)".[3] "For the first forty years of its existence, it was often asserted as near-conventional wisdom that the judgments rendered by the European Court of Human Rights '... have ... not only generally but always been complied with by the Contracting States concerned,'[4] with 'no exceptions' and 'without the need for 'enforcement'."[5]

The Russian Federation signed the ECHR on 28 February 1996.[6] The Federal law ratifying the treaty was adopted on 30 March 1998.[7] Russia accepted the obligation "[to] secure to everyone within [its] jurisdiction the rights and freedoms" described in the ECHR.[8]

"Russia recognized the authority of the ECtHR to ensure observance of this obligation,[9] and the right of individuals to petition the ECtHR alleging violations of the ECHR by the Russian state, a right extraordinary in international human rights law.[10] Accession to the ECtHR has been hailed as a sign of great progress for Russia's human rights record and for its development as a rule of law state."[11]

---

3 Andreas von Staden, *Assessing the Impact of the Judgments of the European Court of Human Rights on Domestic Human Rights Policies,* Annual Meeting of American Political Science Association 1 (2007) Paper presented at the annual meeting of the American Political Science Association, Hyatt Regency Chicago and the Sheraton Chicago Hotel and Towers, Chicago, IL, 30 August 2007 available at: <www.allacademic.com/meta/p212106_index.html>, citing Helfer, Laurence & Anne-Marie Slaughter, *Toward a Theory of Effective Supranational Adjudication,* Yale Law Journal 107:272-391 (1997)

4 *Id.* Citing Rolv Ryssdal, *The Enforcement System Set Up Under the European Convention on Human Rights,* in Mielle K. Bulterman & Martin Kuijer, eds., *Compliance with Judgments of International Courts,* 67 (1996).

5 *Id.* Citing Colin Warbrick, Expantion of Rights protected by the European Convention on Human Rights, in W.E. Butler, ed. *Control over Compliance with International Law,* 140 (1991).

6 See Convention for the Protection of Human Rights and Fundamental Freedoms: Chart of Signatures and Ratifications ETS 5; 213 UNTS 221, available at <http://conventions.coe.int/treaty/Commun/ChercheSig.asp?NT=005&CM=&DF=&CL=ENG>. The Convention was opened for signature in Rome on 4 November 1950, and entered into force following ratification by ten signatories on 3 September 1953.

7 See Federal Law on Ratification of the Convention for the Protection of Human Rights and Fundamental Freedoms and Protocols to it, 30 March 1998, No. 54-FZ, SZ RF [Collected Legislation of the Russian Federation], 1998, No. 14, Art. No. 1514, at 2939-2940.

8 European Convention for the Protection of Human Rights and Fundamental Freedoms, available at <http://conventions.coe.int/treaty/en/treaties/html/005.htm>.

9 *Id.* Art. 19.

10 *Id.* Protocol No. 11.

11 Kahn, Jeffrey, *Russian Compliance with Articles Five & Six of the European Convention of Human Rights as a Barometer of Legal Reform & Human Rights in Russia,* University of Michigan Journal of Law Reform, Vol. 35, No. 3 (2002) Available at: <http://ssrn.com/abstract=1011823>. Citing Marjorie Farquharson, *End*

In the meanwhile, "… Russian constitutional law places international law (in both its treaty and customary law forms) at the highest level of Russia's legal hierarchy.[12] Furthermore, Russian courts may use the interpretation given to treaties by international organs. Thus, in connection with Russia's Council of Europe obligations, Professor Gennady Danilenko noted that there is "no bar to the domestic use of the interpretation of the [ECHR] advanced by the [ECtHR]. The case law of the European Court may thus be gradually transformed into Russian domestic jurisprudence.

Although the vast majority of Russian judges are still likely to find such practice quite unfamiliar, the HACtRF have employed the ECHR and ECtHR case law in its own decisions, encouraging lower courts to do the same."[13]

As applied to litigation regarding VAT's refund HACtRF issued Resolution No. 53, some of which provisions are clearly based on the EU case law.

3 INTERRELATIONS BETWEEN *BULVES* AND RESOLUTION NO. 53

Resolution No. 53 was issued in 2006, whereas ECtHR resolved *Bulves* only in the beginning of 2009. Reasonable question is how could HACtRF have taken *Bulves* into consideration in 2006? In order to draw parallels it is essential to take a look at *Bulves'* analysis.

3.1 Bulves

The case originated in an application against the Republic of Bulgaria filed with the ECtHR on 23 January 2003 under Article 34 of the ECHR by "Bulves" AD, a Bulgarian joint-stock company (applicant company). The applicant company purchased goods from another company (supplier), paid the purchase price including VAT, recorded the purchase in its accounting records for the month of August 2000 and filed its VAT return for that period. The supplier, on the other hand, did not record the sale in its accounting records for the

---

Note: Kalashnikov Versus the Russian Federation, 5 RFE/RL Newsline, 12 December 2001, at <www.rferl.org/newsline/search/> ("In the not too distant future, decisions taken in a quiet Rhineland courtroom could supply much needed voltage to the meandering process of legal reform in the Russian Federation, as they have already done in other parts of Europe."); Bill Bowring, *Russia's Accession to the Council of Europe and Human Rights: Four Years On*, 4 Eur. Hum. Rts. L. Rev. 362, 363 (2000) ("[T]here are perhaps even more convincing grounds for concluding that Russia is undergoing genuine and profound transformation as a direct result of accession, especially in the application of the rule of law.")

12 See Section 4 Art. 15 Constitution of Russian Federation, 12 December 1995, SZ RF [Collected Legislation of the Russian Federation], 2009, No. 4, at p. 445.

13 *Supra* note 11, citing remarks made by Professor Gennady Danilenko at the Ninety-First Annual Meeting of the American Society of International Law (1997).

month of August 2000, but for October 2000, and reported it in its VAT return for the latter period.[14]

The tax authorities conducted a VAT audit of the applicant company covering the period from 10 February 2000 to 31 December 2000. In the course of the inspection, a cross-check of the supplier was conducted in order to ascertain whether it had properly reported and recorded the supply in its accounting records. As a result, the above reporting discrepancy was discovered and the tax authority refused the applicant company the right to deduct the VAT it had paid to its supplier. National courts of all instances dismissed the claims against the tax assessment, whereas the ECtHR granted judgment in favor of the applicant company.[15]

The ECtHR based its analysis on the following the two judgments of ECJ, which examine the entitlement of the recipient of a supply to reimbursement of the VAT charged on such a supply in cases of suspected "carousel fraud". "This type of fraud, a kind of VAT missing trader intra-Community fraud, occurs when goods are imported VAT-free from other Member States, are then re-sold through a series of companies at VAT-inclusive prices and subsequently re-exported to another Member State with the original importer disappearing without paying over to the tax authorities the VAT paid by its customers."[16]

In its judgment of 12 January 2006 in joined cases C-354/03, C-355/03 and C-484/03, *Optigen Ltd (C-354/03), Fulcrum Electronics Ltd (C-355/03) and Bond House Systems Ltd (C-484/03) v. Commissioners of Customs & Excise*: reference for a preliminary ruling from the High Court of Justice (England & Wales), Chancery Division – United Kingdom, European Court Reports 2006, p. I-00483, the ECJ concluded:

> The right to deduct input value added tax of a taxable person who carries out such transactions [which are not themselves vitiated by value added tax fraud]cannot be affected by the fact that in the chain of supply of which those transactions form part another prior or subsequent transaction is vitiated by value added tax fraud, without that taxable person knowing or having any means of knowing.

14 *Supra* note 2, at Section 1-11.
15 *Supra* note 2, at Section 12-19.
16 *Supra* note 2, at Section 30.

In a similar judgment of July 6, 2006 in joined Cases C-439/04 and C-440/04, *Axel Kittel v. Belgian State (C-439/04) and Belgian State v. Recolta Recycling SPRL (C-440/04)* (ECR 2006, p. I-06161), the ECJ went on:

> where it is ascertained, having regard to objective factors, that the supply is to a taxable person who knew or should have known that, by his purchase, he was participating in a transaction connected with fraudulent evasion of value added tax, it is for the national court to refuse that taxable person entitlement to the right to deduct.

Thus, factual or implied knowledge is a crucial element for the taxpayer in order to deduct an input VAT. "If a taxpayer was aware or ought to be aware of the tax fraud committed by the counterparty he has no right for the refund; and whereas a taxpayer was not aware and didn't have to be aware of the fraud he cannot be refused a refund."[17]

Trying to identify this element in *Bulves*, the ECtHR concluded that "the applicant company had absolutely no power to monitor, control or secure compliance by its supplier with its VAT reporting, filing and payment obligations".

Moreover, for *Bulves* ECtHR generated its own rule in order to protect peaceful enjoyment of possessions declared in Article 1 of Protocol No. 1 to ECHR:[18]

> if the national authorities, in the absence of any indication of direct involvement by an individual or entity in fraudulent abuse of a VAT chain of supply, or knowledge thereof, nevertheless penalise the fully compliant recipient of a VAT-taxable supply for the actions or inactions of a supplier over which it has no control and in relation to which it has no means of monitoring or securing compliance, they are going beyond what is reasonable and are upsetting the fair balance that must be maintained between the demands of the general interest of the community and the requirements of the protection of the right of property.

Thus, the ECtHR supplemented the rule generated by CJEC with a *control* element. Fully compliant recipient of a VAT-taxable supply must have no ability to control or monitor its non-complying supplier.

---

17 Astahov S.A., *VAT in European Style.* Your Tax Advocate No. 7 (2009) at 57-62.

18 Under Article 1 of Protocol No. 1 to ECHR "Every natural or legal person is entitled to the peaceful enjoyment of his possessions. No one shall be deprived of his possessions except in the public interest and subject to the conditions provided for by law and by the general principles of international law."

These two elements (knowledge and control) were employed by RSACt Plenum in Resolution No. 53 as well as some lower Arbitrage Courts of Russian Federation.

3.2 *Resolution No 53*

First of all it is important to realize the significance of guidelines issued by HACtRF Plenum for the judicial community in Russia. One of the main HACtRF Plenum functions is the analysis of Arbitrage Courts' implementation of laws and other legal acts and giving guidelines on issues of judicial practice. Resolutions of HACtRF Plenum adopted within its competence are obligatory for all Arbitrage Courts of Russian Federation.[19] Moreover, non-compliance with these guidelines is a basis for overturning a decision.[20]

In order to secure judicial practice uniformity in evaluation of tax benefit's validity, the HACtRF Plenum ruled as follows:

> Counterparty's breach of its tax obligations is not a *prima facie* evidence of unreasonable tax benefit's receipt by the tax payer. Tax benefit might be held unreasonable if tax authority proves that the tax payer acted without due circumspection and care and he should have been aware of its counterparty's breaches in particular due to its interdependency or affiliation with the counterparty.[21]

Thus, along with the breach of the counterparty's tax obligations, the Russian tax authority should prove the following elements to show that the tax benefit sought by the taxpayer is unreasonable:

a. Absence of due diligence (circumspection and care) on behalf of the tax payer;
b. The taxpayer's implied knowledge of the counterparty's breaches evidenced by interdependency or affiliation with the counterparty.

As discussed further, these elements are similar but not the same as were generated by the ECJ in 2006 and used later in 2009 by the ECtHR.

---

19 See Section 1 Art. 13 of Federal Constitutional Law on Arbitrage Courts of Russian Federation, 28 April 1995, No. 1-FKZ, SZ RF [Collected Legislation of the Russian Federation], No. 18, at 1589 (1995).

20 See Section 1 Art. 304 of Arbitration Procedure Code, 14 June 2002 No. 95-FZ SZ RF [Collected Legislation of the Russian Federation], No. 30, at 3012 (2002).

21 *Supra* note 1, at Section 10.

3.3 *Similarities*

De facto HACtRF followed the rule generated by ECJ in its judgment of 12 anuary 2006 in joined cases C-354/03, C-355/03 and C-484/03, *Optigen Ltd (C-354/03), Fulcrum Electronics Ltd (C-355/03) and Bond House Systems Ltd (C-484/03) v. Commissioners of Customs & Excise*: the tax benefit in the form of VAT deduction cannot be affected by the fact of fraud within the chain of suppliers.

The HACtRF also employed implied knowledge of the taxpayer as an exception to this general rule. ECJ used the same element in joined cases C-354/03, C-355/03 and C-484/03, *Optigen Ltd (C-354/03), Fulcrum Electronics Ltd (C-355/03) and Bond House Systems Ltd (C-484/03) v. Commissioners of Customs & Excise* and in joined Cases C-439/04 and C-440/04, *Axel Kittel v. Belgian State (C-439/04) and Belgian State v. Recolta Recycling SPRL (C-440/04).*

Thus, although the HACtRF Plenum does not directly mention the ECJ cases it follows them *de facto.* The ECtHR, which is not bound by the decisions of ECJ, nevertheless cites them and also bases *Bulves* on the said ECJ cases. It sounds unbelievable, but it might be that the HACtRF Plenum issuing Resolution No. 53 in 2006 took into consideration the same ECJ case law as the ECtHR did later in 2009 resolving *Bulves.* Such would be consistent with the contemporary trend toward ever greater use of comparative law, internationally, as persuasive and non-binding evidence of what domestic law might be.

3.4 *Distinctions*

Of course it is worthwhile to mention distinctions crucial for the Russian taxpayer:

Again, it seems like the HACtRF Plenum adopted the initiative suggested by ECtHR, which stated in Section 65 of *Bulves* that "it may be reasonable for domestic legislation to require special diligence by VAT-registered persons in order to prevent such abuse".

The HACtRF Plenum however supplemented the two elements test (control and knowledge) generated by the European Courts with a third element – *due diligence* on behalf of the taxpayer as to its counterparty. Despite the fact that the requirement of circumspection and care is clearly stated, there is still ambiguity how to prove compliance with these abstract duties. Resolution No. 53 does not provide the taxpayer or the tax authority with any list of circumstances which might evidence due diligence on behalf of the taxpayer.

Remarkably, the HACtRF Plenum limited the "implied knowledge" element by specifying the exact situation when it knowledge of wrongfulness may be implied. Thus, in order to prove knowledge of wrongdoing by implication, the Russian tax authority should prove the existence of interdependence or affiliation between the taxpayer and its counterparty.

In sum, "the positions of HACtRF and ECtHR on the issue of VAT's deduction validity have become closer."[22]

4 *Bulves* in Russian VAT Cases

ECtHR case law is not a *binding source* of law in the Russian Federation. However, inspired by similarities between the above mentioned European cases and the guidelines given in Resolution No. 53, the Russian Federal Arbitrazh Courts of some districts do in practice take up the ECtHR case law as persuasive evidence of law and/or as a guide to interpreting domestic law. This fact might give additional weight to the decision if it is scrutinized by the HACtRF.

Common facts are the basis for the outcome of the cases with reference to *Bulves*: the tax authorities refused the taxpayer's VAT's refund because of the bad faith behaviour of the taxpayer's counterparty – *i.e.*, the counterparty did not comply with its VAT obligations. The way the Russian Federal Arbitrage Courts treated *Bulves* was similar, but not the same, in these cases. In some of them, the Russian Federal Arbitrage Courts just mentioned the outcome of the case (overturning the refusal decisions of the tax authority) consistent with the position the ECtHR proclaimed in *Bulves.*[23] In other cases, courts went further, in particular, the Russian Federal Arbitrage Court of the North Caucasus Region concluded that *Bulves* has a precedent value for Russia.[24]

22 Kovalev P.N., Timaev Z.I. *Cooperation with bad faith counterparties: turning-point moment.* Tax Bulletin No. 7 p. 116-121. (2010).

23 See Resolution of Federal Arbitrage Court of Moscow Region No. KA-A40/7280-09-2 dated August 20, 2009 Case No. A40-1471/09-76-6 available at <http://kad.arbitr.ru/?id=4B1F42F9-0C74-422C-B304-524813CDB4B4> Resolution of Federal Arbitrazh Court of Volga Region No. A55-31209/2009 dated 14 October 14, 2010 Case No. A55-31209/2009 available at <http://kad.arbitr.ru/?id=6000C5BE-DC65-449A-A3F7-A3F4B25BA4D9>.

24 See Resolution of Federal Arbitrazh Court of North Caucasus Region dated 15 February 2010 Case No A32-15411/2009-57/92-19/400 available at <http://kad.arbitr.ru/?id=019A55BE-4785-4F71-B354-95EC08E24F46>.

5 CONCLUSION

Alexander Konovalov, the Minister of Justice of the Russian Federation, recently stated "Justice must be administered by taking into account the case law of the European Court of Human Rights".[25] The High *Arbitrazh* Court of the Russian Federation, which is the highest Russian judicial instance over economic disputes, including VAT refund cases, followed *de facto* the main stream of European case law as to the VAT refund though it was not *de jure* obliged to do so.

Thus, "there is nothing to prevent Russian lawyer from presenting violations of the ECHR, and the ECtHR relevant case law, in its arguments before a Russian court. The Russian taxpayer should mention the legal position of the ECtHR and ECJ in Russian Arbitrage Courts: this increases their possibility to resolve the dispute with the Russian tax authorities favorably. In case of further application to ECtHR, it will be essential to understand how the Russian court replies to arguments based on the cited European cases."[26]

25 The minister made this statement in evaluating the progress of efforts to reform the justice system in Russia. See "Alexader Konovalov za noviy oblik Minu'sta". Available at: <www.fparf.ru/news/138.htm>.

26 *Supra* note 17.

Part VII
Afterword

24 The Judiciary in Russia: Is It Possible to Achieve Efficiency, Impartiality and Independence?

Maria Navasardova

1 Introduction

Russia is a uniquely contradictory country. On the one hand, Russia has a great history, a vast territory with enormous natural resources; the Russian people are very intelligent. On the other hand, Russia still suffers from a weak economy, an extremely high level of corruption, a very poor judicial system, enforcement system, and impunity of governmental official, judges, and prosecutors at all levels. The widespread disrespect of the rule of law is a source of other very significant problems, notably in the economy.

I am a citizen of the Russian Federation. I love and want to be proud of my country. That is why I decided to write a chapter on this topic. Unfortunately, a careful study of the Russian judiciary concludes that the level of its progress toward the rule of law (a neutral unbiased judiciary) is at the "stone age". I am an advocate and am forced to encounter the flaws particular to the judicial system. There are numerous problems in this field: lack of methodological competences, political dependency, outright corruption, difficulty of enforcement of judgements, too much or too little publicity, outmoded psychologies and mentalities, at times absent impartiality and many others. In this chapter I describe the principal problems of the Russian judiciary, and propose remedies for overcoming the flaws in the judiciary in Russia.

2 Problems in the Russian Judiciary

Law works perfectly nowhere. To paraphrase Tolstoy, however, all dysfunctional legal systems are dysfunctional in their own ways.[1]

1 Kathryn Hendley, *Varieties of Legal Dualism: Making Sense of the Role of Law in Contemporary Russia*, Legal Studies Research Paper Series, Paper No. 1119, Wisconsin International Law Journal, <http://ssrn.com/abstract=1619478/> (accessed 1 December 2010).

Under Article 1 of the Constitution of the Russian Federation (hereafter "the Constitution"), the Russian Federation is a rule of law state (*pravovoe gosudarstvo*). However, unfortunately, almost every ordinary Russian citizen realizes that is simply a declarative norm.

The idea of a rule of law state arose in the middle of 1980s – the period of perestroika. Professor Aleksandr Iakovlev, who was then a deputy department head at the Institute for State and Law of the Academy of Sciences, but who later became one of Gorbachev's most trusted advisors (Yakovlev 1996), reflected on how to explain Gorbachev's concept of a *pravovoe gosudarstvo* to ordinary citizens.

> How to answer clearly and simply? Perhaps this is the essence: the difference between a rule-of-law-based (*pravovoe*) and a non-rule-of-law-based (*nepravovoe)* state consists in the following. A non-rule-of-law-based state commands by law. In a rule-of-law-based state, state organs are subordinated to law (Kakim dolzhen byt', 1988).[2]

In his speech to the Conference, Gorbachev himself advocated a democratization of the USSR and argued that this would require the establishment of a socialist rule of law (*sotsialisticheskoe pravovoe gosudarstvo*). To put it briefly, the foremost salient feature of a state committed to rule of law is that it effectively ensures the primacy of law. Not a single governmentbody, official, collective, Party organization, public association or individual can be exempt from abiding by the law (Gorbachev 1988: 65).[3]

One of the main purposes of the judicial reform in Russia lasted twenty years was the assertion that judicial power has to be an influential authority independent of the legislative and executive branches: the creation of an independence, impartial and fair court system.

However, unfortunately, this objective has not been achieved. According to polls, the large majority of the Russian people do not consider the courts as a source of justice and defence of their rights and interests. To reach this goal it is necessary to overcome a complex of problems.

3 PROFESSIONALISM AND PROFESSIONAL IDENTITY

It is known that in the Anglo-Saxon system the judge is a middle-aged person with great experience, known to be highly respected by everyone. It is a part of the culture.

2 *Id.*
3 *Id.*

Russia runs to extremes: either judges are too young and inexperienced or are too old and saddled with the soviet mentality. Both variants are obstacles to effective justice. In Russia there is no tradition of respecting judges. In the consciousness of Russians, judges are ordinary people with human weaknesses.

Partly this attitude is supported by the fact that many judges are not highly qualified. Many judges in the commercial courts (*Arbitrazh*) lack experience in dealing with complex commercial matters.[4]

The Russian judiciary also suffers from shortfalls of professional standards and of the corporative spirit which supports judgicial independence in the EU and US. Russian judges depend heavily on local authorities for social and material support. Finally, Russian judges are also part of a strictly hierarchical system.[5]

One of the remedies to overcome this problem is to attract independent lawyers to the judicial system. The source of this could be the Russian Advocate Chamber as one of the few independent institutes in Russia.[6]

4 Partiality and Dependence

Judges are frequently influenced by "suggestions" from governmental authorities, wealthy individuals, and enterprises seeking particular outcomes in cases. In addition, judges are likely to favour large local enterprises over small and medium-sized enterprises, entrepreneurs, and foreigners, since large local enterprises provide employment to the local population and taxes needed by the local governments (and are often controlled by politically well-connected individuals or industrial groups).[7]

Levada-Center conducted a poll all over Russia which shows that the phenomenon of "telefonnoe pravo" (when judicial decision totally depends on the instructions of the gov-

4 Ethan S. Burger,*Corruption In Russia's Arbitrazh Courts*, Volume 14, number 12, December 2004, BNA International, BNA's Eastern Europe Reporter, <http://bnai.com> (accessed 1 December 2010).

5 Энтони Брентон, Россия и верховенство закона, 24 Ноября 2010, <http://eu-russiacentre.ru/our-publications/column/rossiya-i-verxovenstvo-zakona.html> (accessed 1 December 2010).

6 8–9 февраля 2010: Бывшая судья требует перемен и реальной реформы судебной системы России, 12 Февраля 2010, <http://eu-russiacentre.ru/eu-russiacentre-news/press-releases/ex-judge-calls-for-new-blood-and-real-reform-in-russia%e2%80%99s-judicial-system.html> (accessed 3 December 2010).

7 Ethan S. Burger,*Corruption In Russia's Arbitrazh Courts*, Volume 14, number 12, December 2004, BNA International, BNA's Eastern Europe Reporter, <http://bnai.com> (accessed 1 December 2010).

ernment officials) is still wide spread. Only 6% of the respondents believe that the judges are rule only on the basis of the law.[8]

One example of the dependence of the judges is a case of the judge O. Kudeshkina. She was a judge in one of the criminal cases. In the course of proceeding, the Chairman of the Moscow City court interfered in it. She began to instruct the presiding judge, O. Kudeshkina, about how to rule on the case. When judge Kudeshkina rejected to fulfill Chairman's instructions, she was dismissed before expiry of her term of office. She could not find justice in the national courts and applied to the European Court of Human Rights (hereafter "ECtHR"). On 26 February 2009, the ECtHR decided in her favour, pointing out the factual interference of the Chairman in administration of justice.

Judge Kudeshkina affirmed that *corruption* of Judges is not itself the *main* problem in the Russian judiciary. However, in the most significant cases the Russian courts always defend the interests of governmental officials. The dependence of the judicial system supports by the system by itself. The Chairman has a powerful control lever: he distributes cases and awards among the judges, resolves current questions, and initiates disciplinary procedures of judges. At the same time, the Chairman is appointed by the President. Thus, ordinary judges are forced to administer justice looking back to the Chairman. And the latter must correctly interpret the signals of the Kremlin, local authorities, powerful officials or businessmen. Due to this situation, the governmental officials have a guided court.[9]

Hence, it is vicious circle. To change this system a lot of time and very effective cooperation are needed.

5 Corruption

In 2004, the Russian government dramatically increased the wages of its officials and judges, motivated in part by a desire to reduce corruption. What is special about corruption in Russia is its unpredictability and that total investment is at a relatively low level given the country's vast mineral wealth and educated population.[10]

---

8 8–9 февраля 2010: Бывшая судья требует перемен и реальной реформы судебной системы России, 12 Фев 2010, <http://eu-russiacentre.ru/eu-russiacentre-news/press-releases/ex-judge-calls-for-new-blood-and-real-reform-in-russia%e2%80%99s-judicial-system.html> (accessed 15 November 2010).

9 Речь судьи Ольги Кудешкиной, 01 марта 2010, <http://eu-russiacentre.ru/eurc/rech-sudi-olgi-kudeshki-noj.html> (accessed 5 December 2010).

10 Ethan S. Burger,*Corruption In Russia's Arbitrazh Courts*, Volume 14, number 12, December 2004, BNA International, BNA's Eastern Europe Reporter, <http://bnai.com> (accessed 1 December 2010).

"According to most observers, judicial corruption is greater at the trial court level than at the appellate court level. This is not surprising, since it should be easier to bribe a single trial court judge than a panel of appellate judges or members of the Supreme *Arbitrazh* Court. Nonetheless, the procurement of false documents by the other side in a dispute, the lack of a trial transcript to help demonstrate that the trial court's decision was motivated by something other than the legitimate application of law to the facts, and other factors may still discourage many parties from pursuing judicial appeals (particularly where one's opponent is politically well-connected)."[11]

"In common disputes not involving large sums of money, judicial corruption does not appear to be a major problem. Over the last decade, Russian citizens have increasingly begun using the Russian court system to resolve disputes. But this does not necessarily mean they have great faith in the court system. It may mean only that a greater number of commercial disputes are occurring, given the changes in the Russian economy. According to some Russian attorneys, a judge might first examine a case, decide which party should prevail on the merits, and then seek payment for issuing the proper decision. Other judges will simply favor the highest 'bidder' for a favorable result."[12]

"This situation is made possible by the fact that the submission of an appeal of *arbitrazh* trial court decisions is often fruitless, since higher courts are not only reluctant to overturn lower court decisions, but they also are hindered in their ability to conduct effective judicial review because, in most civil law systems, there is no official trial court transcript to examine. Consequently, appellate courts are limited to reviewing decisions for pure errors of law, and refrain from reviewing factual determinations or the misapplication of law to fact."[13]

6 Duration of the Proceeding and Overburdened Courts

The duration of proceedings in civil and criminal cases is a serious problem. Annually, the ECtHR considers numerous complaints against Russia concerning infringement of Article 6 of the European Convention.

The European Court has stated: "It would be inconceivable that Article 6.1 should describe in detail procedural guarantees afforded to litigants – proceedings that are fair, public and

11 *Id.*
12 *Id.*
13 Ethan S. Burger,*Corruption In Russia's Arbitrazh Courts*, Volume 14, number 12, December 2004, BNA International, BNA's Eastern Europe Reporter, <http://bnai.com> (accessed 1 December 2010).

expeditious – without protecting the implementation of judicial decisions; the execution of a judgment must therefore 'be regarded as an integral part of the 'trial' for the purposes of Article 6', and such execution must itself occur within a reasonable time. The European Court believes more generally that the Convention places a positive duty on states 'to organise their legal systems so as to allow the courts to comply with the requirements of Article 6.1 including that of trial within a 'reasonable time'. It has even specified that 'the courts of states parties cannot, without themselves violating Article 6 of the Convention, authorise enforcement of a judgment of a third country which fails to apply the guarantees of Article 6."[14]

In 2004 guidelines were drawn up for moving beyond the concept of 'reasonable time' and determining optimum time frames for each type of proceedings. The key idea is that of the foreseeable time frame', which entails providing accurate information to users or even negotiation with the parties concerned and their lawyers on an acceptable time frame for each case, depending on the procedure adopted.[15]

"Justice delayed is justice denied. Public trust in the judiciary can best be improved by reducing the length and complexity of court proceedings."[16]

Unfortunately, in Russia delays are so frequent as to be normal. Partly the reason is the quantity of cases allocated to one judge: the judges are simply over-burdened. There are also problems with the small staff of the courts, a shortage of linesmen. However, the ECtHR does not consider these arguments as valid causes.[17]

7 Ineffective Enforcement of the Decisions

Another serious problem in Russia is enforcement of judicial decisions. The judicial system can be effective only if the decision is enforced properly and in a timely fashion. Several

14 Jean-Paul Jean & Hélène Pauliat, *An evaluation of the quality of justice in Europe and its developments in France*, Utrecht Law Review, Volume 2, Issue 2,December, 2006, <www.utrechtlawreview.org/> (accessed 12 November 2010).

15 *Id.*

16 Viviane Reding, Justice and Fundamental rights: the Key for Successful Accession to the EU, Conference "Consequences of EU membership for the judiciary" Zagreb, 10 September 2010, <http://europa.eu/rapid/pressReleasesAction.do?reference=SPEECH/10/154&format=HTML&aged=0&language/> (accessed 20 November 2010).

17 Екатерина Торкунова. *Влияниеевропейскойсистемызащитыправчеловеканароссийскоезаконодательства*, <http://alleuropa.ru/index.php?option=com_content&task=view&id=495/> (accessed 10 December 2010).

years ago there was a reform of the bailiff system. It could hardly be said that it changed something radically. However, at least a few first steps in the right direction were made.

8 Measures to Overcome the Flaws

8.1 *Juries*

In December 2008 a new law, which severely restricted the scope for trial by jury was adopted. Henceforth, any crimes which were investigated in accordance with the Crimina Procedural Code by the Federal Security Service (FSB) would no longer come before a jury.[18]

The volume of cases examined before juries in Russia – fewer than six hundred a year – is already unjustifiably low, despite the fact that trial by jury has proved significantly more objective. The principles of adversarial debate and justice are more fully respected in jury trials, because the quality of evidence is subjected to higher demands than before courts without jurors.[19]

Juries may effectively check judicial corruption and thereby help restore faith in judicial institutions and, ultimately, lead emerging democracies closer to the rule of law ideal. However, rule of law reformers have largely rejected jury systems on the ground that juries often disregard or cannot understand the law. Additionally, negative attention on the American jury system has generated popular scepticism as to whether juries can comprehend complex issues and raised concern over a juror's "alleged inclination to make decisions on the basis of emotion" rather than the law. It has also been feared that juries would discourage foreign investment by introducing local prejudice to the judicial system and increasing the risk of unfair or disproportionate verdicts.[20]

Seeking to counter the perceived risk of juries, countries where some type of jury system has been introduced usually use mixed judge-jury systems ("lay judges") or limited the jury to a narrow range of cases, such as serious criminal trials only. That however undercuts the jury's primary benefit: the delivery of a high level of substantive ; the democratization

18 Mara Polyakova, A Few Positive Signs, Generally More of the Same: The Russian Judicial System, 2008 To 2009, The EU-Russia Center Review, The Russian Judicial and Penitentiary System, Issue 11, <http://eu-russiacentre.ru/> (accessed 28 November 2010).

19 *Id.*

20 Brent T. White, *Putting Aside the Rule of Law Myth: Corruption and the Case for Juries in Emerging Democracies*, <https://lawlib.wlu.edu/lexopus/index.aspx?do=search/> (accessed 3 December 2010).

of the law – and the countering of corruption in the judicial system. Despite allegations that juries do not apply the law out of ignorance or emotion, studies have shown that jury verdicts tend to be well-grounded in evidence.[21] Diversity of experience and viewpoints among jury members tend to encourage jurors to deliberate carefully and consider competing explanations – resulting in juries delivering high levels of substantive justice.[22]

In Russia monetary compensation of non-pecuniary damages is insignificant. The state ill esteems the life and health of its citizens. One of the reasons is the mentality of the judges; a well developed but erroneous judicial practice and judicial fear of the reversal of the court's decisions and similar pervasive problems exacerbate this. This problem of non-compensation of non-pecuniary injuries might be best remedied by juries because the jury can better appreciate the actual facts, verify evidence, and insulate the judge from hierarchical (political) power which might otherwise wrongly influence the judicial decision.

8.2 *Alternative Dispute Resolution*

According to aforesaid, it is no surprise that the experienced international lawyers insist on having dispute resolution clauses in their clients' commercial contracts where the value of the contract exceeds a certain amount (*i.e.*, several million dollars, varying by the lawyer and the nature of the transaction) in order to avoid the Russian court system entirely. These dispute resolution clauses usually provide for international arbitration.[23]

Developing alternative remedies to resolve disputes is a good approach to obtain commercial legal certainty in Russia: *e.g.*, arbitration, mediation: the parties themselves choose their arbitrators or mediators. Development of this direction could help solve at least two problems: independence and impartiality of the arbitrators or mediators; and, it would lighten the case-load which burden the state courts.

However, another problem is the enforcement of arbitral awards. Unfortunately, foreign arbitral awards are often difficult to enforce in Russia, either under the 1958 New York Convention on the Recognition and Enforcement of Foreign Arbitral Awards or domestic

---

21 See generally Harry Kalven Jr. & Hans Zeisel, *The American Jury* (1966); see also Theodore Eisenberg *et al.*, *Judge-Jury Agreement in Criminal Cases: A Partial Replication of Kalven & Zeisel's* The American Jury, 2 J. Empirical Legal Studies 171-206 (2005); and Valerie P. Hans *et al.*, *The Hung Jury: The American Jury's Insights and Contemporary Understanding*, 39 Crim. L. Bull. 33, 33-50 (2003).

22 Brent T. White, *Putting Aside the Rule of Law Myth: Corruption and the Case for Juries in Emerging Democracies*, <https://lawlib.wlu.edu/lexopus/index.aspx?do=search/> (accessed 3 December 2010).

23 Ethan S. Burger,*Corruption In Russia's Arbitrazh Courts*, Volume 14, number 12, December 2004, BNA International, BNA's Eastern Europe Reporter, <http://bnai.com> (accessed 1 December 2010).

Russian legislation. Consequently, where the opportunity exists, a victorious party in arbitration may attempt to seize or attach a losing Russian party's assets in third countries that have court systems that will honour the New York Convention's obligations.[24]

The question of foreign arbitral award enforcement is a problem of mentality, judicial practice and distrust of arbitration. I think, first of all, the Supreme Commercial Court (known in Russia as the *Arbitrazh* court – an organ of the state) should issue resolutions (postanovlenie) which would help the lower courts to enforce foreign arbitral awards. Fast and effective enforcement of foreign arbitral awards will positively influence the Russian economy by encouraging foreign investment in Russia and commerce with Russian companies.

8.3 *National Sovereignty*

The Chairman of the Constitutional Court stated that if Russia wants, she can evade the jurisdiction of the ECtHR. Following that logic, the judges announced the "mechanism of the national sovereignty defense", allowing the Russian authorities to avoid enforcing the ECHR decisions which defer from the position of the Constitution Court.[25]

The problem with the "national sovereignty defense" to enforcement of ECtHR decisions inside Russia is that it is irresponsible. The Constitutional Court's decision thereto was political. While no one doubts the sovereignty of Russia, the power of the Kremlin to, if it chooses, rescind its adhesion to the European Convention on Human Rights (ECHR), evading the application of the ECHR is bad for Russian business. Furthermore, politicization of this problem makes it good *legal* decisions less likely. Russian courts have nothing to fear from referring to European law and European practice. Indeed, Russia and the EU are great trading partners and solid legal footing will increase European investment and Russian exports.

8.4 *Specialization of the Judges*

I think some of the problems of the professionalism and competence of the judges could be resolved fairly rapidly by specialization of the judges. When judges are tasked with, *e.g.*, tax, commerce, criminal cases and not forced to be generalists organize judicial training

24 *Id.*
25 Валерий Зорькин готов к обороне: национального правового суверенитета, 22 Ноя 2010, <http://eu-russiacentre.ru/news/valerij-zorkin-gotov-k-oborone-nacionalnogo-pravovogo-suvereniteta.html>.

courses becomes easier and the training becomes more effective. This would be one easily instituted reform which would yield results rapidly.

8.5 *Other Remedies*

The President Dmitriy Medvedev, declaring the new stage of the judicial reform, stated several times that one key objective for Russia is to bring the judicial system and the Constitution. Moreover, President Medvedev publicly admitted that the existing in Russia legal nihilism is one of the principal obstacles to creating a prosperous new Russia which will attract foreign investments.

To change the mentality and psychology not only of the judges, but also of the people is the main objective. To achieve this goal, an effective mechanism is needed. Hence, this too is a vicious circle. However, we have no choice and must move forward to a brighter future for Russia. Just as a vicious circle can spiral downward, so also can a virtuous circle spiral upward. The rule of law will come to Russia:

1. through private law initiatives such as arbitration and mediation.
2. through reform of the judiciary via
   a. judicial (re)training and
   b. juries,
   c. judicial specialization and
3. through the reformation of the politico-legal structure (constitutionalisation) and
4. through the formation of a judicial culture centered on the rule of law as a necessary precondition to greater economic prosperity via increased foreign trade and investment.

9 CONCLUSION

This chapter reveals the main problems in the judicial system in Russia, in particular, partiality and dependence of the judges, corruption, the long duration of proceedings, over-burdened courts, and ineffective enforcement of the decisions. This chapter also considered several remedies for overcoming the flaws of the judiciary: juries, alternative dispute resolution, narrow specialization of the judges, active implementation of ECHR decisions, and trying to change the psychology of the judges and attitude of the people toward the judiciary. Russia is a vast land, with a well educated population and is rich in natural resources. Unfortunately, the legal system lags. This chapter has suggested a few practical and feasible routes to improving the rule of law in Russia and I am very hopeful for Russia's future.

Index

STEVE McCUTCHEON